BUDDHISM IN SINHALESE SOCIETY, 1750–1900

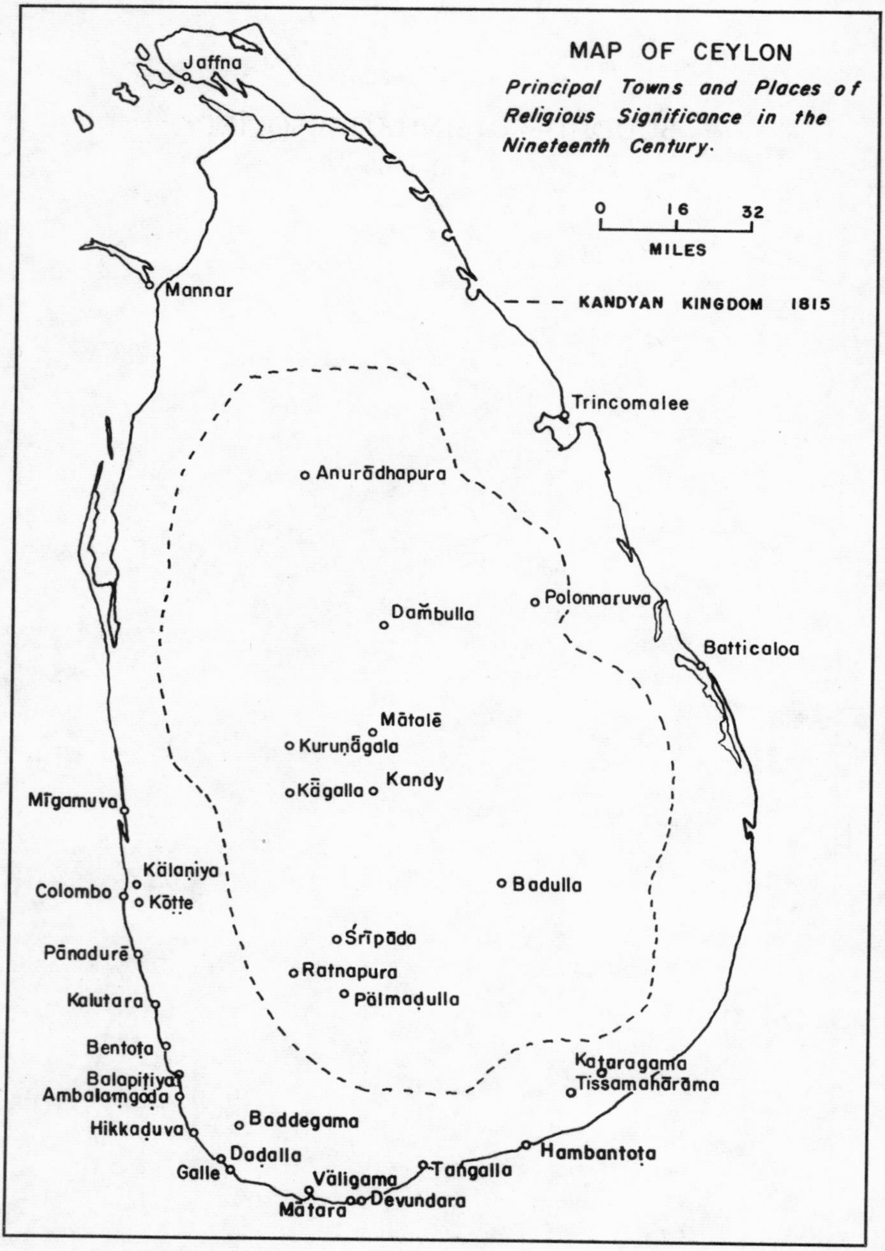
MAP OF CEYLON
Principal Towns and Places of Religious Significance in the Nineteenth Century.
0 16 32
MILES
KANDYAN KINGDOM 1815
Jaffna
Mannar
Trincomalee
Anurādhapura
Polonnaruva
Dam̆bulla
Batticaloa
Mātalē
Kuruṇāgala
Kāgalla
Kandy
Mīgamuva
Kälaṇiya
Colombo
Kōtte
Badulla
Śrīpāda
Pānadurē
Ratnapura
Pälmaḍulla
Kalutara
Bentoṭa
Kataragama
Balapiṭiya
Tissamahārāma
Ambalamgoḍa
Baddegama
Hikkaḍuva
Hambantoṭa
Daḍalla
Galle
Väligama
Tangalla
Devundara
Mātara

BUDDHISM IN SINHALESE SOCIETY 1750–1900

A STUDY OF RELIGIOUS REVIVAL AND CHANGE

KITSIRI MALALGODA

UNIVERSITY OF CALIFORNIA PRESS
BERKELEY · LOS ANGELES · LONDON

University of California Press
Berkeley and Los Angeles, California
University of California Press, Ltd.
London, England

ISBN 0-520-02873-2
Library of Congress Catalog Card Number: 74-22966
Printed in the United States of America

CONTENTS

Spelling and Transliteration vii
Key to Abbreviations ix
Preface xi
Introduction 1

I. The Background 11
- i. Buddhism: Its Transformation and Establishment in Ceylon, 11
- ii. The Impact of the Portuguese and Dutch Missionary Efforts, 28
- iii. Buddhism in the Kandyan Kingdom, 49

Part One. Schisms within the Order and the Rise of New Monastic Fraternities

II. The First Phase: Up to 1815 73
- i. The Nature of the Religious Establishment, 73
- ii. Rebellion in the Kandyan Kingdom, 74
- iii. Kandyan versus Low-country Monks, 82
- iv. Low-caste Protest against the Establishment and the Rise of the Amarapura Fraternity, 87
- v. The Sociological Significance of the Amarapura Fraternity, 100

III. Authority and Dissent in the Siyam Fraternity, 1815–1865 106
- i. The Disestablishment of Buddhism, 106
- ii. Kandyan versus Low-country Monks–The Second Phase: The Rise of the Kalyāṇi Fraternity, 128
- iii. The Amarapura Fraternity in the Kandyan Provinces, 139

IV. The Segmentation of the Amarapura Fraternity, 1815–1865 144
- i. The Problem of Cohesion in the Amarapura Fraternity, 144
- ii. Karāve and Durāve Monks versus Salāgama Monks: The Emergence of the Dhammarakkhitavaṃsa and the Kalyāṇivaṃsa Fraternities, 147
- iii. Salāgama Monks: Division into Mūlavaṃsa and Saddhammavaṃsa Fraternities, 151
- iv. The Rāmañña Fraternity: Its Origin and Its Ideals, 161

V. Decline or Revival? 173
- i. Prophecies of Doom, 173
- ii. The Shift of the Religious Centre, 175

Part Two. Protestant Buddhism

VI. Buddhism Versus Christianity: Beginnings of Buddhist Protest 191
- i. The Challenge: Christian Missions in Ceylon, 1800–1860, 191
- ii. The Buddhist Response, 1800–1860, 205
- iii. The Buddhist Response, 1860–1880, 213

VII. Protest Consolidated 232
- i. Crisis in the Buddhist Response to Christian Missionary Activity, 232
- ii. Lay Participation before 1880, 237
- iii. Lay Participation after 1880: The Buddhist Theosophical Society, 242

Conclusion 256
Appendix I. Chronological Table, 1750–1900 263
Appendix II. Pupillary Succession of Välivița Saraṇaṃkara in the Low Country 266
Bibliography 269
Index 285

SPELLING AND TRANSLITERATION

The text contains numerous Sinhalese, Pali and Sanskrit words. Where exact equivalents are available, the choice of a term of one language in preference to that of another generally depends on the context in which the given term occurs and the source on which the discussion is based. An exception to this rule is the few instances where Sanskrit forms (e.g., nirvana, karma) have secured a place in English usage.

Romanization follows the standard system of transliteration—common to all three languages—which is used in scholarly literature. A term which is expressed in the plural appears either in its original plural form (e.g., *vihāragam*) or in the original singular with an *s* added at the end (e.g., *gaṇinnānses*).

For most of the terms used, conventional or approximate English equivalents are given. The English term *monk*, unless otherwise specified, is used to denote *bhikkhu* (ordained monk) as well as *sāmaṇera* (novice).

Place names are generally given in the forms in which they are known today in Sinhalese. Where there are minor differences between the mid-twentieth-century and nineteenth-century usages, the latter has been preferred (e.g., Huduhumpola and Piḷimatalavva in preference to Suduhumpola and Piḷimatalāva respectively). Some of the well-established Europeanized names, such as Colombo (= Koḷam̆ba) and Kandy (= Maha Nuvara), have been retained; others (e.g., Cotta = Kōṭṭe, Cotton China = Koṭahēna) which are no longer in general usage have been dispensed with except from quotations and from bibliographical references if the Europeanized name appears on the title page.

With regard to personal names: the names of all monks have been transliterated, as have the personal names of most laymen, but not all. The exceptions are those who wrote in English frequently or whose names appear in English documents in the same forms as they themselves wrote them, for example, Gooneratne (= Guṇaratna), Wijesinha (= Vijēsiṃha).

KEY TO ABBREVIATIONS

A.R.	*Administration Reports*
B.M.	British Museum
CALR	*Ceylon Antiquary and Literary Register*
CGG	*Ceylon Government Gazette*
CHJ	*Ceylon Historical Journal*
CJHSS	*Ceylon Journal Of Historical and Social Studies*
C.M.L.	Colombo Museum Library
C.N.A.	Ceylon National Archives
C.O.	Colonial Office documents (at the Public Record Office, London)
CSSH	*Comparative Studies in Society and History*
EZ	*Epigraphia Zeylanica*
JPTS	*Journal of the Pali Text Society*
JRAI	*Journal of the Royal Anthropological Institute*
JRAS	*Journal of the Royal Asiatic Society* (of Great Britain)
JRAS(BB)	*Journal of the Bombay Branch of the Royal Asiatic Society*
JRAS(CB)	*Journal of the Ceylon Branch of the Royal Asiatic Society*
S.P.	Sessional Paper
UCR	*University of Ceylon Review*

PREFACE

This book is a revised and slightly expanded version of a doctoral thesis submitted to the University of Oxford in September 1970. The material on which the thesis was based was collected during the preceding five and a half years at the following libraries and archives: the Sri Lanka National Archives, the Colombo Museum Library, the University of Sri Lanka Library at Peradeniya, the Bodleian group of libraries in Oxford, the Reading Room of the British Museum, and the Public Record Office in London. I am deeply grateful to the staffs of these institutions for their ready and courteous assistance.

My graduate studies in Oxford were made possible by a Rhodes Scholarship, which supported me for three years from 1965 to 1968. Subsequent support from the University of Sri Lanka for a year during 1969–1970 enabled me to bring my studies to completion. My thesis, during its somewhat unusually lengthy period of preparation, was supervised by Dr. Bryan Wilson, and I benefited immensely from his advice and criticisms. He was characteristically generous with his time, knowledge, and experience, and I am also indebted to him for much personal kindness and encouragement. Among others who helped me with my work I should like to make special mention of Dr. Richard Gombrich. He commented on early drafts of the first two chapters and, after the thesis was submitted for examination, he went through the entire typescript with very great care and offered many valuable suggestions for which I am most grateful. The completed thesis, either in its original or revised form, was also read by Professors S. J. Tambiah, Gananath Obeyesekere, K. M. de Silva, and Nur Yalman, and Mrs. Pat Castor. They gave me the benefit of their comments as well as help and suggestions with regard to preparing the work for publication. I deeply appreciate the assistance given by them all which contributed in many ways to making improvements in the final version, but it is only fair to add that practical difficulties or my own obstinacy prevented me from following their advice and suggestions fully. For the gaps and shortcomings that remain in the book and for the particular approach taken in it as a whole I alone, therefore, must take full responsibility.

Revising the thesis for publication was done mainly in Sri Lanka between 1971 and 1973, in the midst of several other commitments and in circumstances which were not the most conducive for academic work. I took the opportunity provided by my presence in Sri Lanka, however, to check many doubtful points, consult some amount of new material, and make a few additions in particular to the latter part of the book. Several new works throwing light on the sociological interpretation of Buddhism appeared in the early 1970s, and at about the same time there were also significant advances in the study of South Asian social institutions like caste as well as in historical studies of nineteenth century Sri Lanka. I have, where it seemed appropriate and feasible, made reference to these most recent works, but, making their acquaintance only in the very late stages of my own research, it was unfortunately not possible for me to make full use of the theoretical insights or factual knowledge provided in them. I hope that this book, from its own perspective, will make a useful addition to this growing body of knowledge.

In 1972, while this book was being prepared for publication, the official name of the country with which the book is concerned was changed from Ceylon to Sri Lanka. Despite this change I have retained the older name in the text of the book as it was by that name that the country was known during the period dealt with in the book and, therefore, it is the one that appears in the sources on which the book is based (with the exception, of course, of Sinhalese and Pali sources). The name Ceylon—which has no unpleasant associations for the citizens of the country—also had a practical advantage in English usage in that it had a well established adjective (Ceylonese), which Sri Lanka did not have in 1972. Thailand, too, is generally referred to in the text of this book by its older name, Siam.

Typing the manuscript at different stages was done by Mrs. M. Miles, Mr. K. Kumarasamy, and Miss Chrissie Hemming. For the care and patience with which they did their work I am much obliged to the three of them, and also to Mr. E. V. Christian who drew the Map of Ceylon and Mr. Carl Peters who prepared the diagram for Appendix II.

Finally, I offer my sincere thanks to the staff of the University of California Press. If not for their efficiency, sustained interest, and gentle yet persistent encouragement, the publication of this book would have been delayed even further.

Auckland
October 1975

KITSIRI MALALGODA

INTRODUCTION

Weber, in his sociology of Buddhism, spoke of a 'transformation' of (ancient) Buddhism; its transformation, that is, from the position of a religious 'technology' of wandering and intellectually schooled mendicant monks to that of a world religion commanding allegiance among large masses of laymen.[1] Basically this transformation involved two things: one, at the level of belief and practice, making accommodations to meet the religious needs of the (predominantly peasant) laity; and two, at the level of religious organization, developing links with secular authorities whose backing was necessary for the propagation and establishment of Buddhism in different Asian communities.

More recent sociological studies of Buddhism, insofar as they are related to Weber's formulations, pertain, in the main, to the problem of how Buddhism prevails as a mass religion in south and southeast Asian peasant communities. The better known of these studies are those of de Young, Kaufman and Tambiah in relation to Thailand;[2] of Nash and Spiro in relation to Burma;[3] and of Obeyesekere, Ames, Yalman and Gombrich in relation to Ceylon.[4] All these studies approach Buddhism from a social

[1] *The Religion of India*, tr. H. H. Gerth and Don Martindale (Glencoe, Ill., 1958), ch. VII.

[2] John E. de Young, *Village Life in Thailand* (Los Angeles, 1955), ch. V; Howard K. Kaufman, *Bangkhuad: A Community Study in Thailand* (New York, 1960), chs. VI, VII, X; S. J. Tambiah, *Buddhism and the Spirit Cults in North-East Thailand* (Cambridge, 1970).

[3] Manning Nash, *The Golden Road to Modernity: Village Life in Contemporary Burma* (New York, 1965), chs. IV, V, VIII; Melford E. Spiro, *Burmese Supernaturalism: A Study in the Explanation and Reduction of Suffering* (Englewood Cliffs, New Jersey, 1967), and *Buddhism and Society: A Great Tradition and Its Burmese Vicissitudes* (New York, 1970).

[4] Gananath Obeyesekere, 'The Great Tradition and the Little in the Perspective of Sinhalese Buddhism', *Journal of Asian Studies*, XXII (1963) 139–53; Michael M. Ames, 'Magical-animism and Buddhism: A Structural Analysis of the Sinhalese Religious System', *ibid.*, XXIII (1964) 21–52; Nur Yalman, 'The Structure of Sinhalese Healing Rituals', *ibid.*, pp. 155–50; and Richard F. Gombrich, *Precept and Practice: Traditional Buddhism in the Rural Highlands of Ceylon* (Oxford, 1971).

anthropological point of view, and they provide ample documentation that the 'accommodations' spotlighted by Weber have indeed occurred at the behavioural level.

These social anthropological approaches to Buddhism have been possible because Buddhist communities continue to be—as they have been in the past—largely peasant societies. At the peasant level, in fact, there has been remarkable continuity in the sphere of religion, as has been explicitly avowed by Ames in relation to Ceylon, the country with which the present study is concerned. Ames writes:

> From the point of view of survival . . . Sinhalese religion seems to be highly successful. It has persisted in one small island perhaps for a longer period than Christianity has persisted anywhere, and with far fewer changes. . . . Inspection of the early written records, myths and legends, scanty as they are, nevertheless strongly suggests that the ancient religion was little different from its contemporary version in basic ideals.[5]

At other levels, however, changes there have been (and Ames does not deny that): indeed, changes significant enough, one might argue, to be viewed as a second major transformation of Buddhism, because these changes have had a direct bearing on both of the key aspects of the first transformation that Weber spoke of. In the first place, during and since the nineteenth century, there emerged in Ceylon numerically small but socially dominant new 'elites' or 'status groups' whose religious needs and interests, as much as their economic bases, were different from those of the traditional peasantry. Secondly, the political milieu of colonial government, in which these changes in the traditional system of stratification occurred, also affected Buddhism in a more immediate and direct way: it brought to an end the backing that had long been given to Buddhism by secular authority. How did these changes affect Buddhism? And how did Buddhism change itself to meet the new circumstances? These questions are of prime concern to the present study.

Recent changes in Buddhism have not gone entirely unnoticed by the social scientist. Religious issues began to figure prominently in Ceylon politics towards the end of the first decade of independence, and attempts have been made to understand and interpret the significance of this

[5] *Op. cit.*, p. 48. See also Gombrich, ch. I.

phenomenon in the context of the broader concerns of the study of 'new nations.' The pioneering study in the regard was by the American political scientist Howard Wriggins: *Ceylon: Dilemmas of a New Nation* (Princeton, New Jersey, 1960), a study which was not confined, however, to the religious dilemmas. A detailed study of the religio-political situation as such has been made more recently by the German orientalist Heinz Bechert.[6] Moreover, two social anthropologists, Ames and Obeyesekere, whose major interests have been in the study of village Buddhism also have begun to show an interest in this problem.[7] These studies provide many useful insights into some of the recent changes in Buddhism; and the study of Bechert provides, in addition, a detailed documentation of events particularly with reference to the post-independence era.

These recent events could perhaps quite legitimately be treated as relatively autonomous at the analytic level, and thus studied in the comparative perspective–as some of these authors have done–as problems related to independent nationhood.[8] Yet a proper grasp of the particular forms that they take in Ceylon would scarcely be possible without a knowledge of their historical antecedents.

The studies mentioned above do recognize the importance of the historical dimension. Indeed, they have themselves made attempts to reconstruct the past, though not with appreciable success, as their reconstructions have been based far too heavily on rather inadequate, and not sufficiently reliable, secondary sources.

There is nothing surprising perhaps in the reluctance of social scientists to get involved in historical research. Yet is seems doubtful whether a social scientist interested in *change* can afford this reluctance, especially in situations where adequate studies by historians, on whose research social

[6] *Buddhismus, Staat und Gesellschaft in den Ländern des Theravāda-Buddhismus*, vol. I (Allgemeines und Ceylon) (Frankfurt am Main and Berlin, 1966).

[7] Michael M. Ames, 'Ideological and Social Change in Ceylon', *Human Organization*, XXII (1963) 45–53; and 'The Impact of Western Education on Religion and Society in Ceylon', *Pacific Affairs*, XL (1967) 19–42. Gananath Obeyesekere, 'Religious Symbolism and Political Change in Ceylon', *Modern Ceylon Studies*, I (1970) 43–63.

[8] The same approach can also be seen in McKim Marriott, 'Cultural Policy in the New States', in Clifford Geertz (ed.), *Old Societies and New States: The Quest for Modernity in Asia and Africa* (Glencoe, Ill., 1963), pp. 27–56; and Donald Eugene Smith (ed.), *South Asian Politics and Religion* (Princeton, New Jersey, 1966), Part IV.

scientists are generally dependent for their background knowledge, are not available. The pressure on social scientists to undertake historical research in such circumstances has been clearly stressed by Shils in a general discussion on the problems related to the study of new nations:

> In Asia and Africa historical studies prosecuted by modern techniques are in their infancy. Sources have not yet been assembled and calendered, bibliographies are deficient, and the basic monographic research has not yet been done. The social scientist who tries to penetrate to the indispensable historical depth finds himself compelled to do historical research of a sort with which his colleagues working on Western societies think they can dispense.[9]

The history of Ceylon is by no means an entirely unexplored field. Quite apart from studies of its ancient and mediaeval history, there have also appeared in recent years several scholarly monographs and articles on the period which is of direct concern to the present study. And in the field of reference works, a superb beginning has been made by H. A. I. Goonetileke in *A Bibliography of Ceylon*.[10] To all these works, the present study is indebted in many ways. Even so, Shils's general observation remains as true of Ceylon as of other Asian and African countries.

Historical studies of nineteenth-century Ceylon, furthermore, have almost entirely been pursued, until very recently, within the framework of British colonial history, a field of study which is no doubt valid and useful in its own right, but which, concerned as it is in the main with the policies of the colonial government, fails by its very nature to provide a balanced picture of the local social institutions as such.

The concern with colonial history on the part of the historian of nineteenth-century Ceylon is partly the result of his eagerness to relate the study of a small country to issues and themes of wider significance. It is also, in part, a consequence of the nature and type of historical sources available for that period: the Colonial Office documents constitute by far the largest, the best catalogued, and the most readily accessible single collection of source material. No serious student of nineteenth-century Ceylon can afford to ignore this collection; it is necessary, all the same, to be aware of its limitations. For the study of certain topics—of which the

[9] 'On the Comparative Study of the New States', in Geertz (ed.), pp. 10–11.

[10] 2 vols. (Inter Documentation Company, Zug, Switzerland, 1970).

formulation of governmental policies is undoubtedly the most important—these documents are indispensable; but for certain others, such as those tackled in this book, they are of very limited value.

This does not mean that Buddhism was of no interest to the colonial government; on the contrary, as we shall see below (especially in chapter III, section i), it was for a long time a subject of great importance to them. What it does suggest is that discussions of Buddhism at the governmental level were not generally carried on with an intimate and sympathetic understanding of the local situation; and that, therefore, unless our interests are confined to the attitudes and prejudices of policy-makers, we must go beyond the official sources.

The best sources, especially for the study of the recent history of the Buddhist order in Ceylon, are to be found in monastic libraries of varying size scattered throughout the island. But as they are so scattered, and are not maintained on professional lines, it is completely beyond the capacity of a single student—even if he is allowed access to them all—to study their rich collections within a reasonable period of time. Attempts to examine these collections and to keep copies of some of the material found among them in a central repository for the benefit of students were first begun under official auspices almost exactly a century ago. In the early decades, however, the interests of these searches were limited mainly to the standard religious, historical and literary works.[11] It was much later, in 1931, with the establishment of the Historical Manuscripts Commission, that the scope of the searches was widened to include other material, such as letters, dedications, acts of appointment, wills and pamphlets. Considering that the commission has now been in existence for four decades, it is not easy to be very enthusiastic about its record (no report has appeared since the third one in 1951, which was in fact ready for the press as early as 1939); but there is no doubt that the commission, with the assistance of the staff of the Department of National Archives, have, amidst numerous difficulties, made available to the reader a vast collection of data which was not easily available to him previously.

[11] See James Alwis, *A Descriptive Catalogue of the Sanskrit, Pali and Sinhalese Literary Works of Ceylon*, vol. I (Colombo, 1870); Louis de Zoysa, *Reports on the Inspection of Temple Libraries* (S.P. XI: 1875), *Report on the Inspection of Temple Libraries* (S.P. XXV: 1879), and *A Catalogue of Pali, Sinhalese and Sanskrit Manuscripts in the Temple Libraries of Ceylon* (Colombo, 1885).

In Part I of this book, 'Schisms within the Order and the Rise of New Monastic Fraternities', I have made extensive use of the material collected by the Historical Manuscripts Commission and now deposited at the Department of National Archives. Buddhists in the early nineteenth century had no printing presses of their own; hence no noteworthy printed sources of primary value are available for the topics covered in that Part. Nor are there good secondary works dealing comprehensively with the history of the Buddhist order during that period. Therefore, a careful examination of the manuscript material was clearly necessary in order to obtain an accurate picture.

With regard to Part II, in contrast, I did not find myself compelled to examine the same sort of material. The British missionaries, from the very beginning, used the printed word as a means of religious propaganda; and so did the Buddhists after the 1860s. In relation to the Buddhist-Christian confrontation, therefore, a substantial body of printed sources is available in the form of tracts, pamphlets, journals and newspapers. There are, in addition, several modern studies (of varying quality) dealing with various aspects of the missionary enterprise. For these reasons, as well as for the reason that my interests were mainly focussed on the Buddhist reaction to Christian missionary activities rather than on Christian missionary activities as such, I have not examined the collections at the archives of missionary organizations, although there is little doubt that, had I been able to afford the necessary time and energy, an examination of them, in particular the diaries kept by the missionaries and the letters that they periodically sent to headquarters, would have enriched the second Part of this study. But as I was dealing, for the sake of sociological perspective, with a period much longer than those generally preferred by professional historians of nineteenth-century Ceylon, an attempt to examine, or re-examine, nearly all the relevant sources available was plainly impracticable.

As in the examination of the sources, so in the choice of topics for discussion, I have been deliberately selective. Chapter I prepares the background; and then Part I deals with the Buddhist order during the century between 1765 and 1865, that is, roughly from the time that higher ordination (*upasampadā*) ceremonies of the Siyam fraternity were confined to Kandy (and to the Goyigama caste) up to the time of the establishment of the Rāmañña fraternity. Special attention is given to the schisms that occurred within the order and the controversies that led to them, and to the doctrinal as well as regional, political and social backgrounds of these controversies and schisms.

The same discussion could have been continued for the post-1865 period. But in Part II attention is shifted to the Buddhist-Christian confrontation on the assumption that the latter had more significant results for Buddhism in Sinhalese society than the contemporary internal changes within the order. The connecting link between Parts I and II is the argument (elaborated in the concluding chapter of Part I) that it was the strength derived from the internal organizational changes in the first half of the nineteenth century that enabled Buddhists to withstand the external threat of British missionary activities in the latter half of the same century.

What is discussed at length in this study as the Buddhist response to the challenge of Christian missionary activities was not the *only* such response that was noticeable in the nineteenth century. Attention will be concentrated rather on that response which had more lasting results. In its origins, though not in its ultimate impact, which was very widespread indeed, it was largely a low-country (rather than Kandyan), urban and semi-urban (rather than rural), modern (rather than traditional) response. In the more traditional and rural parts of the Kandyan areas, there was a very different kind of response, a response not simply to Christianity, but more broadly to Western political dominance as a whole.

Organizationally, the latter was a much less 'rational' response; and by virtue of its political aims, it was not destined to have lasting success after the British had firmly established their strength in the Kandyan areas. It manifested in the form of a series of millennial episodes the aims of which, in Wilson's terms, were clearly 'restorative'.[12] The common millennial dream underlying them all was the emergence of kings through the help of the 'guardian deities' of Ceylon for the redemption of the Sinhalese and their religion. There were several episodes of this nature from the time of the cession of the Kandyan kingdom to the British in 1815 until almost the end of the nineteenth century. Some of them were probably not even noticed by the government; and the rest were quelled without much

[12] Bryan R. Wilson, 'Millennialism in Comparative Perspective', *CSSH*, VI (1963–64) 93–114.

difficulty, except during the very first outbreak in 1817–18, when the effective leadership of the movement was taken over by some Kandyan chiefs and when fighting dragged on for several months.[13] It was only after a ruthless and costly campaign that the British authorities were able to regain their position, and the traumatic experiences of these months lingered on in their minds for several decades. Thus, when the second noteworthy episode of this sort occurred in 1848, the administration panicked and displayed a ferocity that was hardly warranted by the situation.[14] Taken together, these movements constitute a subject that is worthy of detailed historical and sociological study, but that falls outside the scope of this book. I have myself discussed this subject briefly in a separate article.[15]

Another subject which was of importance in relation to the Kandyan areas, and which too has been left out of detailed consideration in this study, is the question of the management, and mismanagement, of 'Buddhist temporalities'. The question arose as a result of the 'disestablishment' of Buddhism, which will be discussed below in chapter III, section i. The main concern in that section, however, will be with the results of disestablishment for the authority structure of the Buddhist order—the way that it reduced the control of the chief monks of Kandy over their subordinates in other parts of the country. In chapter V, section ii, some of the results of the disorganization and misappropriation of temple properties in the Kandyan areas will be taken up for discussion; but there again the emphasis will be on the results, and not on the process itself, nor on the belated and futile attempts of the government to improve the management of the temporalities. Even after 'disestablishment', it was not easy for the government to ignore the problem of temple lands; they amounted in all to about 400,000 acres of tax-free land. The problem that the government had to solve was finding the means of establishing an organization for the proper management of these lands without taking direct administrative responsibility on the government itself; and the

[13] P. E. Pieris, *Sinhalē and the Patriots, 1815–1818* (Colombo, 1950), is a detailed historical study of this period.

[14] See K. M. de Silva (ed.), *Letters on Ceylon, 1848–50: The Administration of Viscount Torrington and the 'Rebellion' of 1848* (Colombo, 1965).

[15] 'Millennialism in Relation to Buddhism', *CSSH*, XII (1970) 424–41.

solution that the Ordinance No. 3 of 1889 sought—after previous attempts in 1846, 1849 and 1877 had been vetoed by the Colonial Office—was providing the necessary legal framework to enable the Buddhists themselves to manage temple property through regional committees of Buddhist laymen and trustees appointed by them.

The increasing involvement of laymen in religious activities, and their involvement as a matter of voluntary participation rather than of feudal duty, were noteworthy features of organizational changes in Buddhism at the time; and the Ordinance No. 3 of 1889, indirectly if not directly, tried to make use of these changes in order to establish a satisfactory system of administration for the temporalities. This experiment proved unsuccessful. Organizational changes in Buddhism, therefore, will be discussed at length in this book, not in relation to the subject of temporalities, but with reference to the new 'associations' or 'societies' which arose in the low country in the latter half of the nineteenth century in close association with, or as a result of, the Buddhist-Christian confrontation. The more successful of these voluntary associations had their beginnings in the 1860s, and they acquired a more lasting character after the establishment of the Buddhist Theosophical Society in 1880. The nature of these associations and their activities will form the subject matter of Part II.

Purely for convenience, the study ends at the end of the nineteenth century. By that time, the Buddhists had learnt to use very effectively the selfsame means which the Christian missionaries had been using against them—education, preaching, and the printing press. The final outcome of the Buddhist-Christian confrontation was therefore already clear. But more varied developments of the Buddhist enthusiasm were yet to be seen: in the temperance movement, in the strengthening of the Sinhalese-Buddhist identity, in the activities of the All Ceylon Buddhist Congress, and so forth. These, however, belong to the first half of the twentieth century, and for this reason will not be discussed in this study. For the same reason, the life and work of that important Buddhist leader, Anagarika Dharmapala (1864–1933), also have been excluded; he did begin to figure prominently in Ceylon Buddhism while he was still in his twenties, but his independent influence cannot be traced, at most, earlier than the last decade of the nineteenth century. The background information provided in this book, it is hoped, will stimulate detailed studies of his personality and career, as well as of the more general developments of Buddhism in Ceylon in the first half of the twentieth century.

Despite sociological training, I have found myself approaching the subject matter of this book more as a historian than a sociologist. I have been content to leave the sociological perspective implicit rather than explicit, and I have focussed my attention primarily on the simple task of getting the main features of the historical record clarified. If, as a result, the book falls between history and sociology, I hope that, for the same reason, it will make a contribution, howsoever small, to both.

Chapter I

THE BACKGROUND

i. BUDDHISM: ITS TRANSFORMATION AND ESTABLISHMENT IN CEYLON

Early Buddhism, by the very nature of its doctrines and practices, had very little potential for popularization at the level of a world religion. Being an extremely radical form of salvation-striving propagated by strictly contemplative mendicant monks who rejected the world, it lacked nearly all the mechanisms which were necessary to 'gather multitudes of confessors' around it.[1] Salvation was accessible only to those who rejected the world—'the homeless'—and only they remained full members of the Community. All the others who remained in the world—'the house-dwelling people'—remained thereby laymen of inferior value. For them there was no strictly *religious* ethic for the guidance of their inner-worldly conduct;[2] no church discipline for the organization of their religious affiliations; and neither a deity nor a cult for the satisfaction of their 'plebeian religious needs'.[3] The driving factor therefore which eventually led Buddhism to

[1] See Max Weber, 'The Social Psychology of World Religions' in *From Max Weber: Essays in Sociology*, tr. & ed. H. H. Gerth and C. W. Mills, 1946 (New York, 1958), pp. 267–69. Weber considered the ability to 'gather multitudes of confessors' to be the main characteristic of a 'world religion'.

[2] Prescriptions for the laity as laid down in the *Dhammika Sutta* and *Sigālovāda Sutta*, etc., had no particular religious bearing in that they were not directly related to the attainment of salvation. Along with many other Indian religions, Buddhism stressed an other-worldly path to salvation. For an elaboration of this thesis, see L. Dumont, 'World Renunciation in Indian Religions', *Contributions to Indian Sociology*, IV (1960) 33–62.

[3] By 'plebeian religious needs' Weber meant the needs 'for emotional experience of the super-worldly and for the emergency aid in external and internal distress', needs which arise out of the recurrent crises of life and which could be satisfied by 'two possible types of soteriology: magic or a saviour'. *The Religion of India*, tr. & ed. H. H. Gerth and Don Martindale (Glencoe, Illinois, 1958), pp. 236–37. In contrast, Weber considered Buddhism a peculiarly 'intellectualist' religion in its origin. As he noted elsewhere: 'Buddhism demonstrates that the need for salvation and ethical religion has yet another source besides the social condition of the disprivileged and the rationalism of the middle classes, which are products of their practical way of life. This additional factor is intellectualism as such, more particularly the metaphysical needs of the human mind as it is driven to reflect on ethical and religious questions, driven not by material need but by an inner compulsion to understand the world as a meaningful cosmos and take up a position toward it'. *The Sociology of Religion*, tr. E. Fischoff, 1963 (London, 1965), pp. 116–17.

transform itself to the status of a world religion was the need to make accommodations to meet these needs and interests of the laity.

Yet this need was inadequate, by itself, to make this transformation a concrete reality. It had to be accompanied by a missionary zeal to conquer the world for the doctrine and an effective authority to consolidate the victories thus gained. Certain elements of missionary enthusiasm may be discerned in Buddhism even in its earliest form, but the essentially apolitical and asocial character that pervaded Buddhism at this early stage hindered the actual realization of this ideal. It was precisely this need that was fulfilled with Emperor Asoka's conversion to Buddhism in the third century B.C. The results of this event were of paramount importance in the later development of Buddhism.

Buddhism was introduced into Ceylon during a period when the connection between Buddhism and political authority was already developed to a high degree under Asoka in India. This feature had a marked impact on the kind of Buddhist institutions that eventually developed in the island. From the very beginning (the first to be won over to Buddhism was the king himself), Buddhism came to be very closely associated with the institution of kingship in Ceylon. Indeed, it has been plausibly argued that the reign of Tissa (250–210 B.C.), who was Asoka's contemporary in Ceylon, established a landmark not merely in the religious but also in the political history of the island. For it witnessed the formal establishment of the institution of kingship, with all its ritualistic paraphernalia, as well as the monarchical form of government in place of the more popular forms of government that had prevailed since the time of the early Aryan settlements.[4] An *abhiṣeka* (consecration) ceremony–a necessary rite of passage in the Indian tradition whereby a prince was acknowledged as sovereign–was held in Ceylon with Asoka's help, and Tissa, as well as a number of his successors, assumed the Mauryan royal title *devānaṃpiya*, meaning 'beloved of the gods'. These political contacts with India preceded the subsequent religious contacts and paved the way for the acceptance and establishment of the doctrines preached by Asoka's missionaries.[5] And if the idea and institution of kingship helped to unite

[4] See S. Paranavitana, 'Two Royal Titles of the Early Sinhalese and the Origin of Kingship in Ancient Ceylon', *JRAS* (1936) 443–62.

[5] *Ibid.*

the country at the political level, the introduction of Buddhism helped to consolidate this unity at the ideological level.

Inferences based on historical and archaeological research have ascertained with considerable success aspects of religious beliefs and practices that prevailed in pre-Buddhist Ceylon.[6] Such beliefs and practices, deriving their elements from a multitude of sources, served the religious needs of the masses who lived in relatively isolated communities. But this primordial and parochial character of religion and society necessarily hindered ideological unification at wider levels, and thus created a gap which became all the more conspicuous when unification was gradually attained at the political level. It was precisely this gap that was filled by the establishment of Buddhism. With this event, over and above the pre-Buddhist 'little tradition' was introduced a Buddhist 'great tradition',[7] a tradition which came to embody the 'central value system',[8] or the official ideology of the kingdom.

The new symbols and institutions, places and objects of worship that cohered around the centre of the 'great community' inspired veneration at the wider social level. The Bodhi tree and the *cetiyas* (in which the corporeal relics of the Buddha were enshrined) became symbols of political unity. Gorgeous ceremonies giving expression to mass religiosity were held in connection with these sacred objects, and the chronicles as well as many other contemporary records are replete with references to them.[9] One of them which rose to pre-eminence was the festival connected with the Tooth Relic, which was brought to Ceylon and received with much

[6] S. Paranavitana, 'Pre-Buddhist Religious Beliefs in Ceylon', *JRAS(CB)*, XXI (1929) 302–28.

[7] The concepts 'great tradition' and 'little tradition', as well as the concepts expressing their societal dimensions–'great community' and 'little community'–have been diffused into anthropological and sociological discussions largely through the work of Robert Redfield. See his *Peasant Society and Culture* (Chicago, 1956) for the best and most explicit formulation of these concepts. For an application of Redfield's concepts to an analysis of Sinhalese Buddhism, see Gananath Obeyesekere, 'The Great Tradition and the Little in the Perspective of Sinhalese Buddhism', *Journal of Asian Studies*, XXII (1963) 139–53.

[8] Edward Shils, 'Centre and Periphery', in *The Logic of Personal Knowledge: Essays Presented to Michael Polanyi* (London, 1961). Although the concepts 'centre' and 'periphery' have grown out of concern with problems of a very different character, in their final forms they correspond in many important respects to Redfield's great and little traditions.

[9] Such references have been incorporated into a coherent account by Paranavitana in 'Buddhist Festivals in Ceylon', in B. C. Law (ed.), *Buddhistic Studies* (Calcutta, 1931), pp. 529–46.

honour and festivity during the reign of Siri-Meghavaṇṇa (A.D. 301–28). It was kept in a shrine within the royal precincts, and proclamations were issued that a grand festival should be celebrated in its honour when the Relic was temporarily removed from the palace to the Abhayagiri monastery each year.[10] Fā-Hsien, who visited Ceylon a few years after the arrival of the Tooth Relic, witnessed this annual festival and has left a graphic account of it.[11] The Tooth Relic eventually became the palladium of the Sinhalese kings and therefore was taken from one city to another when the capital was shifted during the course of Ceylon history. Thus Parākramabāhu I (1153–83) held a grand festival in its honour when it was finally brought to Polonnaruva after a long series of adventures in Rohaṇa, where rival claimants to the throne fought among themselves to take possession of this symbol of sovereignty.[12] The *Daḷadā Sirita* (History of the Tooth Relic), a fourteenth-century prose work, describes in detail the procedure followed on the occasion of its public exposition during the period in which this work was written.[13]

All these accounts clearly point to the immense religio-political significance of festivals of this sort. The patronage extended, and the conspicuous role played by the king himself, symbolized the fundamental unity of the sacred values that held society together. These intermittent rituals bringing the peripheral masses repeatedly in contact with the sacred values of the centre generated that group feeling, the transcendental social factor sui generis that Durkheim so vividly portrayed. 'There can be no society', wrote Durkheim, 'which does not feel the need of upholding and reaffirming at regular intervals the collective sentiments and the collective ideas which make its unity and its personality. Now this moral remaking cannot be achieved except by the means of reunions, assemblies and meetings where the individuals, being closely united to one another, reaffirm in common their common sentiments; hence come ceremonies'.[14]

[10] *Cūlavaṃsa*, tr. by Wilhelm Geiger, and from the German into English by C. M. Rickmers (Colombo, 1953), XXXVII: 92–97.

[11] Fā-Hsien, *A Record of Buddhist Kingdoms*, tr. J. Legge (Oxford, 1886), pp. 105–7.

[12] *Cūlavaṃsa*, LXXIV: 181–248.

[13] The *Daḷadā Sirita*, ed. E. S. Rajasekara (Colombo, 1920). An English translation of a part of this work is given as chapter VI of A. M. Hocart's *The Temple of the Tooth in Kandy* (London, 1931).

[14] Emile Durkheim, *The Elementary Forms of the Religious Life*, tr. J. W. Swain (London, 1915), p. 427.

To be sure, such grandiose ceremonies and rituals, despite their obvious religious, political and social functions, were not those strictly prescribed by the essential tenets of Buddhism. How then were they possible? Did Buddhism come into conflict with them? Or were they tolerated, rationalized or encouraged in terms of the doctrine?

A crucial dilemma inherent in the essential doctrines of Buddhism is the practical inaccessibility of the path to salvation (i.e., world renunciation) and, therefore, the ultimate salvation itself (i.e., nirvana, the cessation of 'suffering' and rebirth), to the mass of mankind. This feature had far-reaching consequences whenever the masses in any country had to be brought under Buddhism. In Ceylon, the solution that emerged was the development of secondary goals for the laity, beneath the (original) primary goals, which continued to be pursued by the radical few who rejected the world. This, of course, did not amount to a rejection of the primary goals by the laity: nirvana was still considered, implicitly and explicitly, the ultimate consummation of all their religious practices and aspirations; and this fundamental belief permeated their lives and actions in innumerable ways. Similarly, the highest veneration was accorded to him who, by renouncing his material possessions and worldly ties, strove arduously for his own immediate salvation. Still, the recognition was inevitably made that this radical path, and therefore the goal itself, were not within the immediate reach of everyone alike. Hence for the laity there arose a formidable gap between the distant salvation ideal and the desire to achieve it, a gap which could well extend to thousands and thousands of rebirths. In this context, the function of secondary goals–especially as embodied in the concept of *puñña kamma* ('merit-making')–was to give religious orientation to actions within this wide and well-nigh imponderable gap. Those who were not morally strong enough to transcend *all* desires (a sine qua non for the attainment of nirvana) were prescribed to cultivate the *desire* for meritorious deeds so that they could improve their chances for better rebirths.[15]

[15] The doctrinal justification for the cultivation of this *desire* was purely as a means to the attainment of the ultimate end. Rebirth in better conditions was believed to place the individual in circumstances favourable to the ultimate path to salvation. *In practice*, however, the means often tended to be transformed into an end in itself. The nature of this paradox and its effects on the Buddhist institutions in Ceylon have been analysed by Michael M. Ames in his paper 'Magical-animism and Buddhism: A Structural Analysis of the Sinhalese Religious System', *Journal of Asian Studies*, XXIII (1964) 21–52.

The ceremonies referred to above, which performed many latent social functions, were thus ascribed a manifest religious function in terms of this new emphasis on merit-making. It should be noted, however, that the significance of this new emphasis was not limited to this field; it lay, in fact, beneath nearly all the religious activities of the laity. As Rahula has observed in his *History of Buddhism in Ceylon*:

Acquiring merit of various kinds, as security for the next world was the motive underlying the religion of the laity, from the king down to the poor peasant. Wealth, health, beauty, longevity, intelligence, power, high-caste and the like, which the people desired, were [believed to be] the results of good karma. People tried, therefore, to do good and to be good in order to obtain these happy conditions. . . . With regard to the laity, the spiritual side is seldom mentioned, either in the Pali commentaries or in the Chronicles, and all their religion seems to be limited to external 'meritorious' deeds.[16]

Sermons preached by the monks for the edification of the laity frequently emphasized these aspects of religious virtues. The *Dakkhiṇā Vibhaṃga Sutta*, which was one of the most popular sermons,[17] indicated the various degrees of merit acquired by giving alms and gifts to fourteen different individual recipients ranging from the Buddha down to the animals, and also the greater merits of seven kinds of alms given to the *saṃgha* (the order of monks) as a community. The *Jātaka* (birth) stories, which provided a popular literature for the laity–in contrast to the Scriptures, which were written in a language unintelligible to the common man –emphasized the same kind of theme, and the stories were given vivid illustration in Sinhalese temple murals.[18] While some literary works, like the *Pūjāvaliya*, were written with the almost exclusive purpose of eulogizing works of merit, the same purpose pervaded many other works, like the *Mahāvaṃsa*. Certain laymen, especially those of noble and royal birth, kept records known as *puñña potthaka* ('merit-books') in which their meritorious deeds were written down. King Duṭṭhagāmaṇī (161–137 B.C.), for instance, had such a merit-book, which was read to him by his

[16] (Colombo, 1956), p. 254.

[17] *Ibid.*, p. 252.

[18] S. Paranavitana, 'Introduction' to *Ceylon: Paintings from Temple, Shrine and Rock*, Unesco World Art Series (New York, 1958).

scribe at his death-bed. Meritorious deeds recorded in it included building *cetiyas*, holding festivals and giving alms to the brotherhood of *bhikkhus*.[19]

The religious activities and interests of the laity were accompanied by corresponding changes in the organization and activities of the *saṃgha*, or the order of monks. The *saṃgha* were called *puññakkhetta* ('merit-field') where one could sow seeds of merit and reap good harvests in the births to come. Hence the order came to be considered an indispensable institution for the religious activities of the laity. The *saṃgha*'s duty it was to expound the doctrine to the laity, and to them were extended much of the charitable gifts of the laity. Apart from private gifts of numerous individuals, public endowments were also made to them for the supply of their material needs, the maintenance of monastic buildings, and for the regular performance of merit-making rituals. These endowments consisted of revenues from lands (sometimes from tanks and irrigation canals) and services of serfs and slaves attached to those lands.[20] This was the development of what Weber called 'monastic landlordism',[21] a development whereby the religious institutions received a feudal character from the ethos of the wider economy and society.

The radical pursuit of other-worldly salvation through incessant commitment to poverty and mendicancy became a distant ideal in the face of these new developments. Though as an *ideal*, it was still held in high esteem, in practice certain accommodations were necessarily made. While certain monks chose the radical path and strove to achieve the primary goals, the others, choosing the less radical path, cultivated the pursuit of secondary goals. The latter specialized in the learning and the preservation of the doctrine while the former practised the rigorous prescriptions laid down in the doctrine. This fundamental conflict between the practice (*paṭipatti*) and the learning (*pariyatti*) of the doctrine, and the functional differentiation of the monks on the basis of this conflict, became very significant features in the early history of Buddhism in Ceylon. The two

[19] *Mahāvaṃsa*, XXXII: 25–26.

[20] For discussions of religious endowments, see W. M. A. Warnasuriya, 'Inscriptional Evidence bearing on the Nature of Religious Endowment in Ancient Ceylon', *UCR*, I (1943) 69–82, II (1944) 92–96; and H. W. Codrington, *Ancient Land Tenure and Revenue in Ceylon* (Colombo, 1938).

[21] *The Religion of India*, p. 257.

different groups have been designated under different names at different times; still the differentiation occurred basically on the same principle.

It was no easy task to find a doctrinal justification for the pursuit of the new secondary goal by members of the *saṃgha*. Doctrinal Buddhism was quite unambiguous on the importance of practice as against the learning of the doctrine.[22] A justification was nonetheless found in terms of the historical circumstances that at one stage gravely threatened the very existence of Buddhism in Ceylon. The turning point was reached as early as the first century B.C. The chronicles and the commentaries record that during this period the political organization of the country was violently disturbed by foreign invasions and internal conflicts; and in addition to these calamities, the whole country was ravaged by an unprecedented famine.[23] With the laymen in no position to support them, the *saṃgha* were reduced to a precarious existence. Some left their monasteries, and certain others were forced to go abroad. Since the *dhamma* (doctrine) was preserved through the oral tradition handed down by the *saṃgha*, any threat to the *saṃgha* meant a threat to the *dhamma* as well. The danger of leaving the *saṃgha* entirely to the uncertain liberality of their supporters —who were bound to be few during periods of political and economic distress—was deeply felt. Hence the practice was established, when stability was ultimately restored, of endowing the *saṃgha* with fixed and regular incomes from lands and other sources of wealth.[24] Similarly, the experiences during the famine brought home to the elders the risks of entrusting the preservation of the Canon to the uncertain life conditions of separate groups of monks. Thus, soon after the famine, they assembled at Aluvihāre in Mātalē and committed to writing the whole *tipiṭaka* and the commentaries thereon so 'that the true doctrine might endure'.[25]

At another conference convened during the same period, the question

[22] The pronouncement in the *Dhammapada* (I: 19–20) that a person of realization, even though he has only a little learning, is superior to one who has great learning but no realization was consistent with the general outlook of the doctrine.

[23] *Mahāvaṃsa*, XXXIII: 37–42.

[24] This innovation was made soon after Sinhalese royal power was restored under Vaṭṭagāmaṇī (89–77 B.C.). The *Mahāvaṃsa* makes a pointed reference to this innovation in the verse following XXXIII: 98. Geiger refers to this verse in a footnote, but excludes it from the text as spurious on insufficient grounds.

[25] *Mahāvaṃsa*, XXXIII: 100–101.

was discussed as to the true basis of the *sāsana*: learning or practice. Although the doctrinal position of Buddhism on this point was unambiguous, 'there were two schools of opinion on the matter: the *Paṃsukūlikas* [the radical group, so named because they wore rag-robes] maintained that practice was the basis of the *Sāsana*; but the *Dhammakathikas* [the 'preachers'] held that learning was the basis. Both sides brought forward arguments and reasons in support of their theories. Ultimately it was decided that learning was the basis of the *Sāsana* and not practice'.[26] Out of this new development there arose a vocational differentiation of monks into *gantha-dhura* (the vocation of 'books', denoting the learning and teaching of the doctrine) and *vipassanā-dhura* (the vocation of meditation).

Another distinction which went parallel to the one mentioned above was the distinction in terms of the respective dwelling areas of the monks: between *arañña-* or *vana-vāsī* (forest dwelling) and *gāmavāsī* (dwelling in monasteries in towns and villages). The *vanavāsīs* chose the radical path of salvation prescribed by doctrinal Buddhism; living in secluded forest-reserves, they devoted their time to meditation. Their right to live in these forests was guaranteed by law and custom. But in contrast to the *gāmavāsīs*, they were not the recipients of munificient gifts from kings or other laymen. They exemplified the ultimate ideals which everybody else hoped to approximate; and contemporary records frequently refer with awed respect to their piety, integrity and determination. But apart from this, they had no particular *social* significance; in every sense they were those who had renounced all their social ties. It was natural therefore that, at the social level, the village- and town-dwelling monks, the *gāmavāsīs*, acquired far greater significance. They showed in themselves the changes in Buddhist ideology and practice which made the world-renouncer come into terms with the world. Living *in* society, they became, though in a special sense, a part *of* society. They were enabled by their constant contacts with the laity and the secular authorities to perform vital religious functions in relation to them. Furthermore, their vocation of learning turned them into a class of professional 'intellectuals', a group of persons indispensable to any form of society.[27]

In this role, they engaged themselves in the systematic pursuit of

[26] Rahula, *History of Buddhism in Ceylon*, p. 158.

learning and thereby sought immediate and constant contact with the sacred values of the great tradition. In addition, they diffused these values, in an attenuated and moderated form, amongst the laity, who needed some means of participation in the central value system of their society but could ill afford the time or energy for its pursuit in any systematic form, engaged as they were in the ordinary business of their lives. Among the *gāmavāsī* monks who practised the *gantha dhura*, therefore, there developed two sorts of specializations: one, the intensive cultivation of the central value system itself, and the other, the diffusion of the basic principles derived from this central value system. While the former group had in their minds the intellectual community itself, the latter group directed their energies to satisfying the needs and interests of the laity. To the performance of these two main functions were geared the educational institutions conducted by the monks.

In the major educational institutions that developed around the capitals of the kingdom, religious studies were pursued on a large and intensive scale. A mastery of the *tipiṭaka* provided the basic groundwork for the scholar, and to it were added the later exegetical works (the commentaries, sub-commentaries and glossaries, etc.) written for the crucial purpose of interpreting the original texts.[28] Most of these works were originally written in, or subsequently translated into, Pali, the lingua franca of the Theravāda intellectuals. The cultivation of Pali helped the establishment of close cultural contacts with other Buddhist countries.[29]

As might be expected of intellectual pursuits of this sort, special emphasis was laid on the study of the more philosophical and metaphysical aspects of Buddhism, the *abhidhamma*, or the 'special doctrine', as they came to be called.[30] The *abhidhamma* was a portion of the Buddhist canon

[27] For a general discussion of the social need for intellectuals and the tasks and functions that they perform in relation to society, see Edward Shils, 'The Intellectuals and the Powers: Some Perspectives for Comparative Analysis', *CSSH*, I (1958) 5–22.

[28] For an examination of these works, see G. P. Malalasekara, *The Pali Literature of Ceylon* (London, 1928).

[29] See Sirima Wickremasinghe, 'Ceylon's Relations with South-East Asia with special reference to Burma', *CJHSS*, III (1960) 38–58; S. Paranavitana, 'Religious Intercourse between Ceylon and Siam in the 13th–15th Centuries', *JRAS(CB)*, XXXII (1932) 190–213; W. Pachow, 'Ancient Cultural Relations between Ceylon and China', *UCR*, XII (1954) 182–91.

that gradually developed out of the original *dhamma* and focussed its attention on the systematization and the interpretative elaboration of the original teachings.[31] The original teachings, as they were handed down from generation to generation, had the character of popular discourses couched in a loose terminology bearing the stamp of the composite audiences to whom they were originally delivered. This feature gave rise to interpretative difficulties, and as a result, controversies of various kinds were common ever since the death of the Buddha. The establishment of Buddhism as the official ideology of Ceylon necessitated a more precise and systematic formulation of the doctrine; and this task of systematization was one of the primary concerns of the monks who engaged themselves in intensive intellectual pursuits.

The doctrine that was expounded to the laity, on the other hand, perpetuated the early tradition of the popular discourse, and was based on the *suttas*, which embodied the early *dhamma*, as against the later *abhidhamma*. In contrast to the latter, which was written in a precise and highly technical vocabulary, the *suttas* made free use of the simile, the metaphor and the anecdote. Many of the popular expositions were written in, or translated into, Sinhalese, the language of the masses. It is recorded that the *sutta piṭaka* itself was translated into Sinhalese during the reign of Buddhadāsa (337–365).[32] Apart from the written, the monks also made extensive use of the oral discourse for the exposition of the doctrine to the laity. Accommodation for preaching was considered an indispensable feature in every *vihāra*, or monastery.

Although the *gantha dhura* originally meant only the learning and teaching of the doctrine, it was widened, as time went on, to embrace many other fields as well. Of particular interest here is the nature of the historical traditions that grew up among the monks. Giving satisfaction to the society's need for contact with its own past, the historical works written by

[30] The scale of remuneration laid down in the Mihintalē Inscriptions of Mahinda IV (956–977) indicates the manner in which learning gained precedence over practice. The teacher of *abhidhamma* was ranked first, with twelve shares, and was followed by the teachers of *sutta* ('discourses') and *vinaya* (disciplinary regulations for the monks) with seven and five shares respectively. *Epigraphia Zeylanica*, I (1904–12) 85.

[31] See the article on 'Abhidhamma' in the *Encyclopaedia of Buddhism*, vol. I, pp. 37–49.

[32] *Mahāvaṃsa*, XXXVII: 175.

the monks elaborated a potent source of legitimacy for the sovereigns as well as the people of Ceylon. This source of legitimacy was based on the concept of *Dhammadīpa*: the belief 'that the island of Ceylon was destined by the Buddha to be the repository of the true doctrine, where the *Saṃgha* and the *Sāsana* would be firmly established and shine in glory'.[33] As a modern observer has put it, 'Rather as the Old Testament [built] up the concept of Israel as a specially chosen people, so [did] the *Mahāvaṃsa* [the best-known historical chronicle of Ceylon] build up the special destiny of the Sinhalese people, and the island of Sri Lanka in relation to Buddhism'.[34]

A strong Buddhist great tradition was thus established at the central level, and through state patronage and the efforts of the town and village monks, its basic principles were successfully diffused among the peripheral masses. Fundamental Buddhist concepts like karma and rebirth penetrated deeply into their basic belief systems and provided them with 'explanations' of 'the problem of the world's imperfections'. Fortune as well as suffering was explained in terms of these mechanistic retributive processes, and prescriptions regarding merit-making showed the laity the way to use these processes to their own advantage. In discussing mass religion, it is important to recognize, however, that this was by no means the whole of its story. Merit-making itself, as was already indicated, was an accommodation made by Buddhism to meet the needs of the laity. Still, the religion of the laity was not exclusively Buddhist even in this compromised and moderated form. In addition to Buddhist beliefs and practices, they indulged in a rich array of 'non-Buddhist' beliefs and practices, which, if taken in isolation, stood in open opposition to the Buddhist ones.

Simultaneous adherence to different traditions has often raised the need for some sort of explanation; and attempts have been made at times to provide explanations in terms of historical diffusion.[35] In explanations of this sort, the 'non-Buddhist' beliefs and practices are traced to 'non-Buddhist' sources: pre-Buddhist, Hindu or Mahāyānist. Such attempts, no

[33] L. S. Perera, 'The Pali Chronicle of Ceylon', in C. H. Philips (ed.), *Historians of India, Pakistan and Ceylon* (London, 1961), p. 33.

[34] B. H. Farmer, *Ceylon: A Divided Nation* (London, 1963), pp. 8.

[35] Such an attempt is implicit, for instance, in Paranavitana's writings: 'Pre-Buddhist Religious Beliefs in Ceylon' (cited above, note 6), and 'Mahāyānism in Ceylon', *Ceylon Journal of Science*, Section G, II (1928–33) 34–71.

doubt, are valuable for historical purposes; but for a study of the religious *system* (from the behavioural perspective) they would not be of equal consequence. Within the religious system, one would expect the relations among its constituent elements to be functional rather than chronological. Furthermore, a strictly diffusionist framework would fail to account for the vital motivational factors that lay behind sustained adherence to seemingly contradictory belief and ritual systems.

Basic among the 'plebeian religious needs', as indicated by Weber, was the need 'for emergency aid in external and internal distress'.[36] Hence the crucial dilemma for Buddhism at the plebeian level was the inadequacy of its basic concepts—as embodied in karma and rebirth—to explain *all* external and internal distress, and the inefficiency of its prescriptions—as embodied in merit-making—as means of alleviating *all* such external and internal distress. Merit-making, to be sure, did guarantee a change of fortune in the lives to come, and perhaps in the present life itself. Yet this guarantee was far from satisfactory as a means 'for *emergency aid* in external and internal distress'. Only two types of soteriology—magic or a saviour—were identified by Weber as satisfactory for meeting this vital need;[37] and the validity of this observation is illustrated by the developments that took place in the Ceylon situation. However devalued or disapproved of by doctrinal Buddhism, magical practices were continually adhered to at the level of the little tradition. And though the Buddha (or the Buddha to be) was not considered a 'saviour' to the same extent as in the Mahāyānist tradition, he was nonetheless transformed into a 'super deity' of a certain sort in the popular belief of the Sinhalese Buddhist.

In addition to karmic causality, circumstances of good and bad fortune were also explained in terms of two other forms of causality: planetary influences and the benevolent or malevolent actions of different types of supernatural beings. In accordance with these beliefs, magical 'technologies' were resorted to in order to control the underlying causal processes: to ward off disaster and to bring forth good fortune.[38] The astrologer

[36] *The Religion of India*, pp. 236–37.

[37] *Ibid.*

[38] Detailed accounts of these beliefs and practices could be found in the sections on 'Popular Religion' in W. Geiger, *Culture of Ceylon in Mediaeval Times* (Wiesbaden, 1960), and M. B. Ariyapala, *Society in Mediaeval Ceylon* (Colombo, 1956).

(*saṃvaccharika*) was consulted to choose auspicious planetary constellations in inaugurating all important tasks; and 'planet gods' were invoked through appropriate rituals to rid the patients of their planetary inflictions. The supernatural beings, in whom the Sinhalese believed, were broadly divided into two main categories: the higher deities (*devas*), who were gradually incorporated into the great tradition, and the lesser spirits, or demons (*yakkhas*), who were manipulated by the magicians to take back the diseases that they had inflicted on human beings.

It is necessary to note, however, that these beliefs and practices did not have an independent existence. The Buddhist great tradition exercised a deep and pervasive influence over the beliefs and practices of the non-Buddhist little tradition, and through the intermixture of these two traditions was formed the Sinhalese Buddhist religious system.[39] All the 'non-Buddhist' supernatural beings derived their legitimacy through warrants (*varan*) received from the 'god above the gods' (*devātideva*), that is, the Buddha, and thereby they were 'converted' and incorporated into the Sinhalese Buddhist pantheon. This process was most evident in the case of the originally Hindu or Mahāyānist gods like Indra, Viṣṇu, Skandha and Avalokiteśvara. In Ceylon, they were divested of their original attributes, and myths linking them with the Buddha and his religion were evolved. They lost their capacity to 'save' human beings, and their actions were confined to protecting Buddhism and to assisting human beings in their worldly affairs.[40]

Even early Buddhism assumed the existence of supernatural beings, but considered them irrelevant to the attainment of salvation. Since, at this early stage, Buddhism was a radical form of other-worldly salvation-striving, propitiatory rituals designed to invoke supernatural beings for

[39] Obeyesekere, 'The Great Tradition and the Little'.

[40] 'Connected with Buddhism of the Island, are temples consecrated to certain gods of the Hindu pantheon, whose character and attributes, as adopted into the Ceylon Buddhist cult, entirely alter their nature and worship paid to them. With the Hindus these gods are immortal, revengeful, licentious: here they are but mortal, well-behaved, guardian deities, and even candidates for Buddhahood. Shrines are erected to them, and offerings made solely to obtain temporary benefits–not by religious supplication to merit reward in a future world. This essential difference between the Hindu and Buddhist notions of gods, common in name to both forms of worship, is rarely understood'. H. C. P. Bell, *Report on the Kegalla District* (Colombo, 1892), p. 18.

this-worldly benefits were depreciated as irrelevant and vulgar practices. As we have already seen, the transformation of Buddhism to the level of a mass religion necessitated a shift from this emphasis on radical salvation-striving; and the resultant secondary goals that came to the fore brought forth with them certain new attitudes towards supernatural beings. The layman who chose the inner-worldly secondary goal had to do something to make the best of the bad bargain that was his worldly existence; and the belief in supernatural beings provided an effective divine instrument for this essentially worldly purpose. Similarly, the belief in gods helped to consolidate the other secondary goal pertaining to the preservation of Buddhism in Ceylon. To the strength of the *saṃgha*, the sovereign and the subjects were added the divine powers of the 'guardian deities' whose bounden duty it was to protect the 'holy island', its people, and most of all, their sacred religion.

All this, however, did not affect the essential doctrinal ideals of Theravāda Buddhism in any significant way. Belief in astrology and in supernatural intervention did not replace the Buddhistic belief in the impersonal mechanisms of the laws of karma. While the former helped to explain good or bad fortune in the immediate perspective, the laws of karma were believed to lie beneath all these processes in the long-term perspective. Similarly, though magical practices helped to alleviate bad fortune and to obtain good in the immediate perspective, they were deemed irrelevant to the ultimate goal of the attainment of salvation. The Buddha was elevated to the rank of a super-deity because all the gods had to be subordinated to him. Hence he was *relevant* to magical practices, as the gods derived their power and authority from him. His permission was necessary to invoke them. No propitiatory rituals, however, were directly performed for him to receive this-worldly benefits. And still less was he considered a 'saviour' in the full sense of the term, who could take the masses to salvation. It was he who showed the path to salvation; but it was ultimately the task of each and every individual to strive for his own personal salvation.

The role of the Buddhist *bhikkhu* was never confused with that of the priest who invoked the gods on behalf of those who sought their help; or with that of the itinerant magician who coerced the demons through the exercise of his magical formulae. The latter two were never accorded the sanctity which was accorded to the *bhikkhu*, and in fact for all purposes they remained mere laymen.

The only significant magical practice that was officially incorporated into Buddhism, and which was performed by the Buddhist monks themselves, was the ceremony known as *paritta*, meaning 'protection'. It was performed in times of public calamity as well as in circumstances of private distress to dispel demonic influences and to bring forth the blessings of the 'three gems'–the Buddha, the *dhamma* (doctrine) and the *saṃgha* (the order of monks). In practice, however, many *bhikkhus* did indulge in magical practices–such as exorcising spirits, making sacrifices, divining by means of omens, and preparing charms–as well as in the 'improper practice' of astrology: all of which were officially condemned as *garhita vidyā* ('despised sciences').[41] Such gaps between official injunctions and actual practices remained almost an endemic feature of the Buddhist order, though the exact proportion of the gap varied from time to time, depending on the relative strength of the great tradition, which, in turn, very often depended on the relative strength of the central political authority.

Whenever a powerful central authority was lacking to channel them to their proper avenues, the selfsame institutional devices which, at their best, elevated the *sāsana* to the level of a pre-eminent social institution, worked to bring it down to corruption and disrepute. The institution of *gāmavāsī* monks, which enabled the *bhikkhus* to establish close contacts with the laity and thereby to gain a role of leadership in society, led them, often for the same reason, to infringe fundamental *vinaya* (disciplinary) regulations. For the benefit of the laity, they started practising a number of 'despised sciences'; and there were numerous though less frequent occasions when individual monks violated their vows of celibacy and maintained wives and children out of monastic funds.[42] To make the *sāsana* a powerful and autonomous institution, it was necessary to endow it with means to supply its material needs; but whenever proper administration was lacking, this practice was liable to numerous abuses. The material benefits of the order

[41] *Katikāvat Sañgarā*, ed. D. B. Jayatilaka (Colombo, 1922), pp. 15 and 19.
[42] *Mahāvaṃsa*, LXXVIII: 3–4.

attracted unscrupulous individuals to the *saṃgha*. Similarly, the pursuit of learning by the *saṃgha*, which led to the preservation of the doctrine as well as to the production of new scholarly works, carried within itself seeds of dissension which proved harmful to the order. Their intellectual pursuits made the monks receptive to outside influences; and especially with the decline of Buddhism in India, the bulk of such outside influences tended to be Mahāyānist, Tāntric or Hindu. Such influences aggravated the interpretative difficulties that generally accompanied the study of the philosophical and metaphysical aspects of Buddhism, and thus paved the path for numerous schisms among the *saṃgha* based on doctrinal as well as on other grounds. So, times were not lacking when the order, in the expressive words of the *Mahāvaṃsa*, was 'sullied by admixture with a hundred false doctrines, rent asunder by the schism of . . . fraternities and flooded with numerous unscrupulous bhikkhus whose sole task [was] the filling of their bellies'.[43]

It should be noted, however, that all these corruptions *in practice* did not lead to scepticism regarding the ideals. On the contrary, the attachment to the ideals was reinforced during periods of crises, and new measures were undertaken to approximate to the ideals when the crises were subdued. The king, as the protector of religion, worked for the 'purification of the order' whenever it was found to be disorganized and corrupt. This was done by a regulative act known as *dhamma kamma*, which was performed by the *saṃgha* on the initiative of the king. The chronicles refer to twelve such regulative acts performed at various times up to the end of the fifteenth century. They were directed to purge the order of heretical doctrines and individuals and thereby preserve the orthodoxy of the order in its beliefs and organization.

The pre-eminent role played by the kings in such 'purifications' was significant, for without the royal authority to back them, reforms of the order could scarcely be successful. The passing of political power over the country to governments which were hostile to Buddhism was bound, therefore, to have important results. This transition was completed in the nineteenth century; but it began as early as the sixteenth.

[43] *Ibid.*, LXXIII: 5–6.

ii. THE IMPACT OF THE PORTUGUESE AND DUTCH MISSIONARY EFFORTS

It was during a period when religious conflict was acute in Europe that the Portuguese, and after them the Dutch, gained control over the maritime provinces of Ceylon along with their other possessions in Asia and Africa. The Protestant Reformation, which broke the formal unity of mediaeval Christendom, nonetheless introduced a new vigour and dynamism into Christianity on both the Catholic and the Protestant sides. If the Dutch in the seventeenth century took pride in Calvinism that provided the religious fervour in their struggle for national independence, the Portuguese of the sixteenth century took similar pride in the success of the measures of their Counter-Reformation. Where the outside world was concerned, the mediaeval dichotomy of mankind into Christians and the heathen continued to hold sway over European minds; and the desire to turn the heathen into Christians figured fairly prominently in the European expansion overseas. To the missionary, in particular, *conquista temporal* was merely the first step towards the final goal of *conquista espiritual*.

An important consequence of the transfer of political power into alien hands, as far as Buddhism in Ceylon was concerned, was the loss of the state patronage which it had enjoyed for centuries, and which, as we have seen earlier, was a necessary condition for the proper functioning of its central institutions. Under the Portuguese and the Dutch, the strength of the state machinery was not merely withdrawn from Buddhism; it was actively used against Buddhism on the side of Christianity.

The distinct advantage of gaining state patronage on the side of Christianity was clearly recognized by the early missionaries. 'It is very difficult to lay the foundations of the faith in a country', confessed one of them; 'but', he continued, 'once the chief personages are seen to receive the gospel others easily listen to it'.[44] *Cujus regio illius religio* was a widely accepted principle in contemporary Europe.

The Franciscans, who were the earliest Christian missionaries in Ceylon, made many efforts to convert the then King of Kōṭṭe, Bhuvanekabāhu VII (1521–51), who was driven by political circumstances into relying more

[44] Quoted in S. G. Perera, 'The Jesuits in Ceylon in the XVI and XVII Centuries', *CALR*, I (1916) 221.

and more on the military strength of the Portuguese.[45] But, though he gave every liberty to the Franciscans to pursue their missionary work in his kingdom, the king himself showed no inclination to embrace the new faith. The Franciscans, however, were able to convert the king's grandson and successor, Dharmapāla (1551–97), who, since his youngest days, had been brought up under their personal guidance. Dharmapāla, who died without issue, bequeathed his kingdom to the King of Portugal, having, by an earlier deed, already transferred the revenues and services of (Buddhist) temple villages to the religious and educational establishments of the Franciscans in Ceylon.[46] Thus, under the Portuguese, Catholicism became the 'established' religion of the maritime provinces, to the exclusion of Buddhism, Hinduism and Islam. And under the Dutch, who succeeded the Portuguese to political power, Reformed (Calvinistic) Christianity became the established religion to the exclusion of all else, including Catholicism.

Both the Portuguese and the Dutch missionary efforts took some coherent and consistent form whenever the religious interests tallied with the political. Dutch opposition to Catholicism and Portuguese opposition to Calvinism were both religious and political. So indeed was the opposition to Buddhism on the part of both these powers. A hard political fact which these colonial rulers had constantly to keep in mind was the existence of an independent Sinhalese kingdom in the central parts of Ceylon, which, despite ups and downs, successfully withstood all encroachments on its sovereignty. Effective Portuguese and Dutch power, in fact, rarely extended beyond twenty miles inland; and a major problem, therefore, which they both had to confront, was the preservation of the loyalties of the subjects in the territories under their control. The prestige of the King of Kandy depended to a large extent on his traditional role as the protector of Buddhism; hence converting the coastal subjects to Christianity was deemed an effective means of weaning them from their potential source of loyalty to Kandy. In particular, the conversion of members of the local nobility was considered vitally important, in view of

[45] Fernão de Queyroz, *The Temporal and Spiritual Conquest of Ceylon* (1687), tr. S. G. Perera (Colombo, 1930), pp. 238 ff.

[46] *Ibid.*, pp. 330–31.

the prestige that they enjoyed in society as well as on account of the indispensability of their loyal services for the carrying out of administrative tasks. The profession of Christianity, therefore, was made a necessary condition for admission into office. Indeed, foreign influences on the nobility spread well beyond the confines of religion to wider cultural spheres.

The dissemination of these influences and the teaching of the principles of Christianity were the primary aims of education, a task which was performed by the clergy. Instruction in schools was primarily religious, and elementary education was necessarily geared to serve the interests of conversion. The school was looked upon as the nucleus of a future congregation; and with many other, non-educational functions also conferred on the schoolmaster, the school, in actual fact, came to be much more than a mere school. It was in the school that baptisms were administered and marriages were solemnized; it was also there that the *tombos*, or registers, of the district were kept and maintained. The schools, therefore, were the depositories of the 'evidence' on which the legal rights of the subjects with regard to inheritance and succession were mainly dependent.[47]

In certain parts of Asia, the attempts of certain Christian missionaries to present Christianity in terms of concepts and categories familiar to Asian minds took an ingenious form. Outstanding were the experiments of the Jesuits, Roberto de Nobili in Madura, India, who lived the life of a brahmin and presented Christianity in a Hindu guise, and Matteo Ricci in China, who sought an alliance with the Chinese literati and advocated the retention of Confucian rites where they were not incompatible with Christian belief and practice.[48] Such attempts were rare among Protestant missionaries; and even among the Catholics they were often frowned on by the orthodox in Rome. Especially in territories directly subject to Western political control, such as Goa and the maritime provinces of Ceylon, the missionaries were less inclined to make compromises than they were in territories which were not subject to their control. In the subject territories, the missionaries expressed unequivocally their opposition to local usages, and their attempts at conversion were consciously directed to

[47] E. W. Perera, 'The School Thombo Holder', *CALR*, I (1915) 89–93.

[48] K. M. Panikkar, *Asia and Western Dominance* (London, 1953), pp. 383–84, 391–94.

achieving a total breakaway from all 'pagan' practices. The cremation of dead bodies, for instance, was forbidden for the Christians; and among the Hindus of Ceylon the story was current that missionaries offered beef to their converts to test their breakaway from traditional beliefs and practices.[49]

Except to the virtuosi at the 'centre' of religious institutions, such exclusiveness was meaningless; the many at the periphery tended to look upon new forms of belief and practice as useful supplements rather than as new substitutes, a tendency which resulted in what Nock has called *adhesion* in contradistinction to *conversion*.[50] The missionaries found it particularly difficult to keep their converts away from the magical beliefs and practices which had intermingled with Buddhism at the level of the little tradition, and which prevailed as part of the daily lives of the masses. Enumerating 'the obstacles to the success of Christianity' in the Galle district, a missionary, in 1732, spoke of 'the public prevalence of idolatry, and the secret adherence to it, under the cloak of Christianity'.

> From their birth to their death, the Singhalese are said to be Buddhists in heart. When a child is born they consult astrologers. Is it sick, they tie charms to its neck, hands and feet. Does it eat rice for the first time, a heathen name is given it, letting go the name at baptism. Would they undertake any work, they must . . . first ascertain the lucky day, the propitious hour. Are they sick, or in adversity, devil ceremonies are performed; do they marry it must be in a good hour, accompanied with all manner of superstitions, do they die, their graves are ornamented with white leaves, and cocoanuts.[51]

The persistence of such traditional beliefs and practices—which has been observed as an almost universal phenomenon among 'converts'—was

[49] See C. R. Boxer, 'Christians and Spices: Portuguese Missionary Methods in Ceylon, 1518–1658', *History Today*, VIII (1958) 346–54; and 'A Note on Portuguese Missionary Methods in the East: 16th–18th Centuries', *CHJ*, X (1960–61) 77–90. The 'beef-test' was common in India too (Panikkar, *op. cit.*, p. 281). In a Hindu society it was indeed a potent test, as tradition degraded beef-eaters to the level of outcastes.

[50] A. D. Nock, *Conversion*, 1933 (Oxford, 1965), p. 7. Nock defined 'conversion' as 'a turning which implies a consciousness that a great change is involved, that the old was wrong and the new is right'. *Ibid.*

[51] Reproduced in J. D. Palm, 'An Account of the Dutch Church in Ceylon, collected from the local records deposited in the Wolfendahl Church, Colombo, Part II', *JRAS(CB)*, III (1847–48) 52–53.

accentuated in Ceylon because of the poor quality of religious instruction that was usually accorded to the converts, and the secular incentives that were widely used as aids to conversion. The closing of administrative offices to those who were not baptized and to those who did not profess Christianity, made all the high and the ambitious eager to baptize themselves and their children, and, though often only nominally, to describe themselves as Christians before the government. Similarly, the advantages that accompanied a 'Christian education', not to mention the fines that were imposed on the truants, made them seek instruction in missionary schools. And the legal recognition given to 'Christian marriages' made them go to church to get their marriage bonds solemnized. The 'Christianity' of the vast majority of them—who, in later times, were known by the significant appellation of Government Christians—was not infrequently a source of embarrassment to the missionaries themselves.

In such circumstances, any attempt to look for reliable statistics of conversion is bound to be futile. Neither the number of individuals who were baptized as Christians, nor the number of students who attended Christian schools, would by any means provide a true figure of the number of Christians. In 1760, for instance, the Ecclesiastical Returns of the Dutch Clergy indicated that 182,226 had been enrolled as Christians at Jaffna; of these only 64 were members of the church; likewise, of 9,820 at Mannar, only 5. And, in the same year, at Galle and Mātara, there were but 36 church members out of a total of 89,077 who had been baptized.[52] Besides, even deliberate exaggeration was not uncommon among the missionaries. As a recent observer has put it: 'One cannot help feeling that the missionaries have been using the multiplication table in the reports they sent home regarding the number of converts they were making. All sorts of contradictory and conflicting statistics are put forward in contemporary records.'[53] Presenting their work in the brightest colours to their superiors

[52] *Ibid.*, p. 67.

[53] S. Arasaratnam, 'Oratorians and Predikants: The Catholic Church in Ceylon under Dutch Rule' (Review Article), *CJHSS*, I (1958) 219. The conflicting and contradictory nature of the statistics in contemporary records may be illustrated with the following instances. In 1556, the Franciscans made the claim that 70,000 fisher-folk in Ceylon had embraced Christianity under their guidance. Half a century later, the total number of Christians in Ceylon was estimated at 30,000. T. B. H. Abeysinghe, Review of W. L. A. Don Peter's *Studies in Ceylon Church History*, *CJHSS*, VII (1964) 98. In 1634, the exact figure of 72,348 was given as the number of Christians in Jaffna; at the end of the same century, the figure was estimated to be about 17,000. R. Boudens, *The Catholic Church in Ceylon under Dutch Rule* (Rome, 1957), pp. 44 and 100.

in Europe was a phenomenon not peculiar to Ceylon; it was characteristic of almost every missionary society at the time.[54]

Despite the rather grave limitations of the absence of reliable statistics, certain broad features of the impact of the Portuguese and Dutch missionary efforts in Ceylon may nonetheless be discerned.

a. One of the most important of them, undoubtedly, was the relative success of Catholic missionary efforts compared with those of the (Dutch) Protestants. This feature was clearly recognized by Tennent in his *Christianity in Ceylon*, which was written in the mid-nineteenth century.

> Whatever may have been the instrumentality resorted to by the Portuguese priesthood, and however objectionable the means adopted by them for the extension of their own form of Christianity, one fact is unquestionable, that the natives became speedily attached to their ceremonies and modes of worship, and hence adhered to them with remarkable tenacity for upwards of three hundred years; whilst even in the midst of their own ministrations, the clergy and missionaries of the reformed church of Holland were overtaken by discouragement; and it is a remarkable fact, that notwithstanding the multitudinous baptisms, and the hundreds of thousands of Singhalese who were enrolled by them as converts, the religion and discipline of the Dutch Presbyterians is now almost extinct among the natives of Ceylon.[55]

The relative success of Catholicism, despite the stern measures taken by the Dutch to suppress it, was indeed a remarkable phenomenon; and it is worth considering some of the factors that facilitated it. One of them, clearly, was the outward similarity of the rich ceremonialism that characterized Catholicism in common with the religious systems that it tried to overthrow. Some Catholic missionaries themselves recognized this similarity and to some extent derived confidence and encouragement from it. The Abbé Dubois, who spent many years as a Catholic missionary in Mysore, India, in writing to a Protestant missionary on 'the impracticability of the conversion of Hindus', observed:

> If any of the several modes of Christian worship were calculated to make an impression and gain ground in the country, it is no doubt the Catholic form which you Protestants call an idolatry in disguise: it has a *Pooga* or sacrifice; . . . it

[54] Panikkar, *Asia and Western Dominance*, pp. 414–15.

[55] J. Emerson Tennent, *Christianity in Ceylon* (London, 1850), p. 67.

has processions, images, statues, *tirtan* or holy water, fasts, *tittys* or feasts, and prayers for the dead, invocation of saints, etc., all of which practices bear more or less resemblance to those in use among the Hindoos.[56]

It is relevant in this connection to note a debate held before Śrī Vīra Parākrama Narendrasiṃha (1707–39), the Sinhalese King of Kandy, between Nanclars de La Nerolle, a French Huguenot, and Fr. Gonçalvez of the Oratorian Catholic Mission. The Calvinist attacked the use of images in Catholic worship, which the priest defended with reference to the Scriptures. Evidently, the king and the Buddhist bystanders were highly impressed by the defence of image worship put up by the Catholic priest.[57] The strict opposition to image worship and mass ceremonialism on the part of the Calvinist church, coupled with its withdrawal of the special intermediary and protective functions of the priesthood, took much of the mass appeal away from this church.

The rise of Dutch power inevitably brought a critical period to Catholicism in Ceylon. The harassment of 'Papists' and the use of secular incentives to gain them for the Reformed church won over a good number of Catholics who were on the periphery of the community. Those who survived these trials were necessarily a hard core of believers who were unified and strengthened through common suffering and sacrifice. Simultaneously, there occurred a marked change in the nature and composition of the Catholic clergy as well. Instead of the European missionary working under the patronage of a Catholic government, there was the Indian missionary from the Oratorian Mission in Goa. He, in contrast to both his European predecessor and the contemporary Dutch predikant, was of necessity driven to a life of barefooted austerity; and his religious effort was entirely voluntary, often within a territory where his religion was officially proscribed. Being Indians, they could move about without getting detected easily; and many of them accepted, with no reservations, the Ceylonese way of life. Their proficiency in Sinhalese and Tamil far surpassed that of the Dutch predikants.[58]

[56] J. A. Dubois, *Letters on the state of Christianity in India* (London, 1823), p. 18. The letter quoted is dated 7 August 1815.

[57] See S. G. Perera, *The Life of Father Jacome Gonçalvez* (Madura, 1942) pp. 50–55.

[58] Edmund Peiris, 'Sinhalese Christian Literature of the XVIIth and XVIIIth Centuries', *JRAS(CB)*, XXXV (1943) 163–81, and 'Tamil Catholic Literature in Ceylon, from the 16th to the 18th Century', *Tamil Culture*, II (1953) 229–44.

Forbidden to enter the Dutch territories, the Catholic priests used the Kandyan kingdom as a springboard for their activities. The kings of Kandy adopted a tolerant attitude towards them, an attitude which was buttressed by their political opposition to the Dutch, and offered refuge to the Catholics and their priests. From Kandy the priests slipped into the maritime provinces from time to time, and went round, in disguise, administering the sacraments to the faithful and organizing Catholic communities in different parts of the Dutch territories. These activities were so well organized that the Catholics had a larger number of priests attending to them in the eighteenth century (even though their presence in the maritime provinces was illegal) than the Protestants ever had.

In about the middle of the eighteenth century, the attitude of the Kandyan court towards the Catholics took a significantly different turn. Within Kandy, apparently from the very beginning, a sizable faction had viewed with disfavour their kings' magnanimity towards the Catholic priests.[59] This faction gained popularity in the wake of the efforts to revive Buddhism during the mid-eighteenth century. Their feelings were enraged, and their case was strengthened by the anti-Buddhist polemical works which were written about this time by the leading Catholic priests.[60] King Śrī Vijaya Rājasiṃha (1739–47), whose position on the throne was somewhat insecure on account of his foreign (South Indian Nayakkar) origin, had no choice but to order the priests out of his kingdom to placate the Buddhists.[61] Fortunately for the Catholics, they were sufficiently well established in the maritime provinces by this time to dispense with the use of Kandy as a springboard. Within a few years, furthermore, the Dutch government gradually became more tolerant towards the Catholics, despite the strong pressure brought upon the

[59] In 1969, because of their opposition, the Catholics were compelled to change the site of their church in Kandy. Boudens, *The Catholic Church in Ceylon*, pp. 99–100.

[60] Prominent among those works were *Budumula*, an examination of Buddhism written by Gonçalvez and presented to the Nayakkar Crown Prince on his accession to the throne, and *Mātara Pratyakṣaya*, a 'refutation' of Buddhism written by the same author on account of a Buddhist-Catholic controversy held in the Mātara district. Boudens, pp. 196–97.

[61] See below, section iii-*c* of this chapter. Śrī Vijaya's successor, Kīrti Śrī Rajasimha, offered to welcome the priests back to Kandy in 1760 at the beginning of hostilities against the Dutch; but the priests, at this time, preferred to give their support to the Dutch in their plans to invade Kandy. Boudens, pp. 159–60.

government by the predikants to revert to the early measures of repression. Catholicism, by then, had ceased to be a serious political threat to the powers of the Dutch, and the government considered it impolitic to check its existence with harsh measures which could lead the Catholic inhabitants to open rebellion against the government.

b. Just as significant as the relative success of Catholicism (as against Calvinism) was the fact that the vast majority of the Ceylonese were *not* converted to the one or the other form of Christianity. The prevalence of deeply institutionalized religious and cultural norms among the populace rendered the propagation of Christianity far more formidable a task than the missionaries had anticipated. Quite apart from this basic and obvious difficulty, there were grave shortcomings in the missionary effort itself.

In the first place, though proselytism was given an important place in the governmental programme, and governmental powers were extensively used to implement this programme, it was hardly ever pursued with the determination and thoroughness that the achievement of such a goal would in fact have required. This was in keeping with the general outlook of contemporary Portuguese and Dutch colonialism. The fact that they were not mere traders, but governors and administrators as well, required them to evolve some positive attitude and policy towards the people whom they governed. They themselves were scarcely prepared, however, for any such responsible undertaking. In terms of effective colonial policy, there was no clear idea of mission, no deep feeling of moral obligation to 'civilize and christianize the heathen'. There were, to be sure, individual administrators who were deeply concerned with such ideals. But their efforts were rarely effective, and in any case, were few and far between. As far as the bulk of the administrators were concerned, there were no positive policies towards the governed; their actions were dictated primarily by considerations of political expediency and economic gain.

Another factor that necessarily cramped the actions of colonial rulers was the existence of a sovereign Sinhalese kingdom in the central regions of Ceylon, which stood in the eyes of the Sinhalese as a bastion of custom and tradition. The attempts to conquer this kingdom created an atmosphere of chronic war and turmoil, an atmosphere which was hardly conducive to 'reformist' activities, or even for that matter, to the basic economic activities in which the rulers were primarily interested. On the other hand, insofar as it could not be conquered, it had to be kept in reasonably good humour, and the attempt to achieve this end necessitated a mitigation of 'reformist' activities, notably in the religious field. Thus, despite opposition from the local predikants and the Batavian authorities, the Dutch government in Ceylon several times placed their ships at the disposal of Kandyan kings to bring *bhikkhus* from Burma and Siam to re-establish *upasampadā* (higher) ordination in Ceylon.[62]

The attempts of the Kandyan kings to uphold and revive Buddhism gave this religion a dignity and self-respect even within the maritime provinces which it might have lacked if the whole country had been governed by a Christian power. Though it was the general policy of the colonial rulers to accentuate the (political) division between the 'low country' and the 'hill country' by spreading Christianity and European culture among the low-country Sinhalese, this policy had its desired effects only on a small section of the total population. While this section more or less faithfully served the colonial government, the rest of the population vacillated between the two governments. All-out drives to suppress Buddhism could alienate their loyalties to the rival power in Kandy; hence, except in the main military and administrative centres, the general attitude of the colonial governments to traditional religious practices remained, in practice, one of leniency and indifference. Buddhism was not allowed to show any outward signs of vitality, mainly for fear of losing Christian converts, but in the rural areas, which really meant the whole country except the few towns and forts, the traditional beliefs and practices persisted without much interruption, though naturally in a weakened state because of the lack of continuous contact with a powerful great tradition. When, in the mid-eighteenth century, attempts to revive the great tradition finally succeeded (in Kandy), such contacts were re-

[62] S. Arasaratnam, 'Vimala Dharma Surya II (1687–1707) and his relations with the Dutch', *CJHSS*, VI (1963) 66; and below, section iii of this chapter. During the period when Kandyan kings were extending their protection to the Catholics, the Dutch government, with even greater reluctance, was compelled in a few instances to mitigate their anti-Catholic policies as well. In 1734, a Catholic priest who was caught within the maritime provinces had to be released because of the king's appeals on his behalf; and, for some time, the Dutch were constrained to adopt a lenient attitude towards Affonso Pereira (the leader of Negombo Catholics) because he stood in good favour with the king. Boudens, pp. 133 and 107.

established, and the low country too—especially the Southern Province—came to be studded with centres of renewed Buddhist activities.[63]

Understandably enough, the relative leniency and indifference of the government was strongly resented by the Christian clergy, who urged it to enforce to their very letter the 'anti-heathenish' laws promulgated by the government. Frustrated in this attempt, they at times went on to petition the home authorities to bring pressure on the Ceylon government. There was, for instance, a prolonged controversy between the clergy and the government over the ancient Buddhist temple at Kälaṇiya, situated only six miles from the main administrative and military centre, Colombo.[64]

Kälaṇiya flourished as one of the major centres of Buddhist worship in the island before the sixteenth century. In 1555, the then King of Kōṭṭe, Dharmapāla, having been converted to Catholicism, transferred the lands belonging to this temple, along with other lands, to the religious and educational establishments of the Franciscans in Ceylon. A few years later, the temple and its shrines were subjected to the ravages of Portuguese soldiers. Towards the end of the seventeenth century, that is, after the Dutch had taken over the maritime provinces, the Dutch predikants sought the permission of the government to build a schoolhouse in the vicinity of the neglected temple. Though the schoolhouse was eventually built, the attraction of Buddhist pilgrims to the Kälaṇiya temple continued to increase, much to the annoyance of the government and the clergy alike. They naturally did not wish to see the existence of a popular and active centre of Buddhist worship so close to their main centre of power. The clergy pressed the government to close the temple down by enforcing the anti-Buddhist *plakkaats* which had been issued from time to time. But the government was reluctant to take such a direct step lest it displease the then King of Kandy, Vimaladharmasūrya II (1687–1707), with whom they preferred to maintain peaceful relations. The Dutch government was prepared to punish Christian converts if they were seen taking part in Buddhist ceremonies; but beyond that it was not prepared to go.

This, in effect, meant a tacit recognition of the rights of Buddhists to

[63] See below, section iii-*c* of this chapter and section ii of chapter V.

[64] The account given below is taken mainly from H. C. P. Bell and A. Mendis Gunasekara, 'Kelani Vihāra and its Inscriptions', *CALR*, I (1916) 145–61.

their own forms of worship, far too generous a concession in the eyes of the clergy. They, accordingly, made direct representations to the directors of the Dutch East India Company. The directors, in 1692, acceded to their appeals. Thus the clergy took charge of the premises, and the Buddhist monks in the temple were ordered to depart.[65]

This was, however, a very unusual instance; rarely did the wishes of the clergy prevail over those of the civil authorities. The subordination of the Church to the interests of the State prevailed as a well-established policy of European companies. As Boxer has observed with regard to the Dutch East India Company:

> Where the interests of the Company and those of the Church clashed the former almost invariably prevailed. As directors wrote [to the Council at Batavia on 12 April 1656]: 'The nature of government is such that it cannot suffer two equally great controlling powers, any more than a body can endure two heads', for which reason the civil power must always have full and unfettered control over the ecclesiastical.[66]

In the administration of Ceylon, there were no significant departures from this generally accepted policy. The clergy were looked upon as individual employees of the government rather than as members of a collective church.[67]

The reluctance of the clergy to accept these conditions, which they considered humiliating, led time and again to scrambles for power and prestige between the secular and the ecclesiastical authorities on issues important as well as trivial. In 1659, there was a quarrel in the Church Council over the question whether the secular representative within it should have a special table with a scarlet cloth on it. The representative claimed it as a symbol of authority. The predikants protested against the claim; and, as a result, it was disallowed. In 1669, the predikants at Jaffna jointly protested against the precedence given to the *disāva* (provincial

[65] *Ibid.*

[66] C. R. Boxer, *The Dutch Seaborne Empire, 1600–1800* (London, 1965), p. 138.

[67] S. Arasaratnam, *Dutch Power in Ceylon, 1658–1687* (Amsterdam, 1958), pp. 222–23. It is worth noting that even in the case of the Kälaṇiya temple, the victory of the clergy was by no means final. Towards the latter half of the eighteenth century, while the Dutch were still in power, Kälaṇiya was restored under the patronage of King Kīrti Śrī Rājasiṃha, and from that time onwards, it continued to flourish as a centre of Buddhist activity. Bell and Gunasekara, *op. cit.*

governor) over them. They referred to an incident where the palanquin bearing the *disāva* had gone ahead of that in which there was a predikant, much to the alleged humiliation of the predikant in the eyes of the onlookers.[68]

Among the more important issues that gave rise to tension was the problem of finances for ecclesiastical and educational purposes. Though the revenues of temple villages and the services of the tenants attached to these villages were transferred to the Franciscans by the converted King of Kōṭṭe, the Franciscans were in fact never allowed to reap the full benefits of this royal gift. The Portuguese secular authorities were not prepared to allow the missionaries to possess or enjoy such vast and powerful economic rights. The bitter complaints of the Franciscans proved to be of no avail.[69] The Augustinians and the Dominicans, who arrived in the island afterwards, were not given any land; they were paid salaries instead. It was this system of paying salaries that was inherited and perpetuated by the Dutch; and though the Dutch were keen on both the education and the conversion of their subjects, they were not prepared to allow this to become a financial drain on the government. No substantial amount was set apart for this task. In fact, they expected schools to be self-sufficient as far as possible. The salaries of schoolmasters quite often had to be paid out of the fines imposed on defaulters. The only significant item of expenditure directly undertaken by the government was the payment of salaries to the predikants who came from Europe.[70]

The restriction of funds for religious purposes was not guided solely by considerations of economy. It was part of the programme of subordinating the Church to the interests of the State. The secular authorities were not inclined to grant much power to the ecclesiastical either in the economic or in any other field. Indeed, evidence seems to suggest that the government officials did not wish to see the clergy develop independent contacts with the people. During the Portuguese times, an instance is recorded where a village 'lord' told a priest who begged him to erect a church in his

[68] Arasaratnam, *Dutch Power*, pp. 224–25.

[69] De Queyroz, *Temporal and Spiritual Conquest of Ceylon*, pp. 1053–57; and P. E. Pieris, *The Portuguese Era*, vol. II (Colombo, 1914), pp. 255 *et. seq.*

[70] Arasaratnam, *Dutch Power*, p. 221.

village: 'Padre, if there were a Church in my village, I would cease to be its Lord'.[71] During the Dutch times, though the predikants claimed the right to visit and inspect village schools, the government refused to allow them to go into villages as often as they liked. The inspection was entrusted to an officer in the civil administration, who could take one of the predikants with him on his tours, although this was not compulsory.[72]

Just as the clergy tried to pose as the champions of the people against the tyranny and oppression of the administrators, the administrators, in turn, made attempts to do the same against the intolerance of the former. And this was frequently given as the reason for refusing them free contact with the people. There were complaints about the manner in which the clergy had exploited village labour for purposes of church-building,[73] as well as about the way they had demanded princely treatment in food and services on their tours of villages. Even more serious allegations were current about the indiscriminate and selfish manner in which they had inflicted fines to ensure church attendance.[74]

Another factor that made it difficult for Christianity to establish itself widely in Ceylon was the absence of a Ceylonese clergy. De Melo has observed:

> The proper establishment of the Church in a country means it is at home in that country. It implies that it has passed from the precarious state in which it lived to the normal state of stability, autonomy and self-sufficiency. . . . Among the various factors or elements that go to bring about this kind of stability, security and self-sufficiency, one of the most important, if not actually the most important, is the formation of a native clergy.[75]

Under the Portuguese administration, there were theological colleges and seminaries conducted by both the Franciscans and the Jesuits.[76] Despite the priestly training given to Ceylonese students at these institu-

[71] Pieris, *op. cit.*, p. 258.

[72] Arasaratnam, *Dutch Power*, p. 223.

[73] De Queyroz, *op. cit.*, pp. 1050 and 1053.

[74] Arasaratnam, *Dutch Power*, p. 224.

[75] Carlos Merces De Melo, *The Recruitment and Formation of Native Clergy in India (16th–19th Centuries)* (Lisbon, 1955), p. xxvii.

[76] S. G. Perera, *Historical Sketches* (Jaffne, 1938), p. 74, and *Jesuits in Ceylon* (Madura, 1941), p. 30.

tions, none of them were admitted to any of the religious orders. The refusal to admit Asians to any of the main religious orders remained in fact, for a very long time, a common feature in the whole of Portuguese Asia.[77]

This was, quite possibly, a result of the stereotypical attitude of suspicion and distrust that the Portuguese generally maintained towards their Asian subjects. Arriving in territories where they were hardly welcome and maintaining themselves in power by the strength of their arms over large subject populations, such an attitude was perhaps only natural among them. This attitude, furthermore, was often compounded with feelings of racial and cultural superiority.[78] Exceptions were made, to be sure, especially in territories which were not directly under their rule. The Chinese and the Japanese were gradually admitted to the religious orders.[79] The same liberality, however, was much delayed in other places. When the Congregation of the Oratory, at last, opened the door to the Indians, the candidates admitted were, significantly, converted brahmins. The devoted labours of a group of them, Joseph Vaz and his brethren, saved Roman Catholicism in Ceylon from near extinction. But Vaz himself, during his long stay in the island, made no attempt to send any Ceylonese abroad to be trained for the priesthood.[80]

The task of training a Ceylonese (Protestant) clergy was tackled with some seriousness under the Dutch administration. This was caused primarily by the paucity of Dutch predikants for missionary work overseas. Of the few who were available for missionary work in Ceylon, very few indeed were even cursorily acquainted with the local languages.[81] Hence,

[77] A similar policy was followed by the same religious orders even longer in Spanish America and in the Philippines.

[78] The claim frequently made by Portuguese writers that their compatriots were free of racial prejudice in their overseas possessions has not survived the test of historical scrutiny. See C. R. Boxer, *Race Relations in Portuguese Colonial Empire, 1415–1825* (Oxford, 1963).

[79] C. R. Boxer, *The Christian Century in Japan, 1549–1650* (Berkeley, 1951), pp. 73, 89–90, 226.

[80] Boudens, *op. cit.*, p. 187.

[81] 'So far as I have been able to ascertain, there were never as many as twenty *predikants* at any given time in Ceylon, and very few of these had either the ability or the inclination to make a thorough study of the indigenous languages and religions. There were some exceptions, such as the Rev. Philippus Baldaeus, who learnt Tamil, and the Rev. Johannes Ruel, who learnt Sinhalese; but their sporadic efforts could make no impression on two such deeply rooted and well-established faiths as Buddhism and Hinduism'. Boxer, *The Dutch Seaborne Empire*, p. 147.

in 1690, a seminary was opened at Nallur in the Northern District to train a local clergy for Tamil-speaking areas; and six years later a second seminary was opened in Colombo to fulfil the same function for Sinhalese-speaking areas.[82] The more promising students of the two seminaries were sent at government expense to Leyden and Utrecht for further training and eventual ordination. Some progress, in this way, was clearly made towards the formation of a Ceylonese clergy; but the numbers thus trained were never so numerous as the founders had optimistically envisaged. The majority of the students who attended the seminaries ended up in secular vocations (as schoolmasters and government clerks) or in the lower ranks of the church as *proponents*.[83] The few who were given the chance to be fully trained and ordained as predikants were barely adequate even to minister to the existing Dutch and Burgher communities, let alone for missionary work among the unconverted. The expenses involved in sending students abroad made the government reluctant to increase their numbers. The few who were given the chance to go to the Netherlands were chosen exclusively from high-caste families.[84]

c. In Europe as well as in Asia, at this time, the religious profession was, in practice if not in theory, a monopoly of the higher strata of society. The restriction of ordination in the Christian churches to members of high-caste families (both in India and in Ceylon) would not appear therefore as surprising.[85] It does, all the same, point to a significant phenomenon: the manner in which the Christian churches, after halfhearted and futile attempts to disregard caste in matters relating to Christianity, came to compromise with this deep-rooted social institution.

The compromises, understandably enough, were more explicit in India than in Ceylon. The Third (1584) and Fifth (1606) Provincial Councils of

[82] *Ibid.*, p. 149.

[83] A *proponent* was 'a clerical officer peculiar to the Church of Holland, with functions intermediate between those of a catechist or deacon of the Church of England and those of a probationer or licentiate of the Church of Scotland'. Tennent, *Christianity in Ceylon*, p. 102.

[84] P. E. Pieris, *Ceylon and the Hollanders* (Tellippalai, 1918), p. 90. A notable example was Henricus Philipsz Panditaratna, the son of Governor Van Gollenesse's Maha Mudaliyar. *Ibid.*

[85] The parallel phenomenon within the Buddhist order, and the low-caste reaction against the high-caste monopoly, will be discussed below in ch. II, sec. iv.

Goa prescribed, inter alia, that candidates for the priesthood should be selected only from the more 'honourable' castes;[86] and a Bull of Pope Gregory XV (1621–23) went to the extent of sanctioning the observance of caste distinctions in the seating arrangements in South Indian churches.[87]

The reasons for these compromises are not difficult to guess, for one of the biggest 'problems' that early Christian missionaries had to encounter in India was the fact that their converts came almost exclusively from the lowest ranks of Hindu society. Though followers of the Hindu religion, these ranks—the low castes and the outcastes—were not full-fledged members of Hindu society. They had very little to lose, except their low status, by breaking away from the Hindu tradition. Hence, mass conversions to other religions—to Islam and to Sikhism in particular—had been rather common among them even before the (large-scale) advent of Christianity.[88] To the high castes, on the other hand, their privileged and central position in Hindu society was ensured only through sustained adherence to the Hindu tradition—to its beliefs and practices, and to its intricate system of prescriptions and taboos. Any breakaway from this tradition meant for them a necessary social degradation; and all those who did not conform to this tradition were judged accordingly by the brahmins. It is not surprising, therefore, that the 'impure' habits of European Christians provoked as much disgust in the orthodox brahmin as those of the Indian low castes. In his 'Notes on the Caste System', Bougle observed:

> The disgust which Europeans inspire in Hindus has frequently been noted. A traveller recounts that a Brahman with whom he was acquainted used to visit him very early in the morning: the Brahman preferred to see him before taking his bath so that he might cleanse himself of the impurities which he had incurred. A Hindu with self-respect would die of thirst rather than drink from the cup which had been used by a 'Mleccha'.[89]

De Nobili's experiment in Madura in the early seventeenth century was

[86] De Melo, *op. cit.*, pp. 144 and 320. The Fifth Council also stipulated that low-caste students in the seminaries should not be taught Latin. *Ibid.*, p. 144.

[87] G. S. Ghurye, *Caste and Class in India*, 2nd ed. (Bombay, 1957), p. 199.

[88] J. H. Hutton, *Caste in India*, 3rd ed. (Bombay, 1961), p. 204.

[89] Originally published (in French) in 1900; translated as 'The Essence and Reality of the Caste System', *Contributions to Indian Sociology*, II (1958) 24.

a conscious effort to cleanse Christianity of this pollutionist stigma.[90] Shunning European company, he lived among Indians and strictly adhered to the prescriptions and taboos that were followed by the brahmins. Acquiring a knowledge of Tamil, the language of those who lived around him, and Sanskrit, the classical language of Hindu scriptures, he proclaimed himself the guru of a new *mārga*, which was orthodox and in the true tradition of Hindu religious thought, yet far superior to anything which had previously been known. To the seminary opened by de Nobili only brahmin pupils were admitted, and the purpose of their training was to send them back to their fellow brahmins and to endeavour to bring them over to the 'true faith'.[91] De Nobili achieved some success, despite strong opposition from his own orthodox brethren. The results, however, were neither widespread nor permanent. The Abbé Dubois, who, in a subsequent period, practised somewhat similar methods in Mysore,[92] reported after a twenty-five year stay in India:

> During the long period I have lived in India in the capacity of a missionary, I have made, with the assistance of a native missionary, in all between two hundred and three hundred converts. . . . Of this number two-thirds were pariahs, or beggars; and the rest were composed of *sudras*, vagrants, and outcasts . . . who, being without resource, turned Christians, chiefly for the purpose of marriage, or with some other interested views.[93]

The relationships between caste and conversion in Ceylon appear considerably different when compared with those in India. In the first place, the recognition of Christianity as the 'government religion' in areas under European control gave this religion a certain dignity which it lacked in areas that were not subject to their rule. Also, the exclusive appointment of Christians to important government offices drove the Sinhalese nobility to profess the 'government religion', at least nominally, in order to preserve their traditional positions of leadership. Conversion to Christianity, while it guaranteed the strengthening of their authority in terms of the values of those newly in power, did not lead—and this was

[90] The attempts of Ricci to build an alliance with the Confucianist literati in China also had the aim of presenting Christianity as a 'respectable' religion.

[91] Vincent Cronin, *A Pearl to India: The Life of Roberto de Nobili* (London, 1959).

[92] Roderick Cameron, 'The Abbé Dubois in India', *History Today*, VIII (1955) 166–68.

[93] Dubois, *Letters*, pp. 133–34 (the letter is dated 16 November 1816).

an important difference from the situation in India–to a necessary and drastic loss of prestige in terms of the traditional values. Concepts of pollution and purity–the essential criteria of status evaluation in the Hindu caste system[94]–did have a relevance even within the Sinhalese system; but in the absence of Hinduism and a dominant caste of brahmins, their actual application was far less rigorous. Implications of this feature were appreciated by Tennent (during a later period) when he wrote:

> In the case of the convert from Buddhism, even under the influence of caste, there is no dread of that fearful vengeance for apostacy which, in the instance of the Hindoo, divests him at one fell swoop of kindred and of friends, of possessions and inheritance, and even of a recognized position amongst civilized men. The Buddhist, when he opens the divine records of Christianity, does not recoil with instinctive prejudice like the Hindoo on discovering that its founder was the son of a carpenter and the associate of fishermen; nor does he shudder as he reads . . . that the temples of Jehovah were consecrated by the blood of oxen and bulls. . . . He does not start at the idea of ascending to the same heaven with the pariah and the outcaste.[95]

In Ceylon, in contrast to India, there were no necessary links between the traditional status system and the traditional religious system. In India the status of each caste was evaluated in terms of brahmanical teachings; in Ceylon no such explicitly formulated standard prevailed for status evaluation. In India the caste system was maintained and consolidated by the priestly authority of the brahmins; in Ceylon no priestly caste existed. The consolidation and legitimation of caste in Ceylon, therefore, was primarily a secular function mainly in the hands of the political authority, the king.[96] As the king was expected to preserve and to conform to what the Pali chronicles repeatedly referred to as 'the path of good and ancient custom', he had no power to interfere with the caste system arbitrarily. Still, within limits, it was his prerogative to ordain appropriate functions to different caste groups.[97] As it happened, it was to this curious role that

[94] H. N. C. Stevenson, 'Status Evaluation in the Hindu Caste System', *JRAI*, LXXXIV (1954) 45–65.

[95] Tennent, *Christianity in Ceylon*, pp. 330–31.

[96] Regarding the 'secularization' of caste in Ceylon, see A. M. Hocart, *Caste: A Comparative Study* (London, 1950), and Ralph Pieris, *Sinhalese Social Organization* (Colombo, 1956), esp. Part V.

[97] *Ibid.* Significantly, even the mythological expositions of the origin of caste current among the Sinhalese (derived from Buddhist *suttas*) traced caste divisions to the decrees of the mythical king–Mahāsammata.

the Portuguese and the Dutch succeeded when they took control of the maritime provinces.

The new state of affairs provided incentives to the more ambitious among the lower castes to acquire power through faithful service to the new masters. It is significant that whereas in India Christianity spread most widely among the lowest strata of society, in Ceylon (certain sections of) the middle ranks were more receptive to the new faith than were the lowest. It is worth examining briefly some of the factors that lay behind this phenomenon.

The rulers were compelled to secure the loyalty of the high caste (Goyigama) nobility as a matter of absolute necessity. The system of administering the colony was a system of indirect rule: a system of rule, that is, which was conducted through the nobility with some conscious direction by the new rulers at the top. It had no chance of success in the absence of the loyalty of the nobility. The means of securing this loyalty, however, presented to the rulers a perpetual dilemma. Basically the dilemma was this. In order not to lose the support of the nobility, they had to be granted substantial privileges (in the form of land grants, titles, honours and medals, etc.); they had to be convinced that they had something to gain by giving their support to an alien regime. Still, these very privileges contrived to increase their power and thus tended to constitute a real threat to the power of their patrons. It has been argued, in fact, that because of the ignorance of Europeans of local custom and usage the nobility wielded greater power under European rule than they did under the rule of Sinhalese kings.[98] Some of them commanded considerable prestige within the Kandyan court too;[99] and a good many of them, in addition to being related to each other, had kinship ties with the Kandyan nobility as well.[100] They had frequent dealings, open as well as secret, with the king and the nobility in Kandy. Decisions to desert the foreign rulers in times of crises were not uncommon among them.[101] The attempt of the rulers to wean the nobility from their loyalties to Kandy through

[98] H. W. Codrington, *A Short History of Ceylon* (London, 1939), pp. 129–30.

[99] The common practice among certain chiefs in the maritime provinces of seeking and receiving titles and honours from Kandyan kings was a source of much annoyance to the European rulers. See P. E. Pieris, 'Appointments within the Kandyan Provinces', *JRAS(CB)*, XXXVI (1945) 113.

[100] *Ibid.*, p. 114.

[101] In this connection, see below, ch. II, sec. ii.

government office, Christianity and other elements of European culture did not prove unreservedly successful.

One possible solution to this problem, as far as the rulers were concerned, was to look for supplementary sources of loyalty within the maritime provinces, and also to try and establish new relationships to check and balance the powers of the nobility. Quite apart from fostering internal rivalry within the Goyigama nobility,[102] another expedient resorted to was the promotion of non-Goyigama individuals to important government offices.[103] The latter were chosen not from the lowest castes but from the castes in the middle ranks of the traditional hierarchy. Particularly important among them were the Karāve and Salāgama castes, neither of which enjoyed high prestige either in the traditional system or in the contemporary Kandyan system. Their avenue for mobility therefore lay in their loyalty to the new rulers.[104]

In terms of their main caste occupations, the Karāvas (fishers) and the Salāgamas (cinnamon-peelers) were less involved in traditional ritual and ceremonial than, for instance, were the Navandanno (smiths), Radav (washers) and Beravāyo (drummers); and, as relative newcomers to the island, they mixed rather more freely with foreigners. 'Many low-caste people', recorded the *Rājāvaliya*, 'unmindful of their low birth, intermarried with the Portuguese and became proselytes'.[105] Of the Karāve caste, specifically, an Oratorian missionary wrote in 1707: 'Many of them are related to the Whites and many of the Mesticos come from them'.[106]

[102] 'It has . . . always been my practice to keep near me some of the Sinhalese chiefs as it would otherwise be difficult to preserve the particular usages of the country among the inhabitants, and also to find out at the same time what was going on, exchanging them sometimes for others of whom the former are jealous. There would otherwise only be a very remote possibility of finding out everything that was happening and of which it was also important to be aware'. *The Memoir of Rycloff Van Goens* (to Jacob Hustaart, 26 December 1663), tr. E. Reimers (Colombo, 1932), p. 19.

[103] During the Portuguese times, there were complaints about the appointment of people to positions for which they were not eligible by right of birth. De Queyroz, *op. cit.*, pp. 1011–14. The same complaint continued during the Dutch times. Arasaratnam, *Dutch Power in Ceylon*, pp. 230–31.

[104] The subject of caste mobility in the maritime provinces will be discussed in some detail in section iv of chapter II (below).

[105] *The Rājāvaliya*, tr. and ed. B. Gunasekara (Colombo, 1900), p. 80.

[106] 'An Account of the Success of the Mission to Ceylon' by Manoel de Miranda, tr. S. G. Perera, *CALR*, VI (1921) 121.

The loyalty of these castes was richly rewarded. A Jesuit missionary describing a baptismal ceremony of five Karāve chiefs from Chilaw in 1606 wrote:

That their baptism might be the more solemn, it was arranged to take place in Malwana, on the feast of our Lady of Victories, which the Captain General observed with great ceremony, when all those who were subject to us in the island had to come with gifts in token of their vassalage. The baptism was conferred in these circumstances to the great pleasure of the Captain General, and other captains who stood sponsors to them, and to our honour and to the honour of the baptised. The General was pleased to grant them many favours and privileges in order to cause the envy of the other gentiles who might thus be led to follow their example.[107]

It was among certain sections of the Karāve caste that Catholicism developed its strongest roots. And it was from this caste that the Dutch received the strongest resistance to their anti-Catholic activities. Yet even within this caste, the change of religious affiliation with the change of rulers in the country was not an uncommon phenomenon; while certain Karāve leaders like Affonso Pereira stuck firmly to the Catholic faith and led the Catholic agitation against the Dutch religious policies, others like D'Andrado adopted Calvinism and strongly supported the new rulers. The adoption of the 'government religion' professed and supported by the current rulers was indeed the general pattern that was common in Ceylon, especially among the mobility-oriented groups and individuals.

iii. BUDDHISM IN THE KANDYAN KINGDOM

a. *The Early Period*

The growth and establishment of European power in the littoral witnessed the shift of the Sinhalese capital to the central highlands of *kanda uḍa raṭa*.[108] Seeking protection in this natural fastness, the Kandyan kingdom maintained its sovereignty under its own kings until the depo-

[107] 'The College of Colombo and its residences', by Hieronymus Gomez, tr. S. G. Perera, *CALR*, II (1916) 21.

[108] 'Kandy' is a European corruption of *Kanda* [*uḍa raṭa*] meaning '[the country above] the mountain'. The Sinhalese name of the capital was Senkaḍagala Sirivardhana Pura; and of the kingdom, Siṃhalē.

sition of Śrī Vikrama Rājasiṃha in 1815. In terms of its ecology, this kingdom differed markedly from all the Sinhalese kingdoms that historically preceded it. Even so, the idea that prevailed that it was the natural successor to all the previous Sinhalese kingdoms[109] necessarily entailed certain features of continuity, particularly in the field of religious institutions. The *bhikkhus* who fled from the coastal regions were warmly received into the Kandyan kingdom and endowed with new temples and land grants to support them.[110] With new temples being built, and the older ones being renovated, Buddhist monasticism gradually established itself within the Kandyan kingdom in more or less the same position it had held in the earlier kingdoms.

By virtue of their religious roles and economic privileges, the Buddhist monks exercised considerable power and influence. At times, they even performed the usual functions of lay officials. King Rājasiṃha's embassy to the Dutch in 1686 was led by the chief monk in Kandy, Kobbǟkaḍuvē Gaṇēbaṇḍāra.[111] During the reign of Rājasiṃha's successor, Vimaladharmasūrya II, the Gaṇēbaṇḍāra exercised even greater influence. He led the Kandyan delegation in their negotiations with the Dutch in 1688; and because of his influence as well as the king's own religiosity, the external policies of Kandy during this reign assumed a definite religious bias.[112] By 1731, the chief monk of the Pōyamalu Vihāre at Kandy, in addition to his ecclesiastical role, occupied two exclusively lay offices, those of Basnāyaka Nilamē and Disāva.[113] The influence of the monks over the general populace played a decisive role, especially in times of political crises.[114]

In its relations with the wider society, therefore, the order of monks

[109] This idea was best expressed in the continuation of the *Mahāvaṃsa* that was written during the reign of Kīrti Śrī Rājasiṃha (1747–82).

[110] 'Palkum̆bura Sannasa', *EZ*, III (1928–33) 241.

[111] S. Arasaratnam, *Dutch Power in Ceylon*, p. 110.

[112] S. Arasaratnam, 'Vimala Dharma Surya II (1687–1707) and his relations with the Dutch', *CJHSS*, VI (1963) 59–70.

[113] C.N.A., 5/63/II (23).

[114] For instance, Ratnālaṃkāra Thera of Devanagala Vihāre played a crucial role in helping Vimaladharmasūrya I to annex the Four Kōralēs to the Kingdom of Kandy after the decline of Sītāvaka. H. C. P. Bell, *Report on the Kegalla District* (S.P. XIX: 1892), pp. 87–88.

played a vital role. Yet, within the order, there was a steady decline in the standards of piety. The growing political influence of the monks indicated, in fact, a general trend towards worldliness. The kings–whose traditional duty it was to maintain the purity of the *sāsana*–were unable to devote undivided attention to this task amidst the chronically turbulent political atmosphere that surrounded their kingdom. Such efforts as they made were generally limited to granting land endowments to various temples and taking measures to preserve the continuity of the order. Hardly any measures were undertaken to institute a proper internal administration regarding the affairs of the *sāsana*. The results were particularly flagrant in the management of temporalities.

In ancient times, though there was no strictly uniform pattern relating to the granting of endowments, the general practice was to grant them to the body of monks as a whole or to different groups of monks who lived in different monasteries. Where the endowments were large, lay wardens (*pirivahanuvās*) were appointed to cultivate the land by means of *ārāmikas* (tenants and slaves),[115] as the monks themselves were prohibited by the *vinaya* rules from performing such mundane activities. In the course of time, however, there emerged definite trends towards the development of private (*pudgalika*) property in land rights among the monks–a development which went contrary to the *vinaya* regulations. This practice was introduced by the kings themselves when they established the precedent of donating land rights to individual monks–often as acts of special favour–with special reference to hereditary possession through pupillary succession.[116] But the trend assumed greater dimensions because of the growing laxity in state superintendance over the management of temple lands. (In times of political decline and instability the state had other priorities.) The appointment of lay wardens ceased, and the effective control over communal temple lands gradually passed into the hands of the resident monks themselves. With the development of greater private

[115]'The Two Tablets of Mahinda IV at Mihintalē' and 'Jetavanārāma Sanskrit Inscription', *EZ*, I (1904–12).

[116]In the earliest (known endowment of this type (in the tenth century), the beneficiary was a monk of Mahāyānist persuasion. See 'The Buddhannahäla Pillar Inscription', *EZ*, I (1904–12) 194 ff.

fortunes in the country, there was, in addition, 'from the thirteenth century onwards, a marked increase in the endowments of private individuals.'[117] Naturally enough, there was no central supervision over the management of these lands either. The development of private ownership and control of temple lands, which thus went on for a few centuries, culminated in Kandyan times when 'it [became] common for one or two resident monks to manage the temple lands'.[118]

Since succession to temple property was regulated in terms of pupillary succession (*śiṣyānuśiṣya paramparā*),[119] the ties between the teacher and his pupil tended to be based on property interests rather than on the prescribed spiritual bonds between the *upajjhāya* and the *saddhivihārika*. As the pupils were often chosen from the teacher's kin-group,[120] property interests came to be bound up with familial interests as well. Succession to temple lands through *sivuru-* or *jñātiśiṣya-paramparā* (according to which the property descended from teacher to pupil, the latter being a relative of the former) became very widespread during the Kandyan period. An illustration of this may be provided with the case of Kobbäkaḍuve Vihāre. The lands belonging to this *vihāre* were granted to Śrīmat Mēnavara Māvela Ratanavalli by King Vikramabāhu (*ca.* 1475–1510) of Kandy with specific instructions for the property to remain in his 'religious descent' (*sāsana paramparā*).[121] In the course of time, 'religious descent' came to be connected with the familial descent of the Kobbäkaḍuve family. A member of this family testified before the Buddhist Temporalities Commission in September

[117] W. M. A. Warnasuriya, 'Inscriptional Evidence Bearing on the Nature of Religious Endowment in Ancient Ceylon', *UCR*, II (1946) 96.

[118] Ralph Pieris, *Sinhalese Social Organization: The Kandyan Period* (Colombo, 1956), p. 74.

[119] Regarding laws of pupillary succession, see Ralph Pieris, 'Title to land in Kandyan Law', in *Sir Paul Pieris Felicitation Volume* (Colombo, 1955); G. W. Woodhouse, 'Sissiyānu Sissiya Paramparāwa, and other Laws relating to Buddhist Priests in Ceylon', *CALR*, III (1918) 174–86, 281–90; and Heinz Bechert, *Buddhismus, Staat und Gesellschaft in den Ländern des Theravāda-Buddhismus*, vol. I (Frankfurt am Main and Berlin, 1966), pp. 224–44.

[120] The choice of pupils from one's kinsmen, especially nephews, has been common among Buddhist monks of Ceylon since early times, and it continues in the present day. Succession to temples on *jñātiśiṣya paramparā* is first to be met with in the Kitsirimevan Käḷaṇi inscription of 1344. See H. C. P. Bell and A. Mendis Gunasekara, 'Kelani Vihāra and its Inscriptions', *CALR*, I (1916) 154.

[121] H. W. Codrington, 'Some Documents of Vikramabāhu of Kandy', *JRAS(CB)*, XXXII (1931) 1.

1876: 'Our family possesses the Kobbekaduwa Vihare. The incumbency must always be held by a member of my family, and for that purpose some member becomes a priest and is specially educated for the office.'[122] As in this case, so in others: all the families connected to such temple offices belonged to the Kandyan aristocracy.[123]

Such a connection guaranteed, to some extent, the continuity of the temple, its incumbency and its property.[124] But it in no way guaranteed the entry of the most devoted and conscientious persons to the order of monks. On the contrary, it led the way for certain persons to join the order merely to preserve the property rights within the family circle. Once a suitable heir could be found, they left the order for more congenial secular pursuits. The working of this process over several generations is admirably documented in the Kaḍadora Grant, which merits quotation *in extenso*:

> Thereupon he [i.e., King Vikramabāhu, *ca.* 1475–1510] got the monks . . . to reside at the holy palace near Mahaväli river, served them with the four-fold requisites, and with the assistance of thirty-five monks who had the Great Elder Dharmakīrti as the chief got three hundred and fifty monks to enter the higher order. Among them was a person who by relationship was a nephew of Dhammañāṇa Thera of Labutala, and who learnt the *dhamma* of the three *piṭakas* under the Great Elder Dharmakīrti. [This person] having won the confidence of this Dharmakīrti Thera received [from him] as an inheritance, Kaḍadora-vihāra, Aratta-vihāra, Alu-vihāra, Ilupändeṇiya-vihāra and Koṭakēdeṇiya-vihāra, and the lands appertaining to them; and he received at the hands of His Majesty the post

[122] *Report of the Commissioners appointed to inquire into the Administration of the Buddhist Temporalities* (S.P. XVII: 1876), p. 5.

[123] Compare with Halévy's observation regarding the Anglican Church in 1815: 'The Anglican clergy was, and was anxious to remain, a branch of the aristocracy. . . . Eleven [bishops] in 1815 were of noble birth. . . . Ten had been tutors or school-masters of a prince, a duke or statesman. . . . Thus did the ecclesiastical constitution of the country harmonize with the political. The landed gentry were masters equally of the ecclesiastical as of the civil administration'. *A History of the English People in 1815*, vol. III (London, 1938), pp. 15–16.

[124] Because the maintenance of the temple, its property and its rites and ceremonies came to be regarded as a duty of the family concerned. In the Kaḍadora Grant—an early eighteenth-century document—whereby Guṇālaṃkāra Dharmakīrti Bhuvanekabā bequeathed his property to his grand-nephew and pupil, Ēkanāyaka Sumaṃgala Ganen, it was stipulated: '. . . this *vihāra* should be developed in the same manner as I did, its rites and ceremonies should be observed. If that is not possible, a meritorious person who is descended from my five brothers and sisters should don robes and improve [the *vihāra*] in accordance with former customs'. 'Kadadora Grant', ed. and tr. C. E. Godakumbura, *JRAS(CB)*, n.s. II (1952) 158.

of *nāyaka* of the Asgiriya-vihāra. He trained a nephew . . . in writing and reading of letters and in the Dharma and the preaching of it, and got him to enter the Order. . . . A short while later he gave up the robes and contracted a marriage with a lady from the family of a nobleman. . . . [From this marriage, he] had a son and him he ordained. . . . This person then received the higher ordination . . . [and] was known as Dharmakīrti Thera. . . . [Dharmakīrti Thera] developed the *vihāra*, enjoyed the lands and having ordained a person who stood in the same relationship as a younger brother to this thera, handed over the *vihāra* lands to him, and then gave up the robes, assumed the name and title of Vikramasekhara Rājapakṣa Mahamudaliyār and took as wife a daughter of the Mahadisāva of Bogamuva. [From this marriage] he got a lucky son and called him Vīrasūrirāla and he was married to a lady who in relationship was a grand-daughter of Rammolaka-adikārama of Uḍunuvara; and in time he had seven children, male and female. A person begotten of this nobleman obtained from the said Vīrasūrirāla the royal grants and other deeds which had come down in succession to the great monks who were by right the owners of this village, carried out the rites and ceremonies pertaining to this *vihāra*. . . .[125]

Many persons who thus entered the order at this time were not properly ordained as monks in terms of the *vinaya* requirements. Known to their contemporaries as *gaṇinnānses*, they represented a new type of monk peculiar to the early Kandyan period, not known before that time or since in the history of Buddhism in Ceylon.

According to the *vinaya* regulations, the order was to consist of two 'grades' of monks: *sāmaṇeras* (novices) and *bhikkhus* (fully ordained monks), the latter being *sāmaṇeras* who had gone through the *upasampadā* (higher ordination) ceremony. *Upasampadā* was not deemed to confer any sacramental or sacerdotal powers on its recipient; it was merely an act of self-dedication to a higher and purer life.[126] Still, the existence of a sufficient number of *bhikkhus* was an absolute necessity for the continuity of the order because, according to the ancient regulations, the admission of a layman to the status of a *sāmaṇera* had to be performed by a *bhikkhu*; and, similarly, the admission of a *sāmaṇera* to the status of a *bhikkhu* required a

[125] *Ibid.*, pp. 153 *et. seq.* Another document akin to this is the 'Daṁbulu Vihāra Tuḍapata' (1726), an English translation of which is given in A. C. Lawrie, *A Gazetteer of the Central Province of Ceylon*, vol. I (Colombo, 1896), pp. 124–27.

[126] A *bhikkhu* was expected to observe 227 monastic rules, and a *sāmaṇera* was expected to observe 10 basic precepts. (The former were an elaborate practical application of the latter.)

chapter of monks consisting of at least five *bhikkhus*.[127] In the absence of an organized ecclesiastical hierarchy within the order, the self-dedication of the *bhikkhus* to higher moral standards and the powers vested in them regarding the admission of new candidates were expected to preserve discipline within the order and keep it free of unworthy individuals. Once a *bhikkhu* admits a layman as a *sāmaṇera* to the order, it was considered his duty to take care of his pupil and instruct him in the doctrine and the disciplinary rules and thereby train him for higher ordination. At the higher ordination ceremony, the novice's knowledge and qualifications were examined, and if admitted to the status of a *bhikkhu*, he was given to the charge of, usually, two more preceptors, under whose guidance and supervision he was expected to acquire his more advanced spiritual training. The important role assigned in the *vinaya* regulations to this type of close and personal relationship between the teacher and his pupil constituted a highly important element of structural cohesion within the Buddhist order.[128]

Sustained adherence to these bonds, and the traditions and practices that were associated with them, required as matters of absolute necessity a favourable social and political atmosphere and devotion and conscientiousness on the part of those who joined the order. In the absence of these conditions, the whole *sāsana* was caught in a vicious circle. Whenever the ordination ceremonies were not regularly performed over a considerable period of time, the number of duly ordained *bhikkhus* steadily declined and eventually it became impossible to gather a sufficient number of them to perform an ordination ceremony. All persons who wished to join the order—merely to succeed to temple property or for more bona fide reasons—had to do it without the necessary rites of passage and without the obligatory connections with spiritual preceptors. Their admission to the order was subject to no proper scrutiny, and their conduct after admission was subject to no regular supervision. The relations between teachers and

[127] The 'president' of this chapter had to be a *thera*, i.e., a *bhikkhu* with not less than ten years' standing from his *upasampadā*. For accounts of the ordination and higher ordination ceremonies, and the texts and translations of the relevant *vinaya* sections, see J. F. Dickson, 'The *Upasampadā-Kammāvācā*, being the Buddhist Manual of the Form and Manner of Ordering of Priests and Deacons: The Pali Text with a Translation and Notes', *JRAS*, n.s., VII (1875) 1–16.

[128] Max Weber, *The Religion of India*, p. 224.

pupils, if there were any, came to be based on 'non-religious' factors such as succession to temple lands, and 'religious' instruction that was passed from teachers to pupils came to be confined to elementary instruction regarding the rites and ceremonies that were traditionally connected with the temples. As a result, a steady decline in the knowledge of the *dhamma* and *vinaya* among the monks inevitably followed. And in the absence of a sufficient knowledge regarding the ideals that they were supposed to pursue, it became impossible for the monks to make any effort to approximate to them.

This process repeated itself three times after the fifteenth century despite the efforts of two kings to arrest it. First, towards the end of the sixteenth century, there was an attempt by Vimaladharmasūrya I (1591–1604), and then, towards the end of the following century, there was another attempt by Vimaladharmasūrya II (1687–1707), to re-establish higher ordination in Ceylon by bringing in monks from that part of Burma known to the Sinhalese as Rakkhaṃga Dēśa and to the Burmese as Arakan.[129] Some temporary success, no doubt, was achieved by these efforts.[130] The results, however, were not of a lasting nature. Writers of subsequent periods, in fact, have raised serious doubts about the very motives that lay behind these ordination ceremonies. Gammullē Ratanapāla, for instance, contended, in the late eighteenth century, that these measures were taken mainly to establish the religious status (and thereby status in relation to temple lands) of a few influential monks rather than to arrest the moral decline within the *sāsana*.[131] Whether these were in fact the motives behind the ordination ceremonies, it would not be easy to decide. It is not surprising, all the same, that the results did suggest an inference of this sort. There

[129] *Cūlavaṃsa*, 94: 15–22, 97: 8–15; D. B. Jayatilaka, 'Sinhalese Embassies to Arakan', *JRAS(CB)*, XXXV (1940) 1–6; and P. E. E. Fernando, 'The "Rakkhanga-Sannas-Cūrnikāva" and the Date of the Arrival of Arakanese Monks in Ceylon', *UCR*, XVII (1959), 41–46.

[130] The accounts left by seventeenth-century European observers like Knox, de Queyroz and the early Dutch visitors, despite their unsympathetic attitudes towards Buddhism, reveal a fairly high standard of piety and discipline within the order. Robert Knox, *An Historical Relation of Ceylon* (1681), ed. James Ryan (Glasgow, 1911); de Queyroz, *Temporal and Spiritual Conquest*, pp. 114 ff; and 'Extracts from the Spilbergen Journal' (July 1602), Annexure B to Donald Ferguson, 'The Earliest Dutch Visits to Ceylon', *JRAS(CB)*, XXX (1927) 379–80.

[131] *Siṃhala Vimānavastu Prakaraṇaya* (1770), ed. Telvattē Mahānāga Sīlānanda (Colombo, 1901), p. 200.

is no evidence that the Arakanese monks remained in the island in order to instruct their Sinhalese pupils in the *dhamma* and the *vinaya*. Nor is there evidence that the Sinhalese monks who received higher ordination in 1697 made any serious effort to instruct their own juniors. It is recorded that thirty-three monks received *upasampadā* ordination, and that one hundred and twenty entered the order as *sāmaṇeras* in 1697.[132] Some of the thirty-three *bhikkhus* eventually left the order,[133] and some of those who remained reverted back to *sāmaṇera* status.[134] The few who remained in *upasampadā* status ordained a few laymen as their pupil *sāmaṇeras*; but no *upasampadā* ceremonies were held after 1697. With the demise of these *bhikkhus*, therefore, it again became impossible for a *sāmaṇera* to receive higher ordination or for a layman to join the order as a duly ordained *sāmaṇera*.[135] Those who did join the order did so without the necessary rites of passage and thus belonged to the category of *gaṇinnānses*. Indeed, most of the monks in the late sixteenth, seventeenth and early eighteenth centuries belonged to the category of *gaṇinnānses*.[136]

The *gaṇinnānses*, in general, professed to observe the ten precepts prescribed for the *sāmaṇeras*. Yet, particularly after the death of Vimaladharmasūrya II in 1707, very little care seems to have been taken by the majority of them in the actual observance of these precepts. The traditional practices and regulations within the order came to be forgotten or openly neglected; and those very practices which had been expressly prohibited to monks became more and more widespread. Quite apart

[132] *Cūlavaṃsa*, 97: 13–15.

[133] Cf. 'Kaḍadora Grant'.

[134] E.g., Välivita Saraṇaṃkara's teacher, Sūriyagoḍa Rājasundara. See Nāhällē Paññāsena and P. B. Sannasgala, ed. *Saṃgharāja Sādhucariyāva* (Colombo, 1947), p. ix.

[135] In 1705, only eight years after the second Arakanese ordination in Ceylon, King Vimaladharmasūrya II requested the Dutch authorities to bring another deputation of Arakanese monks to Ceylon. Although this request was granted and connections were again established with Arakan, the death of the king in July 1707 interrupted any further following up of this path. Arasaratnam, 'Vimala Dharma Surya II', p. 68.

[136] Both Knox (1681) and de Queyroz (1687) referred to *Terrunnānses* ('Tirinaxes' 'Turunnances') and *Gaṇinnānses* ('Gonni' 'Ganezes') as the two major 'groups' within the Buddhist order. They used the term *terunnānses* in a rather nonspecific sense to refer to the few leading *bhikkhus* (the term, derived from *thera*, meant in fact a *bhikkhu* with more than ten years' standing from his *upasampadā*). They were wrong in referring to *all* the other monks as *gaṇinnānses*, as among them there were a few *samaṇeras* as well.

from the more basic precepts, even the outward formalities regarding names and modes of dress, for instance, were manifestly disregarded. The *gaṇinnānses* clothed themselves in white or saffron cloth instead of the orthodox robe prescribed for Buddhist monks. Some of them retained their lay names even after joining the order.[137] More conspicuous, undoubtedly, was their departure from the precept of celibacy; some of them, though certainly not all, maintained wives and children in houses close to their temples out of the incomes derived from temple lands.[138] Moreover, their ignorance of the Buddhist texts led them further and further away from the Buddhistic great tradition towards what the great tradition considered the 'beastly sciences' (*tiraścīna vidyā*) of the little tradition. Indulgence in magic and sorcery, astrology and divination was widespread among them.[139] In fact, during this period, the role of the *gaṇinnānses* tended to be more and more that of a priest or magician than that of a Buddhist monk in its ideal and doctrinal sense.

b. Välivița Saraṇaṃkara and the Silvat Samāgama

While the *sāsana* was at this low ebb, a reformist movement developed within the order, largely through the initiative of a single individual, Välivița Saraṇaṃkara.[140]

Born in 1698, Saraṇaṃkara joined the order at the age of sixteen as a pupil of Sūriyagoḍa Rājasundara, who had received *upasampadā* ordination from the Arakanese monks in 1697. Saraṇaṃkara's teacher exercised considerable influence within the Kandyan kingdom and enjoyed, for some time, the favour of the king, Śrī Vīra Parākrama Narendrasiṃha (1707–39). In 1715, however, he was executed on a charge of treason. Thus left on his own, young Saraṇaṃkara retired to the mountainous area of Alagalla, a few miles from the capital, and devoted these early years to the

[137] P. B. Sannasgala, *Siṃhala Sāhitya Vaṃśaya* (Colombo, 1961), p. 316.

[138] Muṃkoṭuvē Rāḷa, *Saṅgarajavata*, ed. Śri Charles de Silva (Colombo, 1955), v. 59; and *Cūlavaṃsa* 100: 46. The *gaṇinnānses'* wives were referred to as *gaṇēgedaras*, and their sons as *gaṇageḍiyo*. E. R. Sarathchandra, *The Sinhalese Folk Play* (Colombo, 1953), p. 7.

[139] *Saṃgharāja Sādhucariyāva*, p. 2; *Saṅgarajavata*, v. 80; and *Cūlavaṃsa*, 100: 46.

[140] *Saṃgharāja Sādhucariyāva* and *Saṅgarajavata* are two accounts of his life and work written, respectively, in 1779 (in prose) and *ca.* 1780 (in verse). D. B. Jayatilaka's *Saranankara: The Last Sangha-rāja of Ceylon* (Colombo, 1934) relies heavily on these two works. So does Koṭagama Vācissara's *Saraṇaṃkara Saṃgharāja Samaya* (Colombo, 1960). But the latter is a more detailed study, which has consulted several other sources as well.

task of learning the Pali language as a means to reading and understanding the ancient religious texts. By this time, the knowledge of Pali, which had always been an important speciality of the monks, had nearly disappeared amongst them.[141] Saraṇaṃkara's tutor in Pali, in these early years, was a nobleman by the name of Levkē Rāḷahāmi, who had been imprisoned by the king in a village close to Alagalla. Saraṇaṃkara lived in a cave at Alagalla, and, depending on the alms offered by the villagers, engaged himself in the task of pursuing his studies.

During this period, a few companions and followers began to gather around Saraṇaṃkara. The earliest and most intimate of them were Siṭināmaluvē, Ilipängamuvē and Kadirāgoḍa, who remained Saraṇaṃkara's lifelong companions. They formed the nucleus of a new and growing fraternity, which came to be known as the Silvat Samāgama, or 'the fraternity of the pious'. Because of Välivița Saraṇaṃkara's undisputed leadership within it, it was also referred to as the Välivița Samāgama. Although there were a few *sāmaṇeras* within the fraternity, its members were generally referred to as *silvat tänas* ('pious ones') and were thus distinguished from the other *sāmaṇeras* and *gaṇinnānses*.

Under Saraṇaṃkara's guidance and inspiration,[142] they made conscious efforts to break away from the irregular practices which had become prevalent among their contemporaries, and to go back to the ancient regulations and practices prescribed in the *vinaya* texts. Great emphasis was laid on the learning of these texts and on the observance of the rules laid down in them. In recruiting new members to the fraternity, secular factors like caste and family connections were disregarded, and greater care was taken to ensure the piety and devotion of the candidates. Admission to the fraternity brought no material benefits; on the contrary, it required dedication to the ancient ideal of poverty.[143] This condition helped to keep the fraternity free of those individuals who joined the monasteries mainly

[141] It is believed that the only Sinhalese monk who had the ability to converse with the Arakanese monks (who arrived in Ceylon in 1697) in Pali was Vaṭabuluvē Unnānse of Pōyamalu Vihāre. Levkē Rāḷahāmi and Palkumburē Atthadassī, under both of whom Saraṇaṃkara studied Pali grammar, were pupils of this monk. *Saṃgharāja Sādhucariyāva*, p. 3.

[142] Whenever he was away from his pupils, and was therefore unable to supervise their conduct personally, Saraṇaṃkara sent them compendia of advice and instructions (*anuśāsanā vaṭṭōru*). One of them, dated Poson 2273 (June 1730), has been printed in *ibid.*, pp. xvi–xx.

[143] Saraṇaṃkara forbade all his followers to accept money or any other 'unworthy' gifts from their lay devotees, either for their own benefit or for the benefit of their kinsmen. *Ibid.*

for the sake of material benefits. As an effective means of maintaining discipline among the 'pious ones', the traditional fortnightly confessional meetings, which had gone out of vogue among the monks, were reinstituted.[144] Also revived was the practice of mendicancy; and, as a result, the Silvat Samāgama also came to be known as the Piṇḍapātika Samāgama, or 'the mendicant fraternity'.

The growing popularity of the new fraternity among the laity caused considerable jealousy and anxiety among the monks of the wealthy and established monasteries, particularly because some of their own associates and pupils left their old monasteries in order to join the new movement. They became still more resentful of the *silvat tänas*, as the latter shunned their company, considering them worldly and impious, and refused to show marks of respect towards them. Very soon, complaints were made to the king (Narendrasiṃha) alleging the discourtesy of the *silvat tänas*. The greater influence of the established monasteries apparently settled the issue in their favour (the *silvat tänas* were required to pay them the customary respects owed to spiritual superiors); yet the king himself was highly impressed with Saraṇaṃkara's erudition. Though not personally a man of much piety, the king evinced great interest in religious issues and controversies.[145] He decided to extend his patronage to Saraṇaṃkara's educational and religious pursuits. He helped Saraṇaṃkara to establish a monastic educational institution at Niyamakanda, where the resident students were given instruction in grammar, prosody, literature and Buddhist texts. In a few years, this institution turned out to be the progenitor of a renaissance in Sinhalese and Pali literature.[146] According to *Mandāram Pura Puvata*, the king also entrusted the education of his heir–who, being of South Indian origin, was a stranger to Sinhalese laws and customs–to Saraṇaṃkara.[147]

[144] For an account of the 'confessional meeting', see J. F. Dickson, 'The *Pātimokkha*, being the Buddhist Office of the Confession of Priests: the Pali Text, with a translation and notes', *JRAS*, n.s., VIII (1876) 62–130.

[145] In 1712, there was a debate before him between a Calvinist and a Catholic; and again, in 1719, there was a four-cornered debate between a Calvinist, a Catholic, a Muslim and a Buddhist. See R. Boudens, *The Catholic Church in Ceylon under Dutch Rule* (Rome, 1957), pp. 192 *et. seq.* According to *Saṃgharāja Sādhucariyāva*, pp. 7–8, Saraṇaṃkara himself first gained the king's favour by defeating in debate a Hindu brahmin who had visited the court.

[146] P. B. Sannasgala, *Siṃhala Sāhitya Vaṃśaya* (Colombo, 1961), and G. P. Malalasekara, *Pali Literature of Ceylon* (London, 1928).

[147] *Mandāram Pura Puvata*, ed. Labugama Laṃkānanda (Colombo, 1958), v. 511.

c. The Arrival of the Siamese Monks and the Re-establishment of Higher Ordination.

Saraṇaṃkara's greatest ambition, however—to re-establish *upasampadā* ordination in Ceylon—remained unfulfilled during Narendrasiṃha's reign.[148] It was only during the reign of his successor, Śrī Vijaya Rājasiṃha (1739–47), that some positive steps were taken in this direction. If indeed the king was Saraṇaṃkara's pupil before he assumed the throne, it was natural that the teacher exercised considerable influence over him. But even more decisive, probably, was the king's eagerness, on account of his foreign origin, to win the support of the leading Buddhists to his rule.[149] Negotiations were soon commenced with the Dutch to obtain a ship for the journey to a Buddhist country, and in 1741 a delegation led by two of the king's officials and five of Saraṇaṃkara's pupils set off for Siam. The ship foundered off the coast of Pegu, and with no success achieved, two survivors managed to return to Ceylon.[150] In 1745, a second delegation set off from Kandy led by Doranāgama Muhandiram—one of the survivors of the earlier delegation—and two other officials and five of Saraṇaṃkara's pupils. On their way to Siam, Doranāgama fell ill at Batavia; but the delegation proceeded to Siam under the leadership of one of the other two officials, Vilbāgedara Nayide. They reached Siam in 1747, and the request of the King of Ceylon was communicated to the Siamese king, Mahā Tammarāja (Boromkot) II (1733–58). While arrangements were being made for a Siamese mission to visit Ceylon, news reached Siam of the death of King Śrī Vijaya Rājasiṃha. In the absence of a clear assurance regarding the religious policies of his successor, the King of Siam considered it

[148] B. M. Or. 6601 (I) is an appeal written by him to the king in this connection.

[149] Śrī Vijaya Rājasiṃha was the younger brother of the queen of the deceased king (who died without legitimate issue). There was a faction within the Kandyan court led by the disāva of the Three and Four Kōralēs, Levkē Rāḷahāmi, who wished to have Unambuve Baṇḍāra, an illegitimate son of the late king, on the throne. As a result, the choice of a successor remained a problem for more than a year. *Memoir of Joan Gideon Loten* (1757), ed. and tr. E. Reimers (Colombo, 1935), p. 3. In accordance with ancient custom, the new king formally embraced Buddhism on his accession to the throne; and one of his early acts, in addition to supporting Saraṇaṃkara's plea for reviving *upasampadā*, was to get rid of the Catholic priests in Kandy, who had become unpopular with the Buddhists by this time (see above, p. 35). Saraṇaṃkara's personal influence over the king is also shown by the fact that, through his intervention, the relations of Sūriyagoḍa Rājasundara (Saraṇaṃkara's teacher), who had been banished from their ancestral village during the previous reign, were now recalled and restored to their ancestral property. Lawrie, *Gazetteer*, p. 801.

[150] *Saṃgharāja Sādhucariyāva*, p. 12.

unwise to allow the Siamese monks to proceed to Ceylon. Thus disappointed, Vilbāgedara returned to Ceylon.[151]

Śrī Vijaya Rājasiṃha's brother-in-law and successor, Kīrti Śrī Rājasiṃha (1747–82), showed the same zeal as his predecessor in helping to fulfill the long cherished, and twice frustrated, wish of the Buddhists. Being informed by Vilbāgedara of the flourishing state of Buddhism in Siam, he made arrangements with the Dutch for a third delegation to proceed to Siam. This delegation, led by five officials including Vilbāgedara himself, with an entourage of sixty-one other persons, left Ceylon in August 1750, and despite numerous delays on their way, finally arrived in Siam and was presented before the king.[152] The King of Siam agreed to grant the request of the Kandyan king, and necessary arrangements were made for a party consisting of twenty-five monks led by Upāli Thera, and five Siamese envoys together with their attendants to proceed to Ceylon with the Sinhalese envoys. One of the Sinhalese envoys, Paṭṭapola Mohoṭṭāla, died in Siam, and several other events caused delays in the arrival of the Siamese monks in Ceylon. Finally, however, they arrived in 1753, causing great jubilation among all those who awaited their arrival. The Dutch governor of the time, Joan Gideon Loten (1752–57), whose relations with Kandy were not entirely cordial, observed in his *Memoir*: 'But in the year 1753 there was no lack of evidence of good understanding and friendship, the Court being extremely gratified at the long desired arrival of the priests of the Buddhist doctrine from Siam who arrived safely on the 5th of May in a Company's ship at Trincomalee, whence they set out for Kandy'.[153]

The Siamese mission was escorted to the capital by the leading ministers

[151] 'Siyāma Sandēśa Varṇanāva' (B.M. Or. 2702 v).

[152] Besides brief references in works such as the *Cūlavaṃsa* and *Samgharāja Sādhucariyāva*, there are two detailed accounts of this third Sinhalese delegation to Siam written by two officials who were members of the delegation. See P. E. Pieris, 'Kīrti Śrī's Embassy to Siam', *JRAS(CB)*, XVIII (1903) 17–41; and P. E. E. Fernando, 'An Account of the Kandyan Mission sent to Siam in 1750 A.D.', *CJHSS*, II (1959) 37–83. The first is a translation of 'Śyāma Varṇanāva', written by Ällepola Mohoṭṭāla, and the second is a translation of 'Śyāmadūta Varṇanāva', written by Vilbāgedara Muhandiram. Two later works dealing with the same subject are 'Siyāma Sandēśa Varṇanāva' (B.M. Or 2702 v.), written by a grandson of Vilbāgedara; and Tibboṭuvāvē Siddharttha Buddharakkhita, *Siyāmopasampadāvata*, ed. Giridara Ratanajoti (Colombo, 1892). There is an English translation of the last-mentioned work, by W. A. Goonetileke: *Syāmūpasampadā: The adoption of the Siamese order of priesthood in Ceylon* (Bangkok, 1914).

[153] *Op. cit.*, p. 6.

and monks in Kandy and was warmly received by the king himself. Upāli and his associates were given residence at Malvatu Vihāre; and here, at a newly consecrated *sīmā*, they performed their first *upasampadā* ceremony on the full-moon day of Äsaḷa (June-July) 1753. A second *sīmā* was established at Asgiri Vihāre shortly afterwards; and while on pilgrimage in various other parts of the country, the Siamese monks established *sīmās* in other parts of the country as well.[154]

The Siamese ambassadors returned home in 1754;[155] but the monks stayed behind and spent their time, in addition to visiting sacred places, in admitting laymen to the order as *sāmaṇeras* and conferring *upasampadā* on those who had already been admitted as *sāmaṇeras*. Thus there was a steady increase in the number of duly ordained monks in Ceylon. To these new Sinhalese pupils, the Siamese monks gave instruction in the *dhamma* and the *vinaya* and in the customs and ceremonies connected with monastic life. To assist them in their work, the King of Siam sent a second group of monks to Ceylon, under the leadership of Visuddhācariya, who had a thorough training in the techniques of meditation, and Varañāṇamuni, who was well versed in the doctrine and in grammar.[156] This second group of monks arrived in the island in early 1756.[157]

In a letter, dated 15 October 1756, written by the Siamese king's generalissimo to Ähälēpola Adikāram in Ceylon,[158] some information is to be found regarding the reformist activities carried on by the Siamese monks in Ceylon. As becomes evident from this document, their influence spread beyond the confines of monasteries to the religious behaviour of laymen as well. They were particularly instrumental in re-asserting the primacy of Buddhist symbols and practices over those of other religions which had gained ascendancy during Buddhism's period of decline. It is reported, for instance, that they took strong exception to the practice,

[154] *Cūlavaṃsa*, 100: 129; and *Saṃgharāja Sādhucariyāva*, p. 15.

[155] Loten's *Memoir*, p. 7.

[156] *Cūlavaṃsa*, 100: 136–41, 173–75.

[157] *Memoir of Jan Schreuder* (1762), ed. and tr. E. Reimers (Colombo, 1946), p. 16.

[158] The original letter, written in Cambodian characters, is now at Malvatu Vihāre. There is a 'report' on it by S. Paranavitana in the *Second Report of the Ceylon Historical Manuscripts Commission* (S.P. XXI: 1935), pp. 58–61. H. W. Codrington, tr., 'A Letter from the Court of Siam, 1756', *JRAS(CB)*, XXXVI (1945) 97–99, is an English translation made apparently from a Sinhalese summary of the original document.

which had become common especially among the brahmins, of entering places of religious worship without removing their head dresses.[159] It is also believed that the annual *Äsaḷa* festival in Kandy was given its later form mainly through the efforts of the Siamese monks.[160] This festival, as celebrated during the early Kandyan period, was purely an occasion for the ceremonial worship of gods and had no connection with the Temple of the Tooth or with any other Buddhist temple.[161] During the festival, the divinities themselves or their insignia were carried in procession (*perahära*) through the streets of the capital–a sight, it is said, which shocked the Siamese monks, as no similar ceremony was performed in honour of the Buddha. They pressed the king to reorganize the *perahära* and as a result, a new *daḷada* (tooth relic) *perahära* was introduced into the general ritual complex and was given primacy over all the other *perahäras*. The *perahära* in this form symbolically re-established the primacy of Buddhism within the Sinhalese religious system.[162]

The increase in the number of monks in the island following the introduction of Siamese ordination[163] was accompanied by a corresponding increase in the number of monasteries. In the general religious enthusiasm that characterized this period, the monks were helped in these efforts by the king and the nobles as well as by the ordinary villagers. In the smaller villages, the villagers themselves built new *vihāras* or renovated the abandoned ones and invited monks to come and reside in them.[164] The kings and nobles, on the other hand, carried on temple building on a much larger and gradiose scale. 'There is hardly a *vihāra* of any importance in the Kandy district', wrote Coomaraswamy, commenting on King Kīrti Śrī Rājasiṃha's work in this direction, 'which was not restored by him, or newly built'.[165] In this regard, Kīrti Śrī's policies were closely followed by

[159] *Second Report of the Ceylon Historical Manuscripts Commission*, p. 60.

[160] 'Description of the four Principal Kandyan Festivals, compiled from materials furnished by a native chief', *Ceylon Almanac* (1834).

[161] Knox, *op. cit.*, pp. 125–27, gives a graphic description of the *perahära* as it was celebrated during the early period.

[162] For a sociological analysis of the *perahära*, see H. L. Seneviratne, 'The Äsaḷa Perahära in Kandy', *CJHSS*, VI (1963) 169–80.

[163] According to both the *Cūlavaṃsa* and the Siamese document referred to above, 3,000 persons joined the order as *sāmaṇeras* within the first three years (1753–56). During the same period, 600 *sāmaṇeras* received *upasampadā* ordination, according to the Siamese document. The *Cūlavaṃsa*, however, gives the latter figure as 700. *Cūlavaṃsa*, 100: 133–34; S.P. XXI: 1935, p. 59.

[164] Lawrie, *Gazetteer*, *passim*.

[165] Ananda K. Coomaraswamy, *Mediaeval Sinhalese Art* (1908), 2nd ed. (New York, 1956), p. 12.

his brother and successor, Rājādhi Rājasiṃha (1782–98). The acts of both of them, in fact, spread well beyond the confines of the Kandy district—as stated by Coomaraswamy—to practically all parts of the island, including the maritime provinces which were then under the administration of the Dutch East India Company. After the re-establishment of *upasampadā* ordination in 1753, the *gaṇinnānses* and the *upāsakas* who had been looking after temples in different parts of the country flocked to Kandy to receive valid ordination. After being ordained and instructed in the doctrine and the monastic rules for some time, they returned to their own temples, invariably with royal gifts to renew and maintain their temples.

A substantial portion of the economic assets of the king went into the building and repair of Buddhist temples, and in donating lands (*vihāra-gam*) to temples the king lost a considerable amount of his personal revenue and services, as the donations were made out of his own villages (*gabaḍāgam*). The donations, evidently, were not guided solely by religious considerations; they were part of the general process whereby the king exchanged his economic assets for non-economic debts, a process which has been clearly observed in the case of land grants (*nindagam*) to the king's administrators.[166] In fact, the nature of Kīrti Śrī's personal religiosity remains a matter of some doubt despite the glowing tributes paid to him in nearly all the contemporary Sinhalese documents. At any rate, he persisted in Śaivite practices, such as applying ash on his forehead, to which the *Śāsanāvatīrṇa Varṇanāva*[167] traces the ostensible reason for the 'conspiracy' against him in 1760. The more important causes, however, lay deeper than this in the chronic factionalism within the Kandyan court (see below, chapter II, section ii) which acquired a new dimension with the accession of the Nayakkars to the throne. While one faction accepted the new state of affairs and gained the king's favour, a discontented faction conspired to overthrow the king and place a puppet of their own on the throne, citing the king's non-Buddhist origin as their major grievance.

[166] S. B. W. Wickremasekera, 'The Social and Political Organization of the Kandyan Kingdom' (M.A. thesis, London, 1961).

[167] Ed. C. E. Godakumbura (Colombo, 1956), pp. 22–25. Neither the name of the author nor the date of its composition is to be found in the text. On the basis of internal evidence, Hugh Nevill has dated it between 1838 and 1848. *Descriptive Catalogue of Nevill Manuscripts* (at the British Museum), vol. I, no. 20. And the authorship has been attributed by some to Tōlaṃgamuvē Siddhartha (regarding whom see below, ch. III, sec. iii). Kotmalē Saddhammavaṃsa, *Am̆bagahavattē Indāsabhavara Ñāṇasāmi Mahā Nāyaka Svāmindrayan Vahansēgē Jīvana Caritaya* (Kalutara, 1950), Appendix 7B, p. 91.

Apparently, this anti-Nayakkar faction became increasingly ambitious in the wake of the religious revival, patronized, ironically enough, by the Nayakkar king himself. The 'conspiracy' was led by Samanakkoḍi (second Adikāram and Disāva of Sabaragamuva) and Moladaṇḍē (*batvaḍana nilamē*), and was supported by some of the leading monks of Malvatu Vihāre, including Välivița Saraṇaṃkara (*saṃgharāja*) and Tibboṭuvāvē Siddharttha Buddharakkhita (*mahā nāyaka*). Their plan was to assasinate the king and replace him with a Siamese prince who had arrived in the island in 1760.[168]

When the plot was exposed, Kīrti Śrī faced the situation with shrewd judgement. He immediately deported the Siamese prince,[169] executed the officials involved and appointed his own favourites to the vacant offices.[170] The monks, however, were soon pardoned and reinstated in their ecclesiastical offices. Any possible alienation of the mass of Buddhists against him was thus averted, and he continued his policy of making generous religious endowments. His reputation as the greatest patron of Buddhism during the Kandyan period was thus preserved completely intact.

As was natural in a period characterized by a revivalist spirit,[171] both Kīrti Śrī and Rājādhi Rājasiṃha showed particular interest in renovating

[168] C. A. Galpin, 'The Johnston Manuscripts: Relation of a conspiracy against the King of Candy in the year 1760, given by Appoohamy de Lanerolles', *CALR*, II/4 (April 1917) 272–74; A. V. Suraweera, 'The Imprisonment of Sangharāja Saranaṃkara', *Vidyodaya Journal of Arts, Science and Letters*, I/1 (January 1968) 53–57; D. A. Kotelawele, 'New Light on the Life of Sangharaja Welivita Saranankara', *Journal of the Vidyalankara University of Ceylon*, I/1 (January 1972) 119–24.

[169] In the years 1761–65, when relations between Kīrti Śrī and the Dutch were highly explosive, the Dutch governor (van Eck) made several attempts to bring the Siamese prince back to Ceylon and gain control over the Kandyan kingdom by placing him on the throne with the help of the anti-Nayakkar faction. C. N. A. Dutch Records no. 4937 is a report of a Dutch official (Willem van Damast Limberger) who was sent to Siam in this connection. For a brief reconstruction of this part of the episode, see J. H. O. Paulusz, 'Prince Crumpty-Pippit and Governor van Eck', *Journal of the Dutch Burgher Union of Ceylon*, XXI/2 (October 1931) 92–95.

[170] The 'Gäṭaberiya Sannasa' of Kīrti Śrī records the transfer of Moladaṇḍe Nilame's lands to Gōpāla Mudali, who served the king faithfully and played a leading role in uncovering the conspiracy. H. C. P. Bell, *Report on the Kegalla District* (S.P. XIX, 1892), pp. 99–101. Hulaṃgamuvē Buddharakkhita, who provided information regarding Samanakkoḍi's involvement was similarly rewarded. See P. E. E. Fernando, 'India Office Land Grant of King Kīrti Śrī Rājasiṃha', *CJHSS*, III (1960) 72–81.

[171] 'When he [Kīrti Śrī] heard of the doings of former kings, of Parakkamabāhu and others, he recognized it as right and imitated their doings'. *Cūlavaṃsa*, 99: 72.

and rehabilitating the ancient temples and places of religious worship which had been neglected or abandoned over the preceding years. Prominent among them were the *aṭamahāsthāna* ('eight great sacred places') in Anuradhapura, and the ancient shrines at Polonnaruva and Mahiyaṃgana, all of which were in the ancient Rajaraṭa; Samanola Kanda in Sabaragamuva; Ridī Vihāre in the Hat Kōralē; Kälaṇiya in the West; and Mulgirigala in the South.[172] The monks who occupied these ancient shrines eventually ordained and trained pupils of their own, and these pupils, in turn, contributed to the growth of monasticism by occupying smaller shrines which lay close to the more famous ancient shrines.

Many of the monasteries which thus grew up, therefore, were linked to one another through allegiance to common places of origin and through informal ties of pupil-teacher relationships. Over and above this informal organization, a more formal and centralized organization was re-introduced, which derived its legitimacy mainly from the authority of the state. A primary step in this direction was the elevation of the two main monasteries in Kandy—Malvatta and Asgiriya—to pre-eminent positions over all the other monasteries. By this, all monasteries in the island came under the jurisdiction of either Malvatta or Asgiriya.[173] At the head of each

[172] Regarding the restoration of these shrines, see, in addition to the general account given in the *Cūlavaṃsa*, 'Aṭamasthāna Liyavilla' ('Descriptive Catalogue of the Nevill Manuscripts', no. 569); W. Skeen, *Adam's Peak* (Colombo, 1870); H. C. P. Bell and A. Mendis Gunasekara, 'Kelani Vihāra and its Inscriptions', *CALR*, I (1916) 145–61; F. H. Modder, 'Ridi Vihara', *JRAS(CB)*, XIV (1896) 118–24; and Donald Ferguson, 'Mulgirigala', *JRAS(CB)*, XXII (1911) 197–235.

[173] In terms of their origins, Asgiriya belonged to the forest-dwelling (*araññavāsī*) fraternity, and Malvatta belonged to the village-dwelling (*gāmavāsī*). By the middle of the eighteenth century, however, this distinction had lost its original significance, as most of the Asgiriya monks too were in fact village dwelling. It is not easy to ascertain the exact reasons for the creation of these two divisions, equal in status and autonomous within their own spheres. In practice, it is clear, however, that this division harmonized with the general political principle according to which the king prevented the concentration of power at any specific point, as in the case of two chief ministers, or *adikāramas*. See Below, Ch. II, n. 12; and A. M. Hocart, 'Duplication of Office in the Indian State', *Ceylon Journal of Science*, I (1924–28) 205–10. Rivalries indeed did exist between Malvatta and Asgiriya, and helped to some extent to prevent serious conflicts between the king and the *saṃgha* as a whole. During the 1760 'conspiracy', for instance, the Asgiriya monks stood by the king, and the leading Malvatta monks supported the conspiracy. At the early stage, Väliviṭa Saraṇaṃkara, as Saṃgharāja, stood as formal head over both the divisions. But with his death in 1778, the office of Saṃgharāja lapsed, partly because of the difficulty of finding a monk who was acceptable to both divisions alike. For further information regarding the rivalry between Malvatta and Asgiriya, see ch. III, sec. i-*d*. below.

'division' there was a Mahā Nāyaka (Supreme Chief Monk) appointed by the king, who was assisted by two Anu Nāyakas (Deputy Supreme Chief Monks) and a Committee of Nāyakas (Chief Monks) selected from the main monasteries within each division.[174] They exercised general supervision over the monks and the monasteries within their jurisdiction and inquired into the suits that arose from time to time regarding the conduct of monks and the administration of monasteries. When problems arose with regard to succession to monastic property, they intervened in order to examine the relative merits of rival candidates and endeavoured to arrive at workable solutions.[175] Impious monks were expelled by them, and monks found guilty of criminal offences were formally disrobed by the Anu Nāyakas before being given over to be punished by the secular authorities.[176]

Even more important than this power of expulsion were the exclusive powers given to Malvatta and Asgiriya with regard to the admission of novices to higher ordination. Any ordination ceremony, according to the *vinaya* regulations, was valid, irrespective of its exact location, provided it was performed in a duly consecrated *sīmā* and conducted by a chapter of duly ordained monks.[177] In fact, after the arrival of the Siamese monks in 1753, several *sīmās* were established in different parts of the country, and monks were given higher ordination in some of these newly established *sīmās*.[178] For the ostensible reason that 'unworthy' individuals had been

[174] Of the more important shrines and monasteries in the island, the *aṭamahāsthāna* ('eight great sacred places') at Anurādhapura; Samanola Kanda, Kälaṇiya and Ridī Vihāre, and monasteries in the South came under the jurisdiction of Malvatta, while the *solosmahāsthāna* ('sixteen great sacred places') at Polonnaruva; and Mahiyaṃgana, Mutiyaṃgaṇa and Dam̆bulla came under the jurisdiction of Asgiriya.

[175] In terms of the common law of the country, everybody was free to make a final appeal to the king regarding all judicial matters. In cases involving temple property, the king, in addition to appeal jurisdiction, also exercised original jurisdiction. John D'Oyly, *A Sketch of the Constitution of the Kandyan Kingdom*, ed. L. J. B. Turner (Colombo, 1929), pp. 20–21. When such cases required detailed study of the problems involved, the king appointed special officials to inquire into them. Hantiya Nilame, for instance, was appointed by the king to hear and report on all cases involving lands belonging to Asgiri Vihāre. Lawrie, *Gazetteer*, p. 69.

[176] D'Oyly, *op. cit.*, p. 91.

[177] Regarding the concept of *sīmā*, see below, ch. IV, sec. iii.

[178] *Saṃgharāja Sādhucariyāva*, p. 15.

given higher ordination in some of the provincial *sīmās*, *upsampadā* ceremonies were confined to Kandy about the year 1765 by royal command, and provincial monks were instructed to bring their pupils to Kandy to be examined for higher ordination.[179] This indicated a further, and very vital, step in the process of centralizing the affairs of the *sāsana* and in the growth of a strong and centralized religious 'establishment'.

[179] The *upasampadā* 'seasons' at both Malvatta and Asgiriya were, and still are, held during the month between the full moons of Vesak (May) and Poson (June), i.e., immediately before the beginning of both *vassāna*, the 'rainy season', which was of special ritualistic significance for the monks (see below, ch. III sec. ii), and the Äsaḷa festival. One of the latent political functions of the Äsaḷa festival was that, in compelling provincial chiefs to visit the capital during the festival, it "afforded an excellent opportunity for the king to inquire after and comprehend the provincial situation" (Seneviratne, 'The Äsaḷa Perahära', p. 178). Compelling provincial monks to bring their pupils to the capital during the *upasampadā* season similarly helped to reinforce contact between the centre and the periphery of the kingdom. It is worth noting that the *upasampadā* season brought monks to Kandy not merely from the kingdom itself, but also from the territories which were then under the control of the Dutch.

Part One

SCHISMS WITHIN THE ORDER AND THE RISE OF NEW MONASTIC FRATERNITIES

Chapter II

THE FIRST PHASE: UP TO 1815

i. THE NATURE OF THE RELIGIOUS ESTABLISHMENT

The re-introduction of *upasampadā* ordination during the reign of Kīrti Śrī Rājasiṃha, and the reformist activities that followed it, resulted, as we observed in the last chapter, in the institution of a strong and centralized Buddhist establishment with its centre in Kandy. 'In few parts of the world' wrote Davy in 1821, 'is the "establishment" of religion more regularly organized than in Ceylon'.[1] Davy's observation, however, would have been apt for the 1760s and 1770s rather than for the 1820s, for at the time that he made this observation, the authority structure of the 'establishment' had been effectively challenged in the maritime provinces,[2] and in the decades to come, it was destined to be further loosened. Indeed, the relegation of Kandy into the background and the emergence of rival centres of Buddhist activity, especially in the southern and western regions of the island, were features of major consequence in the nineteenth-century religious scene. Not surprisingly, the decline of Kandy in the religious sphere went hand in hand with its decline in the political sphere.

The Kandyan establishment derived its legitimacy not from the *vinaya* regulations, but rather from the monarchical and feudal political structure that characterized society at large.[3] There were indeed conspicuous

[1] John Davy, *An Account of the Interior of Ceylon and of its Inhabitants* (London, 1821), p. 218.

[2] See below, sections iii and iv of this chapter.

[3] The emulation of the feudal political model in order to introduce a new structure of discipline into the Buddhist order was perhaps only to be expected as the traditional *vinaya* (disciplinary) regulations lacked provision for a universal hierarchy of authority. It has been plausibly argued that the organization of the order was modelled on the constitutions of the semi-autonomous tribal republics, like those of the Śākyas, the Mallas and the Vajjis, which existed in India during the Buddha's time. See K. P. Jayaswal, *Hindu Polity* (Calcutta, 1924), pp. 45–55. The Buddha himself grew up as a Śākyan and in his sermons frequently revealed his admiration for the Vajjis, who differed from the Śākyas by virtue of their greater autonomy. Indeed, the term *saṃgha* which came to be applied to the order was currently used to designate such a tribe. D. D. Kosambi, 'Ancient Kosala and Magadha', *JRAS(BB)*, n.s., XXVII (1951–52) 181. The resultant organization had

parallelisms between the political and ecclesiastical establishments.[4] All political authority emanated, in theory, from a specific centre; and so apparently did all ecclesiastical authority. In the sphere of politics, the king appointed the major chiefs and they in turn appointed the lesser ones. In the sphere of religious organization too, the king appointed the chief monks and the latter in turn appointed the incumbents of smaller temples. In neither case were the appointments simply arbitrary, as they both had to be guided by customary rules and regulations. Important monasteries were endowed with land grants in much the same manner as the important chiefs were. The donations were made by the king out of his own lands (*gabaḍāgam*) and in both cases he exchanged his economic assets for non-economic assets of some sort or another. The chiefs who received lands (*nindagam*) were entitled to the dues and services (*rājakāriya*) which were formerly rendered to the Crown by the tenants of those lands. The dues and services were similarly transferred to the monks and monasteries in the case of *vihāragam*, or temple lands. What enabled the chief monks to receive the services of temple tenants and the obedience and respect of subordinate monks was not solely these politico-legal requirements. Yet what made their authority ultimately effective was the kingly power behind it, which, in addition to legitimizing the positions of the chief monks, guaranteed the power of their offices, if necessary by coercive force. Changes in the political establishment, therefore, necessarily entailed changes in the ecclesiastical establishment.

ii. REBELLION IN THE KANDYAN KINGDOM

The Kandyan political system, like many other political systems, was not a

certain democratic features–quite in contrast to the early Christian, e.g., Benedictine, orders which modelled themselves on Roman patriarchies. For a comparative study of Buddhist and Benedictine Rules, see I. B. Horner, 'The Monk: Buddhist and Christian', *Hibbert Journal*, XXXIX (1940–41) 168–78.

[4] See section iv of this chapter (below). The feudal political model was also reflected in the belief system–in the hierarchical model of the Sinhalese pantheon. Major gods, like landlords, had their areas of special jurisdiction; and minor deities, like tenants, owed service to the major gods and constituted their retinue. In ceremonies where the insignia of the major gods were paraded, their (human) attendants carried flags and drums, banners and palanquins–attributes of feudal authority. For an elaboration of this thesis, see Gananath Obeyesekere, 'The Buddhist Pantheon in Ceylon and its extensions', in M. Nash *et al.*, *Anthropological Studies in Theravāda Buddhism* (New Haven, 1966).

system in harmonious equilibrium, but a system which was maintained through internal conflict.[5] Internal conflict, without breaking the system down, worked to retain it in a dynamic balance. The king, though absolute in theory, shared his power in practice with an elite of privileged aristocrats. Conflict between the king and the aristocracy exemplified one possible area of conflict. Direct conflict between these two, however, was a rare occurrence, as the aristocrats themselves were divided into 'factions',[6] a circumstance which enabled the king to enhance his own power by playing off one faction against another. Each aristocratic faction, at the same time, continuously endeavoured to increase its own power at the expense of other factions and of the king.

The fact that the kingdom as a whole was externally in conflict with some European power which was dominant in the coastal regions had important effects on its internal conflict. On the one hand, it tended to bring the different factions together against a common enemy. But, on the other hand, it also left an opening for a discontented faction to aim to increase its own power through a change in the internal state of affairs with outside assistance.

Successive European powers in the coastal regions were facing somewhat similar circumstances in their own areas. Despite direction given at the top by Europeans, the low-country aristocracy constituted an essential part of the administrative machinery. And the relations between European rulers and the low-country aristocracy were similar in many ways to the relations between the king and the aristocracy in the Kandyan kingdom: with the difference, however, that discontented aristocratic

[5] For sociological discussions of conflict as an institutionalized feature of social relations, see Simmel's classic essay *Conflict* (1908), tr. Kurt H. Wolff (Glencoe, Ill. 1955), and Lewis A. Coser, *The Functions of Social Conflict* (London, 1956). In a succession of books and articles Gluckman has elaborated the same thesis in relation to African tribes. See particularly his *Order and Rebellion in Tribal Africa* (London, 1963). For an examination of the Kandyan political system from a similar standpoint, see S. B. W. Wickremasekera, 'The Social and Political Organization of the Kandyan Kingdom' (M.A. thesis, London, 1961).

[6] 'Factions', despite their importance in politics, defy precise definition because of their composite nature and their lack of coincidence with more persistent–kinship, caste or territorial–groupings. Within the Kandyan court, kinship ties were related to the formation of factions. (The aristocrats had to obtain the king's permission in contracting a marriage, and in this way the king controlled one factor which contributed to the formation of factions.) But the relationship was not a precise one; close kin could well be members of different factions.

factions in the low country turned to the King of Kandy even more easily–he being considered the king of the whole of Ceylon[7]–than their counterparts in Kandy turned to the Europeans. This threat to their security was in fact one reason why European powers were keen to subjugate the Kandyan kingdom.

Desertions from one side to the other were not uncommon; and the desire to subjugate the other was common to each side. But, despite the shifting of boundaries from time to time, the coexistence of two powers continued as almost an inevitable feature for two centuries. The kings of Kandy were able to gain substantial victories in the coastal regions, especially in times when their influence was high and discontent with colonial governments was widespread in those regions.[8] But such victories were only temporary. With no naval power to back their exploits on land, it was impossible for the Kandyans to make a complete and lasting conquest of the coastal regions. Effective control over these territories, therefore, passed from the hands of one European naval power to another–from the Portuguese to the Dutch, and from the Dutch to the British–depending on the changing fortunes of those powers both in Europe and in overseas territories. By supporting the Dutch to oust the Portuguese, and again the British to oust the Dutch, the kings of Kandy aimed to increase their own power. But in this they were disappointed. Once the new power was well established in the coastal regions, it quite easily stepped into the shoes of its European predecessor without giving much thought to the contracts made with the kings, whose support was crucial for them only during their entry into the island. The transfer of power from one European power to another, therefore, implied no material change in the basic structure of politics. The perennial game of tug-of-war between the coastal and interior powers was played basically according to the same rules.

If it was impossible for the Kandyans to make a lasting conquest of the coastal regions, it was no more possible for the Europeans to make a lasting

[7] Buddhist monks in the coastal regions received their ecclesiastical offices from the King of Kandy (see section iii, below). It was also not unusual for Sinhalese aristocrats in these regions to receive titles and honours from the king. P. E. Pieris, 'Appointments within the Kandyan Provinces', *JRAS(CB)*, XXXVI (1945) 113.

[8] Minor insurrections and Kandyan incursions were recurrent events in the maritime provinces. For an account of a major episode of this sort, see J. H. O. Paulusz, 'The Outbreak of the Kandyan-Dutch War in 1761 and the Great Rebellion', *JRAS(CB)*, n.s., III (1953) 29–52.

conquest of the Kandyan kingdom. There were military expeditions to the interior under all three European powers, some of which quite easily occupied the capital. But such conquests were even less lasting, and in the end, far more disastrous than Kandyan conquests of the coastal regions. Whereas the Kandyans, when attacked on the coastal plains, could make a speedy retreat into their own kingdom, European armies that occupied Kandy were hemmed in from all sides by rivers, mountains and forests. With communications cut, provisions running short, and sickness and desertions rapidly increasing, they were eventually left to the doubtful mercy of the Kandyans returning to their capital.

The key to gaining control over the kingdom lay, therefore, not in military actions pure and simple but in the effective manoeuvring of its internal conflicts with the aim thereby of upsetting the balance which was maintained through conflicts. This strategy had already been tried out to some extent by the Dutch,[9] though with no tangible success. The British, after some preliminary blunders, resorted to this form of tactics with far greater efficiency;[10] and their task being made simpler by a growing

[9] The *Memoirs* left by retiring Dutch governors for the guidance of their successors in office frequently contained outlines of factionalisms within the court and instructions as to which of the factions were potentially amenable to Dutch influence. The commonest method used to gain the friendship of the members of such factions was sending them valuable presents. But in one instance there was even an attempt to make available to one such faction—which had previously made an abortive 'rebellion' against the reigning monarch—a puppet to be placed on the throne with Dutch collusion. See above, p. 66. Placing a puppet of their own on the throne was one of the commonest methods by which various factions attempted to increase their powers.

[10] The preliminary blunders were committed during the governorship of Frederic North, the first British governor in Ceylon (1798–1805). Encouraged by the dissensions in Kandy, North first aimed to extend British power through a treaty which was most unfavourable to the Kandyans. When, after protracted negotiations, this diplomatic effort failed in 1802, the governor decided to gain control over the kingdom by placing a puppet of his own on the throne. The expedition undertaken to achieve this in 1803 ended in complete disaster. With the departure of North and the arrival of Maitland in 1805, a different strategy was adopted against Kandy. John D'Oyly, a member of the Civil Service, who had acquired a good knowledge of Sinhalese, was put in charge of all dealings with Kandy instead of the Maha Mudali (the highest Sinhalese official in the administration) who had performed that function ex officio since the Dutch times. Wars as well as peaceful embassies, both of which involved high expenses, were given up; and less money was more 'effectively' spent to reward spies and to supply presents to individual Kandyan chiefs. D'Oyly's *Diary*, ed. H. W. Codrington (Colombo, 1917), throws light on the manner in which these activities were carried on. For detailed discussions of relations between the British and the Kandyan kingdom, see P. E. Pieris, *Tri Sinhala: The Last Phase 1795–1815*, 2nd ed. (Colombo, 1939), and Colvin R. de Silva, *Ceylon under the British Occupation, 1795–1833*, 3rd impression (Colombo, 1953), chs. III, IV, V.

political crisis within the kingdom, they finally succeeded in the year 1815.

The balance within the Kandyan political system could be upset by either of two courses: one, a concentration of power in the hands of the king, leading to a position of 'despotism'; and the other, an overwhelming supremacy of an aristocratic faction, leading to a position of 'oligarchy'.[11] Most of the political crises in the history of the kingdom had their roots in tendencies towards the one or the other of these extremes. The political troubles during the reign of Śrī Vikrama Rājasiṃha (1798–1815), the last king of Kandy, which are of concern to us here, arose out of a sudden shift from a position of near oligarchy to that of near despotism.

Śrī Vikrama began his reign young (he was only eighteen years of age at the time) and inexperienced, hardly more than a puppet of a powerful and ambitious aristocratic faction led by the first Adikāram,[12] Piḷimatalavvē, who aimed by this move to increase his own powers. Indeed, Śrī Vikrama was chosen, despite the better claims of the late king's brother-in-law, prince Muttusāmi, particularly to serve this purpose.

For some time, the powers of Piḷimatalavvē and his faction were supreme. His opponents were either reconciled to his party or imprisoned, exiled or killed. The more important offices which thus became vacant were given to his close allies.[13] But this supremacy did not last long. Śrī Vikrama, once he was established on the throne, soon started placing checks on Piḷimatalavvē's power and taking more and more power into his own hands. Piḷimatalavvē and his allies were the first to be hit because they were the most powerful faction within the court, and therefore, that which constituted the greatest threat to royal power; but the king's manoeuvres soon came to involve the whole aristocracy. Starting from the defensive position of redeeming himself from the role of a puppet, the king was finally led to a position of having to assert his independence with increasing vigour and determination. The process soon acquired a momentum of its own. In order to free himself from the aristocrats who

[11] Wickremasekera, *op. cit.*

[12] There were two *(maha) adikāramas* (chief ministers) in the kingdom, styled *pallegampahē* and *uḍugampahē*. They held equal powers within their respective jurisdictions, but *pallegampahē* enjoyed precedence and was therefore referred to as first Adikāram (or Adigar) in British documents.

[13] The most important among them was the office of *uḍugampahē adikāram* given to Piḷimatalavvē's son-in-law and close ally, Mīgastänne, after the murder of Ärävvāvala, Piḷimatalavvē's main rival.

had put him on the throne, the king had to take measures to curb their power and influence. The aristocrats who had high ambitions at the time of his accession were thereby embittered; and they attempted to right their situation through a change in the structure of power with outside (British) assistance or internal insurrections or both. This led the king to trust them less and less and to attempt to curb their powers more and more.

The stock tactics for controlling the aristocracy were freely resorted to by the king. Piḷimatalavvē's attempts to build connections with the royal family, with the ultimate aim of gaining the throne for himself, met continual rebuffs.[14] The gap which prevailed for some time, as a result of the liquidation of the leaders of Piḷimatalavvē's rival faction, was soon filled by the elevation of Levkē, a rival of Piḷimatalavvē, to the position of the Chief of Ūva and by giving him an important place within the court. Ähälēpola, who succeeded Piḷimatalavvē as first adikāram in 1811, was similarly kept in check to some extent through Molligoḍa, who was appointed the second Adikāram in 1813. Members of each faction were employed to enquire into complaints against adherents of the other. A close watch was kept on the movements of the aristocrats, and to prevent them from developing their influence in the provinces, they were constantly moved from one *disāva*[15] to another. Two of the extensive and troublesome *disāvas*, Hat Kōralē (in 1808) and Sabaragamuva (in 1814), were split up. To reduce the wealth of the aristocrats, certain dues like the *marāla* (death duty) which had long been in abeyance were revived, and

[14] In 1801, Piḷimatalavvē gave his daughter in concubinage to the king in the hope that she would be made queen; but the king married two daughters of one of his own kinsmen, Gampola Nāyakkar, an inveterate enemy of the first adikāram. De Silva, *op. cit.*, p. 129. In 1805, Piḷimatalavvē's son was married to a daughter of the late king by one of his junior wives. Such unions being considered contrary to custom—the presence of aristocrats with royal blood, and therefore claims to the throne, being a potential threat to the king—the king disapproved of the marriage and banished Piḷimatalavvē's son from the court. Pieris, *Tri Sinhala*, p. 83.

[15] The kingdom consisted of twenty-one divisions: nine smaller divisions in the immediate neighbourhood of the capital, which—with the exception of two—were known as *raṭas*; and twelve larger divisions in the provinces, which were known as *disāvas*. The *disāvas* were less subject to central supervision than were the *raṭas*, and the powers of the aristocracy were extensive in them. Here they had their traditional *valavvas* (manor houses) and hereditary lands and large local followings (consisting mostly of the tenants of those lands) who, by virtue of services rendered to aristocratic families for several generations, had strong feelings of attachment and loyalty towards them. See Ralph Pieris, *Sinhalese Social Organization: The Kandyan Period* (Colombo, 1956), p. 64.

the customary payments made by the chiefs on their appointment to offices were increased. The king also increased the strength of his personal bodyguard from seven to twenty-three companies.[16]

Conflict between the king and the aristocracy, as was noted earlier, was a 'normal' feature of the Kandyan political system; but conflict between the king and the aristocracy *as a whole* was a situation of crisis indeed. Against a unified aristocracy, the king, who had no efficient standing army and whose revenues were very limited, would be quite helpless—a circumstance which was normally averted only by the deeply entrenched factionalisms within the aristocracy.[17] Śrī Vikrama's final downfall lay in a temporary unification of the main elements of the aristocracy, who, seeing their position threatened, chose to change their master with the implicit aim of establishing their powers on a more secure footing.

The first to turn against the king was his initial benefactor, Piḷimatalavvē. After his intrigues with Governor North, which led to the disastrous British expedition in 1803, his influence over the king steadily declined. In 1811 he made his final desperate bid to gain power through a conspiracy to assassinate the king. His plans went awry and he was executed. Ähälēpola, Piḷimatalavvē's nephew and second Adikāram, had been suspected of complicity in the 1811 conspiracy. He was pardoned and promoted to succeed Piḷimatalavvē as the first Adikāram; but the king never gave him his confidence. This mistrust was not undeserved, for Ähälēpola himself entered into fresh intrigues with the British in the same manner and for the same ends as Piḷimatalavvē. When the final breach with the king came in 1814, Ähälēpola escaped the fate which befell his predecessor. The rebellion in his support in the border provinces of Sabaragamuva and Tun Kōralē failed; but Ähälēpola and his leading supporters managed to flee into British territory, where a warm welcome awaited them.

The king employed Molligoḍa, Ähälēpola's major rival, to quell the rebellion, a task which he completed to the king's satisfaction. Ähälēpola's

[16] *Ibid.*, p. 105. This stipendiary (*paḍikāra*) class of militia consisted largely of Malays and Malabars.

[17] 'The chief strength of the court of Kandy consisted in the common jealousy of the aristocracy towards each other'. Henry Marshall, *Ceylon: A general Description of the Island and its Inhabitants* (London, 1851), p. 28.

office as well as some of his lands were given to Molligoḍa.[18] Meanwhile, preparations were being made in the British territories to gain control over Kandy with the assistance of Ähälēpola who, as a former first Adikāram, had an intimate knowledge of the strength as well as the weaknesses of the kingdom. Both he and D'Oyly resumed communications with Kandyan chiefs, a good number of whom were now being further estranged from the king as a result of the purges that followed Ähälēpola's defection. Their first success was with the Disāva of Tun Kōralē, the younger brother of the new first Adikāram. Communications with Molligoḍa himself showed his willingness to join the new alliance, a decision which turned the tide against the king. The king, possibly counting on Molligoḍa's rivalry with Ähälēpola, depended heavily on him. Just as he was charged to quell the rebellion at Sabaragamuva earlier, he was now ordered to take control over Tun Kōralē after his brother's defection. Furthermore, his own *disāva* of Hatara Kōralē was crucial to the security of Kandy, as it guarded the entrance to the kingdom from the enemy stronghold in the western coastal regions.[19] As there was no attempt to guard this vital frontier, the British forces, accompanied by the rebel Sinhalese chiefs, entered the capital with no resistance. On 18 February 1815, the king, abandoned by all his major chiefs, was captured by Ähälēpola's men. On 2 March 1815, at a 'Convention' held in Kandy, the chiefs, acting on behalf of the inhabitants, ceded the Kandyan provinces to the British Crown, subject to a treaty signed by both parties.[20]

This event had momentous results for the traditional institutions of the Kandyan kingdom, including its religious establishment. We shall turn to

[18] See 'Molligoḍa Sannasa', in H. C. P. Bell, *Report on the Kegalla District* (S.P. XIX: 1892), pp. 101–3.

[19] It was in recognition of the valour of the Hatara Kōralē forces in the struggles against the Portuguese that Rājasiṃha II, in the seventeenth century, granted them the Royal *ira haňda koḍiya* (the banner of the sun and moon) and assigned this *disāva* precedence over all the other *disāvas*. P. E. Pieris, *Sinhalē and the Patriots* (Colombo, 1950), pp. 23–24. The esteem in which Hatara Kōralē was held is indicated by the reference in the Molligoḍa *sannasa* (of May 1814) to 'the army of the most truthworthy ever victorious Maha Disāva of Satara Kōralē.'

[20] For details see Pieris, *Tri Sinhala*. Molligoḍa's defection to the British poses a problem as, quite apart from holding the highest possible position under the king, he was also Ähalēpola's main rival, both before as well as after the deposition of the king. Probably the best explanation of his behaviour was provided by the deposed king himself; when asked by William Granville, the British officer who was conducting him to his exile in South India, 'whether the first adigar, Molligody,

these results at the beginning of the next chapter. First we shall examine the changes that took place in the context of the inherently limited nature of Kandyan authority–even prior to its final breakdown–as a result of the division of the country into two powers, interior and coastal.

iii. KANDYAN VERSUS LOW-COUNTRY MONKS

The political division of the country into coastal and interior regions before 1815 placed the low-country monks in a rather ambiguous position in their relations with political authorities. For although these monks received their ecclesiastical offices, and the honours and titles attached to them, from the kings of Kandy, they in fact lived in territories where the kings had no effective authority to enforce these grants. The monks were compelled, therefore, to solicit the colonial administrators–first the Dutch, and later the British–to recognize and confirm such offices, honours and titles received from Kandy.[21] A chief monk was entitled, in the first place, to command the obedience and respect of the other monks within his jurisdiction. His rights were not limited, however, to this purely religious sphere. He was also entitled, by virtue of his office, to such traditional honours as travelling in palanquins accompanied by flags and drums, and to such services as receiving *aḍukku* (cooked provisions) and coolies from the headmen of the areas he happened to pass through.[22] The enforcement of these rights required the approval, if not the active support, of the effective political authority within the area concerned.

The colonial administrators, mindful of the connections that the monks maintained with Kandy and the pervasive influence that they exercised over the Buddhist populace, took conscious steps to keep them in good humour and to win them over, if possible, to their own governments. The

was a favourite of his. He said, "Yes, Molligody is a good man, but not a clever one. He has sworn to serve the English, and you may depend upon him [a prediction which proved to be correct], because he is a man of his word. He would never have abandoned me if he could have helped it'. 'Journal of Reminiscences relating to the late king of Kandy when on his voyage from Colombo to Madras in 1816, a prisoner-of-war on board His Majesty's Ship "Cornwallis" ', *Ceylon Literary Register*, 3rd series, III (1933–34) 494 (entry dated 1 February 1816).

[21] See, for instance, the letter of Mettapiṭiyē Saṃgharakkhita to the Dutch Commander at Galle, dated 13 June 1789 (C.N.A. Galle Records, vol. 1241), and the petition of Mahagoḍa Indasāra, Chief Monk of the Districts of Galle and Colombo, to Governor Maitland, n.d., *ca.* 1805, C.M.L. Johnston Papers, No. 168.

[22] *Ibid.*

Dutch government, especially after the Kandyan invasion of the early 1760s, made positive efforts to show friendly gestures towards Buddhist monks. Governor Falck (1765–85), who assumed office immediately after the period of intense hostility with the Kandyans, paid a visit to the leading Buddhist temple in the Dutch settlements, Mulgirigala Vihāre, about the year 1765.[23] Not long afterwards, a circular was sent by the Dutch Disāva of Mātara to Mulgirigala and its subordinate temples informing them of 'the goodwill of the Government towards the Buddhist religion and the desire of the Government to support the Buddhist religion and the Buddhist temples'.[24] Towards the end of their rule in Ceylon, one of the Dutch governors, van de Graff (1785–93), even went to the extent of recommending a monthly stipend of twenty-five rix dollars to one of the leading Buddhist monks in the Southern Province, Karatoṭa Dhammārāma (1737–1827).[25]

The same sort of diplomatic and outwardly friendly attitude was continued by the early British governor, Thomas Maitland (1805–12). About Mulgirigala, Maitland wrote to the Collector of Revenue in the area:

> The Priests who officiate in the Temple have prodigious influence in the Country, and the Dutch Government frequently experienced the effects of it in your Province– It is a political Engine which the King of Kandi is continually endeavouring to keep in his favour, and which we ought by good management, to turn to our own Advantage– You must therefore do everything you can to cultivate the Friendship and gain the confidence of the Priests of that Temple.[26]

Maitland advised the collector to visit the place himself and to explain to the monks 'most distinctly, that Government is determined not only to tolerate but to support them in the exercise of their religion and to bestow such honours, as are most congenial to their feelings upon all those who are distinguished by the extent of their learning, and the propriety of their conduct'.[27]

Maitland also proposed the establishment of a committee of Buddhist

[23] Donald Ferguson, 'Mulgirigala', *JRAS(CB)*, XXII (1911) 218.

[24] *Third Report of the Ceylon Historical Manuscripts Commission* (S.P. XIX: 1951), p. 12.

[25] Veheragampiṭa Nandārāma, *Karatoṭa Vata* (Mātara, 1940), p. 19. See also John F. Tillekaratne, 'The Life of Karatoṭa Kīrti Srī Dhammārāma, High Priest of Matara in the Southern Province of the Island of Ceylon', *The Orientalist*, III (1889) 204–7.

[26] C.O. 59/27. The letter is dated 31 January 1807.

[27] *Ibid.*

monks in the Southern Province 'to whom all cases . . . relative whether to the Priests themselves, or their lands and their religious ceremonies were to be referred for decision'.[28] In his letter to the collector of revenue, the governor confided that his intentions for doing so were 'first, to convince the People, that the Greatest respect and attention shall be shown to their religious prejudices and customs– Secondly, to give the Priests themselves a fellow feeling with our Government, and of course an interest in supporting its Authority among the inhabitants.'[29] The monk who was chosen to lead this committee was the same Karatoṭa Dhammārāma who had received a stipend under the Dutch administration–an erudite, able and ambitious monk whose relations with Kandy were not entirely cordial.[30]

Karatoṭa's relations with Kandy were initially strained mainly because of a controversy that arose during the reign of Rājādhi Rājasiṃha (1782–98) regarding the incumbency of the much venerated shrine of Śrīpāda (The Sacred Foot Print) in the Sabaragamu *disāva*. The shrine, along with the temple village of Kuṭṭāpiṭiya for its maintenance had been entrusted to the pupillary succession of the Saṃgharāja Välivița Saraṇaṃkara during the reign of Kīrti Śrī Rājasiṃha (1747–82).[31] During the Saṃgharāja's lifetime, and under his own instructions, the affairs of the

[28] *Ibid.*

[29] *Ibid.*

[30] Alexander Johnston, who for several years served in the Judicial Establishment of Ceylon, referred to the 'very judicious manner' in which the committee of monks under Karatoṭa enquired into the cases that came before them, and 'the soundness of the principles on which the members of it relied in framing their decisions', and ascribed to the success of this committee the reason for having felt confident in recommending the introduction of trial by jury into Ceylon. Alexander Johnston's 'Reply' to 'The Address by the Chiefs and all the subordinate Priests of Budhoo . . . ' in *Important Public Documents, to and from Sir Alexander Johnston, 1802–1819* (n.d.). Johnston was particularly impressed with Karatoṭa and got a portrait of the latter painted for himself. P. E. Pieris, *Notes on Some Sinhalese Families*, Part IV (Colombo, 1911), p. 30. John D'Oyly, while he was stationed in Mātara between 1803 and 1805 came into close contact with Karatoṭa and gained a knowledge of the Sinhalese language under him, a knowledge which was to be of great assistance to him in his subsequent career. See the editor's 'biographical note' in *The Diary of John D'Oyly*, ed. H. W. Codrington (Colombo, 1917). Maitland's letter of 31 January 1807 to D'Oyly's successor at Mātara, extracts from which were quoted above, reveal an unusually intimate and accurate knowledge of the local elite (chiefs and monks)–their rivalries and alliances. In all probability, D'Oyly himself was the real author of that letter.

[31] See H. C. P. Bell, *Report on the Kuṭṭāpiṭiya Sannasa* (Kandy, 1925). The village of Pälmaḍulla was also added to the shrine subsequently.

shrine were managed, in succession, by three of his low-country pupils: Mālimbaḍa Dhammadhara, Vēhällē Dhammadinna, and Kum̆burupiṭiyē Guṇaratana.[32] As the latter two monks held, in addition, the office of the chief monk of the low country,[33] a link developed, through usage, between the two offices. No immediate change was enforced at the demise of the Saṃgharāja in 1778: Kum̆burupiṭiyē continued to hold both offices. But with the latter's death in (or soon after) 1779,[34] the two offices were separated from each other, largely through the influence of Moratoṭa Dhammakkhandha (1735–1811) who, at this time, was Anu Nāyaka of Malvatta Vihāre and *rājaguru* (tutor) to the new king, Rājādhi Rājasiṃha. Karatoṭa Dhammārāma, who was appointed the chief monk of the low country in succession to Kum̆burupiṭiyē, was thus deprived of control over Śrīpāda; and, greatly disappointed, he left the Kandyan kingdom and returned to the Southern Province in 1785. His subsequent contacts with the colonial administrators tended to worsen his relations with Kandy. As president of the newly established low-country Committee of Monks, he received a stipend from the British administration; and Moratoṭa, who by this time had risen to the rank of Mahā Nāyaka, informed the king (Śrī Vikrama Rājasiṃha, 1798–1815) of this 'unfaithful' act, and deprived Karatoṭa of the revenues he had regularly obtained from the village of Pallebädda in Sabaragamuva, which, some years earlier, had been granted to him by Rājādhi Rājasiṃha in recognition of his talents as a poet.[35] It appears, furthermore, that Kandy ceased to recognize Karatoṭa as the chief

[32] *Saṃgharāja Sādhucariyāva*, ed. P. B. Sannasgala and Nāhällē Paññāsena (Colombo, 1947), pp. 20–22.

[33] *Ibid.*

[34] The exact date of his death is not known. 1779 was the year in which he wrote his will from his sick-bed. A copy of the will is given in Kiriällē Jñāṇavimala, *Saparagamuvē Päraṇi Liyavili* (Colombo, 1942), p. 93.

[35] The composition which particularly impressed the king was a poem extolling the virtues of the Buddha known as 'Bhārasa Kāvya', which consisted of twelve alliterative stanzas all of which were included within a single diagram and within which they were readable from left to right and vice versa, and from top to bottom and vice versa. See James Alwis, 'Introduction' to his translation of *The Sidath Sangarawa* (Colombo, 1852), pp. cvii–cxv. For 'Pallebädda Sannasa', see Jñāṇavimala, *op. cit.*, pp. 107–8. It is believed that Karatoṭa composed 'Bhārasa Kāvya' (in 1786) in order to regain the king's favour, having previously incurred his displeasure–presumably–in making attempts to gain the incumbency of Śrīpāda against the wishes of the king's tutor, Moratoṭa. Regarding the withdrawal of the Pallebädda revenues from Karatoṭa, see his two petitions to Maitland and to Johnston. C. M. L. Johnston Papers, nos. 33 and 167.

monk of the low country and appointed another monk to the same office while he was still alive.[36]

Meanwhile, Śrīpāda was managed by the Mahā Nāyakas of Malvatta, but the controversy regarding its incumbency remained unsolved[37] and gained a new vigour after the cession of the Kandyan kingdom to the British in 1815. The matter came up before the Board of Commissioners in Kandy in the later part of 1825; and in the following year, the control of the shrine was taken away from Malvatta Vihāre and given back to the low-country monks on the recommendation of George Turnour, the Agent of Government at Sabaragamuva, who was directed by the commissioners to make a special inquiry into the case.[38] The new recipient of the shrine was Gāllē Medhaṃkara (?–1836), a pupil of Karatoṭa. The decision was unpopular with the Kandyan monks, and they continued to send in petitions against it.[39]

Quite apart from the specific issue of the incumbency of Śrīpāda, the appointment of a provincial chief monk who was unacceptable to the Kandyan monks also raised the wider issue regarding the authority of the Kandyan monks, who traditionally exercised control over the monks in the whole island.[40] It is hardly surprising, therefore, that all the leading Kandyan monks, led by the Mahā Nāyakas and the Anu Nāyakas of Malvatta and Asgiriya, in their joint petition to the Commission of Enquiry in 1829 felt the need to assert this aspect of their authority in the strongest terms and to urge the government not to undermine it.[41] As far as the large majority of the low-country monks were concerned, however,

[36] 'Kamburupitiye [Kuḍā] Unnanse is appointed Nayaka of Pata Rata [Low-Country].' *The Diary of John D'Oyly*, 21 February 1812.

[37] In addition to the controversy between the Malvatta and the low-country monks, there was another controversy within Malvatta Temple itself between Moratoṭa (and, after his death, his pupils) and Väliviṭa (Kuḍā) Saraṇaṃkara. See *The Second Report of the Historical Manuscripts Commission* (S.P. XXI: 1935), pp. 48–49.

[38] The Board of Commissioners, Kandy, to George Turnour, 16 December 1825; and Turnour to the Board of Commissioners, 15 January 1826. C.N.A.

[39] Turnour to the Board of Commissioners, 27 February 1827 (C.N.A.), refers to one such petition. During the period 1829–30 the Malvatta monks sent two petitions to the Colebrooke Commission on the same subject. C.O. 416–31 (petition no. 418) and 416/32 (no. 628).

[40] Evidently this was not unknown to the British administrators. As early as 1800, Governor North wrote of the 'High Priest of Candy whose Authority extends over all the Priests and Temples of Budha in the Island. . . .' North to Governor General in Council, Fort William, Secret Despatch of 4 August 1800, C.O. 54/2.

[41] Petition no. 372, C.O. 416/31.

despite their disagreements and controversies with Kandy, the basic issue was not in doubt. They continued to give at least formal recognition to the authority of the Mahā Nāyakas, and annually sent their pupils to Kandy to be examined for higher ordination. It was only towards the middle of the nineteenth century that controversies involving further issues—in the background of a steadily weakening Kandyan establishment—finally led and enabled some monks in the low country to reject the authority of the Mahā Nāyakas and to organize a fraternity of their own. These developments will receive attention in the next chapter. While this group of monks could well have been accommodated, albeit in a subordinate position, within the existing order, there was another group of monks in the low country—monks of low-caste social origins—who were almost totally unacceptable to the establishment. The protest activities to which these low-caste monks were driven historically preceded those of the other group, and it is to them that we shall turn our attention now.

It is perhaps worth emphasizing that the term 'low caste' as used in this study is not intended in any way as a pejorative; its use is necessitated purely by the social fact of inequality. The numerically preponderant, and socially and politically dominant, Goyigamas (subjectively) considered these castes as 'low' (*aḍu* or *hīna*); and in terms of (objective) secular as well as ritual criteria too, the status of these castes was lower than that of the Goyigamas. Of course, not all the non-Goyigamas—though collectively referred to here, for lack of a better generic term, as 'low castes'—were of equal rank; and some of them refused to accept the positions that the Goyigamas (and other castes) wished to keep them in. How this came about, and the results that it produced in the sphere of religious organization are problems that will be examined next.

iv. LOW-CASTE PROTEST AGAINST THE ESTABLISHMENT AND THE RISE OF THE AMARAPURA FRATERNITY.

The low-caste protest against the religious establishment in Kandy which resulted in the rise of the Amarapura fraternity (*nikāya*)[42] also took place in the coastal regions of the island, and for this reason may be considered

[42] The term *nikāya* is generally translated as 'sect'. I have preferred, however, to translate it as 'fraternity', as the term 'sect' would be misleading in this context, in view of the manner in which it is currently used (following Weber and Troeltsch) in discussions of sociology of religion.

part of the general conflict between the monks of the two regions. But in this instance, in contrast to the instances considered in the preceding section, the conflicting parties also belonged to different castes, a circumstance which intensified the conflict and rendered the final breach practically unavoidable.

In theory, of course, Buddhist monks were 'casteless', for caste is a social category, and hence of no relevance to those who had renounced the society. Yet, in practice, this ideal was rarely realized—at any rate not during the period that we are concerned with—for reasons that will be examined shortly. On entering the order, monks showed no signs of losing their caste identities;[43] on the contrary, they continued to be highly conscious of their caste. Hence, incidentally, the justification for using such expressions as *Salāgama monk* and *Karāve monk* in this book, for those were expressions that the monks themselves used at the time.

The political division of the island was directly relevant for the success of the new low-caste fraternity in that its centre of activity was (geographically) beyond the effective authority of the King of Kandy, whose coercive powers could otherwise have been used against it; but just as significant for the emergence of the new fraternity was an *indirect* result of the political division, namely, the collective upward mobility of certain low castes under colonial rule which resulted in their attempts to challenge high-caste monopolies in many fields, including that of religion.

The immediate cause for conflict was the refusal by the chief monks in Kandy to grant higher (*upasampadā*) ordination to those monks who had non-Goyigama social origins, a refusal which was legitimized by a royal decree attributed to Kīrti Śrī Rājasiṃha. Although the exact sequence of events which led to the promulgation of such a decree is not accurately known,[44] the refusal of *upasampadā* to low-caste monks, despite its evident conflict with *vinaya* regulations, does not come altogether as a surprise.

[43] Though, in theory, they were supposed to do so—just as rivers of different names lose their names and identities on entering the ocean and are left with only the common identity of the great ocean. *The Book of the Discipline*, vol. V, tr. I. B. Horner (London, 1953), p. 334.

[44] Davy (*An Account of the Interior of Ceylon* . . ., p. 219) records the tradition that it was due to the fact that high-caste laymen were disinclined to pay respects to monks who, before their admission to monkhood, belonged to one or the other of the low castes. There is another tradition, however, which holds that the decree was promulgated because low-caste monks unforgetful of their humble origins, paid respects to lay individuals, especially the king and his officials, by pros-

The choice of an other-worldly path within a caste-society, it has been observed, provided the surest means for any individual to transcend all social barriers and receive the adulation of all strata in his society.[45] Though this observation has generally been true in relation to individual world-renouncers, such as, for instance Indian *sannyāsis*, it has tended to be much less true in relation to world-renouncers *organized* into religious orders. In Ceylon, as in all the other Buddhist countries, the (organized) religious order became a *social* institution–in contrast to a mere aggregation of individuals who had broken off their ties with society –with the result that the clear bifurcation that prevailed in theory between the religious and the social spheres was blurred in actual practice. The order itself became an institution commanding much esteem within society; hence, the intrusion of the criteria of esteem that prevailed in the wider society into the monastic order followed as an almost inevitable consequence.[46]

Attention has already been drawn (in section i of this chapter) to the parallelisms that existed between the religious establishment and the feudal *political* structure that characterized society at large. Clear reflections of the wider feudal *economy* with its intricate division of labour based on the caste system may be similarly seen in the administrative arrangements relating to monastic estates. The Goyigama tenants attached to these estates cultivated the *muttețțu* fields, and a portion of the crop was paid to the temple for the maintenance of its resident monks. The other castes too performed their respective services and received in return a quantity of raw rice or a piece of cultivable land within the temple domain. Thus, attached to temple lands there were different groups of Navandanno to build and repair temple buildings and to supply craftsmen and painters for temple decorations; people of the Baḍahäla caste to supply bricks, tiles and earthen

---

trating themselves in their presence and thus degraded the order. This account is related in the *Mandāram Pura Puvata* (vv. 823–62) and agrees with a prose account printed in the 'Introduction' to Labugama Laṃkānanda's edition of this work (Colombo, 1958), pp. xiii–xv. Both traditions–no matter which one is correct–illustrate the difficulty which will be examined shortly of isolating the order of monks from its social surroundings.

[45] E. R. Leach (ed.), *Aspects of Caste in South India, Ceylon and North-West Pakistan* (Cambridge, 1960), p. 6.

[46] As was already noted (pp. 42–44 above), Christian churches too, at this time, restricted membership of the clergy to the higher castes.

vessels; Hunnō to provide lime and plaster for the walls and floors of monastic buildings; Radav to furnish clean cloth and lampwicks for temple ceremonies; Beravāyō to provide drummers, pipers and dancers at festivals; Paduvō to carry goods and bear the palanquins of chief monks; and so on. In relation to the services of these different caste groups, the chief monk stood in a position similar to that of a feudal lord. General feudal practices, like the *däkuma* at which the tenants annually appeared before the landlord with presents and betel leaves, were duly observed in temple lands too.[47]

By ancient tradition, the persons who deserved such honours and services were the people of the high-caste (Goyigama) nobility. Hence, all the important chiefs were chosen from this caste. In view of the significant parallelisms that existed between the roles of the chiefs and of the chief monks, it would appear hardly surprising that membership of the order too came to be limited to this caste. The *upasampadā* ceremony, which signified the admission of a novice (*sāmaṇera*) to full membership of the order, was celebrated in Kandy as a Royal Festival (*Vāhala Pinkama*). The candidate was referred to as *Vāhala Nāga*, or 'Royal Candidate'; and just before being invested in his new status, he was dressed in princely finery and paraded through the streets of the capital,[48] in a manner that could well cause envy even among those who claimed to be the noblest within the kingdom.

It is probable that the practice of recruiting at least the more important monks within the order from the higher strata of society was fairly common in Ceylon since the earliest times. The definite rule that the candidates' caste (*jāti-gotra*) should be enquired into at the ordination ceremony first occurs in the *Daṁbadeṇi Katikāvata* of the thirteenth century.[49] Queyroz and Knox, both seventeenth-century observers, mention that only persons 'noble birth' were chosen to be *terunnāsēs*.[50] It may be argued, therefore, that what had in fact prevailed as the informally established practice was merely formalized during Kīrti Śrī's time. What is

[47] Several documents throwing light on the administration of temple lands are given (in English translation) in A. C. Lawrie, *A Gazetteer of the Central Province of Ceylon*, 2 vols. (Colombo, 1896–98), *passim*. For accounts of Kandyan feudalism, see Ralph Pieris, *op. cit.*, and Wickremasekera, *op. cit.*

[48] Davy, *op. cit.*, p. 220.

[49] D. B. Jayatilaka (ed.), *Katikāvat Saňgarā* (Colombo, 1922), pp. 9 and 10.

[50] Fernão de Queyroz, *The Temporal and Spiritual Conquest of Ceylon* (1687), tr. S. G. Perera (Colombo, 1930), p. 114; Robert Knox, *An Historical Relation of Ceylon* (1681), ed. James Ryan (Glasgow, 1911), p. 117.

important, however, is that henceforth it became rigid in its actual application.

The radical spirit that characterized certain sections of the order at the time of the arrival of the Siamese monks in Ceylon had its effects on the early ordination ceremonies; and hence, caste exclusivism was not rigidly adhered to at this stage. Quite a number of Saraṇaṃkara's pupils of the Silvat Samāgama belonged to non-Goyigama castes, and some of them managed to obtain *upasampadā* at this time. Prominent among them were the two leading low-country pupils of Saraṇaṃkara, Siṭināmaluvē Dhammajoti and Vēhällē Dhammadinna.[51] This liberality, however, did not last long; the order soon drifted back to its privileged and established position. The Silvat Samāgama, which at one stage spearheaded the pursuit of radical ideals within the order, experienced a general attenuation in its commitment to radical ideals and was gradually absorbed into the establishment. Saraṇaṃkara himself became the formal head of the establishment; he was also the recipient of many a material gift.[52]

The Kandyan monks themselves were well aware that their caste exclusivism did not derive its legitimacy from the ancient *vinaya* regulations. Answering the question 'Men of what *nagaran* [castes] are qualified to enter on the duties of the religious life?'—which was included in a questionnaire addressed to them by Iman Willem Falck, the Dutch governor (1765–85)—the monks replied: 'It does not appear in the books that the religious life is not open to men of any *nagaran*, nevertheless at the present time in the Sinhala Raṭa [Kandyan kingdom] the admission of a person of low *nagaran* is prohibited.'[53]

Since the authority of 'the books' could easily be quoted against this prohibition, a rationale for protest movements was inherent in the situation. Their success only required an adequate number of *bhikkhus* willing to initiate low-caste individuals as *sāmaṇeras* into the order; a keenness on the part of low-caste individuals to enter into religious life; sufficient

[51] It is believed that Siṭināmaluvē belonged to the Durāve caste and that Vēhällē belonged to the Näkäti caste. Polvattē Buddhadatta, *Samīpātītayehi Bauddhācāryayō* (Ambalaṃgoḍa, 1950), p. 4. It should be noted, however, that, though there is general agreement with regard to Siṭināmaluvē's caste, the same degree of agreement is not to be found with regard to Vēhällē's caste.

[52] For details, see Tirāṇagama Ratanasāra, *Saṅgaraja Vatagota* (Maharagama, 1963).

[53] This document is dated 12 August 1769. A complete English translation of it is appended to P. E. Pieris, *Sinhalē and the Patriots* (Colombo, 1950), pp. 577–87.

means in the hands of their patrons to send them abroad, if necessary, to receive *upasampadā*; and freedom from the authority of the King of Kandy, whose power could be used against protest movements—conditions which were amply satisfied in the low country.

Although the overwhelming majority of the leading monks in the low country (who received higher ordination at Kandy) belonged to the Goyigama caste, they did not belong to the aristocratic segments of this caste as did the leading monks in the Kandyan kingdom. In the low country, the highest segments of the Goyigama caste held administrative offices under colonial governments, and therefore, they had to profess Christianity, though often only nominally. Many of them maintained close friendships with Buddhist monks and patronized their religious and literary activities;[54] but they hardly ever showed a keenness to join the religious life themselves. Such a step would have entailed for them a loss of government office with no corresponding gain in any other field. For although a handful of the low-country temples were wealthy, the vast majority of them were not. The monks in the low country had to depend more on their piety and learning to command social esteem, in contrast to their counterparts in Kandy, who already possessed it by virtue of their family connections and monastic wealth.[55] Many of the low-country monks derived their spiritual succession through the non-Goyigama Siṭināmaluvē, and not being part of a wealthy feudal elite, they were less concerned with perpetuating the order through their own kinsmen. They admitted pupils from a wider social compass; and among their pupils were the non-Goyigama novices who, being unable to obtain *upasampadā* ordination within the existing fraternity, went on to establish a new fraternity of their own.

The new fraternity was started, not by monks from all the non-Goyigama castes, but mainly by monks from three castes—Salāgama (alternatively Halāgama, Chālia), Karāve and Durāve—which were preponderant

[54] P. E. Pieris, *Ceylon and the Hollanders* (Tellippalai, 1918), pp. 136 ff., and P. B. J. Hevawasam, *Mātara Yugayē Sāhityadharayan hā Sāhitya Nibandhana* (Colombo, 1966), *passim*.

[55] It is not surprising, therefore, that the religious and literary revival which began in the time of Välivița Saraṇaṃkara persisted for a longer period outside than within the Kandyan kingdom. See the works cited in the preceding footnote, and ch. V, sec. ii (below).

in the low country. None of these castes enjoyed high prestige in the Kandyan kingdom;[56] but in the coastal regions, under the Portuguese and the Dutch, they rose to prominence in the caste hierarchy. This was helped largely by their high concentration in certain localities;[57] but equally important was the freedom from the authority of the Goyigama chiefs which they achieved under colonial rule.

In the Kandyan kingdom, although the non-Goyigama castes had their own headmen (called *vidānēs* and *durayās*), the *baddas* ('departments') to which they were attached for the performance of their caste duties were under the management of Goyigama chiefs.[58] They were thus obliged to receive orders from and serve Goyigama chiefs in addition to serving the king. Similar arrangements persisted in the low country, too, with regard to some of the smaller castes low down in the caste hierarchy.[59] In the case of the larger and economically more important castes, however, the Europeans took them directly under their control, and thereby freed them from their traditional obligations to Goyigama chiefs.[60] These castes

[56] In the Kandyan kingdom, members of the Salāgama and Durāve castes could not grow beards nor wear *ohori* (cloths worn by women above the waist and thrown backwards over the shoulder). D'Oyly's *Diary*, 16 June 1812. The Karāvas, being predominantly a coastal caste, were not even mentioned in the seventeenth-century account of Knox. Some Karāvas subsequently migrated to the interior and rose to some prominence in the caste hierarchy along with the rising economic importance of the *maḍigē* (transport) department to which they were attached. Davy (*op. cit.*, p. 112) ranked them first among the non-Goyigama castes while conceding that the Navandanno 'occupied according to some, the first rank among the low castes'.

[57] Numerical preponderance, as Srinivas has shown, has been one of the primary conditions for the emergence of 'dominant' castes. 'The Social System of a Mysore Village', in McKim Marriott (ed.), *Village India: Studies in the Little Community* (Chicago, 1955).

[58] The Koṭṭalbadda (artificers' department) was frequently under the supervision of the Disāva of Sabaragamuva (Jñāṇavimala, *op. cit.*, pp. 125, 150, 151–52); and the Maḍigēbadda and the Kuruvēbadda (transport and elephant departments respectively) were frequently under the supervision of the Disāva of Hatara Kōralē. John D'Oyly, *A Sketch of the Constitution of the Kandyan Kingdom* (1835), ed. L. J. B. Turner (Colombo, 1929), p. 16.

[59] The Hinnāvō caste at Potupiṭiya, for instance, had to serve the (Goyigama) Basnāyaka of Colombo. C.O. 416/5.

[60] A notable exception was the Durāve caste, some members of which, being attached to the Kuruvēbadda, were under the direction of the (Goyigama) Gajanāyaka. But even within this department, titles and honours were sometimes bestowed on Durāve headmen which apparently they were not traditionally entitled to. A deed of grant (dated 3 March 1772) promoting a Durāve headman to the rank of Mudali specifically stated that it was being done 'out of order and over the heads of others'. R. G. Anthonisz, *Report on the Dutch Records* (Colombo, 1907), pp. 55–56.

thereby achieved a shortcut to enhance their positions, through faithful services to Europeans rather than to their Goyigama superiors. Such services, being invaluable both politically and economically, were consistently encouraged by the rulers and rewarded with titles and honours which had traditionally been Goyigama monopolies. The privileges which they achieved in this manner stood in significant contrast to their low status in the Kandyan kingdom, a feature which is made clear by the following entry in D'Oyly's *Diary*. The entry, relating to representations made to the British governor by the *mohoṭṭālas* (secretaries) of four Kandyan provinces, reads:

> That they hear, the Low Country Mod[elia]rs of Karawe, Durawe, Halagame and other Low Casts have been created, and are accustomed there to travel in Palanquins– In the Kandyan Country, such things are never permitted, and they request, that no Persons of these Low Casts may be allowed to assume such Honours within the Kandyan Territory, but only the niyama Mudiyansela [genuine aristocrats] of the Goyigama.[61]

Of the three castes–Salāgama, Karāve and Durāve–the first to challenge Goyigama monopolies both in the secular and the religious spheres was the Salāgama caste,[62] by far the most 'favoured' low caste in the low country. Being attached to the Cinnamon Department (Mahabadda), which, by virtue of its economic importance, rose to a supreme position under the Portuguese and the Dutch, the powers and privileges of the caste rose along with the growing importance of this department. The first Dutch governor in Ceylon wrote of them:

> For the peeling of the cinnamon a certain class of people of this Island has been set apart called *Chjahalias*, a despised people among the inhabitants but to be made much of by us owing to the profits which they bring the Honourable Company and the fact that no cinnamon can be obtained except through them, wherefore they are provided with good holdings and maintenance.[63]

[61] *Op. cit.*, 19 March 1815. The governor readily agreed, saying: 'Your ancient Customs shall undoubtedly be observed, and the Persons of inferior Cast shall be forbidden to use such Honours and Distinctions within the Kandyan Provinces'. *Ibid.*

[62] For accounts of the origin and the early history of this caste, see Alexander Johnston, 'Account of a Flag representing the Introduction of the Caste of Chalias or Cinnamon-peelers into Ceylon', *Transactions of the Royal Asiatic Society of Great Britain and Ireland*, III (1835) 332–34; the petition presented to General Diogo de Melo de Castro, reproduced in Queyroz, *op. cit.*, pp. 1018 ff.; and *Memoir of Jan Schreuder* (1762), tr. and ed. E. Reimers (Colombo, 1946), pp. 73–74.

[63] *Memoir of Joan Maetsuyker* (1650), tr. and ed. E. Reimers (Colombo, 1927), p. 10.

It should be noted, however, that the lot of the Kuruñdukāra (cinnamon-peeler) section of this caste was by no means a pleasant one under the Portuguese and the Dutch. They were compelled to spend more than six months of the year in unhealthy forests, away from their families and villages. Yet in return for these toilsome services they were granted several caste privileges,[64] many of which, in fact, they extorted from their rulers by virtue of their economic indispensability.[65] Salāgama headmen who belonged to the Panividakāra (messenger) segment of the caste were given particularly high rewards as their services were necessary in the day-to-day administration of the cinnamon department (which included tasks like compiling registers of peelers under their commmand, organizing and superintending their work, and collecting dues at the end of the harvesting season). Rewards granted to them included high offices in the administration, extensive maintenance lands, military escorts, *paṭabäñdi* ('frontlet-tied') names and gold medals[66]—in short, the paraphernalia of power and prestige which were best exemplified in the Goyigama model which the other castes tried to emulate.[67]

The importance of the Salāgamas was realized not merely by the Europeans but also by the Kandyans. During times of discontent among the cinnamon-peelers, inciting them to rebellion or encouraging them to flee into Kandyan territory had been a fairly common practice among the

[64] The petition submitted by this caste to the Commission of Enquiry in 1829 (C.O. 416/5, no. B.2) contains a list of these privileges.

[65] In their dealings with the administration, the cinnamon peelers (consisting of males above twelve years of age) acted almost in the fashion of an organized trade union. Sending petitions and delegations, and in the absence of redress, threatening to stop work or actual stoppages were common tactics resorted by by them. Governor Van Imhoff warned his successor 'that these people never cease to complain and petition, although they are better off than any of the other inhabitants of Ceylon; and that they always come with their complaints when it is time to commence the peeling'. *Memoir* (1740), tr. and ed. R. G. Anthonisz (Colombo, 1911), p. 50. Not being inclined to risk the loss of revenue from cinnamon, the administration was in many instances compelled to give way.

[66] For an account of the Salāgama families who held high offices in the administration and the numerous rewards granted to them, see Sampson Rajapakse, *A Memoir, with a sketch of the Salagama Sinhalese, their Chiefs and Clans* (Colombo, 1912).

[67] Bertolacci wrote of the Salāgama caste: 'Prone to insult the castes which are superior to them, they have long aimed at attaining the privileges of the Vellales [Goyigamas]. . . .' *A view of the Commercial, Agricultural, and Financial Interests of Ceylon* (London, 1817), p. 243. Emulating the higher castes has always been a major feature in processes of caste mobility. See D. F. Pocock, 'The Movement of Castes', *Man*, LV (1955) 71–72; and M. N. Srinivas, *Social Change in Modern India* (Berkeley and Los Angeles, 1966).

more militant sections of the Kandyans.[68] In times of acute conflict between the two powers, this practice was vigorously followed by them with the aim of crippling their enemy's main source of revenue. During the troubles of 1760–61, the political and economic factors were apparently supplemented by the religious, and the agents sent by the Kandyans to Välitara, the main centre of Salāgama power, were two Buddhist monks who went on to carry on propaganda in this area urging the people to rise against the Dutch.[69] The Välitara area, which eventually witnessed the growth of the first low-caste fraternity, thus came into some sort of immediate and direct contact with the religious spirit that characterized the mid-eighteenth century Kandyan kingdom.

The success of the new fraternity also required the assistance of wealthy and influential patrons, a task which came to be performed by Salāgama headmen. The tendency to seek patrons among local headmen was a feature common to nearly all the low-country monks, as the patronage of the King of Kandy, though highly valued, was not readily available to them. Some of the headmen themselves were lay pupils of these monks; hence close ties of friendship between monks and laymen were quite common during this time.[70] The patronage given by the headmen was generally repaid by the monks by eulogizing them in their literary works and helping to spread their influence among the local populace. Thus the very same headmen who had to profess Christianity in order to please their European superiors, had good reason to support Buddhist activities in their areas, as a means of gaining popularity among their native subordinates. With regard to supporting Buddhist activities, the lead was given by the Goyigama headmen of the Southern Province, notably by members of the Ilangakkōn, De Saram and Ēkanāyaka families.[71] They were soon

[68] 'Memoir of Van Gollonesse' (1751), tr. in C.O. 54/125, fols. 125, 241–44.

[69] Regarding these two monks, see J. H. O. Paulusz (ed. and tr.), *Secret Minutes of the Dutch Political Council, 1762* (Colombo, 1954), pp. 63–64, 68, 76.

[70] P. E. Pieris, *Ceylon and the Hollanders*, p. 136.

[71] 'Matara still contained great families . . . willing to play the part of generous Maecenas. Some members of these families were themselves no mean scholars; they, as the Hollanders so frequently complained, were educated at home by Buddhist priests'. *Ibid.* Contemporary works, like *Kavmiṇikoňḍola* (1773), written by Pattāyamē Lēkam on the invitation of Don Joan Abhayasirivardhana Ilangakkōn Mudali, and *Kavmutuhara* (1778), written by Sāliäla Maṇiratana on the invitation of Abhayaratna Ēkanāyaka Muhandiram, contain profuse eulogies of the religious activities of these families.

followed in this by the headmen of the Salāgama caste; they too wished to have a group of monks who, by birth, were attached to the Salāgama caste.[72] And since the status of the patrons was bound to be enhanced by the status of their clients, it soon became incumbent on these headmen to ensure the high status of their clients. Helping them to obtain higher ordination was a primary step in ensuring their high status in the religious sphere.

Since the establishment in Kandy was unwilling to deviate from their caste exclusivism at this time, the low-caste monks were compelled to organize *upasampadā* ceremonies on their own with the assistance of their own patrons. The first *upasampadā* ceremony of this sort was held at Toṭagamu Vihāre in 1772, and it was followed in 1798 by another at Tangalla.[73] Both were vehemently disapproved of by the establishment in Kandy,[74] and as time went on, even those who received higher ordination at these ceremonies found themselves not entirely pleased with the manner in which they achieved it. Not inclined to be a permanent 'rebel' group, they went on to seek respectability–if not through the authority of the King of Kandy, then at least through the authority of a king of some other Buddhist country and that of the colonial government, which constituted the effective political power in the territories where they lived.

Thus, in the year 1799, Aṁbagahapiṭiyē Ñāṇavimala, a Salāgama monk who lived in the Ambarukkhārāmaya at Välitara,[75] proceeded to Burma with five *sāmaṇeras* (novices) and three lay devotees with the aim of obtaining higher ordination there. The journey was financed by Aṁ-

[72] The first monk to occupy such a role was Dikvällē Buddharakkhita who, in 1778, wrote *Kāvyadīpanī* at the request of Simon de Zoysa Sirivardhana, a Mudali of the Cinnamon Department. This work panegyrizes at length the patron as well as his paternal and maternal ancestors. See vv. 34–70 of Māpalānē Paññālaṃkāra's edition of this work (Colombo, 1913). Dikvällē was a pupil of Siṭināmaluvē Dhammajoti (*Ibid.*, v. 75).

[73] H. J. M. Vikramaratna Sēnānāyaka, *Amarapura Śrī Saddhammavaṃsa Nikāya piḷibaňda ati saṃkṣipta Itihāsa Katāva* (Ambalaṃgoḍa, 1928), pp. 2–3.

[74] In a letter (undated) to a group of Karāve and Durāve laymen in the low country, Moratoṭa Dhammakkhandha (who was the Mahā Nāyaka of Malvatta between 1787 and 1811) accused the Salāgama monks of having bribed the 'sinful and impious Vagēgoḍa [Dhammakusala]' into presiding over the *upasampadā* ceremony at Toṭagamuva. C.N.A. 5/63/8/(3).

[75] It is believed that he had his early education under Bōvala Dhammānanda and that he was admitted to the order by the Saṃgharāja Välivița Saraṇaṃkara upon Bōvala's recommendation. Buddhadatta, *op. cit.* (1950), p. 21.

bagahapiṭiyē's patron, Haljōti Dines de Zoysa Jayatilaka Sirivardhana, a leading Salāgama headman in the Välitara area.[76] Upon their arrival in Amarapura, the then capital of Burma, the Ceylonese party was received by the reigning monarch Bodawpaya (1782–1819) himself; and with his patronage, they were given higher ordination by a chapter of Burmese monks presided over by Saṃgharāja Ñānābhivaṃsa in 1800. After being instructed by their Burmese preceptors for some months, they returned to Ceylon in 1803, bringing with them a number of Pali texts and a letter from the Saṃgharāja to the *bhikkhus* of Ceylon.[77] Soon after their arrival, they established a *sīmā* at Balapiṭiya; and under the presidentship of Aggasāra, the most senior of the Burmese monks who came with them, granted *upasampadā* to many novices who had been unable to obtain it from the establishment in Kandy. The new fraternity which thus began came to be known as the Amarapura Nikāya, and was distinguished from the Kandyan establishment, which, because of its original connection with Siam, henceforth came to be known as the Siyam Nikāya.[78]

Although the new fraternity was thus started in Ceylon, it needed time as well as the efforts of another monk–who was evidently far more ambitious a person than its founder, Am̆bagahapiṭiyē–for the new fraternity to gain some form of formal recognition from the British authorities in the maritime provinces. This second monk was Kapugama Dhammakkhandha, also of the Salāgama caste and enjoying the patronage of the highest headman of his caste, Adrian de Abrew Vijayagunaratna Rājapakṣa.[79] While residing in the Vālukārāmaya at Daḍalla, Kapugama came to know of the successful return of Am̆bagahapiṭiyē and decided to proceed to Burma himself in order to obtain higher ordination in a similar fashion. With his patron's assistance, he set off from Ceylon in 1807 with

[76] Regarding whom, see Rajapakse, *op. cit.*

[77] This letter, after recapitulating the history of religious contacts between Burma and Ceylon, describes the manner in which the Ceylonese monks were received and granted higher ordination in Burma in 1800. For the text of this letter, see I. P. Minayeff (ed.), 'The Sandesa-Kathā', *J.P.T.S.* (1885) 17–28. These events are also briefly referred to in the *Sāsanavaṃsa* written in Burma by Paññāsāmi in 1861, edited by Mable Bode (London, 1897), p. 135.

[78] The term *samāgama* was used as a synonym for *nikāya* in the nineteenth century; since then it seems to have gone out of vogue.

[79] Regarding this highly influential patron of Kapugama, see Rajapakse, *op. cit.*

six other monks and three lay devotees, and returned, after two years, with his mission successfully completed.[80] In addition to higher ordination, Kapugama also received from the king and the Saṃgharāja of Burma an act of appointment to the office of Gaṇācariya (Chief Monk) with the title 'Saddhammavaṃsapāla Dhammasenāpati Mahādhamma Rājaguru' and a letter addressed to the governor of the maritime provinces of Ceylon asking the latter to confirm the said appointment.

Kapugama eventually managed to obtain a certificate in confirmation of this appointment. This certificate (dated 14 January 1814), however, made no explicit reference to the new fraternity. It merely stated:

> Whereas the Sinhalese Priest Dhammakkanda unnanse having proceeded to Ava, has brought from thence and produced a letter addressed to His Excellency the Governor, together with a commission and signet from which it appears, that he has been nominated by the Emperor of Ava to the office of Ganachariya, and has received certain ornaments and honorary Distinctions.
>
> This is to certify, that the said Dhammakkhanda unnanse has permission to assume and use within the British territories on the Island of Ceylon, the ornaments and honorary Distinctions thus conferred upon him, without interruption, in so far as the same is consistent with existing regulations.[81]

The first formal recognition of the new fraternity as such could be seen only in the Act of Appointment granted to the founder of the Amarapura fraternity, Aṁbagahapiṭiyē, in 1825.[82] A few years earlier, the practice of

80 Their journey to Burma and the events which followed are described in the *Daḍalusāsanavaṃsa*. See also the letter written by Bōpāgoḍa Ñāṇālaṃkāra to Mirissē Dhammānanda (dated 14 October 1863), reproduced in Buddhadatta, *op. cit.* (1950), pp. 50–51. Bōpāgoḍa was one of the six monks who accompanied Kapugama on his journey to Burma in 1807.

81 C.N.A. 5/63/45/(2). Mrs. Elizabeth Harvard who (with her husband, who was a Wesleyan missionary in Ceylon) visited Kapugama's temple, wrote to her parents in England (26 August 1816): 'I afterwards went, with our party, to inspect the Priest's dwelling-house, and his library, which is a very extensive and valuable one, containing many royal and noble presents which he received in the countries where he has travelled'. W. M. Harvard, *Memoirs of Mrs. Elizabeth Harvard*, 3rd ed. (London, 1833), p. 65.

82 C.N.A. 5/63/21/(2). Even this appointment was limited to 'the Office of High Priest in and over the *Buddhist Priests belonging to the Mahabadda* of the Maritime districts of Ceylon' (emphasis added). The first appointment over the entire Amarapura fraternity (of the Maritime Districts) was made, after Aṁbagahapiṭiyē's death, in 1835. See the Act of Appointment granted to Bōpāgoḍa Sumana, dated 25 February 1835, reproduced in Vikramaratna Sēnānāyaka, *op. cit.*, Appendix III.

granting written acts of appointments had been introduced by the British administration;[83] and since Kapugama had left the order by this time,[84] Aṁbagahapiṭiyē became the obvious choice.

But even before this formal appointment, Aṁbagahapiṭiyē (as the senior Sinhalese pupil of the Burmese Saṃgharāja) seems to have been informally recognized as their leader by the members of the new fraternity, and, accordingly, consulted in the conduct of their religious affairs. Thus Attuḍāvē Dhammarakkhita, the first Durāve monk to obtain *upasampadā* in Burma,[85] felt obliged to inform Aṁbagahapiṭiyē of the higher ordination ceremony which he performed in Devundara some time after his return to the island. In his reply[86] Aṁbagahapiṭiyē expressed his satisfaction at the manner in which the ceremony had been performed, and asked Attuḍāvē to supervise the religious activities of the monks in his own area. He was also instructed, in the same letter, to work in cooperation with Kataluvē Guṇaratana, the first Karāve monk to obtain *upasampadā* in Burma.[87]

V. THE SOCIOLOGICAL SIGNIFICANCE OF THE AMARAPURA FRATERNITY

In the discussion of the traditional religious system in chapter I, section i, reference was made to some of the features that developed within the

[83] See below, ch. III, sec. i.

[84] In his efforts to get the (above mentioned) 'Certificate' from the government, Kapugama came into contact with George Bisset, an Anglican clergyman who was Governor Brownrigg's brother-in-law. Bisset and the Wesleyan missionary Harvard persuaded Kapugama to give up his robes and embrace Christianity, which he did in June 1816. At his baptism, Bisset and Harvard acted as his sponsors, and he was named George (Nadoris de Silva) after the former. Immediately after his baptism, he was appointed a Mohoṭṭi Mudali in the Cinnamon Department by the governor; and in this secular office he soon began to show–in even more accentuated form–the same sort of ambition and drive as he had shown as a monk. A short account of his life is given in Henry Long's letter (dated 9 March 1911) in the *Ceylon Independent* of 30 March 1911. This account is based on a biography of this important convert written by Harvard, a copy of which had been in the correspondent's possession. For some further information regarding George Nadoris de Silva, see n. 95, below.

[85] He proceeded to Burma in 1807, and having obtained *upasampadā* in the following year, remained in Burma for five years as a pupil of the Burmese Saṃgharāja prior to his return to Ceylon. For an account of his life, see Pälänē Vajirañāṇa, *Śri Dharmarakṣita Caritaya* (Colombo, 1930).

[86] Dated Äsaḷa 2361 Buddhist era (July 1817), C.N.A. 5/63/106/(3).

[87] Kataluvē Guṇaratana left for Burma in September 1807, obtained higher ordination in March 1809, and returned to Ceylon in June 1810. See Polvattē Buddhadatta, *Kalyāṇi Śāsanavaṃśaya* (Colombo, 1935).

Buddhist order in Ceylon–such as village-dwelling (*gāmavāsī*) fraternities and monastic landlordism–which, at their best, helped to raise the order to the level of a pre-eminent social institution, but which, at the same time, carried within them seeds of corruption that contrived to disorganize the order and bring it into disrepute in the absence of proper control and supervision. Reference was also made to the reformist activities undertaken by the kings from time to time, which attempted to 'purify' the order of heresy and corruption and preserve its orthodoxy in relation to both its beliefs and practices.[88] As the activities of the Silvat Samāgama of the Kandyan period amply illustrated, the *origins* of such reform activities were not necessarily linked to acts of royal piety. The long-established written tradition–which contained not merely the texts of the disciplinary regulations and the commentaries thereon, but also records of the numerous vicissitudes that the order had gone through–helped to preserve the ideals of monkhood even during periods of acute political and religious crises and paved the way for periodic revivalist movements. Yet, as the later history of the Silvat Samāgama itself clearly demonstrated, a thoroughgoing reform or reorganization of the order in the traditional framework necessarily required royal patronage to render the reform effective and complete.

In this context, the successful emergence of the Amarapura fraternity at the beginning of the nineteenth century stands unique in the history of monasticism in Ceylon. The new fraternity, on the one hand, did not depend on the patronage of the King of Kandy to make its reformist activity a success; on the other hand, in adopting as its raison d'être the protest against a royal decree (relating to caste exclusivism) it successfully questioned for the first time the right of secular authorities to regulate the affairs of the order.[89]

It is necessary to note, however, that in opposing secular interference the new fraternity was not playing the role of a privileged religious establishment which competed with secular authorities to gain control over the scarce means for power–as were, for instance, the Gregorian

[88] See pp. 26–27.

[89] 'They do not acknowledge the authority of the royal edicts to introduce novelties into their religion, neither do they acknowledge the Buddhist hierarchy'. A. de Silva, 'On the Corruptions of Buddhism and the Different Tenets, Opinions and Principles of the Amarapoora and Siamese Sects', Appendix XII to Ribeyro's *History of Ceylon* (1685), retranslated from the French edition (with an Appendix containing chapters illustrative of the Past & Present Conditions of the Island) by George Lee (Colombo, 1847), pp. 276–77.

reformers of early twelfth-century Europe who too opposed secular interference and visualized a utopia in which the papacy dominated secular rulers.[90] It was, more simply, a fraternity of the traditionally disinherited who challenged the right of the establishment, both religious and political, to keep them permanently excluded. In this regard it showed a common feature observed in many other religious movements, the best documented being the Christian sectarian movements. Wilson writes:

> The specific factors of stimulus of sect emergence are usually found in the stresses and tensions differently experienced within the total society. Change in the economic position of a particular group (which may be a change only in relative position); disturbance of normal social relations . . . ; the failure of the social system to accommodate particular age, sex and status groups–all these are possible stimuli in the emergence of sects.[91]

The changes that occurred in the status structure of the low-country Sinhalese prior to and at the time of the emergence of the Amarapura fraternity have already been referred to.[92] The declining consensus regarding the status–in this case, caste–hierarchy can be seen in the explicit claim made by the Salāgama headman Adrian de Abrew Rājapakṣa that 'it is certain that . . . the *Challias* descended from a very high [*brahmin*] cast and that they have always been held in great estimation',[93] during a time when Goyigama headmen were inclined to rank them ninth in the caste hierarchy.[94] It is also not without significance that, personal ambitions apart, a founder member of the Amarapura fraternity (who was a one-time protégé of Rājapakṣa) was later involved in efforts to free the Kandyan

[90] Norman F. Cantor, *Church, Kingship and Lay Investiture in England, 1089–1135* (Princeton, 1958), p. 7.

[91] Bryan R. Wilson, 'An Analysis of Sect Development', *American Sociological Review*, XXIV (1959) 8.

[92] Section iv (above) of this chapter.

[93] 'Abridgement of the history of the CHALIAS, by Adrian Ragia Pakse, a Chief of that Cast', appended to J. Joinville, 'On the Religion and Manners of the People of Ceylon', *Asiatick Researches*, VII (1801) 444–45.

[94] 'Translation of Report by the Fourth Maha Modliar on the subject of Casts etc.' (dated Colombo, 8 June 1818), enclosure no. 8 to Despatch no. 290 of 17 July 1818, Brownrigg to Bathurst, C.O. 54/71.

Salāgamas from the domination of Goyigama headmen,[95] a phenomenon which apparently had its parallels among the coastal Karāvas as well.[96]

The new fraternity also shared with sectarian movements the manner in which its ideals were formulated. 'The object of the Amarapoora priests' wrote a contemporary observer, 'is to bring back the doctrines of Buddhism to their pristine purity, by disentangling them from caste, polytheism, and other corruptions to which they have been subject for ages'.[97] Troeltsch wrote of Christian sects: 'They . . . always appeal to the Gospel and to Primitive Christianity, and accuse the Church of having fallen away from its ideal'.[98]

This Buddhist revivalism differed significantly from Christian sectarian movements, however, in that, in accordance with the 'logic'[99] and the historical antecedents of Buddhism, its primary concern was with the reform of the order rather than with an establishment of a 'priesthood of all believers'. Still, it is worth noting that the very existence of the revivalist fraternity facilitated expressions of lay religiosity (through the traditional Buddhist channels) in increasingly large segments of the population. The wealthy and influential laymen of the Salāgama, Karāve and Durāve castes who helped the founders of the Amarapura fraternity to obtain higher

[95] This person was George Nadoris de Silva mentioned above (n. 84). He was sent to the Kandyan provinces by Governor Brownrigg during the troubles of 1817–18; and over there he managed to gain a reputation for his loyalty to the British government. In 1819 he was publicly honoured for his loyal services (CGG, 4 June 1819). But his attempts, prior to this, to get himself appointed Maha Mudali over the Kandyan Salāgamas was summarily dismissed by the governor with the comment: 'He is an ambitious creature; what he desires with regard to Mahabadde never could be agreed to' (Brownrigg to Bisset, 6 September 1818). Regarding George Nadoris de Silva's activities in the Kandyan provinces, see P. E. Pieris, *Sinhalē and the Patriots*, esp. pp. 290, 314, 544.

[96] Ilangakkōn Mudali of Mātara, on learning that the Mahavidāne Mudali of the Karāvas in Mātara was likely to be appointed their only and principal Chief and Interpreter, wrote to the Maha Mudali of Colombo on 19 August 1801 urging him 'to implore His Excellency the Governor not to change the old standing privileges of the Wellales and the subjection of the Fishers to the Chiefs of the Corles and Pattoes and to myself'. A copy of this letter in the possession of Sir Paul E. Pieris has been partially reproduced in *ibid.*, p. 314.

[97] A. de Silva, *op. cit.*, p. 276.

[98] *The Social Teachings of the Christian Churches*, tr. O. Wyon (London, 1931), vol. I, p. 334.

[99] For a discussion of the forms of institutional arrangements implied by the 'logic' of different world religions, see David A. Martin, *Pacifism: An Historical and Sociological Study* (London, 1965), Part I.

ordination in Burma soon started building more and more temples to accommodate the monks of the growing fraternity.[100] The connections that the Amarapura monks had with these castes in terms of their social origins helped to bring forth closer cooperation between the monks and their lay devotees; and, in the course of time, this sort of cooperation gradually spread into certain other castes as well. In the latter part of the nineteenth century it was observed, for instance:

> The jaggery people (*Vahumpura*) near Galle have built a temple, and their pupil-priests in yellow robes and with begging bowls in their hands are now seen obtaining the food of mendicants from the hands of their own friends. The profound meditative air of the young mendicants, and the evident pride with which their friends give alms and honour the new priesthood are very striking.[101]

Although the high concentration of certain castes in certain localities would have helped the development of such links between monks and their lay patrons, it would be wrong to assume that the Amarapura monks received the patronage only of those castes which they were related to by birth. Being a new and 'rebellious' fraternity, they had no royal endowments with which to support themselves; they depended heavily on the laity for their subsistence. It seems very likely that the relatively radical nature of their religious practices impressed many a laymen irrespective of caste distinctions. An anthropologist writes of present-day Ceylon: 'I know many villagers of *Goigama* caste who prefer to give alms to monks of the Amarapura or Ramanya Nikaya rather than to those of the Siyan Nikaya because they believe that the former are less worldly'.[102] There is no reason to assume that circumstances were very different then, for mass admiration of ascetic practices has always been a well-established feature of Buddhism in Ceylon.[103]

[100] D. P. Vīraratna, *Upavihāravaṃsaya hevat Lakdiva Paurāṇika Siddhasthāna* (Colombo, 1930).

[101] L. Nell, 'A Huniyam Image', *JRAS(CB)*, VII (1881) 116.

[102] Gananath Obeyesekere, 'Theodicy, Sin and Salvation in a Sociology of Buddhism', in E. R. Leach (ed.), *Dialectic in Practical Religion* (Cambridge, 1968), p. 35.

[103] The appearance of ascetic fraternities, for this reason, has invariably been a source of some embarrassment for the 'established' fraternities. See, for instance, the previous discussion of the Silvat Samāgama of the Kandyan period (pp. 59–60 above). A mid-twentieth century ascetic fraternity has been discussed by Nur Yalman in 'The Ascetic Buddhist Monks of Ceylon', *Ethnology*, I (1962) 305–28.

Asceticism, except in its Puritan 'this-worldly' version, has universally been the concern of a few, the many being capable only of admiring the charismatic qualities obtained through asceticism. Reischauer has admirably summarised the position of the Buddhist layman in this regard:

> While the layman may not be ready to forsake the world himself he admires the man who has done so, and he feels that some day, either in his old age or in some future rebirth he, too, will take this important step. In the meantime, it behoves him to do the next best thing and loyally support those who have taken the Buddha's teaching seriously.[104]

Paradoxically, the ultimate result of this emphasis on asceticism on the part of the new fraternity was not increasing other-worldliness, but rather increasing involvement in their social surroundings.[105] Closer dependence on the laity meant that the monks had to perform their 'parish' obligations: preaching, officiating at death ceremonies and the like. Greater emphasis on the study of the doctrine and the *vinaya* regulations entailed deeper involvement in the social life of the community of monks, with the resultant controversies with monks within as well as outside the fraternity.[106] The new revivalist spirit also made the Amarapura monks sharply aware of the external threats to Buddhism, a circumstance which led many of them in the latter half of the nineteenth century to get themselves deeply involved in polemics with Christian missionaries. Bishop Copleston, who during his stay in Ceylon frequently witnessed such polemics, wrote: 'This sect, the Amarapura, is at present the most prominent in controversy, street preaching, and all that is aggressive. It is among them that the Theosophists have found their chief allies'.[107]

[104] A. K. Reischauer, 'Buddhism', in E. J. Jurji (ed.), *The Great Religions of the Modern World* (Princeton, 1946), p. 118. Knox (*An Historical Relation of Ceylon*, p. 102) wrote specifically of the Sinhalese: 'They do much extol and commend Chastity, Temperance, and Truth in words and actions; and confess that it is out of weakness and infirmity, that they cannot practice the same, acknowledging that the contrary Vices are to be abhorred. . . . They do love and delight in those Men that are most Devout and Precise in their Matters'.

[105] Certain paradoxical features of Buddhist asceticism have been discussed in more general terms in Obeyesekere, *op. cit.* (1968), esp. pp. 34–37.

[106] See chapter IV, below.

[107] R. S. Copleston, *Buddhism: Primitive and Present in Magadha and in Ceylon* (London, 1892), pp. 433–34.

Chapter III

AUTHORITY AND DISSENT IN THE SIYAM FRATERNITY, 1815–1865

i. THE DISESTABLISHMENT OF BUDDHISM

What occurred in Kandy in 1815 – to use a distinction made by Gluckman in a different context – was a *rebellion* to replace a particular king, not a *revolution* to destroy kingship itself as an institution and replace it with some new form of political organization.[1] Weber, though not using the same terminology, made substantially the same distinction while discussing 'traditional authority' when he wrote: 'When resistance [to traditional authority] occurs, it is directed against the person of the chief. . . . The accusation is that he has failed to observe the traditional limits of his authority. Opposition is not directed against the system as such'.[2]

The Sinhalese chiefs who rebelled against Śrī Vikrama Rājasiṃha justified their actions in terms of the alleged personal cruelty and oppression of the king, a justification which received the wholehearted support and encouragement of their British allies. The Proclamation issued by the Governor-in-Council on 10 January 1815, at the beginning of the invasion of Kandy, declared hostilities 'not against the Kandyan nation . . . [but] against that tyrannical power alone'.[3] The agreement of the two parties was very soon given concrete expression in the 'Convention' of 2 March 1815, which announced: 'That the Rajah Sri Wikreme Rajah Sinha, by the habitual violation of the Chief and most sacred Duties of a Sovereign, has forfeited all claims to that title or the Powers annexed to the same, and is

[1] Max Gluckman, *Order and Rebellion in Tribal Africa* (London, 1963), p. 8.

[2] Max Weber, *The Theory of Social and Economic Organization*, tr. A. M. Henderson and Talcott Parsons (New York, 1947), p. 342.

[3] CGG, 13 January 1815.

declared fallen and deposed from the Office of King'.[4] In his place—and for the due performance of the chief and most sacred duties of a sovereign—'The Dominion of the Kandyan Provinces [was] vested in the Sovereign of the British Empire . . . to be exercised through the Governors or Lieut. Governors of Ceylon for the time being and their accredited agents'.[5] This dynastic change however was not expected to bring forth any other changes, for the same clause continued:

> . . . saving to the Adikars, Dessaves, Mohottales, Corals, Vidaans and all other Chief and subordinate Native Headmen lawfully appointed by authority of the British Government, the Rights, Privileges and Powers of their respective Offices, and to all classes of the People the safety of their persons and property, with the Civil Rights and immunities, according to the Laws, Institutions and Customs established and in force amongst them.[6]

If the Kandyan chiefs were anxious to preserve their traditional powers and privileges on a firm footing, they were no less anxious to guarantee the safety of their religion. Indeed, all available evidence clearly points to their particular concern over the future of their religion, a concern not unexpected considering their awareness of what their religion had had to endure in the hands of three European powers. Whenever in the preceding two centuries European armies had penetrated into the Kandyan kingdom, religious shrines and monasteries had invariably been the first to be looted and destroyed. The resultant bitterness on the part of the Kandyans is briefly, but plainly, expressed in their official chronicle, the *Cūlavaṃsa*. 'Heretical evil-doers, cruel and brutal. . . . They broke into the towns, into the relic shrines and monasteries, destroyed the image houses, Bodhi trees, Buddha statues and so on, did great harm to the laity

[4] Clause 2 of the 'Convention'. A contemporary copy of this document is to be found as an enclosure to Despatch of 5 November 1816, Brownrigg to Bathurst, C.O. 54/61. This document came to be spoken of as An Act of Convention because it was agreed to at a 'convention' in Kandy. It constituted, however, nothing more or less than a 'treaty', the effect of which was to bring about a conditional surrender of the Kingdom of Kandy. See Colvin R. de Silva, *Ceylon under the British Occupation, 1795–1833*, 3rd impression (Colombo, 1953), esp. p. 164; and P. E. Pieris, 'Appointments within the Kandyan Provinces', *JRAS(CB)*, XXXVI (1945) 112.

[5] Clause 4.

[6] *Ibid.*

and the Order', this chronicle wrote of the Portuguese.[7] Referring to the Dutch expedition to Kandy in 1765, the same work wrote: 'Like cruel armies of yakkhas [demons], they forced their way into the town and destroyed the sacred books and everything else'.[8]

The activities of the British since their arrival in the island hardly helped to foster a more favourable attitude. What happened in Kandy when the British forces occupied the capital in 1803 may be gleaned from the following brief reference left by a monk who at great risk smuggled away to safety a copy of the *Mahāvagga Vinaya* which had been offered to the Brotherhood at Malvatta five months before the invasion.

> On the day in the month of Navam of the year two thousand three hundred and forty five of the Buddhist Era on which the English people entered the Capital, when thieves removed the goods and cloths of the Pōyagē and stole the bags and wraps in which the books were encased, I, Ram̆bukkana Sobhita Unnānsē, took the same and brought it safely across the Hantāne forest.[9]

Outside the capital, the troops in the same year destroyed the Aluvihāre in Mātalē,[10] the site where Buddhist literature was first committed to writing in the first century B.C.; and plundered the Saman Dēvālaya in Sabaragamuva, an ancient shrine which had once been destroyed by the Portuguese in the sixteenth century, and was rebuilt and re-endowed by Rājasiṃha II in the seventeenth century.[11] All was not well even in the year 1815, despite the undertaking given by the governor that 'in their march through the country, the most rigorous discipline will be observed by the British troops; . . . Their [i.e., the inhabitants'] religion shall be sacred and

[7] *Cūlavaṃsa*, Part II, tr. by Wilhelm Geiger, and from German into English by C. Mabel Rickmers (Colombo, 1953), 95: 5–8.

[8] *Ibid.*, 99: 125.

[9] This volume is now in the Colombo Museum Library. The relevant passage appears with a faulty English translation in W. A. de Silva's *Catalogue of Palm Leaf Manuscripts in the Colombo Museum*, vol. I (Colombo, 1938). I have reproduced here (in a slightly amended form) P. E. Pieris' translation in *Tri Sinhala: The Last Phase, 1796–1815*, 2nd ed. (Colombo, 1939), p. 49.

[10] A. C. Lawrie, *A Gazetteer of the Central Province of Ceylon*, vol. I (Colombo, 1896), p. 32.

[11] For an account of the Dēvālaya, see H. C. P. Bell, 'Maha Saman Dēvālē and its Sannasa', *CALR*, II (1916–17) 36–46. James Cordiner in his *Description of Ceylon*, vol. II (London, 1807), pp. 246–52, has recorded the circumstances in which the shrine came to be plundered by the British soldiers while the Malays and coolies refused to touch the money although there was much more than the British could take away.

their temples respected'.[12] In the relatively isolated southeastern regions of the kingdom, where the watchful eyes of high-ranking officials and Sinhalese chiefs were lacking, the troops got out of hand and overran the whole area, treating it like some enemy territory. Among the shrines plundered were two *vihārēs*, one at Bōgoḍa and the other at Älla, and the Kataragama Dēvālaya at Badulla, a much venerated shrine which, like the Saman Dēvālaya mentioned above, had been restored and re-endowed by Rājasiṃha II, soon after Constantino de Sa, the Portuguese general who burnt the original building down, met with his destruction at Vällavāya in 1630.[13]

Considering these circumstances, it is hardly surprising that the chiefs were particularly anxious to obtain a guarantee regarding the future of their religion—a guarantee which they received in the most emphatic terms. The fifth clause of the Convention declared: 'The Religion of Boodhoo professed by the Chiefs and Inhabitants of these Provinces is declared inviolable, and its Rites, Ministers and Places of Worship are to be maintained and protected.' The unequivocal nature of this clause caused Governor Brownrigg himself some qualms, and he felt obliged to give his reasons to the Colonial Office. 'In truth', he wrote to Bathurst, 'our secure possession of the country hinged upon this point. . . . I found it necessary to quiet all uneasiness respecting it, by an article of guarantee couched in the most unqualified terms'.[14]

Yet even with this very definite undertaking, it was not without some difficulty that the governor was able to win the confidence of the actual religious functionaries, the *bhikkhus* (monks) and *kapurālas* (priests),[15] who did not share the desire of the chiefs to depose Śrī Vikrama Rājasiṃha and who in the past had been the direct victims of the sacrilegious acts of European troops. They were apprehensive about the safety of the sacred objects under their care and were sceptical of the ability and willingness of

[12] The Proclamation of 10 January 1815, CGG, 13 January 1815.

[13] P. E. Pieris, *Sinhalē and the Patriots, 1815–1818* (Colombo, 1950), pp. 61 and 614–15.

[14] Brownrigg to Bathurst, 15 March 1815, C.O. 54/55.

[15] *Kapurālas* were 'priests' in the sense of being intermediaries between the deities of the *dēvalēs* in which they functioned and the devotees who sought divine assistance. In practically every other respect, however, they remained mere laymen. They conformed to certain rules of purity during religious ceremonies, but they did not belong to an organized religious order and they were never accorded the sanctity generally accorded to *bhikkhus*.

the British government to continue the age-old traditions unchanged. The monks in their conversations with the chiefs frequently expressed fear about the safety of the Tooth Relic,[16] and some even freely expressed the view that a Sinhalese king was necessary for the security of religion.[17]

Both Brownrigg and D'Oyly–who soon after the Convention was appointed 'Accredited Agent of the British Government in the Kandyan Provinces' with the appellation of 'Resident' for convenience–knew of these anxieties and made every effort to dispel them. The governor himself met the monks of Malvatta and Asgiriya twice with flattering ceremony: once on the tenth of March, the day on which the Convention was actually signed; and again, on the nineteenth, on the eve of his departure from Kandy. On both occasions he assured the monks that the protection and security promised to their religion would never be wanting.[18] After the governor's departure, D'Oyly met the *kapurālas* of the four *dēvālēs* in Kandy and gave them similar assurances regarding the worship of gods.[19]

The British government thus undertook, as the successor to the Kandyan throne, to perform the traditional functions of Kandyan kings, of which maintaining the established religion was just one, though undoubtedly a very important one. Expecting persons of non-Buddhist origins to support and protect Buddhism, despite the initial suspicions that the monks had regarding the British, was not without precedent among the Kandyans; for, quite apart from the numerous instances in the early history of the Sinhalese,[20] the last four kings of Kandy were of Hindu origin. Indeed, as the religious activities of these (Nāyakkar) kings amply illustrated, supporting the established religion provided a potent source of legitimacy and popularity for alien rulers.[21] This was apparently known to the British, who, at least at the stage of their early promises, used it to their own advantage. Śrī Vikrama Rājasiṃha was accused of having caused 'Injuries . . . to the world and to Religion', injuries which would soon be rectified, assured the governor, under the newly established British

[16] *The Diary of John D'Oyly*, ed. H. W. Codrington (Colombo, 1917), 27 March, and 3 April 1815.

[17] *Ibid.*

[18] *Ibid.*, 10 March and 19 March 1815.

[19] *Ibid.*, 8 April 1815.

[20] See Walpola Rahula, *History of Buddhism in Ceylon* (Colombo, 1956), pp. 62 ff.

[21] See above, pp. 61 and 65–66.

authority.[22] 'We are not come to this Country' said D'Oyly, addressing the *kapurālas* in Kandy, 'to destroy the Religion of Buddha and the Gods, which have prevailed from ancient Time in this Country, but to protect and promote it'.[23]

For some time, though with decreasing enthusiasm, some effort was made to conform to these undertakings which amounted to nothing less than maintaining the established position of Buddhism in the Kandyan provinces. At the minimum, this required making appointments to *vihārēs* and *dēvālēs* on the authority of the government; but its effective operation needed, in fact, governmental backing in many other respects, including the personal participation of high-ranking officials in religious ceremonies. Such participation presupposed some amount of sympathy on the part of those who held authority with the customs and institutions of the people whom they governed; something, it is hardly necessary to say, which was characteristically lacking among colonial administrators of this time. In the absence of such sympathy, what led them to perform such 'unpleasant' duties were considerations of political and administrative expediency,[24] considerations which remained important in the Kandyan provinces for a long time, but which became less and less compelling as the British gradually strengthened their position within the internal power structure of Kandy.

As far as the internal power structure of Kandy was concerned, although the transfer of power in 1815 was only a rebellion at the time it actually occurred, its ultimate consequences were revolutionary. The British, soon after their accession to the Kandyan throne, were faced with

[22] Brownrigg's address to the chiefs and people of the Raṭapaha (five Districts) on 19 March 1815, D'Oyly's *Diary*.

[23] *Ibid.*, 8 April 1815.

[24] It was evidently such considerations that originally compelled Brownrigg to give a firm guarantee to Buddhism as embodied in the fifth clause of the Convention and to get this clause confirmed in its original form by the Colonial Office. Having given his solemn undertakings to the Kandyans that the protection promised to their religion would never be wanting, he wrote to his own superiors at the Colonial Office: 'I am so far from considering the Kandyan People as permanently debarred from the light of Christianity, that I think it requires no great share of foresight to predict that the gloom of ignorance and superstition which has enveloped that unfortunate Region will at no distant period be materially dissipated by the gradual and insensible diffusion of religious knowledge'. Brownrigg to Bathurst, 1 June 1816, C.O. 54/60.

the perennial problem of all Kandyan sovereigns, the problem of controlling the powerful aristocracy, and in order to maintain themselves firmly in power, they were compelled to adopt a policy of undermining the powers of the aristocracy, often in manifest violation of the undertakings given to them in 1815.[25] In fact the Kandyan chiefs in deciding to transfer their allegiance to the British sovereign made a drastic miscalculation insofar as they were attempting thereby to perpetuate their traditional powers and privileges; for, in the place of Śrī Vikrama Rājasiṃha who had threatened their powers merely with the limited resources of a Kandyan king, they now chose an imperial power with virtually unlimited resources in both men and money. In the absence of sufficient material strength of their own to defend their claims, the treaty that they entered into with the British eventually proved to be hardly anything more than a mere scrap of paper. Thus the cyclical processes so characteristic of Kandyan politics in the pre-1815 period came to be replaced by a more or less linear process in the post-1815 period, as manifested in the gradual concentration of power in the hands of the expanding British bureaucracy at the expense of the powers of the declining traditional aristocracy.

The support that certain chiefs gave to some of the (anti-British) millennial movements[26] was in some ways a reaction to this process. In the end, however, the failure of these movements simply provided the administration with convenient opportunities to use this support–proved or merely alleged–to remove from office some of the more inflential chiefs[27]

[25] The *bona fides* of this undertaking (clause 4 of the Convention) seems no less dubious than that of the undertaking regarding religious institutions. For instance, while replying to the criticisms of the Convention by Hardinge Giffard (the Advocate Fiscal)–mainly on the grounds that it preserved the judicial functions of the chiefs and excluded the Kandyan provinces from the jurisdiction of the Supreme Court–Brownrigg stressed the necessity of introducing changes with great caution and after careful study with measures that would 'gradually and insensibly supersede the deeprooted prejudices of these people without their perceiving them to be attacked'. Brownrigg to Bathurst, 15 March 1815, C.O. 54/55. The governor, in other words, was playing for time to undermine the institutions whose safety he had solemnly guaranteed.

[26] Regarding which see above, pp. 7–8.

[27] Of the eleven chiefs who signed the Convention, only two (the elder Molligoḍa, *ob.* 1823, and Ratvatte, *ob.* 1827) managed to have uninterrupted careers. Of the others, two were sentenced to capital punishment by court martial in 1818, which sentence was executed in the case of one (Käppiṭipola) and commuted to banishment in the case of the other (Piḷimatalavve Jr.). (The latter was allowed to return in early 1833, and died two years later). Three were arrested and confined in Colombo, of whom one (Kapuvatte, *ob.* 1824), though restored to freedom in 1820, was denied the positions of Second Adikaram and Disāva of Sabaragamuva, which he held earlier;

and to introduce new and revolutionary measures, aimed, among other things, at reducing the powers of the traditional system of offices. An effective beginning in this direction was made by the lengthy Proclamation of 21 November 1818[28] which was issued soon after the protracted troubles of 1817–18. With this, the chiefs lost nearly all their judicial powers and a good deal of their traditional privileges, emoluments and administrative powers. The details of these changes–summed up by the governor as aimed at reducing the chiefs 'from an aristocratic faction . . . to the rank and office of stipendiary organs for effecting the regulations and orders of the supreme executive authority'[29]–and the other changes which steadily followed them over the years need not detain us here. What is relevant here is that the nature of the 1815 rebellion was radically transformed within a period of only three years. The chiefs were no longer an autonomous body who (as leaders of their people) deposed their king and by treaty substituted another king in his place. Innovations, though rare, were not unknown in the old Kandyan kingdom. But 'before innovations of importance [were] carried into Effect it [was] customary [for the King] to consult the principal chiefs, and frequently the Principal Priests'.[30] This was no longer the standard practice in the Kandyan provinces. Decision making, removed from the hands of the traditional leaders of the area, became henceforth the business of the colonial administrator and his superiors at the Colonial Office.

Results of this process gradually became evident in the sphere of

---

the second (Millāve) died in confinement in 1821; and the last, Ähälēpola, the architect of the British success in the Kandyan kingdom in 1815, was kept in confinement for seven years without a trial and then deported to Mauritius (where he died in 1829). The younger Molligoḍa and Dūllāve, who survived the troubles of 1817–18 and who were subsequently rewarded for their loyalty, had chequered careers. The former, at the height of his power, was arrested in 1834, dismissed from the offices he held, and tried for treason on flimsy evidence. Aquitted at the trial, he lived just long enough (*ob.* 1845) to be reappointed Disāva of Hatara Kōralē ten years later in a belated, halfhearted and futile attempt on the part of the government to win the confidence of the chiefs. Dūllāve too, though not put on trial, had come under suspicion in 1834. Divested afterwards of his offices in the provincial administration, he survived his colleagues of 1815 to witness the 'rebellion' of 1848. In that year, he was imprisoned for a while and removed from the position of Diyavaḍana Nilame. He died in the following year.

28 CGG, 28 November 1818.

29 Brownrigg to the Board, 25 September 1818, enclosure to Brownrigg to Bathurst, 8 January 1819, C.O. 54/73.

30 John D'Oyly, *A Sketch of the Constitution of the Kandyan Kingdom* (1835), ed. L. J. B. Turner (Colombo, 1929), p. 1.

religion too. But in the religious sphere, in contrast to the political, the administration acted with greater caution and the Kandyans themselves pressed their claims with greater earnestness. In contrast to all the other clauses of the Kandyan Convention, therefore, the fifth clause became the focus of much debate both public and private right through the nineteenth century.

The earliest criticisms of the fifth clause were mainly concentrated on the use of the word 'inviolable' to describe the position of Buddhism, a position which the Christian missionaries feared would hinder their intended efforts to convert the Kandyan population. The missionaries made representations to the Colonial Office, notably through William Wilberforce, the Evangelical, and the governor was compelled to defend the clause on the ground that the word 'inviolable' was rendered into Sinhalese by a phrase signifying 'not to be broken down'.[31] Although the governor had earlier admitted that the guarantee to Buddhism was couched in language 'more emphatical than would have been my choice',[32] he was not moved by these criticisms to change its wording immediately. He did seize the opportunity provided by the troubles of 1817–18 to pacify these critics by extending protection to the peaceable exercise of *all* religions: still the special position of Buddhism remained unchanged.[33] Traditional religious institutions were expressly excluded from the operation of the major innovations which were introduced by the Proclamation of 21 November 1818. Thus temple lands (*vihāragam* and *dēvālagam*) remained exempt from taxation,[34] and the tenants of those lands were required to perform their customary services (*rājakāriya*) to the temples.[35] The government, by continuing to make appointments to religious offices, legitimized the authority of the incumbents of those offices to exact the obedience and services of their subordinates.[36]

Lieutenant-Colonel Colebrooke in his *Report on the Administration of the Government of Ceylon* (dated 24 December 1831) expressed his disapproval of the governmental backing given to Buddhism, but suggested no radical

[31] Brownrigg to Wilberforce, 13 June 1816, C.O. 54/60.

[32] Brownrigg to Bathurst, 15 March 1815, C.O. 54/55.

[33] Clause 16 of the Proclamation of 21 November 1818, CGG, 28 November 1818.

[34] *Ibid.*, clause 21.

[35] *Ibid.*, clause 30.

[36] *Ibid.*, clauses 7 and 10.

or immediate changes.[37] The home government in transmitting the report to the Ceylon authorities advised the latter to avoid any direct sanction of 'Pagan worship'; but, realizing the delicate nature of the issues involved, left the initiative with regard to any changes entirely in the hands of the Ceylon authorities.[38] The Order-in-Council abolishing *rājakāriya* which followed Colebrooke's general recommendations specifically excluded temple lands from its operation, as those services were essential for the functioning of religious institutions.[39]

In the course of time, however, the adherence to the undertakings of 1815 became less and less enthusiastic and more and more impersonal. During the early years, the tactful resident, John D'Oyly, who in contrast to his compatriots in Ceylon took the trouble to acquire a command of the language and a knowledge of the institutions of the people he had to govern, made efforts to perform the duties in the spirit in which they were undertaken. But after his death in 1824, these duties–transferred to the Judicial Commissioner in that year, and later (in 1833) to the Government Agent of the Central Province–were never performed with the same amount of interest or understanding. These changes were accompanied by a definite change of policy on the part of the Colonial Office, which, as a result of a campaign begun by the Christian missionaries in the late 1830s, gave specific instructions to the Ceylon government to withdraw all support given to Buddhism.[40] But even prior to this change of *policy*, the performance of the British administration in Ceylon lagged far behind the expectations of the Kandyans, expectations which they entertained in terms of the undertakings given to them in 1815. The declining enthusiasm on the part of the British administration which finally culminated in

[37] See *The Colebrooke-Cameron Papers*, ed. G. C. Mendis, vol. I (Oxford, 1956), p. 37.

[38] Goderich to Horton, no. 79 of 14 September 1832, C.O. 54/74. Printed *ibid.*, p. 244.

[39] Order-in-Council, at the Court of St. James, 12 April 1832, CGG, 29 September 1832. Reprinted *ibid.*, p. 240.

[40] The campaign began in Ceylon in the monthly periodical *The Friend*, which appeared from July 1837 to December 1845, edited by Robert Spence Hardy of the Wesleyan Mission, and published by the Colombo Auxiliary Religious Tract Society. It attracted wider attention and support soon after Hardy put forward his ideas in a pamphlet called *The British Government and the Idolatry of Ceylon* in 1839. The politics of this campaign from 1839 up to 1844 when the ideas of the missionaries gained full acceptance at the Colonial Office has been thoroughly dealt with by K. M. de Silva in *Social Policy and Missionary Organizations in Ceylon, 1840–1855* (London, 1965), esp. ch. II.

their attempt to withdraw from all connections with Buddhism, and some of the results of this withdrawal, may be illustrated with the following instances.

a. The Kandyan kings used to send provisions daily from the Royal Store (Maha Gabaḍāva) to the two colleges of monks, Malvatta and Asgiriya. This custom, the governor assured the monks on 19 March 1815, would continue unchanged.[41] This assurance was honoured during the early years;[42] and D'Oyly even offered *dāna* (alms) to the monks in much the same fashion as had been done by the Kandyan kings. He wrote in his diary on 13 April 1815:

Priests in particular attend to identify the Property of the Temple viz: Weyliwita–Tibbotuwave–Kotikapola of Malvatte Wihara–Owitipana and Kotagama, of Asgiriya. . . . As the Priests were called early to the Palace, I caused a Danaya to be prepared and given to them at the Pattrippuwa in the best Kandyan Manner, with 4 Kinds of Rice, 31 of Curry, and 12 of Cakes &c.–and sent some of it to Kobbeykaduwe Nayake Unnanse, who is unable, from sickness to attend.

Though by these measures D'Oyly succeeded in gaining the confidence of the Kandyans,[43] he became unpopular, for the same reason, among his compatriots in Ceylon. Hardinge Giffard, the Advocate Fiscal, wrote home on 28 November 1817: 'He is said to be deeply versed in the Sinhalese language and customs, and to be nearly if not actually a convert to the superstition of Buddhism'.[44]

The practice of sending provisions to the two colleges was abandoned in 1832, when, as a result of the tenurial reforms of that year, the royal villages (*gabaḍāgam*), which till then had supplied the provisions, became liable to be alienated. The produce of *gabaḍāgam* had also been utilized for other religious purposes, making customary gifts during religious festivals both

[41] D'Oyly's *Diary*.

[42] Things given to the monks included paddy, salt, robes and small cash allowances. See the 'Return of allowances granted either in money or in kind by the colonial government of Ceylon to the several priests of the temples in Kandy', sent by H. Wright, the Judicial Commissioner, to the Commission of Enquiry, 6 September 1830, C.O. 416/21.

[43] On D'Oyly's death, Governor Barnes decided to let the residency lapse because D'Oyly could not be replaced; 'for the confidence of the Kandyan people in him was supreme', he wrote to Bathurst on 10 June 1824. C.O. 54/86.

[44] 'Letters of Hardinge Giffard', Appendix T to P. E. Pieris, *Sinhalē and the Patriots*, p. 653.

in Kandy and in the provinces being the most important. Though the government, in 1832, abandoned the practice of making direct payments in kind, it nonetheless recognized its obligation to support the traditional religious institutions. Thus, in lieu of the direct payments which were then withdrawn, Governor Horton arranged to make an annual monetary grant of about £310.

This grant had to be sanctioned annually by the Legislative Council; and the missionaries raised objections against it on the ground that it amounted to a 'Christian legislature' allocating funds to support 'heathenism'.[45] In 1844, Governor Campbell made it known to the Colonial Office that it would be difficult to justify a refusal of this trifling grant, as the government levied the greater part of its revenue from Buddhists.[46] This defence of the grant found no support at the Colonial Office, and at their insistence the grant was withdrawn in May 1847.[47] Two years later, after the troubles of 1848,[48] the Colonial Office allowed a grant of lands in compensation for the discontinued monetary contribution.[49] After considerable delay, this grant was finally made in February 1858; however, as no proper arrangements were made by the Ceylon government for the management of these lands, before long some of them passed into alien hands.[50]

b. 'The possession and exhibition of the Tooth relic of Bhood' wrote Colebrooke, 'is regarded by the natives of the Kandyan provinces as the most important of the prerogatives of the Kings of Kandy to which the British Government has succeeded'.[51] The immense religio-political significance of the Tooth Relic was realized by the British at the time of their

[45] Robert Spence Hardy, *The British Government and the Idolatry of Ceylon* (Colombo, 1839).

[46] Campbell to Stanley, no. 14 of 24 January 1844, C.O. 54/210. Out of public funds, the government, at this time, maintained a (largely Anglican) 'ecclesiastical establishment'. The annual salary paid to its head alone amounted to £2,000.

[47] 'Expenditure on account of the Buddhist and other Ceremonies at Kandy hitherto paid by Government, but entirely withdrawn since May 1847', Enclosure no. 2 of Despatch no. 133 of 14 October 1847, Torrington to Grey. C.O. 54/238.

[48] Regarding which, see K. M. de Silva (ed.), *Letters on Ceylon: The Administration of Viscount Torrington and the 'Rebellion' of 1848* (Colombo, 1965).

[49] Grey to Torrington, no. 384 of 23 April 1849, C.O. 55/261.

[50] Ranjit T. Heṭṭimulla, *Daḷadā Puvata* (Kandy, 1960), pp. 90–91.

[51] *The Colebrooke-Cameron Papers*, p. 37.

entry into the Kandyan kingdom; and soon after the 'Convention' they negotiated with the Kandyans for the return of the Relic as well as the insignia of the four gods–Nātha, Viṣṇu, Kataragama and Pattini–which had been removed to safety at the approach of British troops. The insignia of the gods were returned with due ceremony on 7 April 1815, and on the following day, D'Oyly personally distributed the offerings customarily sent to the four *dēvālēs*.[52] After some delay, on 24 April, the Tooth Relic was brought back to its sanctuary, the Daḷadā Māligāva, in a magnificent procession;[53] and that night, with deep relief, D'Oyly wrote to Brownrigg: 'We have this day obtained the surest proof of the confidence of the Kandyan nation and their Acquiescence in the Dominion of the British Government'.[54] The keys to the shrine (where the Tooth Relic was kept) which had been in the possession of the Kandyan kings were now in the custody of the resident, and the task of guarding the Relic and the moveable property of the shrine was now assigned to a Sinhalese government official and a regular soldier.

The official custody of the Tooth Relic as well as the governmental backing given to the ceremonies connected with it soon attracted the resentment of the European Christian community in Ceylon, and gradually the administrators themselves began to minimize their involvement. When a grand *daḷadā* festival was held in 1828, the ceremonies were officially superintended by the Revenue Commissioner in Kandy, George Turnour; and Governor Barnes himself witnessed and participated in the ceremonies, just as Governor Brownrigg had done on a previous occasion in 1817.[55] But on this later occasion, when an application was made by the Kandyan chiefs to Governor Barnes soliciting him to provide a military salute for the festival and to make a customary gift to the Relic, the governor rejected the application 'on the ground that he would do

[52] D'Oyly's *Diary*, 8 April 1815.

[53] An eye-witness account of this procession by Lieutenant W. H. Lyttleton is given in J. W. Bennett, *Ceylon and its Capabilities* (London, 1843), pp. 412–13.

[54] Quoted in Brownrigg to Bathurst, no. 104 of 20 July 1815. C.O. 54/55.

[55] A description of the 1817 festival (based on a Sinhalese account supplied by Millāvē) was published in the CGG of 13 September 1817. A detailed eye-witness account of the 1828 festival, too, has been written, and an abridged English translation of this (communicated by Colebrooke) appeared in the *JRAS*, III (1836) 161–64. The full Sinhalese account has been published more recently in *Prabhāṣodaya* (1935) 227–28, 259–62.

nothing which could imply identity in the Buddhist faith on the part of the authorities'.[56] In fact, neither request was unusual, not merely in view of the established Kandyan custom, but also on account of the precedents established by D'Oyly. For when the Relic was originally brought back to Kandy in 1815, it was received with a salute from the temple gingalls, which was returned by the artillery of the British garrison; and soon after the Relic was deposited in the sanctuary, D'Oyly made an offering on behalf of the new king's representative.[57]

In 1843, when the campaign against the connection of the government with Buddhism had already gathered considerable momentum, the mere presence of the governor (Colin Campbell) and the Acting Government Agent of the Central Province (C. R. Buller) at an exposition of the Tooth Relic caused a stir in missionary circles.[58] Their campaign—ardently supported by the evangelical James Stephen, who at this time was the Permanent Under-Secretary at the Colonial Office, and who fought 'their [i.e., the missionaries'] case for them better than they could have done themselves'[59]—made a complete conquest of the Colonial Office; and in the following year, specific instructions were given prohibiting government officials from taking any part in the exhibition of the Relic.[60] Furthermore, the Ceylon government was instructed to give up the custody of the Relic altogether with no 'unnecessary delay'.[61]

The Colonial Office gave no instructions stating to whom the custody of the Relic should be handed over, and the Kandyans were unanimously opposed to violating the immemorial tradition of keeping the custody of the Relic with the highest political authority in the island. The Kandyans

[56] George Turnour's letter (dated 21 July 1838) to *The Friend*, II (1838) 38–40.

[57] See the account in Bennett, *op. cit.* D'Oyly's offering was a musical clock which had been brought out some time earlier as a gift to Śrī Vikrama Rājasiṃha. Even at that early stage, there were some who were not quite impressed by D'Oyly's diplomacy. Hardinge Giffard, in the letter quoted earlier (n. 44), wrote: 'To gratify their priests . . . the British resident went in solemn procession to their principal temple in Kandi, walked barefooted up to the altar, and made offerings to their idol—all in his official character. This I believe is the first instance for four centuries of a representative of a British Government publicly sacrificing in an Heathen temple'.

[58] See J. Peggs, *The Present State of the British Connection with Idolatry in Ceylon* (London, 1853). This pamphlet was an expanded version of a memorandum written to the Colonial Office in 1843.

[59] K. M. de Silva, *Social Policy*, p. 102.

[60] Stanley to Campbell, no. 210 of 24 July 1844. C.O. 55/

[61] *Ibid.*

registered their opposition both in conferences with the governor and government officials as well as in petitions sent to the governor and to the Queen of England.[62] But since their opposition had no effect whatsoever, they ultimately gave in with the greatest reluctance to Governor Torrington's proposal to have the custody of the Daḷadā Māligāva (Temple of the Tooth Relic) vested in a committee consisting of the Diyavaḍana Nilamē of the Temple and the Mahā Nāyakas of Malvatta and Asgiriya. This proposal was put into effect, and the Temple was handed over to the committee on 2 October 1847.[63]

c. The festivals connected with the Daḷadā Māligāva and other temples as well as the day-to-day maintenance of all the major temples required a large labour force which was mobilized in terms of an intricate system of land tenure. Although the age-old custom was sufficient to induce many tenants to perform their tenurial obligations, some amount of compulsion was necessary in the case of those who were lax. This compulsion was traditionally exercised by the chiefs on behalf of the king; but after the Proclamation of 21 November 1818, the chiefs no longer had a legal right to act in this capacity, having been deprived of their former judicial authority. Hence, when necessary, it devolved directly on the British authorities to compel obedience. This they apparently did during the early years, as they 'considered it politic to give them [the Buddhists] every support and countenance',[64] but not entirely in a manner that brought satisfaction to those who were in charge of temples. All the major temples had *lēkam miṭi* where the possessions of the temples and the services attached to all the allotments of land were minutely registered. The government made no serious attempt to study these registers, nor to enforce all the services registered in them. 'The laxity of the people, and the

[62] Governor Campbell held a conference with Kandyan chiefs and monks on 23 April 1845. Campbell to Stanley, no. 120 of 8 May 1845, C.O. 54/217. Again, on 10 November, there was another conference in Kandy where the government was represented by P. E. Woodhouse, the Assistant Colonial Secretary. Minutes of this conference were enclosed with the despatch of Campbell to Stanley, no. 37 of 7 February 1846. Also enclosed with the same despatch were the petitions of the Kandyans to the governor, dated 4 July 1845, and to the Queen of England, dated 7 January 1846 (with 1941 signatures).

[63] Torrington to Grey, nos. 133 and 134 of 14 October 1847. C.O. 54/229.

[64] The evidence of George Turnour, the Revenue Commissioner of the Kandyan Provinces, before the Colebrooke Commission, Kandy, 2 September 1829. C.O. 416/20.

remissness of the government officers in enforcing the orders for their attendance, has been urged as a subject of complaint by the Chiefs', wrote Colebrooke in 1831.[65]

Although he made note of this complaint, Colebrooke made no recommendations to rectify it; indeed he was clearly opposed to traditional systems of land tenure and to governmental interference in enforcing them. His major recommendations on land tenure, as we have already noted, were not applied to temple lands; but innovations in the tenure of other (i.e., non-temple) lands rendered it difficult—and made the administrators reluctant—to maintain pockets of tradition attached to temple lands. Thus in 1834, just two years after the abolition of *rājakāriya*, Governor Horton (while reaffirming the government's undertaking to support Buddhism) made it known in a general Proclamation that the government would no longer enforce the attendance of temple tenants at religious festivals.[66]

Part of the tenurial obligations of the tenants consisted of keeping the temples in constant repair; and in enforcing this aspect of their obligations the government showed the least interest. Davy, who toured Kandy in 1817 in his capacity as Governor Brownrigg's physician, wrote: 'Though from the time of our entrance into Kandy our object has been to improve the town, what we have done has generally had a contrary effect. We have pulled down much and built up little; and taking no interest in the temples, we have entirely neglected their repair'.[67]

d. When the government became reluctant to support the traditional rights of temple authorities, the only way that the latter could enforce their rights was by resorting to courts of law. Though the monks did resort to courts of law when it was necessary, they did so with some reluctance, as legal procedures invariably entailed expenses as well as numerous delays; and also because a litigant monk generally lost his popularity with the

[65] *The Colebrooke-Cameron Papers*, pp. 35–36.

[66] Proclamation of 9 August 1834, CGG 16 August 1834. This new attitude stood in sharp contrast to the attitude adopted sixteen years earlier in the Proclamation of 21 November 1818 which said: '. . . the attendance on the Great Feast, which certain persons were bound to give, be continued to be given punctually and gratuitously' (clause 30).

[67] John Davy, *An Account of the Interior of Ceylon and of its Inhabitants* (London, 1821), p. 276. See also his remarks (p. 328) on the pathetic state of the *dēvālēs* and the Palace at the one-time Royal residence of Hañguranketa.

laity.[68] In any case, a monk could successfully resort to law only if his rights were firmly recognized by law–by virtue of a valid appointment from the government.

The manner in which a chief monk was appointed in the Kandyan kingdom has been described thus by Karatoṭa Dhammārāma in a letter to Alexander Johnston:

> A virtuous and wise Priest of rank who is fully acquainted with the religion is chosen out and brought before the King, whereupon the first Adigar by order of the King says in the presence of the Chiefs and High Priests that he the said Priest is appointed Chief Priest to such Temple, but a Commission in writing is never granted to him, and after that he the said Priest gets all the lands, wages, flags, umbrellas, and men belonging to that Temple who were granted to his Predecessor and afterward all the Priests belonging to that Temple appear before him and abide under his orders.[69]

The same sort of procedure was followed in (and immediately after) 1815, with the governor or the resident taking the place of the king; but the British bureaucrat in his office being both ill-equipped and disinclined to play the role of the Sinhalese king in his court, the personal appointment was soon replaced by the impersonal 'Act of Appointment' in writing.[70] Yet in the selection of nominees for temple offices, the British

[68] Christian missionaries who campaigned against the government's connection with Buddhism knew of this, and no doubt liked to see it happen: 'The possession of lands by the priesthood, and the disputes that continually arise between the incumbents and their retainers, cause the priests to be frequently seen in the courts of law which has had a tendency to bring them into disrepute with the more thoughtful of their adherents'. R. Spence Hardy, *Eastern Monachism* (London, 1850), p. 32. Many years later, Governor Gordon observed: 'Many of the strongest enemies of Buddhism ... desire abstinence from all legislative intervention, being aware that existing abuses throw an amount of discredit on the Buddhist clergy, from which they do not desire to see them freed; and perceiving that if things go on as they now are, the pecuniary resources of the Buddhist monastic establishments, which they desire to see exhausted, will not long hold out'. *Address to the Legislative Council*, 31 October 1888.

[69] Johnston Papers, C.M.L. The document is undated, but is prior to 1809 when Johnston returned to England to come back in 1811 as Chief Justice.

[70] In terms of clause 10 of the Proclamation of 21 November 1818, it became necessary for all chiefs to hold written Instruments of Appointment. The same condition was not immediately extended to temple offices; thus, on 11 December 1818, the Board of Commissioners considering the appointment of Kiralagama Unnānse to Asgiri Alut Vihāre concluded that 'it has not been customary to appoint Priests, Principals of Temples by a written Instrument and does not consider it necessary to introduce such a practice'. Such a practice, however, was soon introduced; and when

officials continued to play a major role, as evidenced by the statement of John Downing, the Judicial Commissioner in Kandy, before the Colebrooke Commission. Enumerating his functions in the sphere of superintending the management of temples, he mentioned as one of his duties 'bringing before the Board the names of candidates for office, either as Priests or Chiefs, and the Board recommends them to the Governor who appoints them'.[71]

The Acts of Appointment granted to the chief monks by the governors more or less followed the standard formulae of contemporary British Acts of Appointment. The one granted to Koṭagama Guṇaratana Unnānsē by Governor Wilmot Horton on 17 September 1835, for instance, reads:

> By virtue of the Powers in Us vested by His Majesty, and reposing especial confidence in your zeal, piety, learning, and loyalty, We have given and granted, and by these Presents do give and grant to you, the said Kotegame Gooneratene Teroonnansey, the office of Mahanayeke Unnansey of Asgiry Wihare in Kandy during pleasure. . . . And all priests and other persons whom it may concern, are hereby peremptorily commanded to respect and obey you, the said Kotegame Gooneratene Teroonnansey, as Mahanayeke Unnansey of Asgiry Wihare in Kandy, so long as you shall hold the said office and to pay you all honours not abrogated by Us, which you are entitled to in virtue thereof, by the customs of the Kandyan Provinces.[72]

The selection and appointment of chief monks by British officials was one of the things to which Spence Hardy raised objection in the pamphlet referred to above, and his arguments in this respect, in contrast to his other arguments, found almost immediate acceptance with the Ceylon government. Governor MacKenzie, making this public duty an issue of

on 12 May 1820, Välivița (Kuḍā) Saraṇaṃkara was appointed Mahā Nāyaka of Malvatta and Nāyaka of Śrīpāda, he was given two written 'Acts' in relation to the two offices. Revenue Commissioner's Diary, 19 May 1820.

[71] Dated, Kandy, 15 September 1829, C.O. 416/20 (G. 13). 'Extracts from the Proceedings of the Board of Commissioners for Kandyan Affairs' (C.O. 416/21) contains information relating to the manner in which the Commissioners evaluated the relative merits of the candidates for the incumbency of Malvatta Vihāre and selected one to be recommended to the governor.

[72] This 'Act' is printed in full in *Correspondence relating to Buddhist Temporalities Ordinance*, S.P. IV: 1907, p. 14. K. M. de Silva (*Social Policy*, p. 126, n. 2) is off the mark when he says that these 'Acts' (or 'warrants') 'generally copied the somewhat flowery language of the letters of appointment of Kandyan days'. As we have noted, there were no letters of appointment in 'Kandyan days'.

conscience, refused to sign Acts of Appointment for temple offices, and sought to repeal the tenth clause of the Proclamation of 21 November 1818, which was supposed to make such signing necessary.[73] However, he had no time to accomplish this. Therefore, in March 1841, on the eve of his departure from Ceylon, he laid down a written protest against any governor of Ceylon being called upon to make appointments to temple offices.[74]

Even after this protest, the government, on a few occasions, did make appointments to temple offices; but the appointments thus made did not cover even the barest minimum. 'Temples are without Head Priests; those *who act* cannot legally enforce their rights and are cheated of their dues' admitted Governor Torrington in 1848.[75] The temples affected included not only the provincial *vihāres* but also Asgiriya, which had to be without a Mahā Nāyaka from 1845–49, and again from 1851–53.[76]

The resultant disorganization of temple affairs soon became evident to the government; and after much discussion and numerous appeals by the Kandyans, it was finally decided in 1853 to issue 'Certificates' to chief monks instead of 'Acts', the issue of which had been discontinued. This decision was taken in the midst of very strong missionary opposition;[77] and the differences between the Acts and the Certificates indicate in some way the concessions granted to the missionary point of view. Since the references in the Acts to the governor 'reposing especial confidence' in the 'zeal, piety, learning, and loyalty' of the person appointed were interpreted as admission by the government of responsibility for the person appointed, the Certificates completely omitted this formula. The responsibility of selecting a candidate became henceforth entirely the business of the monks themselves; and the Certificate granted to such a candidate merely stated: 'Whereas . . . , has been elected by the Priests of . . . to be the Chief Priest

[73] Proceedings of the Executive Council, 17 October 1840.

[74] *Ibid.*, 24 March 1841.

[75] Torrington to Grey, 11 August 1848, in K. M. de Silve (ed.), *Letters on Ceylon*.

[76] See the petition of Kandyan chiefs and *bhikkhus* to Earl Grey, dated 5 January 1852, enclosure, Anderson to Grey, no. 16 of 13 January 1852, C.O. 54/288; and the two letters of Asgiriya monks to the Government Agent of the Central Province, dated 5 February and 21 April 1852, enclosures, Anderson to Pakington, no. 61 of 6 August 1852, C.O. 54/290.

[77] For details, see K. M. de Silva, *Social Policy*, pp. 116 ff.

of the said Temple: It is hereby declared that the said election of . . . to be the Chief Priest of . . . is recognized by the Government'.[78]

Also, the Certificate, in contrast to the Act, had no clause commanding the chief monk's subordinates to obey and respect him and to pay him the honours that he was entitled to in virtue of his office, which meant that hereafter the government assumed no responsibility, even at the merely formal level, for enforcing the authority of the chief monks. The chief monks themselves had to do their best to assert their authority in relation to their subordinates; and in the case of those who persisted in their insubordination, they either had to remain silent or seek costly and uncertain redress through courts of law. This had highly significant results for the authority structure of the ecclesiastical establishment. The contrast between the two periods–the early period when the ecclesiastical establishment was backed by the government and the later period when it was left to its own devices–may be illustrated with the following examples.

Some amount of rivalry existed between Malvatta and Asgiriya from the time of King Kīrti Śrī Rājasiṃha,[79] and this rivalry took a new turn in the early 1820s when the Malvatta monks began to challenge quite openly the validity of the *sīmā* ('consecrated boundary') where the ordination ceremonies of the Asgiriya chapter were performed. In response to the Malvatta challenge, Yaṭanvala Sunanda, the Mahā Nāyaka of Asgiriya (1824–35), made a proclamation defending the *sīmā* at Asgiriya. The Malvatta monks, led by Koṭikāpola Ratanajoti, their Mahā Nāyaka (1825–26), addressed a petition to the governor through the Board of Commissioners in Kandy in 1825 protesting against Yaṭanvala's proclamation;[80] and in the following year, they wrote a book called *Sīmā Saṃkara Vinodanī* reiterating their criticisms of the Asgiriya *sīmā*.[81] This

[78] The Colonial Secretary to the Government Agent, Central Province, no. 152 of 7 April 1853, printed in S.P. IV: 1907, pp. 11–12.

[79] One major reason for this rivalry was that when ecclesiastical affairs were reorganized during the reign of this king, some temples over which Asgiriya, the older establishment, made claims were handed over to Malvatta. See above, ch. I, n. 174, and *Third Report of the Historical Manuscripts Commission*, S.P. XIX: 1951, p. 23.

[80] Appendix VI to Kotmalē Saddhammavaṃsa *Aṁbagahavattē Indāsabhavara Ñāṇasāmi Mahā Nāyaka Svāmīndrayan Vahansēgē Jīvana Caritaya* (Kalutara, 1950), pp. 85–87.

[81] C.M.L., M. 4; B.M., Or. 6603/216 and 232.

was followed by a second proclamation by Yaṭanvala and others attacking Malvatta in 1826.[82] In all probability, it was these exchanges that the Judicial Commissioner in Kandy had in his mind when he testified before the Colebrooke Commission in 1829: 'There have been some dispute between the two principal wiharres in Kandy–but the subject has not been considered of such importance as to require the direct interference of Government'.[83]

Among those who joined in this criticism of the Asgiriya *sīmā* was Mayilavävē Guṇaratana, the chief monk of Huduhumpola Vihāre,[84] a temple which was under the jurisdiction of Asgiriya. Mayilavävē indeed went further: since he had no faith in the validity of the *sīmā* where he received ordination, he got himself and his pupils reordained by the monks of the Amarapura fraternity at Daḍalla. The Asgiriya monks, who did not recognize the Amarapura fraternity, considered this an act of 'heresy'; they excluded Mayilavävē from the Asgiriya chapter and sought to remove him from his office at Huduhumpola. They had no immediate success; but on their insistence, the government, in 1836, dismissed Mayilavävē's pupil, Ram̆bukvällē Sobhita–who, in 1829, had succeeded his teacher to Huduhumpola, and following him, had got himself reordained by the Amarapura fraternity–from his office at Huduhumpola and gave over the office to Vāriyapola, a monk who was acceptable to the Asgiriya monks. Furthermore, when Ram̆bukvällē refused to surrender the temple to Vāriyapola, the Government Agent of the Central Province raised an action against him in the Kandy District Court in 1837 to have him ejected.

Ram̆bukvällē died before the case was tried, whereupon the nine resident monks (pupils of Mayilavävē and Ram̆bukvallē) were substituted as defendants. The District Judge decided against the government; but the decision was reversed, on appeal, by the Supreme Court in 1838.[85]

All this happened while the government was still prepared to uphold the authority of the Mahā Nāyakas. What happened when the government withdrew the support which had been given to the authority of the Mahā Nāyakas? When the government ceased to supervise the administration of temple lands, there were many monks who dealt as they pleased

[82] Appendix VII to Kotmalē Saddhammavaṃsa, *op. cit.*, pp. 89–91.

[83] C.O. 416/20.

[84] Mayilavävē and his pupils signed the Malvatta peittion to the governor referred to above.

[85] The details are given in Lawrie, *Gazetteer*, pp. 361ff. See also section iii (below) of this chapter.

with the lands under their custody, in manners highly prejudicial to the interests of the religious institutions to which the lands were attached. The Mahā Nāyakas occasionally made efforts to reprimand the malefactors, but with hardly any success.

Goḍamunnē Ratanajoti, a monk of the Huduhumpola temple, for instance, leased out lands belonging to the temple and appropriated the rent. Though asked by the chief monk of the temple, Pērādeṇiyē Indajoti (who held a Government Certificate dated 1869 in recognition of his office) to hand over the money to the temple, he refused to do so. Pērādeṇiyē made complaints to the Mahā Nāyaka of Asgiriya and the latter summoned Goḍamunnē to appear at Asgiriya for an enquiry. Though it was repeated three times, Goḍamunnē ignored the summons with complete impunity.[86]

Dam̆bulu Vihāre, a temple more ancient and wealthier than Huduhumpola, and also belonging to the Asgiriya chapter, held large tracts of forest land, which were meant to supply the timber for the maintenance of the temple and also to meet the needs of the temple tenants. The chief monk of this temple, with no regard to the interests of which he was the custodian, sold the timber in one of the forests to a low-country carpenter and omitted to pay the money into the temple chest. The villagers made complaints to the Service Tenures Commissioner, but all that the commissioner could do was to bring the complaint to the notice of the Mahā Nāyaka. The Mahā Nāyaka instructed Dūllǟvē Luku Baṇḍā (president of the Village Tribunals of Mātalē North) to inspect the lands and send a report. Dūllǟvē's report confirmed the complaints of the villagers; still the Mahā Nāyaka found himself powerless to remove the monk from his office.[87]

With these two major instances of insubordination fresh in his mind, the Mahā Nāyaka of Asgiriya (Vattegama Sumaṃgala, 1869–85), when asked by the Buddhist Temporalities Commission, 'Do you find the priests readily submit themselves to the authority of their ecclesiastical superiors?', replied, 'Since . . . 1852 . . . there has been an end to all authority on the part of the Mahā Nāyaka'.[88]

[86] *Report of the Commissioners appointed to inquire into the administration of the Buddhist Temporalities*, S.P. XVIII: 1876, pp. 1, 10, 17.

[87] *Ibid.*, pp. 4, 17; and *Report of the Service Tenures Commissioner*, A.R. 1871, p. 371.

[88] S.P. XVIII: 1876, p. 17.

Dam̆bulu Vihāre, for a long time, had been very closely associated with Asgiriya; and Huduhumpola Vihāre was situated just a mile and a half from Kandy. If by the middle of the nineteenth century Kandy had begun to lose its hold over places of this sort, which were very much part of their traditional domain, it would hardly come as a surprise that their authority was even weaker in the more distant territories in the southern and western parts of the island.

ii. KANDYAN VERSUS LOW-COUNTRY MONKS—THE SECOND PHASE: THE RISE OF THE KALYĀṆI FRATERNITY.

In section iii of the last chapter we examined conflicts between Kandyan and low-country monks during the time of Karatoṭa Dhammārāma (1737–1827) which reached a critical point in 1826 with the appointment of Gāllē Medhaṃkara (?–1836), a pupil of Karatoṭa, to the incumbency of Śrīpāda despite the opposition of Kandyan monks. This conflict, as was then observed, led to no formal schism between the two groups. Yet, not long afterwards, a new controversy arose between the two groups, started this time by another pupil of Karatoṭa, Bentara Atthadassī (?–1862), who lived at Vanavāsa Vihāre in Bentara, which did lead to such a schism. It is to this controversy and to its resultant schism that we turn our attention now.

Bentaṛa, about the year 1831, put forward some new ideas concerning three main points which were of considerable importance to the Buddhist monkhood: new ideas which by virtue of their departure from what was then generally accepted as regular and proper, and also, by virtue of the reputation that their author enjoyed as a monk of learning, were destined, from the very beginning, to lead to a major controversy.

Of the three points that Bentara brought into controversy, one was about *sāṃghika dāna*, or alms given to the order of monks. Giving alms, as a means of acquiring merit, was one of the acts prescribed for the Buddhist laity, and the amount of merit to be gained by such giving was deemed to differ depending on the type of recipient. Particularly rewarding, according to the *Dakkhiṇā Vibhaṃga Sutta* (The Discourse on the Analysis of Offerings), which distinguished between different types of givers and recipients, was alms given to the *saṃgha*, the order of monks.[89] For obvious

[89] *Majjhima Nikāya*, vol. III, ed. Robert Chalmers (London, 1899), no. 142.

reasons, no layman could offer alms to the *entire* order; in actual fact, giving was always to a few specific monks. In theory, *sāṃghika dāna*, or alms to the (entire) order, was nonetheless possible, as even a few monks (five or more) could *represent* the order and accept alms on behalf of the order. In extending invitations to monks for alms-giving ceremonies, the laymen, ideally, had to make their invitations 'collective', that is, they had to invite a certain number of monks within one monastery (or more) with no reference as to the particular individuals who were to accept the invitation. This meant that the monks themselves, and not the laymen, made the decision on behalf of the order as to who should accept the invitation. Though this was the ideal, it was not uncommon in actual fact for laymen to have their 'favourite' monks in different temples, and therefore to convene these 'favourites' for alms-giving purposes by inviting each of them individually. It was about this practice that Bentara raised issue with his contemporaries. He contended that in such circumstances *dāna* (giving) to the monks was not *sāṃghika* (collective) but *pudgalika* (individual), and therefore less meritorious.

Bentara's other two points concerned the mode of reckoning months and seasons–hence the calendar–which was of crucial importance for the observance of a complex of Buddhist rituals.

Early Buddhists did not develop an astronomical system of their own; they derived their system from the theories which were current in India at the time.[90] It was from the Vedic system that they derived the lunar month and the notion of *uposatha*, that is, the notion that every new-moon day and full-moon day should be held sacred and set apart for religious observances. For the Buddhist laity, *uposatha* (eventually increased to four days in each month by adding the two intermediate quarter-moon days) became the occasion to refrain from mundane activity and observe the eight precepts, that is, three precepts in addition to the five that they were expected to follow every day. For the monkhood, *uposatha* meant (in addition to ministering to the needs of the laity) the occasion for their fortnightly confessional gatherings. On this occasion, monks within a clearly defined boundary met in an *uposathāgāra* (confessional hall); here they recited the *Pātimokkha* containing two hundred and twenty-seven

[90] E. J. Thomas, 'Sun, Moon and Stars (Buddhist)', *Encyclopaedia of Religion and Ethics*, XII.

rules for *upasampadā* monks, mutually confessed transgressions of those rules, agreed on punishments and so forth.[91]

Another notion borrowed from the Vedic system was the observance of the three seasons of the year: Gimhāna (Summer), Vassāna (the rainy season) and Hemanta (Winter). Of the three seasons, the most important for ritual purposes was the rainy season. Just as *uposatha* implied an intensification of religious preoccupations (on the part of both laymen and monks) in comparison with the other days of the month, so did *vassāna* imply a somewhat similar intensification in comparison with the other two seasons of the year. During this season, beginning on the day after the full moon of Āsāḷha (June-July) and ending with the full moon of Kattikā (October-November), the monks were expected to observe a retreat known as *vassa* for a period of three months. During this period of retreat, the monk was expected to remain in one village devoting his time to his own educational and spiritual progress as well as to that of the villagers around him. And the villagers themselves were expected to attend diligently to the material requirements of the monk. The termination of the retreat, *pavāraṇā*, was followed by the ceremonial presentation of *kaṭhina*, a robe, by the villagers to the particular monk who had been spending *vassa* among them.[92]

Since the observance of these rites were dependent on the calendar, the unity of the order required acceptance of a uniform calendar. Disagreements on important calendrical events could only lead to schisms, as did disagreements relating to the mode of reckoning Easter, to cite a parallel in early mediaeval Europe.[93]

Although the basic units of the Buddhist calendar–the two phases of the moon–were unambiguous, there was room for disagreement as to when one month ended and another began: more specifically, whether a month ended with full moon or new moon. Both methods had been in use in India since the Vedic times.[94]

[91] For an account of the *uposatha* ceremony, together with the relevant Pali texts and their English translations, see J. F. Dickson, 'The *Pātimokkha*, being the Buddhist Office of the Confession of Priests', *JRAS*, n.s., VIII (1876) 62–130.

[92] For an account of the ritual complex of *vassa*, see J. F. Dickson, 'Notes illustrative of Buddhism as the daily religion of the Buddhists of Ceylon', *JRAS(CB)*, VIII (1884) 207–31.

[93] J. G. Carleton, 'Calendar (Christian)', *Encyclopaedia of Religion and Ethics*, III, 88–90.

[94] R. Sewell and S. B. Dikshit, *The Indian Calendar* (London, 1896).

The mode of reckoning months naturally had implications for the mode of reckoning seasons and years. Since the lunar month was shorter than the solar month, it was necessary, from time to time, to have an intercalary month (*adhikamāsa*) to bring the lunar year into harmony with the solar year. The exact point of intercalation depended on the mode of reckoning months; and the intercalation, in turn, determined the reckoning of seasons; and through that it also determined the dates on which to start and end the periods of *vassa*.

Both on the mode of reckoning months and on the dates for the observance of *vassa* Bentara disagreed with his contemporaries who were following the traditions founded on the Buddhist exegetical works. Although Bentara's arguments were by no means confined to the question of the intercalary month (his point about *sāṃghika dāna* had nothing whatsoever to do with it), by virtue of the central importance of this issue, the controversy started by him came to be known as the Adhikamāsa Vādaya, or the 'Controversy on the Intercalary Month'. The astrological and doctrinal intricacies of this controversy will be of no concern here.[95] Concern will be with the course that the controversy took and the results it produced for the Buddhist order in Ceylon.

Since Bentara's opinions on the three points mentioned above differed from those which were then generally held by monks of both the Siyam and the Amarapura fraternities, Bentara was invited, in 1837, by Valagedara Dhammadassī (the chief monk of the Siyam fraternity in the Galle District) for a discussion on those points. Bentara accepted this invitation; and at a meeting convened by Valagedara, where monks of both the Siyam and the Amarapura fraternities as well as some laymen led by Mudaliyar Guṇatilaka Amarasirivardhana were present, Bentara and Valagedara debated the three controversial points. No agreement was reached at the end of this discussion; each party remained unconvinced by the arguments put forward by the other. On 10 June 1837, Bentara prepared, at the request of Mudaliyar Guṇatilaka Amarasirivardhana, a document containing a summary of the discussion held on this occasion, with an addendum embodying his own final observations.[96] This document was circulated among the

[95] A very brief reference to some of the astrological issues may be found in C. Alwis, 'On the Principles of Sinhalese Chronology', *JRAS(CB)*, III (1856–58) 190–91.

[96] C.N.A. 5/63/8/(23).

leading monks of the time; yet, at this stage, Bentara seems to have received no support from any of them.[97] Seeing his inability to convince his Ceylonese brethren, Bentara turned his eyes towards Siam, hoping to obtain a favourable decision from there.

The religious contacts between Ceylon and Siam which were established in the mid-eighteenth century with the inauguration of the Siyam fraternity in Kandy did not persist very long. A Siamese prince, as we have noted earlier, was involved in a conspiracy against King Kīrti Śrī Rājasiṃha in 1760.[98] But even apart from this unpleasant incident, the political conditions in neither country were conducive to the maintenance of uninterrupted contacts with the other. The political crisis in the Kandyan kingdom which culminated in the overthrow of the Nāyakkar dynasty in 1815 has been told earlier.[99] The destinies of Siam in the late eighteenth century were scarcely more promising. The perennial wars with Burma resulted, in 1767, in an utterly humiliating defeat for the Siamese; their land was occupied, and their four-hundred-year-old capital, Ayodhya, was looted and burnt, never to be rebuilt. 'Old Siam' was restored on a firm footing only with the accession of the new Chakri dynasty to power in 1782 with Ratanakosinda (Bangkok) as the capital.[100]

With the return to political stability, a revival of religious activities began under the first king of the new dynasty, Rama I (1782–1809), and continued with increasing vigour under his successors, Rama II (1809–24) and Rama III (1824–51).[101] In the wake of this revival, the old contacts with Ceylon were revived: the *Mahāvaṃsa* was translated into Siamese during the reign of Rama I;[102] and in 1816 a good-will mission of eight Siamese monks arrived in Ceylon and returned home in 1818.[103] In 1840 five Ceylonese monks visited Siam,[104] and from this year onwards there

[97] See, e.g., the observations of Bōpāgoḍa Sumana (the Nāyaka of Amarapura fraternity), dated 5 March 1838, given in Mādampē Dhammatilaka, *Adhimāsa Lakṣanaya saha Yācādhimāsa Nirṇayē Doṣanirṇaya* (Ambalaṃgoḍa, 1909), p. 16.

[98] Above, p. 66.

[99] Above, ch. II, sec. ii.

[100] Prince Dhani Nivat, 'The Reconstruction of Rama I of the Chakri Dynasty', *Journal of the Siam Society*, XLIII (1955) 21–47.

[101] Walter F. Vella, *Siam under Rama III, 1824–1851* (New York, 1957), esp. ch. III.

[102] Dhani Nivat, *op. cit.*, pp. 34–35.

[103] R. Lingat, 'History of Wat Mahādhātu', *Journal of the Siam Society*, XXIV (1930) 11–12.

[104] R. Lingat, 'History of Wat Pavaraniveça', *ibid.*, XXVI (1933) 81–82.

were uninterrupted contacts between the two countries for several decades, with monks from each country visiting the other and carrying numerous messages to and fro.[105]

For the Siamese monks contacts with Ceylon were important because they still looked upon Ceylon as the centre of Buddhism and repository of its sacred literature.[106] For the Ceylonese monks in turn contacts with Siam had a very special significance; not having a king of their own, they were now looking for royal surrogates, and the kingdom of Siam provided them with an ideal which was close to their image of their own past. True enough, the Ceylonese monks had the British sovereigns and their representatives in Ceylon—and, at the formal level, they in fact treated them with the same kind of deference as was due to Sinhalese monarchs—but the hostility of alien rulers towards Buddhism was not unknown to Ceylonese monks; it was, in fact, a subject of complaint to their more fortunate Siamese brethren.[107]

With the loosening of the authority structure of the ecclesiastical establishment in Ceylon, Siam also became some sort of a court of appeal to the Ceylonese monks. The voice of the Mahā Nāyakas no longer carried the same weight as in the past; it lacked its traditional royal backing, or for that matter, even the backing of the colonial government. In situations of conflict, therefore, it became common for all parties to appeal to Siam for their decision. This practice in no way implied that all parties were willing to abide by decisions which were to be given by Siam; still a decision in one's favour was looked upon by each party as a source of great strength and confidence.[108]

Bentara tried to get a message across to Siam, first in 1840, and again in 1843, but with no success. Finally, in 1844, he succeeded in sending two messages: one to the King of Siam,[109] and the other to the ten chief monks of the Dhammayuttika fraternity led by Vajirañāṇa.[110] In both messages

[105] *Pāli Sandesāvalī*, ed. Polvattē Buddhadatta (Ambalaṃgoḍa, 1962), *passim*.

[106] Lingat, 'Wat Pavaraniveça', p. 81.

[107] *Pāli Sandesāvalī*, pp. 207, 265.

[108] As we shall see later (ch. IV, sec. iii), Burma played very much a similar role in relation to some of the internal conflicts within the Amarapura fraternity.

[109] Appendices 10 (the Pali original) and 11 (a Sinhalese translation) to Kotmalē Saddhammavaṃsa, *op. cit.*

[110] Document no. 13 in *Pāli Sandesāvalī*. Vajirañāṇa was none other than Prince Mongkut (1804–68), the highest ranking prince in Siam in his time, who was in the monkhood at the time of

he referred to the dissensions within the order in Ceylon, and asked for help from Siam to bring about unity. In his message to Vajirañāṇa and other monks, he also wrote at length on such problems as those relating to the *adhikamāsa* and solicited the opinions of Siamese monks on them. Bentara's two messages were soon followed by a message to Vajirañāṇa from the monks of Malvatta and Asgiriya, who made it clear that they were not in sympathy with Bentara's point of view.[111]

Bentara received no support from Siamese monks. Indeed, though no reply from Siam on this matter is available, evidence indicates that the Siamese monks upheld the position of those who were opposed to him.[112] Yet Bentara was in no mood to give up his position.

A further public debate took place in 1850 at Kalutara with Bentara on one side and two young and highly promising scholars of the time, Hikkaḍuvē Sumaṃgala (1826–1911) and Baṭuvantuḍāvē Devarakṣita (1819–92) on the other.[113] In the following year, the second round of the same debate was held at the Kōṭṭe temple with Bentara and Baṭuvantuḍāvē representing the two sides.

Both Hikkaḍuvē and Baṭuvantuḍāvē remained unconvinced by Bentara's arguments at the end of these debates. Bentara did have some success, however, in that, at about this time, he managed to gain the support of two very important monks in the Colombo district: one of them was Maligaspē Maṃgala (?–1872) of the Kōṭṭe temple, who at this time was chief monk of the Siyam fraternity in the Colombo District; the other was Valānē Siddhārttha (1811–68) of Parama Dhamma Cetiya Vihāre in Ratmalāna, a

his father's death in 1824 and who decided to remain there when his half-brother, Rama III, succeeded to the throne. He was known as Vajirañāṇa from the time of his *upasampadā* until the year 1851, when he left the monkhood to succeed Rama III to the throne. During the period of his monkhood, he gained a well-deserved reputation for his learning as well as for his reformist zeal. See Lingat, 'Wat Pavaraniveça'. He had an equally remarkable career as King of Siam from 1851 to 1868. Yet, in the Western world, he came to be known mainly through the caricature of him presented by the English governess to his children, Anna Leonowens, in her two books: *An English Governess at the Court of Siam* (Boston, 1870) and *The Romance of the Harem* (Philadelphia, 1872). For recent and more sympathetic attempts to grasp the character of this remarkable man, see Alexander B. Griswold, 'King Mongkut in Perspective', *Journal of the Siam Society*, XLV (1957) 1–14, and Abbot Low Moffat, *Mongkut, the King of Siam* (New York, 1961). Both as monk and later as king, Mongkut maintained a very extensive correspondence with people in different parts of the world. Amongst them were some of the leading Ceylonese monks at the time.

111 *Pāli Sandesāvalī*, document no. 14.

112 Yagirala Prajñānanda, *Śrī Sumaṃgala Caritaya*, vol. II (Colombo, 1947), p. 508.

113 Mādampē Dhammatilaka, *op. cit.*, p. i.

pupil of Gāllē Medhaṃkara of Śrīpāda and teacher to both Hikkaḍuvē and Baṭuvantuḍāvē, who were opposed to Bentara.

On 27 July 1851, Maligaspē, making use of his position as chief monk, issued a proclamation to the monks in his area instructing them to start observing *vassa* on a date which was in accord with the system of calculation preferred by Bentara. This proclamation provoked a spate of criticism in the low country[114] as well as in Kandy. The monks of Malvatta sent a long letter to Maligaspē criticising Bentara's system of calculation; and this letter being handed over to Bentara, he wrote a point-by-point reply to Malvatta on 4 November 1851.[115]

The controversy continued in the next few years through the exchange of letters and tracts (in manuscript, as Buddhists at this stage had no printing presses of their own). In 1854, Bentara wrote *Māsādhimāsa Dīpanī* expounding his position, to which Hikkaḍuvē wrote a reply entitled *Līnārttha Dīpanī*.[116] Bentara's counter-reply to the latter, called *Adhimāsa Prakaśinī*,[117] was written in the later part of 1855, just a few months after his eventful trip to Kandy, on which we must briefly focus our attention now.

On 19 May 1855, Bentara wrote to Parakum̆burē Vipassī, the Mahā Nāyaka of Malvatta, indicating his desire to visit Kandy at the end of the month together with about fourteen other monks, both *upasampadā* and *sāmaṇera*, in order to worship the Tooth Relic, and also to discuss 'matters of mutual concern', meaning no doubt disagreements regarding the *adhikamāsa*.[118] Though not mentioned in this letter, another reason why he went up to Kandy at this time was to obtain *upasampadā* for his pupils; because of his disagreements with the Kandyan monks, Bentara had not visited Kandy for some two decades, as a result of which some of his pupils who were old enough to receive *upasampadā* had had to remain unordained.[119]

[114] See, e.g., the letter to Maligaspē dated 25 August 1851 from a group of laymen and monks who described themselves as 'Prajñāvanta Dharmavādīn', in Yagirala Prajñānanda, *op. cit.*, pp. 508–10.

[115] *Ibid.*, pp. 430–42.

[116] Printed in full, *ibid.*, pp. 531–55.

[117] C.N.A. 5/63/39/(3).

[118] This letter is given in Yagirala Prajñānanda, *op. cit.*, p. 415.

[119] Amongst them were three monks who gained considerable fame later on: Potuvila Indajoti, Yātrāmullē Dhammārāma and Am̆bagahavattē Saraṇaṃkara. See Kotmalē Saddhammavaṃsa, *op. cit.*, pp. 7, 9.

As he planned, Bentara visited Kandy with his associates and pupils; and the controversial issues were taken up for discussion. Among those who represented Malvatta at these discussions was Hikkaḍuvē, who apparently had been especially invited to Kandy for the occasion.[120] The discussions continued for three days; but rather than leading the two parties to any kind of agreement, they created even greater ill-feeling and mutual hostility. On the third day, Bentara left the assembly hall, and a few days later went back to the low country. The Malvatta monks, soon afterwards, issued a proclamation addressed to all their low-country brethren instructing them not to follow the system of calculation suggested by Bentara.[121] In this proclamation they described Bentara's system as entirely arbitrary and contrary to *vinaya*. Bentara's break with Kandy thus became final and complete.

The organization of a rival (low-country) fraternity got under way immediately after Bentara's return to the low country. On the full-moon day of Poson (June) 1855, the splinter group met at the Kōṭṭe temple where Bentara's supporter, Maligaspē, was the chief incumbent, and decided to call themselves Śrī Kalyāṇi Sāmagrīdharma Saṃgha Sabhā, which may be freely rendered as Kalyāṇi Fraternity. Among its members were, in addition to Bentara and Maligaspē, Valānē Siddharttha mentioned previously, Pānadurē Sumaṃgala of the Indasārārāmaya at Mahaaruggoḍa, and Päpiliyānē Sīlavaṃsa of Śrī Mahā Vihāre at Galgoḍa.[122] They decided to grant *upasampadā* to low-country (Goyigama) monks within the low country itself, at Kälaṇiya (Sanskrit, Kalyāṇi), a place six miles from Colombo which for several centuries had been closely associated with Buddhism in Ceylon.[123]

Since the cooperation of the temple at Kälaṇiya would be invaluable for the performance of *upasampadā* ceremonies in that area, Bentara, Maligaspē and others tried to win over to the new fraternity the chief incumbent of this temple, Māpiṭigama Saṃgharakkhita. Māpiṭigama, however, not merely refused to give his cooperation; he even actively worked against the new fraternity. When Maligaspē wrote to Kandy

[120] Yagirala Prajñānanda, *op. cit.*, p. 415.

[121] C.N.A. 5/63/57/(1), printed in *ibid.*, pp. 415–16.

[122] Labugama Laṃkānanda, *Jayavardhanapura Kōṭṭē Śrī Kalyāṇi Sāmagrīdharma Mahā Saṃgha Sabhāva* (Colombo, 1964), p. 9.

[123] Regarding the history of Kälaṇiya, see H. C. P. Bell and A. Mendis Gunasekara, 'Kelani Vihāra and its Inscriptions', *CALR*, I (1916) 145–61; and pp. 38–39, above.

asking the Mahā Nāyaka to send five monks to officiate at the proposed *upasampadā* ceremony at Kälaṇiya (on the Vesak full-moon day of 1856),[124] Māpiṭigama addressed a letter to the Mahā Nāyaka affirming his own loyalty to Kandy and urging the Mahā Nāyaka to disallow the proposed ceremony at Kälaṇiya.[125] A similar letter was also written by Hikkaḍuvē at about the same time.[126] Both Māpiṭigama and Hikkaḍuvē in their letters insisted that the well-established practice of performing *upasampadā* ceremonies of the Siyam fraternity only at Kandy should be maintained unimpaired.

On 12 May 1856, after a delay of more than three months, the Mahā Nāyaka of Malvatta sent a reply to Maligaspē's letter of 5 February. In this reply, he declined to comply with Maligaspē's request (to send five Kandyan monks to officiate at Kälaṇiya). Also, as could have been anticipated, he expressed his unwillingness to give his sanction to an *upasampadā* ceremony performed anywhere else than at Kandy.[127]

Before the arrival of this letter, however, all necessary arrangements had been made by Maligaspē and others to hold the *upasampadā* ceremony at Kälaṇiya as planned. Since Māpiṭigama was unwilling to place his temple at their disposal, Maligaspē obtained a piece of land close to the Kälaṇi river from a wealthy layman in the area, Mulhiriyāvē Lēkam, and had the necessary buildings erected there.[128] Paying no regard to the Mahā Nāyaka's letter, the first *upasampadā* ceremony of the new fraternity was performed on 22 May 1856. At this ceremony, twenty-one novices were given higher ordination, with Bentara and Maligaspē acting as *upādhyāyas*, and Pānadurē, Päpiliyānē and Valānē together with five other monks —Uḍugampola Ratanapāla of the Bellanvila temple, Baddegama Saraṇaṃkara of the Pāmankaḍa temple, Talaṃgama Sumaṃgala, Kataluvē Atthadassī and Boraläsgamuvē Piyadassī—acting as *karmācāryayas*.[129]

[124] Maligaspē wrote two letters to this effect. The second letter, dated 5 February 1856, is given in Labugama Laṃkānanda, *op. cit.*, pp. 11–13.

[125] C.N.A. 5/63/57/(2). This letter is dated 14 March 1856.

[126] Parts of this letter are given in Yagirala Prajñānanda, *op. cit.*, pp. 63–64, and Labugama Laṃkānanda, *op. cit.*, pp. 13–14. In neither place is the exact date given. The reference in the letter to the 'forthcoming' Sinhalese New Year suggests that it was written some time before the middle of April (1856).

[127] This letter is given in Labugama Laṃkānanda, *op. cit.*, pp. 15–16.

[128] *Ibid.*, pp. 9–10.

[129] *Ibid.*, pp. 16–18.

The inevitable retaliation followed from those who were opposed to the new fraternity. Māpiṭigama, whose temple, as we have noted earlier, was situated in the area where the *upasampadā* ceremony was held, and whose power and influence presumably were affected by the success of the new fraternity, wrote to Kandy on 8 June 1856 urging the Mahā Nāyaka to instruct all the monks in his area to dissociate themselves from the monks of the new fraternity.[130] The Mahā Nāyaka, of course, needed very little persuasion in this matter. On 13 July, he, together with the Mahā Nāyaka of Asgiriya, wrote to the monks who had been loyal to Kandy, condemning the *upasampadā* ceremony of the schismatic (*bhedakāra*) monks, and exhorting them to suspend all contact with those monks pending a final decision from Kandy.[131]

This order obviously implied that Maligaspē could no longer function as the chief monk of the Siyam fraternity in the Colombo District. In his place, Vādduvē Dhammānanda, a monk who had been loyal to Kandy, was instructed by the Mahā Nāyaka to perform those functions and was given an 'appointment' to that effect.[132]

Beyond this the Mahā Nāyaka could do very little. On the most important issue, namely, that of preventing the performance of *upasampadā* ceremonies somewhere other than at Kandy, he could do nothing. There were appeals from the low-country loyalists that the Mahā Nāyaka should petition the governor and the Queen of England on this matter, as it involved a breach of established custom as well as a threat to the authority of the Mahā Nāyaka.[133] As the basis of such petitions they presumably had in mind the undertakings given by the British government in the Kandyan Convention of 1815. But the Mahā Nāyaka himself does not seem to have taken any action in this regard; by the 1850s, he may very well have realized the futility of such appeals to the British government.

[130] C.N.A. 5/63/57/(2); partially reproduced in *ibid.*, p. 20.

[131] C.N.A. 5/63/57/(4); partially reproduced in Labugama Laṃkānanda, *op. cit.*, pp. 20–21.

[132] Maligaspē to Pälpolagē Juan and other laymen, 1 January 1865, in Yagirala Prajñānanda, *op. cit.*, pp. 505–6; and Vādduvē to the Mahā Nāyaka, 24 April 1869, *ibid.*, pp. 70–71.

[133] Hikkaḍuvē to the Mahā Nāyaka, *ca.* April 1856 (referred to above), and Valagedara Dhammadassī (Chief Monk of the Galle District) to the Mahā Nāyaka, 25 April 1858, C.N.A. 5/63/57/(5), printed in Yagirala Prajñānanda, *op. cit.*, 62–63.

iii. THE AMARAPURA FRATERNITY IN THE KANDYAN PROVINCES

With the end of the old Kandyan kingdom in 1815 and the resultant weakening of the authority structure of the Kandyan ecclesiastical establishment, the Amarapura fraternity, which up to 1815 had been confined to the low country, gradually began to expand its activities into the Kandyan provinces. The initiative for this expansion came only in part from the low-caste monks who had established the Amarapura fraternity in the low country at the beginning of the century. It came far more strongly from certain monks in the Kandyan provinces who originally belonged to the Siyam fraternity, but who, for one reason or another, were in conflict with their ecclesiastical superiors. They, in contrast to their low-country brethren, belonged to the Goyigama caste. And for them the existence of the Amarapura fraternity with its radical ideology was an easy and ready-made avenue for the expression and organization of their protest against the establishment.

Reference has already been made to the case of the Huduhumpola temple where two successive chief monks, Mayilavävē Guṇaratana and Ram̆bukvällē Sobhita, got themselves reordained within the Amarapura fraternity.[134] About the same time, another monk of the Asgiriya chapter, Tōlaṃgamuvē Siddhārttha, who lived in the Asgiriya temple itself as a pupil of the Mahā Nāyaka, Yaṭanvela Sunanda, joined in the criticism of the Asgiriya *sīmā*; and having incurred the displeasure of his teacher, he left Asgiriya and obtained reordination within the Amarapura fraternity at Balapiṭiya in 1834. Very soon he became the most vociferous opponent of the Siyam fraternity as well as the most vigorous champion of the Amarapura fraternity in the Kandyan provinces. He had considerable success, particularly in the border province of Sabaragamuva, where the local chiefs gave him their support. 'Suffragam', wrote de Silva, who had spent six years in this area as a schoolteacher, 'may at present be regarded as the chief seat of this [Amarapura] reformation, and where the difference in the tenets and principles of the two sects [Siyam and Amarapura] is wider and greater than anywhere else, though the Amarapoora sect originated with the Chalia priests of the district of Ambalangoda and Galle, about

[134] Section i-*d* (above) of this chapter.

40 years ago'.[135] And 'Tolangomua, a priest who was originally of the Asgiriya establishment in Kandy', he observed, 'may be regarded as the great champion of the Amarapoora sect at Suffragam and as the strictest reformer of the corruptions'.[136]

Sabaragamuva, situated in the border regions of the old Kandyan kingdom, had a long tradition of relative autonomy; and some of its chiefs had been noted for their rebelliousness against the authority of the kings of Kandy. It was in this province that Ähälēpola in 1814 launched the rebellion against Śrī Vikrama Rājasiṃha, as a result of which the king divided the *disāva* into two parts to reduce the powers of its provincial chief.[137] The British, with similar intentions, divided it further–into three parts–in 1818.[138] In religious matters too it appears that the chiefs of this area were not inclined to give their wholehearted support to the authority of the Mahā Nāyakas in Kandy. In 1825 they were in support of taking the incumbency of Śrīpāda away from the Mahā Nāyaka of Malvatta and giving it over to Gāllē Medhaṃkara, who was a low-country monk.[139] And now, in the next decade, they were ready to give their patronage to Tōlaṃgamuvē, who was quite openly protesting against the religious establishment in Kandy. De Silva, who was quoted earlier, wrote in another place:

> The inhabitants of Suffragam at conquest of Kandy by the British as other Kandyans were Buddhists of the sect called Siamese–the form of Buddhistical faith that had been established long ago by their kings; but of late a change has taken place. . . . The doctrines of the sect of Buddhists called Amarapoora . . . have made rapid progress in the Kandyan provinces, more particularly in Suffragam. It was introduced into this district by the exertions of Nugewelle Bandar, commonly called Adigar, a nephew of late Doloswella Dissawa. As this individual (Nugewelle Bandar) was related to almost all the respectable families of Suffragam, and being a Pali scholar, many of the respectable families at once

[135] A. de Silva, 'On the Corruption of Buddhism and the Different Tenets, Opinions and Principles of the Amarapoora and Siamese Sects', Appendix XII to George Lee's translation of John Ribeyro's *History of Ceylon* (Colombo, 1847).

[136] *Ibid.*

[137] Above, p. 79.

[138] Ralph Pieris, *Sinhalese Social Organization* (Colombo, 1956), p. 127.

[139] The 'Report' of Mahavalatännē, Dolosvala and Delgoḍa to the Agent of Government at Sabaragamuva, 27 August 1825, C.N.A.

became converts to this reformed and orthodox Buddhism, so much so, that 30 priests at once underwent *upasampada* ordination of Amarapura sect in 1837: and since, all the influential persons have come into the pale of Amarapura faith.[140]

As a Christian, perhaps, de Silva in this memorandum somewhat misrepresents the position of the Amarapura Nikāya in viewing it as a 'sect' into which *laymen* were converted rather than as a fraternity to which *monks* affiliated themselves. Yet, a similar misrepresentation could be found even in the comments, made in the course of a conference in Kandy, by the monks of the Malvatta and Asgiriya temples—if we can place reliance on the minutes of the conference, which have been recorded in English by a government official. At this conference, which was held in October 1847 to discuss plans for the management of Buddhist affairs, the monks are reported as having told Governor Torrington that 'they have every wish to be on good terms with the Chiefs, but they fear the Chiefs have not much good feeling towards them. Some of them indeed belong to a different sect, not the Siamese sect but the Amarapoora sect, which is not pure Buddhist'.[141]

Notwithstanding these remarks, the position of laymen in relation to *nikāyas* (which have been erroneously translated as 'sects') was not as members, but simply as patrons (*dāyakas*). It is by no means unlikely that some (Goyigama) chiefs preferred to patronize the Amarapura fraternity, having in all probability been impressed with their more radical ideals and practices; but giving their patronage to monks of one fraternity in no way prevented them from extending it, if they so wished, to monks of another fraternity. What seems generally true of the Sabaragamuva chiefs is that they tended to patronize pious and learned monks with no great regard to their fraternity or to their social origins.

The expansion of the Amarapura fraternity in the Kandyan provinces was perhaps hindered to some extent by the action of the government and the decision of the Supreme Court in relation to the Huduhumpola Temple. The government made a case for the dismissal of Ram̆bukvällē[142] on the ground that the Kandyan Convention of 1815 bound the govern-

[140] 'Memorandum' of 9 January 1845 to P. Anstruther (President of the Central Commission), enclosure no. 4, Campbell to Stanley, no. 96 of 8 May 1845, C.O. 54/217.

[141] Enclosure no. 3 to Despatch no. 133 of 14 October 1847, Torrington to Grey, C.O. 54/239.

[142] For the events which led to it, see above, section i-*d* of this chapter.

ment to maintain and protect Buddhism as it was *then* professed by the chiefs and inhabitants of the Kandyan provinces, and that therefore Ram̆bukvällē had forfeited his right to the temple by joining a fraternity which was not in existence in the Kandyan provinces in 1815.[143] This plea was upheld by the Supreme Court, who observed:

> It appearing . . . that one sect, viz., the Siam alone, has existed in Kandy, and that at the time of the foundation of this temple the sovereign was Siamese, the chief of the Asgiri establishment (of which this is avowedly a dependency in matters of faith) Siamese, and the founder of this particular temple Siamese, the Court is of opinion that it would be acting *contra formam doni*, contrary to the undoubted intentions of the founder and of the persons who have endowed this temple with lands, and contrary to the plain construction of the Treaty of 1815, were it to allow this property to pass into the hands of persons who cannot but be deemed to profess an heretical faith by the Siamese Buddhists.[144]

The results of this decision, though of some importance, were not really crucial with regard to the expansion of the Amarapura fraternity in the Kandyan provinces. The decision no doubt dissuaded monks in the older and well-endowed temples from joining the new fraternity. It seems very likely, however, that the appeal of the new fraternity was not so much to these monks (who already had a central place in the traditional religious establishment), as to the monks in the poorer temples who were in the periphery of the establishment. Among them, allegiance to the new fraternity gradually spread over the years, and the decision of the Supreme Court in no way stood as a barrier against them. For the decision of the Supreme Court was merely concerned with the property rights of the Siyam fraternity and not with its authority structure, a fact which was made clear in the judgement itself in the following words:

> There is nothing in its [i.e., the Court's] decree or in the reasons on which it is founded to prevent the Amarapura sect from propagating their sentiments, from buying, building, from occupying pansalas and vihares within the Kandyan territories. The Court merely determines that they cannot usurp the

[143] The relevant portion of the plaint (dated 15 March 1837) instituted by the Government Agent of the Central Province in the District Court of Kandy (case no. 8950) is reproduced in P. E. Pieris, *Sinhalē and the Patriots*, pp. 569–70.

[144] 'The Crown vs. Rambukwelle Unnanse', quoted in Lawrie, *Gazetteer*. The judgement is dated 28 December 1838.

property of others and turn it to purposes evidently opposed to the religious wishes of the holders of such property.[145]

In addition to Sabaragamuva, the adjoining province of Ūva also became an active centre of Amarapura activity by the middle of the nineteenth century.[146]

None of the Amarapura monks in the Kandyan provinces, in contrast to their brethren in the low country, proceeded to Burma for higher ordination. The earliest among them to join the fraternity, like Mayilavävē and Tōlaṃgamuvē, came down to the low country for higher ordination. When, later on, they organized higher ordination ceremonies of their own in the Kandyan provinces, they performed these ceremonies under the presidency of Bōgahapiṭiyē Dhammajoti, a low-country Salāgama monk who had gone to Burma and returned to the island in 1811 with higher ordination.[147] Bōgahapiṭiyē spent the latter part of his life in the Kandyan provinces. Though he received no formal act of appointment from the government, he has come to be regarded as the first chief monk and founder of the Amarapura fraternity in the Kandyan provinces.[148]

145 *Ibid.*

146 Välitara Dhīrālaṃkāra, 'Mahā Vihāra Vaṃśaya hā Amarapura Nikāya', *Itihāsa Kathā*, II (1926) 205.

147 *Ibid.*, pp. 204–5.

148 *Ibid.*

Chapter IV

THE SEGMENTATION OF THE AMARAPURA FRATERNITY, 1815–1865

i. THE PROBLEM OF COHESION IN THE AMARAPURA FRATERNITY

The Amarapura fraternity, from its very beginning, was not destined to have an ecclesiastical organization even remotely resembling that of the Siyam fraternity. Whereas the Siyam fraternity was established in the middle of the eighteenth century with the help of just one group of (Siamese) monks who were brought to Ceylon from Siam, the Amarapura fraternity had its origins in five different groups of (Ceylonese) monks who went to Burma and returned with higher ordination at different times during the first two decades of the nineteenth century. Thus, even at the time of its enthusiastic beginning, the Amarapura fraternity had more the character of a loose federation of fraternities than that of a unified and centralized fraternity, to which the Siyam fraternity approximated at the time of its establishment. In fact, although all the five groups of Ceylonese monks who returned from Burma came to be looked upon as belonging to one Amarapura fraternity, not all of them had their higher ordination at the city of Amarapura in Burma.[1] Even their Burmese preceptors, therefore, did not belong to one clear and immediate line of pupillary succession. In contrast, all the Siyam fraternity monks could, and did, trace their immediate spiritual ancestry to just one person – the monk Upāli who led the Siamese mission to Ceylon in 1753.[2]

Of even greater significance in relation to this contrast between the

[1] Kapugama Dhammakkhandha had his higher ordination at Ratanapura (Avā), and Kataluvē Guṇaratana at Haṃsāvatī (Pegu) in Rāmañña (Lower Burma). Polvattē Buddhadatta, 'Lakdiva Buruma Nikāyē Itihāsaya', in N. A. Jayawickrama (ed.), *Paranavitana Felicitation Volume* (Colombo, 1965), pp. 37–38.

[2] The Siyam fraternity officially refers to itself as Śyāmopāli Mahā Nikāya, meaning 'the great fraternity of Upāli of Siam'.

Siyam and the Amarapura fraternities is the fact that while all the founders of the Siyam fraternity (with the negligible exception of one or two individuals) belonged to just one caste (Goyigama), the founders of the Amarapura fraternity belonged to three different castes. Of the five groups of monks who went to Burma, three were Salāgama, the other two Karāve and Durāve respectively. Upon their return to the island, these five groups certainly experienced considerable interaction, and at times even worked in close collaboration with one another. At the same time, they maintained their separate identities. They had different *sīmās* for the performance of their higher-ordination ceremonies, and this helped them to maintain, and perpetuate, different lines of pupillary succession. And the pupils of the founders (and later on, of their successors) were almost invariably recruited within the ranks of their own castes.[3]

Furthermore, in contrast to the Siyam fraternity, which (traditionally) had one major patron, the King of Kandy, the Amarapura fraternity had no such overwhelming figure from whom patronage was forthcoming. Its different branches had different patrons, usually local headmen, and since these patrons themselves came from different localities and belonged to different castes, there was no pressure from them on the monks to amalgamate as one unified fraternity.

There was one noteworthy effort on the part of Salāgama headmen to unify the different groups of Salāgama monks, an effort which had a good chance of success, as the Salāgamas, though internally divided into sub-castes, appeared as one caste vis-à-vis the other castes. Besides, the Salāgamas alone had a chief monk formally appointed over them by the government. Yet this attempt to unify them—as we shall see in section iii, below—had but a very temporary success. The chief monk of the fraternity, though formally appointed by the government, had no actual governmental backing in the enforcement of his authority. And he could scarcely have expected any such backing during a time when the government was

[3] Even the practice of ordaining a close kinsman as one's chief-pupil, a practice which was common in the Siyam fraternity, especially in the Kandyan provinces, was not uncommon in the Amarapura fraternity. For instance, the chief-pupil of Aṁbagahapitiyē Ñāṇavimala, Bēratuḍuvē Dhammādhāra, was his nephew; and the chief pupil of Bēratuḍuve, Aṁbagahapiṭiyē Vimalasāra, was in turn *his* nephew (and therefore, Aṁbagahapiṭiyē Ñāṇavimala's grand-nephew). Polvattē Buddhadatta, *Samīpātītayehi Bauddhācārayayō* (Ambalaṃgoḍa, 1950), pp. 25 and 110.

busy withdrawing the support it had given–under more pressing obligations–to the authority of the chief monks of the Siyam fraternity.

Even the Siyam fraternity, despite its homogeneity (in relation to caste), and despite its tradition of centralized authority, did not entirely succeed –as we saw in the last chapter–in preserving its unity in the nineteenth century. There were conflicts between its two major colleges; and there were also conflicts, with more lasting results, between its Kandyan and low-country branches. That the Amarapura fraternity, which from its very beginning was far more heterogeneous in its composition and which, moreover, was lacking in a structure of centralized authority, had had to face problems of a similar nature–and in far greater intensity–hardly comes, therefore, as a surprise. What is significant is that the result of these problems was not a complete *disorganization* of the Amarapura fraternity; the result was rather a process of *segmentation* into more or less clear, identifiable and viable units.

The Amarapura fraternity was described in 1861 by Laṃkāgoḍa Dhīrānanda (of whom more later, in section iii of this chapter) in a message to the Saṃgharāja of Burma[4] as consisting of four groups of monks: (1) a Salāgama group, (2) a Karāve group, (3) a Durāve group–all in the coastal regions, and (4) a Goyigama group in the 'hilly regions', who, having left the Siyam fraternity to which they originally belonged, received ordination from monks in group (1).

At the time that Laṃkāgoḍa wrote this message, he himself was deeply involved in a controversy within the Salāgama group, a controversy which, soon afterwards, split that group into two: a higher-Salāgama group and a lower-Salāgama group.

In addition, there was a fifth group of monks–not mentioned by Laṃkāgoḍa, understandably, since they were not conspicuous as a *separate* group in 1861–namely, a group of Goyigama monks in the low country, who, having left the Siyam fraternity, were at this time with the Amarapura fraternity, but who, not long afterwards, were to leave the Amarapura fraternity as well and organize an entirely new fraternity–the Rāmañña fraternity.

It is to the unravelling of the story of this segmentation that the rest of this chapter will be devoted.

[4] *Pāli Sandesāvalī*, ed. Polvattē Buddhadatta (Ambalaṃgoḍa, 1962), document no. 23.

ii. KARĀVE AND DURĀVE MONKS VERSUS SALĀGAMA MONKS: THE EMERGENCE OF THE DHAMMARAKKHITAVAṂSA AND THE KALYĀṆIVAṂSA FRATERNITIES

Salāgama monks, as has been noted,[5] were the first among the non-Goyigama monks in Ceylon to proceed to Burma and return with *upasampadā* ordination. The Karāve and the Durāve monks who returned to the island not long afterwards[6] had close contacts with these Salāgama monks, and during the early days at any rate, worked in close collaboration with them. They did not feel inclined, however, to submit entirely to the authority of the Salāgama monks; indeed, evidence seems to indicate clearly that, from the very beginning, they were keen to obtain for their own groups some form of governmental recognition similar to that which had been granted to the Salāgama monks.

Thus on 15 November 1814–ten months after Kapugama Dhammakkhandha (Salāgama) had obtained a 'Certificate' from the government in confirmation of the office, title and honours that he had received from the King of Burma[7]–the leading monks of the Karāve and the Durāve castes held a meeting at Kōṭṭegoḍa in the Southern Province of Ceylon and selected a Karāve monk, Vilēgoḍa Puññasāra of Ambalaṃgoḍa, as their chief monk; in the following year they petitioned the government, praying for official confirmation of that selection.[8] This petition failed to procure an Act of Appointment for Vilēgoḍa. In the following years, he petitioned the government with remarkable perseverance, repeatedly asking for an Act of Appointment.[9] When, in the year 1825, the government appointed a chief monk over the Salāgama monks,[10] Vilēgoḍa insisted on his claims with added vigour, now asking to be appointed at least over the Karāve monks, if not over both the Karāve and the Durāve monks.[11] In a petition (dated 4 June 1829) addressed to the Colebrooke Commission, he wrote:

[5] Pp. 94 ff.

[6] Pp. 100, above.

[7] P. 99, above.

[8] C.N.A. 5/63/47/(158). This petition, dated 15 June 1815, was signed by 31 *bhikkhus* (including Kataluvē Guṇaratana and Attuḍāvē Dhammarakkhita, who, respectively, led the Karāve and Durāve missions to Burma) and 23 *sāmaṇeras* of the two castes.

[9] C.N.A. 5/63/44/(142), (145), (149).

[10] See above, p. 99.

[11] C.N.A. 5/63/44/(143).

Your Honor's Petitioner does not want himself to be made head Priest, but as he is considered as the principal of this [Karāve] cast and as such he is instructed with the management of the Religious duties, he is anxious to obtain for his cast also, the same liberties enjoyed by other casts of this Island, namely, the Vellale [Goyigama] and Mahabadde [Salagāma], in order that this cast of people alone may not be deprived from the benefit of worshipping their Religion.[12] . . . The Petitioner cannot imagine [he observed further] why the Priests of this [Karave] cast cannot have a head over them while Government has appointed one for the Mahabadde which is a lower cast than that of the Petitioner's.[13]

The tendency to regard the Salāgamas as inferior to themselves was common to both the Karāvas and the Durāvas, and this was a factor which made them somewhat reluctant, even initially, to give their whole-hearted support to the Salāgama efforts to challenge Goyigama monopolies. The Karāvas and the Durāvas were hardly less keen than the Salāgamas to acquire the coveted Goyigama privileges; yet they were not keen to do so under Salāgama leadership. Indeed, if compelled to choose they rather preferred the authority of the Goyigamas to that of the Salāgamas. It was no doubt for this reason that, even as early as 1772, when the Salāgamas organized an *upasampadā* ceremony at Toṭagamuva in opposition to the authority of the Kandyan chief monks,[14] the Karāve and Durāve headmen, rather than encouraging the monks of their castes to obtain *upasampadā* along with the Salāgama monks, made an appeal to the Mahā Nāyaka of Malvatta, praying him to use his influence over the king to obtain his approval for the ordination of Karāve and Durāve monks at Kandy.[15] Only when this appeal failed did they help their monks to proceed to Burma and obtain *upasampadā*–in the same manner as Salāgama headmen had helped their own monks a few years earlier. Upon their return to the island, the Karāve and Durāve monks wished, as was noted earlier, to be placed under their own chief monks properly appointed by the government. Failing this, they apparently preferred to be under the

[12] C.O. 416/30 (petition no. 190).

[13] *Ibid.* This petition was supported by another (dated 1 July 1829) signed by some Karāve laymen of the Colombo, Galle and Mātara districts, C.N.A. 5/63/44/(155).

[14] See above, p. 97.

[15] Though this letter is not available, its contents can be inferred from the Mahā Nāyaka's reply, C.N.A. 5/63/8/(3).

authority of Goyigama chief monks rather than that of Salāgama ones. Vilēgoḍa, in the petition quoted above, having referred to the relative inferiority of the Salāgamas, continued: 'If this [i.e., the appointment of a Karāve chief monk] cannot be allowed to them, they [the Karāve monks] will remain satisfied by being placed under the Head Priests of the Vellale Cast provided they will be ordained . . . and can enjoy all the Religious Rights without reserve'.[16]

The government, however, paid no heed to these requests; it did not appoint a Karāve chief monk, nor did it take any action towards placing Karāve monks under the formal jurisdiction of Goyigama chief monks. All that it did was to appoint, in 1835, a Salāgama monk, Bōpāgoḍa Sumana, as chief monk over the entire Amarapura fraternity in succession to Aṁbagahapiṭiyē Ñāṇavimala who, in 1825, had been appointed over only the Salāgama monks.[17] This was clearly not what the Karāve and the Durāve monks wanted. They made no formal protest against the authority of Bōpāgoḍa Sumana; there was no need for them to do so, as Bōpāgoḍa, quite understandably, did not presume to have much authority over them. Nor did they stage a dramatic or sudden withdrawal; there was really no 'unified' fraternity for them to withdraw themselves from. They simply continued to maintain, and in time consolidate, their separate identities.

The Durāvas began, quite early, to go their own way, and they had some initial support from the Salāgamas. When the first Durāve monk who went to Burma (in 1807), Attuḍāvē Dhammarakkhita, returned to the island (*ca.* 1813), an *upasampadā* ceremony was performed under his presidency at Devundara; and Aṁbagahapiṭiyē Ñāṇavimala, the Salāgama founder of the Amarapura fraternity, was duly informed of this ceremony. Aṁbagahapiṭiyē, in his reply,[18] expressed satisfaction at the manner in which the ceremony had been performed and asked Attuḍāvē to supervise the religious activities of the Amarapura monks in his own area. He also suggested that the new group of monks under Attuḍāvē's leadership be called, after the name of its leader, Dhammarakkhitavaṃsa Amarapura Nikāya (The Dhammarakkhita 'lineage' of the Amarapura fraternity).

[16] C.O. 416/30 (petition no. 190).
[17] See above, ch. II, n. 82.
[18] C.N.A. 5/63/106/(3).

Am̆bagahapiṭiyē, of course, made no suggestion that membership of this 'lineage' should be limited to the Durāve caste. But that, not surprisingly, was what in fact happened.

Of the three non-Goyigama castes who were involved in founding the Amarapura fraternity, the Durāve caste was the smallest[19] as well as the least powerful. Similarly, of the different branches of the Amarapura fraternity, the one which consisted of Durāve monks, the Dhammarakkhitavaṃsa, was also the least prominent on the religious scene at this time. Their activities were largely confined to the southernmost region of Ceylon, in certain parts of which the Durāvas were numerically preponderant. Their main centre was at Devundara where they had their first *upasampadā* ceremony. Mīripänna, a village six miles south of Galle, also came to be closely associated with them because of the fame of the Durāve incumbent of the temple there, Mīripännē Dhammaratana (1768–1851), who was well known in his time as a Sinhalese poet.[20]

The Karāve monks, in contrast to the Durāve monks, had their headquarters (Doḍandūva) closer to that of the Salāgama monks. Hence they had more day-to-day contact with the Salāgama monks than did the Durāve monks. These contacts included, and no doubt were reinforced by, the joint performance, occasionally, of important ecclesiastical acts.[21] Yet the awareness among Karāve monks of their separate identity was in no way diminished by this, as was shown above with reference to their attempts to have their own chief monks. It is worth recalling, furthermore, that although the Karāve monks were generally looked upon as belonging to the Amarapura fraternity, their leader and founder, Kataluvē Guṇaratana, was ordained not at Amarapura but at Haṃsāvatī in Rāmañña. Their Burmese preceptors, therefore, were not the same as those of the majority of their (non-Karāve) Amarapura brethren in Ceylon. By virtue of their original connection with Rāmañña, the Karāve monks, at times, used the designation Rāmañña Fraternity to distinguish themselves from

[19] At the (partial) census of 1824, there were 19,655 Durāvas, as against 26,301 Salāgamas and 55,293 Karāvas in the Chilaw, Colombo, Galle and Tangalla districts. (The number of Goyigamas in the same area was 191,500.) *Return of the Population of the Island of Ceylon* (Colombo, 1827).

[20] 'As a Sinhalese poet he is unrivalled at the present day', wrote James Alwis in 1850. 'On the Elu Language, its Poetry and its Poets', *JRAS(CB)*, II (1850) 149. For a brief account of his life and work, see Carolis de Silva, *The Life of Dhammaratana of Miripenna* (Galle, 1868).

[21] *Pāli Sandesāvalī*, documents no. 19 and 20.

the other branches of the Amarapura fraternity.[22] They gave up this designation, in all probability, some time after 1864 when a new fraternity under that name appeared in the island (see section iv, below), and thereafter adopted the name Kalyāṇivaṃsa after the name of the *sīmā* (at Haṃsāvatī) where their founder was ordained in 1809.[23]

From their original centre at Doḍandūva, the Kalyāṇivaṃsa gradually spread northwards along the coastline into areas like Kalutara and Pānadurē, where the Karāve caste was numerically preponderant and–particularly in the latter half of the nineteenth century–economically dominant. The fraternity expanded steadily from the original group of 9 monks in 1810 up to 100 monks by the middle of the century, and then up to 150 and 200 respectively at the end of the next two decades.[24]

iii. SALĀGAMA MONKS: DIVISION INTO MŪLAVAṂSA AND SADDHAMMAVAṂSA FRATERNITIES.

Salāgama monks of the coastal regions belonged to two major lines of pupillary succession: (1) that of Am̆bagahapiṭiyē Ñāṇavimala, who returned from Burma in 1803; and (2) that of Kapugama Dhammakkhandha, who returned in 1809.[25]

The first of these lines had their main temple at Välitara and their *sīmā* (the consecrated boundary where *upasampadā* ceremonies were performed) on the river Mādu at Balapiṭiya. The second line had their main temple at Daḍalla and their *sīmā* on the river Giṃ at Giṃtoṭa. Though there was no enmity between these two groups of monks, they generally maintained their distinct identities and performed their ecclesiastical acts separately.

Salāgama laymen who disliked this separateness showed a keenness to unify the two groups; and apparently they succeeded in bringing about

[22] *Ibid.*, document no. 5.

[23] The *sīmā* at Haṃsāvatī was known as 'Kalyāṇi' because it was consecrated by a group of Burmese monks who obtained *upasampadā* ordination at Kalyāṇi (Kälaṇiya) in Ceylon in the fifteenth century. See Taw Sein Ko, 'A Preliminary Study of the Kalyani Inscriptions', *Indian Antiquary*, XXII (1893) pp. 11 ff. Hence, incidentally, the similarity of the names of 'Kalyāṇivaṃsa' and of the Siyam fraternity splinter (see above, ch. III, sec. ii) which had its first ordination ceremony at Kälaṇiya in 1856.

[24] *Pāli Sandesāvalī*, documents no. 5, 19, 20, 26.

[25] See above, pp. 97–99. Pupils of the third Salāgama monk who returned from Burma, Bōgahapiṭiyē Dhammajoti, were (as was noted in ch. III, sec. iii) mainly in the Kandyan provinces.

this unity not long after Kapugama Dhammakkhandha, the founder of the second line of monks, had given up his robes and embraced Christianity in 1816.[26] In the early 1820s they invited the Daḍalla monks, who were then under the leadership of Bōpāgoḍa Sumana, the chief pupil of Kapugama, to Välitara; after a five-day conference, they persuaded the Daḍalla monks to unite themselves with the Välitara monks.[27] Afterwards, on the appeal of both the monks and the leading laymen of the caste, Am̆bagahapiṭiyē, the founder of the first line of monks, was formally appointed chief monk over all the Salāgama monks by the government in 1825.[28] When Am̆bagahapiṭiyē died in 1834, the office of chief monk was granted to (the aforementioned) Bōpāgoḍa Sumana.[29]

It was during Bōpāgoḍa's term of office, which lasted until his death in 1864, that the great schism within the Salāgama section of the Amarapura fraternity occurred. This schism saw the end of the short-lived unity of the Salāgamas. The leading figure behind the schism was Laṃkāgoḍa Dhīrānanda, the chief pupil of Bōpāgoḍa. Laṃkāgoḍa belonged to the higher of the Salāgama subcastes,[30] and as the new splinter group which began under his leadership got itself organized into an autonomous fraternity, its membership tended to be restricted to this higher subcaste.[31] Yet the importance of the caste factor at the time that the schism actually began is not easy to ascertain. The major point at issue, then, was the validity of the *sīmā* of the unified Salāgama fraternity.

[26] Regarding his conversion, see above, ch. II, n. 84.

[27] Polvattē Buddhadatta, *op. cit.* (1950), p. 52.

[28] C.N.A. 5/63/21/(2).

[29] The Act of Appointment granted to him is reproduced in H. J. M. Vikramaratna Sēnānāyaka, *Amarapura Śrī Saddhammavaṃsa Nikāya piḷibañda ati saṃkṣipta Itihāsa Katāva* (Ambalaṃgoḍa, 1928), Appendix III.

[30] The Salāgamas, at the end of the eighteenth century, were clearly divided into four subcastes: (1) Panividakārayo (messengers), (2) Hēvāyo (soldiers), (3) Kuruñdukārayo (cinnamon-peelers), (4) Uliyakkārayo (coolies). The barriers between these subcastes were maintained by law during the Dutch administration (C.O. 416/5). In the early years of the British administration, the laws regulating these distinctions ceased to be operative, and gradually the two smaller subcastes, (1) and (4), were absorbed into the larger two, (2) and (3). The new twofold division persisted right through the nineteenth century and is of importance even today. See Bryce Ryan, *Caste in Modern Ceylon* (New Brunswick, New Jersey, 1953), p. 110.

[31] The (sub) caste difference of Laṃkāgoḍa's pupils comes out clearly in the dispute that took place in the late nineteenth century between them and the pupils of Bōpāgoḍa over the possession of Jayasēkarārāmaya at Demaṭagoḍa, the temple that Laṃkāgoḍa occupied at the time of his death in January 1871. C.N.A. 5/63/36/(3).

Before unification, as has been noted, there were two *sīmās* belonging to Salāgama monks: one at Balapiṭiya belonging to Välitara monks, the other at Giṃtoṭa belonging to Daḍalla monks. Soon after the achievement of formal unity, the need to have just one *sīmā* was increasingly felt, for having one *sīmā* was a primary prerequisite for maintaining the formal unity of a fraternity. The one-*sīmā* rule, so long as it could be enforced, compelled the provincial monks to send their pupils annually to the religious 'centre' for higher ordination; and this enabled the chief monks (as illustrated clearly by the Malvatu and Asgiri branches of the Siyam fraternity) not merely to be in repeated contact with the provincial monks, but also to exercise some form of formal and informal control over them.[32]

When the question of having one *sīmā* came up for discussion, the Välitara monks led by Bēratuḍuvē Dhammādhāra, the nephew and chief pupil of their founder, insisted on having the *sīmā* at Balapiṭiya as the *sīmā* of the unified fraternity—with good reason no doubt as this was the earliest *sīmā* established by the Amarapura monks in Ceylon. At first they received no support from the chief monk, Bōpāgoḍa, who, perhaps out of loyalty to his own Daḍalla branch, remained indifferent to their proposal. In fact, in the year 1839, no *upasampadā* ceremonies were held at Balapiṭiya, as Bōpāgoḍa refused to be there during the *upasampadā* season. After some protest by Bēratuḍuvē and his associates,[33] however, he agreed to having Balapiṭiya as the *sīmā* of the unified fraternity. And, in order to meet the needs of the larger (unified) fraternity, the old *sīmā* was enlarged in 1845 so that it could accommodate about a hundred monks at a time. It was the validity of this (enlarged) *sīmā* that Laṃkāgoḍa challenged in 1851.

That Laṃkāgoḍa's challenge soon led to a prolonged controversy, and eventually to schism, is hardly surprising, for the validity of a *sīmā* was of crucial importance to all the monks associated with that *sīmā*. We have, on several previous occasions, referred to the importance of *upasampadā* for the Buddhist order.[34] The importance of *sīmā* was closely related to this, for it was in a *sīmā* that *upasampadā*, as indeed all the other major

[32] No wonder, therefore, that soon after the coastal Salāgama monks had achieved their unity, accusations were levelled against Bōgahapiṭiyē Dhammajoti, the Salāgama monk who was living in the Kandyan provinces, for his practice of performing *upasampadā* ceremonies in different parts of the country. Balapiṭiyē Dhīrānanda and Bēratuḍuvē Dhammādhāra to Bōpāgoḍa Sumana, 28 April 1840, C.N.A. 5/63/47/(88).

[33] *Ibid.*

[34] See esp. pp. 54–55, above.

ecclesiastical acts (*saṃgha kamma*), were performed. The invalidity of a *sīmā* necessarily entailed the invalidity of all the acts performed in that *sīmā*. Thus, a monk who had undergone *upasampadā* ceremonial in a faulty *sīmā* had no right to claim *bhikkhu* status; no right to participate in the communal rites of *bhikkhus*; no right to ordain pupils and thereby perpetuate the fraternity; and so on.

Sīmā, in ordinary usage, means simply a boundary; but in this context it means, more specifically, a boundary demarcating the 'sacred' area (where ecclesiastical acts were performed) from the 'profane' outer world. For this very reason, the boundary had to be very precise and clear-cut. Definitions of different types of boundaries and of different ways of making them constitute the subject matter of a substantial portion of *vinaya* literature.[35] One of these types, which was fairly extensively used in Ceylon, was the *udakukkhepa sīmā*, or the 'boundary fixed by the throwing of water'. The chapter of monks, in this case, assembled on a raft or in a (temporary or permanent) building in the middle of a river (or a lake), and the boundary was fixed by one of the monks, of moderate strength, throwing out water in the four directions. The area inside the four furthermost points where water fell was considered the *sīmā*.

The *sīmā* of Balapiṭiya was of this type. Its basic structure consisted of several pillars in the middle of the river Mādu over which a temporary hall was built during each *upasampadā* season. At the time that this *sīmā* was enlarged in 1845 (to meet the needs of the larger unified fraternity), a bridge was built to approach it from the river bank. This bridge did not actually connect the bank to the building in the middle of the river; it stopped a few feet outside, as otherwise it would have intruded into the 'sacred area'. From the bridge, the monks approached the building over a plank, which was taken away before the commencement of ecclesiastical acts.

Laṃkāgoḍa's contentions were focussed on this bridge. He maintained that although the bridge itself was not connected to the building, a part of

[35] These works, overwhelmingly exegetical rather than canonical, illustrate the increasingly important place that ritual and procedure came to occupy in the Buddhist order. The historical development of the concept of *sīmā* and its importance to the Buddhist monkhood have been examined by Kam̆burupiṭiyē Ariyasēna in 'Sīmāva hā ehi aitihāsika saṃvardhanaya piḷiban̆da tulanātmaka vimarśanayak' (Ph.D. thesis, University of Ceylon, 1967).

it did intrude into the 'sacred area' (demarcated by the throwing of water), thus rendering the boundary *saṃkara* (confused) and therefore irregular and invalid.

Laṃkāgoḍa was considered an authority on *vinaya*; his Sinhalese paraphrase of Buddhadatta's commentary *Vinaya Vinicchaya*, completed in about 1844, was widely acclaimed at the time as a work of great scholarship.[36] His particular concern with problems relating to *vinaya* could be seen in the lengthy epistles exchanged by him with Vajirañāṇa of Siam.[37] In virtue of both his knowledge and ability, he was frequently consulted by his own teacher, Bōpāgoḍa, in the management of the ecclesiastical affairs of the fraternity.

It was, naturally, to Bōpāgoḍa that Laṃkāgoḍa first explained his objections to the Balapiṭiya *sīmā*. At this stage, the teacher was apparently convinced by the pupil's arguments. Together, in 1852, they took to Doḍandūva some twenty Daḍalla monks who had obtained higher ordination at the allegedly faulty *sīmā* and got them reordained with the assistance of the Karāve chief monk, Koggala Dhammasāra of Śayilabimbārāmaya at Doḍandūva.[38]

Soon afterwards, Laṃkāgoḍa wrote to Bēratuḍuvē explaining the need for giving reordination to those among the Välitara monks too who had obtained ordination at Balapiṭiya. When this letter arrived, Bēratuḍuvē assembled the Välitara monks and discussed its contents with them. Some monks, it seems, agreed with Laṃkāgoḍa's arguments and expressed their willingness to undergo reordination; but the others, led by Kahavē Ñāṇānanda, Bēratuḍuvē's chief pupil, expressed their disagreement with Laṃkāgoḍa, and sent him a challenge to prove his case in the midst of a general assembly of monks.[39]

Thus began the Sīmāsaṃkara Vādaya, or the 'Controversy on the Confused Boundary', with its two sides: Saṃkaravādīn ('Confusionists'), led by Laṃkāgoḍa, claiming that the boundary at Balapiṭiya was 'con-

[36] Only the first part of this work, called *Viniścayārttha Dīpanī*, has appeared in print, edited by Talallē Dhīrānanda (Colombo, 1937). The introduction to this edition contains a short biographical sketch of the author.

[37] *Pāli Sandesāvalī*, document no. 24.

[38] *Guṇaratanatissa Sāsanavaṃsa*, quoted in Polvattē Buddhadatta, *op. cit.* (1950), pp. 53–54.

[39] Laṃkāgoḍa Dhīrānanda to the Saṃgharāja of Burma, Buddhist era 2404 (1861), in *Pāli Sandesāvalī*, document no. 23.

CHART

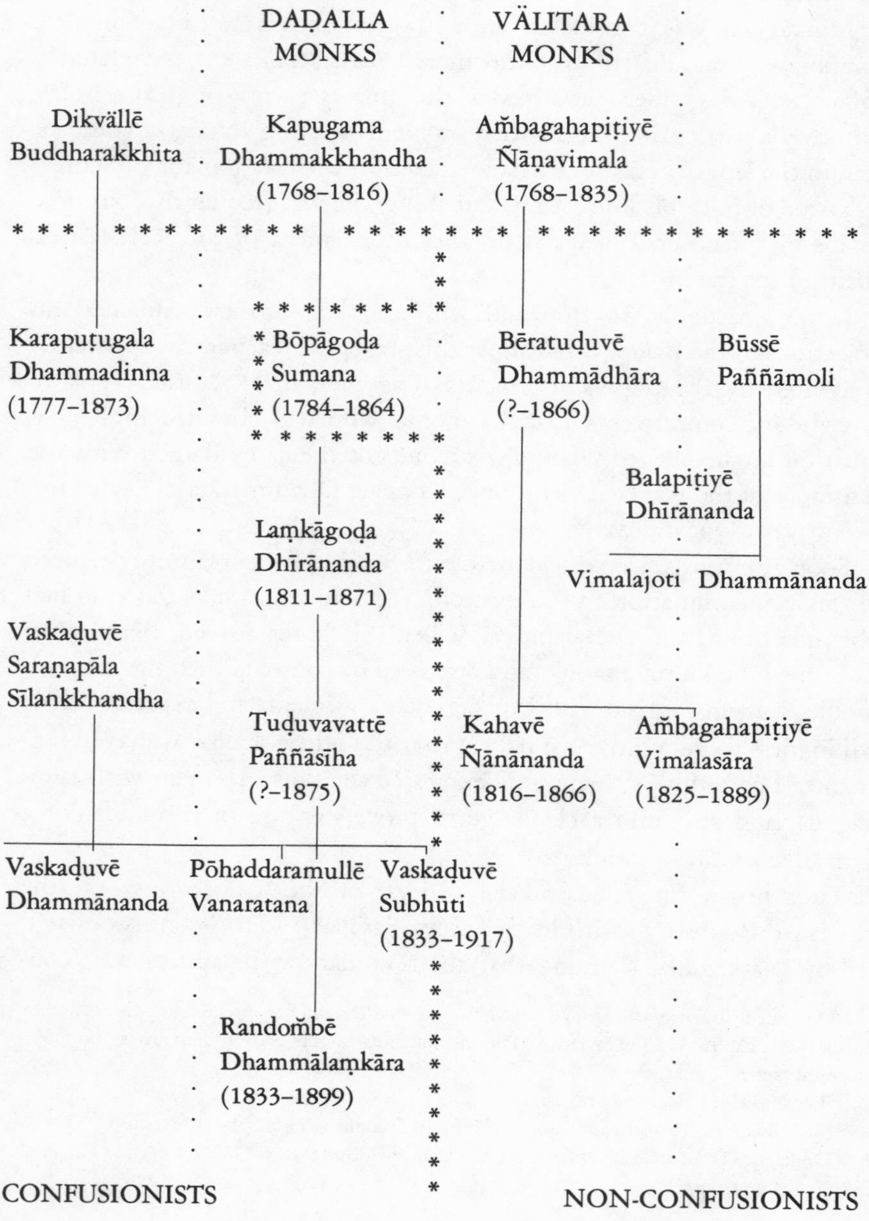

DAḌALLA MONKS
VÄLITARA MONKS
Dikvällē Buddharakkhita
Kapugama Dhammakkhandha (1768–1816)
Aṁbagahapiṭiyē Ñāṇavimala (1768–1835)
Karapuṭugala Dhammadinna (1777–1873)
Bōpāgoḍa Sumana (1784–1864)
Bēratuḍuvē Dhammādhāra (?–1866)
Būssē Paññāmoli
Balapiṭiyē Dhīrānanda
Laṃkāgoḍa Dhīrānanda (1811–1871)
Vimalajoti
Dhammānanda
Vaskaḍuvē Saraṇapāla Sīlankkhandha
Tuḍuvavattē Paññāsīha (?–1875)
Kahavē Ñāṇānanda (1816–1866)
Aṁbagahapiṭiyē Vimalasāra (1825–1889)
Vaskaḍuvē Dhammānanda
Pōhaddaramullē Vanaratana
Vaskaḍuvē Subhūti (1833–1917)
Randoṁbē Dhammālaṃkāra (1833–1899)
CONFUSIONISTS
NON-CONFUSIONISTS

fused', and therefore irregular and invalid; and the Asaṃkaravādīn ('Non-confusionists'), led by Kahavē, defending the validity of the *sīmā* at Balapiṭiya.

The first debate between the two sides was held at Dūvē Vihāre in 1852. Laṃkāgoḍa and Kahavē spoke. No agreement was arrived at; but after this first debate, Bōpāgoḍa, who till then had supported Laṃkāgoḍa, crossed over and joined the 'Non-confusionists'.[40] The manner in which the leading Salāgama monks thereafter divided themselves on the issues of this controversy may be shown in the accompanying chart.

It will be seen that the original division of the Salāgama monks, into Välitara and Daḍalla branches, was directly relevant to the new factionalism: with the major exception of Bōpāgoḍa, all the leading non-confusionists belonged to the Välitara branch while all the leading confusionists belonged to the Daḍalla branch. The Välitara branch, as the older of the two, had a larger membership. Besides, the confusionist cause was not a 'popular' one, since its challenge to the status quo brought discomfort to many a Salāgama monk. The desire to hold the larger group of Salāgama monks under his own sway was, quite possibly, one of the considerations that led Bōpāgoḍa to throw his own weight behind the non-confusionists.

A second debate between the two sides was held in the following year (1853) at Talpiṭiya Vihāre in Kalutara, and then a third in July 1854 at Būssē Vihāre.[41] From the point of view of settling the dispute, these debates were of no use whatsoever. On the contrary, they tended to polarize the two sides more and more. Laṃkāgoḍa, about this time, left Vālukārāmaya at Daḍalla, where Bōpāgoḍa was the chief incumbent, and took up residence at Manḍalārāmaya in Ratgama.

On 1 March 1855, Bōpāgoḍa, by now the real leader of the non-confusionists, invited Laṃkāgoḍa for a further debate. This letter evoked no response from its recipient. Bōpāgoḍa, therefore, followed it up with two more letters to the same effect, dated 3 and 9 May respectively. Laṃkāgoḍa replied at last on the twenty-eighth[42] indicating his lack of interest in debating the same issues all over again, as they had been debated, with no

[40] *Ibid.*

[41] *Ibid.*

[42] These letters have not been traced; but the sequence of events is given in Bōpāgoḍa's Proclamation, which will be cited shortly.

useful outcome, on three previous occasions. If it were really necessary, he was prepared to argue his case again in the midst of an entirely new assembly of monks; but not, he emphasized, in the midst of the same old group of monks.[43]

This, in effect, was an expression of no confidence in Bōpāgoḍa and his non-confusionist supporters; and they, in fact, took it in that spirit. Egged on by his supporters, Bōpāgoḍa acted swiftly. On 30 May, he issued a proclamation suspending Laṃkāgoḍa from the fraternity and prohibiting, on the threat of expulsion, all loyalist monks from being associated in any way with him or any of his confusionist colleagues and pupils.[44] Laṃkāgoḍa was openly accused of causing schism (*bheda*) in the order, a very grave offence (according to *vinaya* regulations) for any monk to be accused of.

The confusionists were in no mood to recant. On the contrary, they now began to canvass support for their cause more actively than ever before. They made overtures to Karāve monks, yet found no favourable response.[45] From the ranks of their Salāgama brethren, however, they were able to muster about a hundred monks behind them. On 29 June 1855, all these monks assembled at Ganēgoḍälla Vihāre in Kosgoḍa (at the invitation of Laṃkāgoḍa's supporter, Karapuṭugala Dhammadinna), and here they gave a written pledge in support of Laṃkāgoḍa and resolved not to associate themselves with those monks who had been ordained at—what they claimed to be—the faulty *sīmā*. The consensus of this meeting was embodied in a pamphlet called 'Saṃkara Viniścaya', which was issued immediately afterwards.[46]

The confusionists were keen to justify their standpoint with reference to the opinions of an independent arbitrator. Thus, just as Bentara Atthadassī in 1845 had referred the 'Adhikamāsa Controversy' for the consideration of Siamese monks, Laṃkāgoḍa and his supporters now decided to solicit the

[43] Laṃkāgoḍa to the Saṃgharāja of Burma, *op. cit.*

[44] C.N.A. 5/63/1/(35).

[45] Laṃkāgoḍato Uḍugampiṭiyē Sumana and Doḍandūvē Piyaratana, 11 June 1855, printed in full in Polvattē Buddhadatta, *op. cit.* (1950), pp. 62–63. It is not possible to find out what reply, if any Uḍugampiṭiyē and Doḍandūvē sent to Laṃkāgoḍa's letter. But three years later, in a letter to the Saṃgharāja of Burma, they made it clear that they were not in sympathy with the confusionist point of view. *Pāli Sandesāvalī*, document no. 20.

[46] C.M.L., A.H. 5.

opinions of Burmese monks on the 'Sīmāsaṃkara Controversy'. In 1856 they sent a special delegation to Burma for this purpose. The delegation consisted of two monks: Vaskaḍuvē Dhammakkhandha and Pōhaddaramullē Vanaratana, pupils of one of Laṃkāgoḍa's allies, Vaskaḍuvē Saraṇapāla Sīlakkhandha. The two monks arrived in Burma in 1857, and the Saṃgharāja of Burma, Ñeyyadhamma, having heard their account and consulted many a relevant religious text, 'declared the existence of the defect of confusion [at the Balapiṭiya *sīmā*] . . . and gave them also a letter containing a message [to the Ceylonese monks]'.[47] This was a significant victory for the confusionists. Copies of the decision given by the Burmese Saṃgharāja were distributed by them among all the monks who had an interest in the controversy.[48]

The non-confusionists refused to be impressed. They, having already replied to the *Saṃkara Viniścaya* with a pamphlet of their own called *Kumaticcheda Viniścaya*,[49] complained that their opponents had misled the Saṃgharāja by not having placed before him all the facts relevant to the controversy; and in order to present the non-confusionist version of the controversy, they immediately sent forth a delegation of their own to Burma, consisting again of two monks, Vimalajoti and Dhammānanda, pupils of Būssē Paññāmoli.

These two monks arrived in Burma in 1858, and soon entered into discussions with the Saṃgharāja.[50] They failed in their attempt to obtain a new ruling on the Sīmāsaṃkara Controversy; the Saṃgharāja stood quite firmly by his original decision. But, having no inclination to take sides, and thereby worsen a schism which was already there among his Sinhalese brethren, he did what he could do in the circumstances not to displease the non-confusionists and to bring about some settlement between the two sides. He treated the Sinhalese delegation with the highest cordiality; and

[47] Paññāsāmi, *Sāsanavaṃsa* (1861), tr. B. C. Law (London, 1952), p. 160. The Saṃgharāja's message, known as 'Sīmā Vivāda Vinicchaya Kathā', has been published, edited by I. P. Minayeff, in the *Journal of the Pali Text Society* (1887), pp. 17–34. Minayeff obtained his copy of the message from Vaskaḍuvē Subhūti, a fellow-pupil of the two delegates who brought it from Burma.

[48] Tuḍuvavattē Paññāsīha (on the instructions of Laṃkāgoḍa and Karapuṭugala) to Mirissē Dhammānanda and Uḍugampiṭiyē Sumana, 10 May 1859, in Polvattē Buddhadatta, *op. cit.* (1950), p. 57.

[49] C.N.A. 5/63/1/(4).

[50] *Sāsanavaṃsa*, p. 160.

upon their return in 1860, he sent through them a very courteous message to Bōpāgoḍa (who was his senior by several years) emphasizing his concern for the amicable settlement of disputes among his Sinhalese brethren. He also sent several gifts to Bōpāgoḍa, together with a new Act of Appointment under the seal of the King of Burma elevating him to the rank of 'Jinorasa Amaravaṃsadhaja Mahādhammarājādhirājaguru'.[51]

In the meantime, the Saṃgharāja, on his own initiative, wrote a letter to the influential Amarapura monk, Bulatgama Sumana—who generally kept aloof from these controversies and who, throughout this period, was doing his best to maintain some sort of unity among Sinhalese monks—asking him to bring the two sides together for a conference and thereby help them to settle the dispute peaceably. Bulatgama soon began to act upon this request. In July 1861 he arranged a meeting between the two sides on neutral ground, in a temple belonging to Karāve monks at Ambalaṃgoḍa. Here he read the letter sent to him by the Saṃgharāja, and appealed to both sides to unite themselves in deference to the Saṃgharāja's appeal. Both parties formally expressed their willingness to do so; but as the meeting progressed it became evident that no real unity was possible without a mutually acceptable solution to the vexed Sīmāsaṃkara Controversy. Neither side was willing to compromise its original stand with regard to that controversy; hence, amidst the squabbles that this problem inevitably gave rise to, the meeting broke up, with the purpose for which it was convened entirely unattained.[52]

There were attempts, even afterwards, to bring the two sides together. But these attempts were no more successful than the one just referred to. Nor did the Sīmāsaṃkara Controversy come to an end with the demise of its early leaders: Bōpāgoḍa in 1864 and Laṃkāgoḍa in 1871. Their pupils and followers continued it with undiminished vigour.[53]

[51] Polvattē Buddhadatta, *op. cit.* (1950), p. 56.

[52] Laṃkāgoḍa to the Saṃgharāja of Burma, *op. cit.*

[53] Correspondence with Burma on the issues of the controversy continued in the 1860s and 1870s; and in 1878 a special envoy was sent by the king and the monks of Burma to have discussions with the two sides and bring about a settlement. This envoy, Jāgara, spent about seven months in Ceylon, but failed to restore the unity of the Salāgama monks. Soon after his departure, Aṁbagahapiṭiyē Vimalasāra, at this time the leader of the non-confusionists, wrote a defence of their position called *Sīmālakkhana Dīpanī* (Colombo, 1881), and to this, the leader of the confusionists, Randoṁbē Dhammālaṃkāra, replied with a work called *Sīmā Naya Dappana* (Colombo, 1885). The 'Introduction' to the latter work contains a brief history of the Sīmāsaṃkara Controversy from the confusionist point of view.

Indeed the conflict, which first began with Laṃkāgoḍa's challenge on the Balapiṭiya *sīmā* in 1851, was never really resolved; nor was the schism that it gave rise to effectively averted. After his suspension by Bōpāgoḍa (possibly even a little earlier), Laṃkāgoḍa began to perform all ecclesiastical acts with his own group of followers. In time, this new splinter group gradually organized itself into a separate fraternity. They called themselves the Saddhammavaṃsa fraternity, after Laṃkāgoḍa's title, Saddhammavaṃsapāla, which was also held, before him, by Kapugama Dhammakkhandha, the founder of the Daḍalla line of monks, who received it from the King of Burma in 1809.[54]

The larger group of Salāgama monks who remained under Bōpāgoḍa's leadership were known henceforth as the Mūlavaṃsa fraternity: 'Mūlavaṃsa' (meaning 'Original Lineage') because the majority of them derived their pupillary succession from Am̆bagahapiṭiyē Ñāṇavimala, the founder of the earliest group of Amarapura monks in Ceylon.

iv. THE RĀMAÑÑA FRATERNITY: ITS ORIGIN AND ITS IDEALS

The preceding two sections have been devoted to the major segments of the Amarapura fraternity in the low country: its Durāve, Karāve and Salāgama segments. Each of these segments had its distinctive name, which revealed nothing of its caste basis; but as we have seen, caste distinctions did play an important part in this process of segmentation.

The Karāve, Salāgama and Durāve castes were (and are) the major non-Goyigama castes in the low country. Hence it is not surprising that monks of these three castes came to comprise the major segments of the Amarapura fraternity. Speaking of the Amarapura fraternity as a whole, it is worth noting that though its membership was drawn *predominantly* from these three castes, admission into the fraternity was in no way limited to them *exclusively*. Quite possibly, there were within it a few monks from castes below the ranks of the three mentioned above;[55] and–particularly relevant to this discussion–there were also a few Goyigama monks who originally belonged to the Siyam fraternity, but who, later on, transferred their allegiance to the Amarapura fraternity.

The transfer of allegiance (from the Siyam to the Amarapura fraternity)

[54] See above, p. 99.

[55] One of these groups, the Vahumpuras, gained some prominence in the latter part of the nineteenth century (see above, p. 104).

on the part of certain Goyigama monks was not an entirely new phenomenon. It occurred fairly early in the Kandyan provinces; and as we have seen earlier, the growth of the Amarapura fraternity in those provinces depended heavily on it.[56] But in the low country it was a relatively late occurrence. While in the Kandyan provinces this transfer took place largely in the context of the controversies between Malvatta and Asgiriya in the second and third decades of the nineteenth century, the parallel process in the low country took place only in the next two decades in the context of an entirely different controversy, the Adhikamāsa Controversy, which too, like the Malvatu-Asgiri controversy, was causing divisions within the Siyam fraternity.

The low-country Goyigama monks who thus joined the Amarapura fraternity found themselves in a position markedly different from that of their Kandyan counterparts. While the Kandyan group of monks gradually organized themselves as a separate branch of the Amarapura fraternity and remained, mainly by virtue of their geographical separation, free of the controversies that were raging amongst the low-country Amarapura monks, the low-country group of Goyigama monks found themselves in the midst of a fraternity as sharply divided as the Siyam fraternity (which they had left) ever was, over a controversy of their own—the Sīmāsaṃkara Controversy. This left them disillusioned with what unmistakably appeared to them to be petty and ritualistic concerns of both the fraternities in existence in Ceylon at the time, and drove some of them to found an entirely new fraternity for the pursuit of the higher ideals of monkhood. The result of their effort was the third major fraternity in Ceylon, the Rāmañña fraternity.

The founder of the new fraternity was a monk named Aṁbagahavattē Saraṇaṃkara. He was helped in matters relating to the actual organization of the new fraternity by two other monks, Puvakdanḍāvē Paññānanda and Varāpiṭiyē Sumitta.

Aṁbagahavattē, born in 1832 at Akmīmana, a village in the Southern Province of Ceylon, joined the Siyam fraternity in 1847 as a pupil of one of his maternal uncles, Akmīmana Sobhita of Tuvakkugala Vihāre in Galle.[57]

[56] See above, ch. III, sec. iii.

[57] The main source for the following account is Aṁbagahavattē's biography: Kotmalē Saddhammavaṃsa, *Aṁbagahavattē Indāsabhavara Ñāṇasāmi Mahā Nāyaka Svāmīndrayan Vahansēgē Jīvana Caritaya* (Kalutara, 1950).

Having had his early training under this teacher, he proceeded to Vanavāsa Vihāre in Bentara in 1850 for more advanced studies under the then chief incumbent of that temple, Bentara Atthadassī. Bentara, it will be recalled, was at this time involved in the Adhikamāsa Controversy,[58] and this controversy made a deep impression on the young *sāmaṇera* who was studying at his feet. Aṁbagahavattē accompanied the master on his trip to Kandy in May 1855 (which brought about the latter's final breach with Kandy); he was also one of the earliest recipients of higher ordination under the auspices of the Kalyāṇi fraternity, which was organized soon after Bentara's return from Kandy. Aṁbagahavattē was not particularly happy with the ordination that he received, nor with the new fraternity that he belonged to. When, at about this time, his (original) teacher, Akmīmana, left the Siyam fraternity and joined the Amarapura fraternity as a pupil of Tōlaṃgamuvē, Aṁbagahavattē followed suit and joined the Amarapura fraternity himself as a pupil of Bulatgama Sumana in 1857.

The Amarapura fraternity, as we have seen, was involved at this time in the Sīmāsaṃkara Controversy; and just a few months after Aṁbagahavattē's entry into the fraternity, the 'confusionist' delegation to Burma–Pōhaddaramullē Vanaratana and Vaskaḍuvē Dhammakkhandha –returned to Ceylon bringing with them the Burmese Saṃgharāja's decision on the controversy. Aṁbagahavattē met these two monks; and being impressed with their account of the state of Buddhism in Burma, decided to go there himself.

His new teacher, Bulatgama, who had good contacts in Burma, helped him in making preparations for the journey, and gave him a letter of introduction to the Burmese Saṃgharāja. On 10 October 1860, Aṁbagahavattē left Ceylon together with four companions–two *bhikkhus* and two *sāmaṇeras*–and three lay devotees to look after them during the journey. Aṁbagahavattē's four companions were, like himself, monks who had originally been in the Siyam fraternity and who, later on, had joined the Amarapura fraternity. Two of them were his fellow pupils: one, Kōdāgoḍa Sumaṃgala, under Akmīmana Sobhita; the other, Pälpola Dhammadassī, under Bentara Atthadassī. The other two companions, Dīpēgoḍa Sīlakkhandha and Väligama Dhammapāla, were pupils of two of Akmīmana's pupils, Maligaspē Dhammapāla and Pannamgoḍa respectively.

[58] See above, ch. III, sec. ii.

Aṁbagahavattē and his party arrived in Ratanapuṇṇa (Mandalay) on 24 February 1861. On 11 June the two *bhikkhus*, Dīpēgoḍa and Pälpola, were given *daḷhī kamma* (confirmation of *upasampadā*); and, on the following day, the three *sāmaṇeras*, Aṁbagahavattē, Kōdāgoḍa and Väligama, were given *upasampadā*.[59] After that, having spent about a year under their Burmese preceptors, and having renewed their ordination at the Kalyāṇi *sīmā* in Rāmañña, they left Burma and arrived back in Ceylon on 18 August 1862. Aṁbagahavattē brought with him two messages: one addressed to his teacher, Bulatgama; the other, longer one, addressed to all the monks of Ceylon, giving details of their sojourn in Burma.[60]

About a month after Aṁbagahavattē's return, Puvakdanḍāvē Paññānanda, the monk who, later on, was to help him in founding the Rāmañña fraternity, left for Burma with his party of fourteen *bhikkhus*, two *sāmaṇeras* and four lay devotees. Puvakdanḍāvē too, like Aṁbagahavattē, had first joined the order as a member of the Siyam fraternity and had subsequently left that fraternity and joined the Amarapura fraternity—as a pupil of Vitārandeṇiyē Indasāra. This elderly Amarapura monk, Vitārandeṇiyē, was due to proceed to Burma along with his pupils on this mission; but he died while preparations were being made for the journey. The party that eventually left for Burma consisted of six of his pupils (including Puvakdanḍāvē) and eight of his pupils' pupils.

The destination of the Ceylonese party was Haṃsāvatī (Pegu) in Rāmañña (Lower Burma), and they took with them two letters of introduction: one from Bulatgama Sumana, who had helped the earlier delegation; the other from Uḍugampiṭiyē Sumana and Doḍandūvē Piyaratana, two leading Karāve monks, who, through the founder of their fraternity, Kataluvē Guṇaratana (who received his ordination at Rāmañña in 1809), had fraternal connections with the monks in Rāmañña.[61]

Puvakdanḍāvē and his party arrived in Haṃsāvatī in early 1863; and

[59] Along with *upasampadā* they were also given new names; but only Aṁbagahavattē continued to use his new name, Indāsabhavara Ñāṇasāmi, after his return to Ceylon.

[60] These two messages are given as Appendices (nos. XIX and XXI) to Kotmalē Saddhammavaṃsa, *op. cit.* The message to Bulatgama was written by the Saṃgharāja's pupil, Paññasāmi, the same monk who wrote the *Sāsanavaṃsa* in 1861. In that work (a history of Buddhism in Burma) Paññāsāmi included a brief note on the visit of Aṁbagahavattē and his party. See B. C. Law's translation (London, 1952), p. 161.

[61] A Sinhalese translation of the letter given by Uḍugampiṭiyē and Doḍandūvē appears in Polvattē Buddhadatta, *Kalyāṇi Sāsanavaṃsa* (Colombo, 1935), pp. 96–106.

having obtained higher ordination from the monks in that region, all but two of them returned to Ceylon in the latter part of the same year. They brought with them a message addressed to Bulatgama Sumana giving details of their stay in Rāmañña.[62] The two monks who stayed behind returned in the following year, bringing with them a document containing a brief outline of the 'spiritual genealogy' (*ācāri paramparā*) of the monks in Rāmañña. This document was addressed to Uḍugampiṭiyē Sumana and Doḍandūvē Piyaratana (mentioned above):[63] as leaders of the Karāve monks in Ceylon, these two monks had been rather anxious to obtain this 'genealogy', as it was to Rāmañña monks that they themselves traced their spiritual ancestry.

The two groups of monks who had recently returned from Burma, under the leadership of Aṁbagahavattē and Puvakdanḍāvē respectively, numbered in all more than twenty fully ordained monks; and they were soon joined by a third group from the Kandyan provinces led by Varāpiṭiyē Sumitta, a monk senior by several years to both Aṁbagahavattē and Puvakdanḍāvē.

Varāpiṭiyē Sumitta was one of thirty-five Sinhalese monks who went to Siam in 1844. They all went there with the Siamese delegation that arrived in Ceylon in that year, and returned with the religious texts that they had borrowed from monastic libraries in Ceylon.[64] At the time that he left Ceylon, Varāpiṭiyē was forty-four years of age, and for twenty-two years he had been a fully ordained monk of the Malvatu chapter of the Siyam fraternity. But soon after his arrival in Siam, he got himself freshly ordained by the monks of the Dhammayuttika fraternity in Siam (which was then under the leadership of Vajirañāṇa), and remained there as a member of that fraternity. He returned to Ceylon with some of his Sinhalese companions in 1852 (not long after the leader of their fraternity, Vajirañāṇa, had given up his robes and succeeded to the throne of Siam), and lived with the companions in his native Mātalē district. It was here that he was met by Aṁbagahavattē in the early part of 1864 while the latter was on a pilgrimage in the central and north-central parts of the island.[65]

Aṁbagahavattē invited Varāpiṭiyē to preside at the *upasampadā* cere-

[62] Kotmalē Saddhammavaṃsa, *op. cit.*, Appendix XXIV.

[63] *Pāli Sandesāvalī*, document no. 22.

[64] R. Lingat, 'History of Wat Pavaraniveça', *Journal of the Siam Society*, XXVI (1933) 82.

[65] Kotmalē Saddhammavaṃsa, *op. cit.*, pp. 67–70.

mony that he and Puvakdanḍāvē were planning to hold shortly; the invitee was eminently suited to play this role by virtue of his seniority. Varāpiṭiyē accepted the invitation, and on 12 June 1864 the *upasampadā* ceremony was performed as planned at a newly consecrated *sīmā* at Mahamōdara in Galle with the participation of Aṁbagahavattē, Puvakdanḍāvē, Varāpiṭiyē, and all their companions and followers.[66]

This may be considered (as is generally done) the formal beginning of the Rāmañña fraternity; but it should be noted that there was no *immediate* separation from the Amarapura fraternity, in which many of these monks had their teachers and old associates. Particularly close, understandably, were their contacts with the Karāve monks, who had as good a claim as these monks to call themselves Rāmaññas.[67] But these contacts did not remain close very long. The separation began to take manifest form in the late 1860s, and the new group of monks made their exit final and complete by moving completely outside the broad organizational framework of the Amarapura fraternity. Thus, while the Durāve, Karāve and Salāgama monks remained, despite their mutual exclusiveness, as branches, or what we have called segments, of the same Amarapura fraternity, the new group (with its Goyigama leadership) became an entirely new 'fraternity'–in opposition to the two (Siyam and Amarapura) fraternities in existence at the time.

In this role they raised the cry of 'reform' in much the same fashion as it had been raised half a century earlier by the Amarapura fraternity against the Siyam fraternity. How this role of the Rāmañña fraternity appeared to a sympathetic outsider may be seen in the comments on the fraternity and its founder made by Olcott in his *Diary Leaves*. Olcott came to know the founder (Aṁbagahavattē) rather well in the last few years of the latter's life, and was, in fact, one of those who witnessed his cremation on 3 February 1886.[68] Reviewing briefly the recent history of the Buddhist order in Ceylon, Olcott wrote:

> The priests [of the Siyam fraternity], being mainly of high social rank, would not confer ordination upon candidates of lower caste, so the more energetic and learned of these went to the King of Burma and got what they sought from the

[66] *Ibid.*, pp. 72–75.

[67] Polvattē Buddhadatta, *op. cit.* (1935).

[68] H. S. Olcott, *Old Diary Leaves*, vol. III (Madras, 1929), pp. 343 ff.

chief priests. This formed the Amarapoora Nikaya. But in the course of time that happened which always happens in the religious affairs of men: piety relaxed, learning became confined to the minority, idleness and sanctimoniousness prevailed, and now and again a monk who grieved over the decay of true religion would break out in protest. . . . Ambagahawatte was one of these protesting rebels; he gave up his connection with the Amarapoora Nikaya, went abroad and took a fresh ordination, and founded the Ramanya Nikaya. . . .[69]

His rallying cry was, of course, Reform. . . . He set the example of austerity of life, observing strictly the rule of Vinaya, and requiring the same of those who chose to follow him. From the start he made an impression, his sect gradually grew strong, and, although he has been dead several years [written in 1900], it has prospered and now embraces a large body of zealous and able monks.[70]

Although the Rāmañña fraternity was described here as embracing 'a large body of . . . monks', in comparison with the Siyam and the Amarapura fraternities, it was certainly not large. In fact, it was (and still is) the smallest of the three fraternities. Its strength, however, was not in its numbers, but in its radical spirit. Its smallness, quite possibly, helped it to maintain this radical spirit. As a small fraternity, it was more manageable and more readily amenable to close supervision by its leaders than a large fraternity. It was also less troubled, at least partly for the same reason, by the fissiparous tendencies which were manifest in the Siyam and the Amarapura fraternities.

The 'reformism' of the Rāmañña fraternity persisted, on the whole, longer than that of the (earlier) Amarapura fraternity; one reason for this, it could be supposed, was that it was more strongly motivated by religious ideals pure and simple. Religious ideals did play no mean part in the emergence of the Amarapura fraternity; still, they were closely intermixed with the (secular) caste factor—the desire on the part of lower castes to appropriate traditional high-caste monopolies. No similar process underlined the rise of the Rāmañña fraternity. At the time that this fraternity emerged into the religious scene, the four major castes in the island—Goyigama, Karāve, Salāgama and Durāve—had already found their niches in the divisions within the existing order. The new fraternity, therefore,

[69] *Ibid.*, p. 344.

[70] *Ibid.*, vol. II (Madras, 1928), pp. 297–98.

became welcome ground for the more religiously motivated, of whatever caste background.

The influence of the Rāmañña fraternity spread not merely in the low country, where it originated, but also in the outlying areas of the old Kandyan kingdom, particularly in Mātalē, Hat Kōraḷē and Nuvara Kalāviya, where some of the more radically oriented monks transferred their allegiance from the Siyam to the new fraternity.[71] A significant feature about the latter group of monks was the enthusiasm for the *araññavāsī* ('forest dwelling', as against *gāmavāsī*, 'village dwelling') vocation which some of them developed under the inspiration of Puvakdanḍāvē Paññānanda, who had his own *arañña* at Kirinda (in the Southern Province) even before the formal establishment of the Rāmañña fraternity.[72] Two of the new recruits from the Siyam fraternity gained much fame as *araññavāsī* monks. The first, Ulaṃkulamē Saraṇaṃkara, became a legendary figure in his own lifetime; numerous stories were current at the time about his life in the jungle and encounters with wild beasts.[73] The second, Ilukvattē Medhaṃkara, was described by Olcott as 'a young man, truly holy in his life and aims to a degree that I have never seen equalled among the bhikkhus of Ceylon. A part of each year it was his custom to retire into the forest and spend the time in meditation, subsisting on berries and such other food as came in his way'.[74]

Yet, despite this preference that some of its members showed for the *araññavāsī* vocation, the Rāmañña fraternity, in general, was by no means a simple 'back to the forest' movement. Reform of the community of monks and of the community of laymen remained very much their concern. This concern inevitably brought them into conflict with the other two fraternities and involved them in prolonged controversies with them. These new controversies differed markedly from the earlier ones, in which the Siyam and the Amarapura fraternities were involved, in that

[71] Mātalē Sāsanatilaka, *Rāmañña Vaṃśaya* (Colombo, 1964), pp. 51 ff.

[72] *Ibid.*

[73] Nitalava Ñāṇissara, *Śrī Saraṇaṃkara Mahā Sthavira Caritaya* (Mīrigama, 1928).

[74] *Old Diary Leaves*, vol. III, p. 388. Ilukvattē was the leading Buddhist representative at the opening ceremony of the Theosophical Society Library at Adyar in December 1886. *Ibid.* There is a short biography of him written by his pupil, Uḍugampola Suvaṇṇajoti, called *Ilukvattē Medhaṃkarasabha Svāmīn Vahansēgē Jīvita Katāva* (Colombo, 1889).

they were concerned with issues of much wider interest. I shall refer here briefly only to the two most important.

a. The first one was known as the Dēvapūjā Vādaya, or 'the Controversy on the propitiation of deities'. The position of deities (*dēvas*) in Sinhalese Buddhism has previously been discussed at some length;[75] a detailed discussion of the subject, therefore, is unnecessary here. To give but a mere summary: (1) Buddhism recognized the existence of these supernatural beings and their ability to help human beings; (2) it did not credit them, however, with powers to 'save' human beings; (3) the deities were considered irrelevant therefore to the seeker of ultimate salvation; but (4) at the level of the masses, the propitiation of deities was not merely a tolerated but even an accepted practice in Buddhism. To this it should be added that, although not all the *dēvālēs* (shrines dedicated to deities) were associated with Buddhist temples, it was not uncommon for Buddhist temples to have *dēvālēs* within their precincts (though always in a position inferior to the shrines devoted to the Buddha). This was particularly so in the case of the older temples which were in the custody of the Siyam fraternity. But it seems quite likely that even the more recent Amarapura fraternity had, in the course of time, come to follow this pattern in their own temples.

It was in this context that the Rāmañña fraternity, in their enthusiasm for the more radical ideals of Buddhism, began to denounce the propitiation of *dēvas* as well as the tolerance shown towards this practice and the encouragement given to it by the other two fraternities. The actual 'controversy' began in 1871 with the active participation of the founder of the Rāmañña fraternity (Aṁbagahavattē) himself,[76] and continued intermittently during the next three or four decades.[77]

[75] See above, pp. 23–25.

[76] Six letters written by Hikkaḍuvē Sumaṃgala to Aṁbagahavattē (between March 1871 and November 1876) concerning, inter alia, the 'Dēvapūjā Controversy' are given in Yagirala Prajñānanda, *Śrī Sumaṃgala Caritaya*, vol. II (Colombo, 1947), pp. 692–99, 699–701, 707–9, 709–10, 712–14, 714–16.

[77] The two most important pamphlets which appeared in print in connection with the Controversy were Uḍugampola Suvaṇṇajoti, *Bauddha Labdhi Viśodhaniya* (Colombo, 1898), which is an exposition of the Rāmañña point of view, and the reply to that, Toṭagamuvē Paññāmoli, *Sadācāra Vibhāvaniya* (Colombo, 1904).

The standpoint of the Rāmañña fraternity in relation to the 'Dēvapūjā Controversy' was by no means a popular one; the propitiation of deities was a practice too well established in popular Buddhism closely related to the felt needs of the laity to be given up suddenly in a burst of enthusiasm. But some support they certainly did have, not merely among the monkhood but also among some of the more sophisticated Buddhist laymen, who, about this time, came to play an increasingly important role in the religious affairs of the country. The attitudes and activities of these laymen will receive greater attention in Part II of this study. For the moment, it will suffice to quote just one of them, Louis Corneille Wijesinha, a Pali scholar and convert from Christianity who was active in Buddhist affairs. In 1876, while 'the propitiation of deities' was a much discussed issue, he asserted before the Buddhist Temporalities Commission: 'Among the more intelligent classes of Buddhists there is little or no belief in dewale worship, but among the lower classes . . . there is a superstitious belief that there is a possibility of averting the anger of the presiding deity in cases of sickness or calamity, and of propitiating his favour'.[78]

b. Secondly, the monks of the Rāmañña fraternity, in their enthusiasm for the strict observance of *vinaya* regulations, called the mass of non-Rāmañña monks *samaṇa dussīlas* (impious monks) and exhorted the laity not to support them. Supporting impious monks would bring no merit on the laity, but only demerit, they contended. It was this contention that led to the controversy known as the Dussīla Vādaya, or 'the Controversy on the impious (monks)'. The Rāmañña standpoint gained no support from the *Dakkhiṇā Vibhaṃga Sutta* ('Discourse on the Analysis of Offerings'), which was the standard canonical authority on the subject, nor from the noncanonical *Milindapañha*, which had examined this specific issue in greater detail.

[78] *Report of the Commissioners appointed to inquire into the administration of the Buddhist Temporalities* (S.P. XVII: 1876), p. 20. On pp. 47–52 *ibid.* there is a petition addressed by some *dēvāla* tenants in Sabaragamuva to the governor and the Legislative Council where more statements like the above are made. Wijesinha himself was the author of those statements, and in formulating them, Aṁbagahavattē was one of the monks whom he consulted (*ibid.*, p. 53). There is an able reply to that petition on pp. 55–58 by Iddamalgoḍa Basnāyaka Nilamē with extensive citations of Buddhist scriptures, which suggest that he was helped in its preparation by a scholarly Buddhist monk – most probably Hikkaḍuvē Sumaṃgala, who was closely acquainted with him.

In the *Milindapañha*—which is written in the form of a series of Socratic dialogues between the Greek Bactrian king of North India, Menander (second century B.C.), and the Buddhist monk, Nāgasena—the monk says in reply to a question from the king:

> Even, O king, when thoroughly fallen, a guilty Samana yet sanctifies the gifts of the supporters of the faith—just as water, however thick, will wash away slush and mud and dirt and stains—just as hot, and even boiling water will put a mighty blazing fire out—just as food, however nasty, will allay the faintness of hunger. For thus, O king, hath it been said by the god over all gods in the most excellent Majjhima Nikāya in the chapter on gifts (the *Dakkhinā Vibhaṃga*):
>
> 'Whene'er a good man, with believing heart,
> Presents what he hath earned in righteousness
> To th' unrighteous,—in full confidence
> On the great fruit to follow the good act—
> Such gift is, by the giver, sanctified'.[79]

The *Milindapañha* was a work highly respected over the centuries. It was known to, and had been quoted with approval by, the great commentator of the fifth century, Buddhaghosa.[80] During the much more recent period that we are concerned with here, it attracted particular attention because a Sinhalese translation of it (made *ca.* 1777–78 by Hīnaṭikuṁburē Sumaṃgala, a pupil of Attaragama Rājaguru Baṇḍāra, who was himself a pupil of Välivita Saraṇaṃkara) appeared in print in 1878.[81] The Rāmañña monks, however, were unimpressed by all this. They simply refused to accept the authority of *Milindapañha* on this point.[82]

The doctrinal implications of this refusal were profound.[83] But our

[79] *The Questions of King Milinda*, tr. T. W. Rhys Davids, Part II (Oxford, 1894), p. 83–84.

[80] *Ibid.*

[81] Edited by Mohoṭṭivattē Guṇānanda et al., (Colombo, 1878).

[82] 'Descriptive Catalogue of Nevill Manuscripts (at the British Museum)', vol. I, no. 168 (*Milinda Praśnaya*).

[83] Among the major publications on the Dussīla Controversy were: Mohoṭṭivattē Guṇānanda, *Dussīla Dāna Vibhāga* (Colombo, 1887), and the (anonymous) reply to that from the Rāmañña fraternity, *Dussīla Dāna Viniścaya* (Colombo, 1887); Uḍugampola Suvaṇṇajoti, *Dussīla Saṃgraha Bhedaya* (Colombo, 1888); P. A. Peiris, *Śramaṇa Dussīla Saraṇāgamana Vibhāgaya* (Colombo, 1893), and the reply to that, S. L. Perera, *Rāmañña Vāda Bhaṃgaya* (Colombo, 1893); Uḍugampola Suvaṇṇajoti, *Bhikṣu Sīlaya* (Colombo, 1893); H. L. Adrian Appuhāmi, *Dussīla Mardanaya* (Colombo, 1895); and (anonymous) *Dussīla Katura* (Colombo, 1897). See also Yagirala Prjñānanda, *op. cit.*, p. 646, and Panamvela Rāhula, *Bädigama Nāhimiyō* (Mātara, 1967), *passim.*

concern here is rather with the more immediate practical results of the 'Dussīla Controversy', namely, that it made the laymen more watchful of the behaviour of the monks, and made the monks themselves more careful of how they appeared to the laity on whose charity they were dependent. In this respect, the Rāmañña fraternity, though a small fraternity, was certainly an 'influential' one, as Copleston observed at the time.[84] Both in their precepts and in their practices, they exemplified 'the historic role of great ascetics' that Durkheim spoke of. They showed that 'it is necessary that an elite put the end too high, if the crowd is not to put it too low. It is necessary that some exaggerate, if the average is to remain at a fitting level'.[85]

The most significant *general* phenomenon that the early history of the Rāmañña fraternity bore witness to was the ability of Buddhist ideals to survive, and not merely to survive but also to gain adherence, even when the external (political) conditions, to all appearances, were highly unfavourable. Some further aspects of the same general phenomenon will be taken up in the next chapter.

[84] *Buddhism: Primitive and Present in Magadha and in Ceylon* (London, 1892), p. 432.

[85] *The Elementary Forms of the Religious Life*, tr. J. W. Swain (London, 1915), p. 356.

Chapter V

DECLINE OR REVIVAL?

i. PROPHECIES OF DOOM

The apocalyptic vision of the eventual, and indeed inevitable, triumph of Christianity over all other religions was very much a part of the early nineteenth-century evangelical frame of mind, and this vision was widely prevalent among both the missionaries and the administrators of Ceylon at the time. This belief was, in fact, one of the basic presumptions that guided the thinking of those who advocated the 'disestablishment' of Buddhism; in their opinion, Buddhism, which was already in a state of decline and which was destined to disappear altogether, was being 'artificially' maintained by means of governmental backing given to it. It was Hardy who first articulated this presumption into an argument for disestablishment in 1839.[1] Very soon it gained the support not merely of his missionary colleagues, but also of influential administrators both in Ceylon and in England. Tennent, the Colonial Secretary, for instance, asserted with confidence that the severance of the state's connection with Buddhism would in reality mean 'the withdrawal of the only stay that could much longer have retarded its decay'.[2]

If those who were removed from the local scene, such as officials at the Colonial Office (who eventually gave orders to disestablish Buddhism), adhered to this presumption purely on 'dogmatic' grounds, others who were more familiar with the local situation found enough evidence *in situ* to validate the presumption. For one thing, Buddhist monks themselves were fully convinced of the 'indispensability' of governmental backing for the maintenance of Buddhism; and they gave expression to this conviction over and over again when they insisted that the government conform to

[1] R. Spence Hardy, *The British Government and the Idolatry of Ceylon* (Colombo, 1839), p. 44.

[2] Quoted in K. M. de Silva, *Social Policy and Missionary Organizations in Ceylon, 1840–1855* (London, 1965), pp. 105–6.

the undertakings given to them in the Kandyan Convention. And, of course, hardly anybody could fail to see signs of 'decline' in Buddhism in the immediate results of the disestablishment: the disorganization of temple property and the irregular performance of temple rituals; the declining authority of the Mahā Nāyakas and the increase of schisms and controversies. The general tenor of the ideas that many Christians at the time held regarding the future of Buddhism was well expressed by Forbes as early as 1840 when he wrote: 'I anticipate that Buddhism, shorn of its splendour, unaided by authority, and torn by internal dissension, will not long have power to retain even its present slight control over the actions of its votaries . . . , and that it will fall into disuse before Christianity is prepared to step into its place'.[3]

When the process of disestablishment was finally accomplished, predictions of this sort were made with even greater confidence. The prominent Sinhalese Christian, James Alwis, while discussing the 'prospects of Buddhism' in the course of a lecture which he delivered in Colombo on 25 October 1861, declared: 'There are, indeed, good grounds for believing that Buddhism will, at no very distant period, disappear from this Island'.[4] Alwis gave due credit to the colonial government for having helped to bring about this state of affairs, and stated (somewhat surprisingly, perhaps, considering his interest in popularizing the pursuit of orientalist studies): 'A powerful means by which Buddhism is failing in the stand it had originally made in this Island is the discouragement which is offered to the native Pundits. They do not, under the British Government, derive any of the benefits or enjoy the privileges which were conferred on them in a bye-gone day'.[5] He went on to quote with approval a statement made by Hardy in 1850 (in *Eastern Monachism*, p. 366): ' "This process of decay is already apparent in Ceylon. There being no outward stimulus to exertion, the priests exhibit no enthusiasm of study, and many of them are unable to read at all." ' Alwis merely added an explanatory note to Hardy's concluding sentence: 'I believe he meant the Pali works of Buddhism'.[6]

[3] *Eleven Years in Ceylon*, vol. I (London, 1840), p. 291.

[4] 'Buddhism: Its Origin, History and Doctrines' (first published in Colombo, 1862), reprinted in JPTS, (1883), p. 31.

[5] *Ibid.*

[6] *Ibid.*

ii. THE SHIFT OF THE RELIGIOUS CENTRE

It would not be entirely unreasonable to assume, however, that in making pronouncements like the above Alwis was guided more by the dogmatic convictions of his Christian contemporaries than by his own good knowledge of the local situation. As a keen orientalist he had close contacts with the learned Buddhist monks of his time—he himself acquired his knowledge of Sinhalese, Pali and Sanskrit under the guidance of the former monk, Baṭuvantuḍāvē Devarakṣita—and he could scarcely have failed to be impressed by their learning and scholarship. Indeed, in a lecture on the Pali language, delivered just over a month after the above lecture on Buddhism had been delivered, he admitted:

> Although a dead language, the Pali has been carefully cultivated in Ceylon. From the period it became the sacred language of the Sinhalese, Kings and Princes have encouraged its study; nobles and statesmen have vied with each other to excel in its composition; and laymen and priests have produced some of the most elegant works in it. The names of Batuwantudāve, Hikkaduwe, Lankāgoda, Dodanpahala, Valāne, Bentota, Kahave, and [Väligama] Sumangala, amongst a host of others, are indeed familiar to Pali scholars, as those of the learned who are *even now* able to produce compositions by no means inferior to those of a Buddhaghosa or a Parakkrama.[7]

Thus, contrary to the opinions expressed by Hardy and many other Europeans in Ceylon, the interest in and the knowledge of Buddhist scriptures were by no means lacking among the Buddhist monks of Ceylon in the middle of the nineteenth century. George Turnour, who was more qualified than any other Englishman in his time to speak on the subject, wrote in 1837: 'In no part of the world, perhaps, are there greater facilities for acquiring a knowledge of Pali afforded, than in Ceylon. Though the historical data contained in that language have hitherto been under-

[7] 'The Buddhist Scriptures and their Language, the Pali', reprinted *ibid.*, pp. 60–61. Alwis's orientalist studies were strongly motivated by a desire to redeem his country's heritage from the slights cast upon it by missionaries like Hardy. See M. Y. Gooneratne, *English Literature in Ceylon, 1815–1878* (Dehiwala, 1968), esp. p. 97. Two of Alwis's younger contemporaries, Louis Corneille Wijesinha and Edmund Rowland Gooneratne, were led by the same desire, and through the orientalist path, to give up their adherence to Christianity and to espouse Buddhism. Alwis's faith in Christianity never wavered; and in the religious sphere, the influence of Hardy and other missionaries continued to be strong in him. Hence his simultaneous adherence to two very different points of view.

rated, or imperfectly illustrated, the doctrinal and metaphysical works on Buddhism are still extensively, and critically studied by the native priesthood'.[8]

Yet monastic education, despite its importance not merely for the monks but also for large masses of laymen,[9] received no encouragement at all from the government. This neglect was guided partly by religious considerations: enthusiasm for Christianity, and its invariable concomitant, hostility towards Buddhism. The separation of the laity from the influence of the monks was deemed a necessary prelude to their conversion to Christianity. It was guided also by another consideration, the emphasis on English as the proper medium of instruction, particularly after Colebrooke's recommendations of 1831. Colebrooke insisted on education in English for two reasons: it would be a means of preparing candidates for public employment; and it would serve as an aid to 'the natives to cultivate European attainments'.[10] Viewing the English language as a civilizing and christianizing force was common at the time; and Colebrooke, though not a very articulate exponent of this view, nonetheless had implicit faith in it. It should be noted that not all those who were actually in charge of education in Ceylon–administrators and missionaries–were unqualified supporters of education in English;[11] yet they all were in agreement in looking upon education as a means of propagating Christianity. Hence, even those who advocated education in the vernaculars never turned their attention to Buddhist monastic schools. Indeed, the Wesleyans, who from the outset were the most persistent advocates of vernacular education, first began teaching in Sinhalese (in 1817), according to Tennent, with the very

[8] 'Introduction' to *The Mahāwanso in Roman Characters with the Translation subjoined* (Cotta, 1837), p. xxv.

[9] The high rate of literacy maintained by means of free instruction imparted in monasteries was attested to by Davy, who made his study of the Kandyan provinces soon after their cession to the British in 1815. He wrote: 'Very many of the natives are said to be grammatically acquainted with Singalese; every Upasampada priest should be, and is more or less acquainted with Pali, and a few of them are conversant with Sanskrit. Reading and writing are far from uncommon acquirements, and are almost as general as in England amongst the male part of the population'. *An Account of the Interior of Ceylon and of its Inhabitants* (London, 1821), p. 237. See also Forbes, *Eleven Years*, vol. II, p. 245.

[10] 'Report on the Administration of the Government of Ceylon' (24 December 1831), in *The Colebrooke-Cameron Papers*, ed. G. C. Mendis (Oxford, 1956), p. 71.

[11] K. M. de Silva, *Social Policy*, pp. 145 *et seq.*

objective 'of superseding the Buddhist priesthood in this department'.[12] Although in the larger part of the island there were no schools other than monastic schools, Colebrooke refused to appreciate their importance and dismissed them curtly in one sentence: 'The education afforded by the native priesthood in their temples and colleges scarcely merits any notice'.[13] For several decades to come, this remained the official attitude towards monastic schools.[14]

There were, to be sure, many temples, particularly in the Kandyan provinces, which were sufficiently wealthy in their own right to have carried on their educational functions even with no assistance from the government. But in the general disorganization of temple affairs that followed the disestablishment of Buddhism, monastic wealth, instead of being an asset to religious institutions, tended to have the reverse effect. As the government had no interest in ensuring that monastic property was properly managed and utilized for purposes for which it was intended, the incumbent of each temple was left with the 'right' of doing virtually what he pleased with the lands of his temple. This became particularly so after Ordinance No. 10 of 1856, which was intended 'to provide for the settlement of claims to exemption from taxation of all temple lands in the Kandyan provinces, and for the due registration of all lands belonging to such temples'. After a futile attempt in the early 1840s to interfere with the immunities of temple lands and to render them alienable,[15] the attention of the government was concentrated on the registration of temple lands; and it was in order to achieve this that the Ordinance No. 10 of 1856 was enforced. This was motivated, however, out of interest not so much in temple lands as in non-temple lands. Temple lands were not taxable; hence it was necessary for the government to ensure that no taxable lands were included in this category with the intention of evading taxes. In fact, along

[12] *Christianity in Ceylon* (London, 1850), p. 295.

[13] *The Colebrooke-Cameron Papers*, p. 74.

[14] A subcommittee of the Legislative Council appointed 'to inquire into and report upon the state and prospects of Education in the Island' reported in 1867: 'There is scarcely any useful knowledge disseminated in such schools, and whatever is taught in them is so intertwined with error, and superstition, that the aim and end of all Primary Instruction would be defeated, if it were left to be propagated by the teaching of either Buddhist or Hindu priests'. S.P. VIII: 1867, p. 13.

[15] Regarding which, see K. M. de Silva, 'The Development of British Policy on Temple Lands in Ceylon, 1840–55', *JRAS(CB)*, n.s., VIII (1963) 312–29.

with registration, the government gave up all interest in temple lands.[16] The result was that temple authorities who hitherto had been entitled merely to the usufruct of the lands dedicated to them, were now vested with absolute rights. Many monks in the Kandyan provinces found it irresistible to use these rights to their personal advantage.[17] And there was no effective authority to stop them: the ecclesiastical authorities were much weaker than they had been before,[18] and the secular authorities (i.e., the government) remained inactive in this regard for a long time to come.[19]

In these circumstances, temple property did become assets to individual monks, but not to the institutions to which they were attached. Thus, strange as it may seem, the poorer temples in the low country had a better chance of performing their traditional religious and educational functions than the wealthier ones in the Kandyan provinces, as was clearly stated by a district administrator in one of the Kandyan provinces in 1871:

> There is a very noteworthy difference between the Kandyan and the low-country priesthood. In the low-country the priests depend for their subsistence upon the alms and benefactions of the people, and they are therefore more strict in the observance of the rules of their religion, and more desirous of eminence in learning for an ignorant or immoral priest would not gain the respect or the affection of the people upon whose charity he subsists. The Kandyan priesthood, on the other hand, is supported by the produce of the royal benefactions and endowments, and lead a life of careless and sensual . . . religion. Each priest looks upon his vihārē as his private property, and considers that the offerings of the people and the produce of the lands are to be devoted to his personal enjoyment. The result is that the temples are all in a ruinous state, and the lands are being gradually alienated.[20]

This was, evidently, a broad generalization, and naturally it is not free of the limitations of such a generalization. Yet, as a generalization, it was nonetheless valid, and has the support of a considerable volume of other

[16] *Report of the Commissioners appointed to inquire into the administration of the Buddhist Temporalities* (S.P. XVIII: 1876), pp. viii–ix.

[17] *Ibid., passim.*

[18] See above, pp. 123–127.

[19] See above, pp. 8–9.

[20] L. F. Lee, 'Annual Report on the Kegalla District', *Administration Reports: 1871*.

evidence. For instance, practically every witness–lay and cleric, Kandyan and low-country–who appeared before the Buddhist Temporalities Commission in 1876, testified to the 'worldliness' of the Kandyan monks and to their mismanagement of monastic property and to the neglect of their educational duties. C. B. Dunuwille, the Diyavaḍana Nilamē (Chief Lay Custodian) of the Temple of the Tooth Relic, when he was asked, 'Do you consider that the priests neglect their duty?' replied: 'Yes; the temples were built and the lands were granted to them for the purpose of studying and teaching religion both to the priests and the laity, which duties are now utterly disregarded, the priests employing their time in other pursuits, such as trade and the management of temporal affairs of the temple'.[21] Dūllǟvē Loku Baṇḍā (grandson of the Disāva of Valapanē who signed the Kandyan Convention), president of the Village Tribunals of Mātalē North, stated: 'There is evidence of the maintenance of schools attached to temples in history and in the memory of the people. This practice has now been abandoned. I myself learnt my alphabet in Ehelapola pansala with about twenty other boys. Now there is no one. . . . I learnt Sinhalese in Kandy at Kotugodella Vihare. There is no longer any teaching there'.[22]

Even the two highest colleges, Malvatta and Asgiriya, were not unaffected by this general decline, Ram̃bukvällē Sonuttara of Malvatte Vihāre testified: 'Six of the twenty priests of the Malwatte Vihare know Pali, and of the twenty priests at Asgiria only three. In the Kandyan times it was very rare for any one of these priests to be ignorant of Pali'.[23]

Clearly, as far as the temples in and around Kandy were concerned, the conditions depicted by Turnour in 1837 did not survive in the next generation.[24] The most revealing in this connection, perhaps, was the evidence of the leading low-country monk, Hikkaḍuvē Sumaṃgala. Hik-

[21] S.P. XVII: 1876, p. 34.

[22] *Ibid.*, pp. 3–4.

[23] *Ibid.*, p. 9.

[24] Turnour began his Pali studies in 1826 at Sabaragamuva (where he was the Agent of Government) and continued them at Kandy (to where he was transferred in 1828). At Kandy, he possessed, as he put it, 'the advantage from my official position, of almost daily intercourse with the heads of the Buddhistical church, of access to their libraries, and of their assistance both in the selection of the works I consulted, and in the explanation of the passages which required elucidation'. Turnour, *op. cit.*, p. lviii. His comments therefore were mainly, if not exclusively, about these monks.

daḍuvē, in 1873, had opened Vidyodaya College in Colombo; when he was asked, 'How is it that it has been necessary for you to found this college in the low-country when there are already the two great colleges of Malwatta and Asgiria in Kandy, specially endowed for the education of the priesthood?' he replied: 'I am aware that these two colleges were established for the purpose, and that in point of fact in former days they actually did serve it, but that is now not the case, and we have found it necessary to establish a college elsewhere to meet the want. My college is unendowed; it is supported mainly by subscriptions'.[25]

Hikkaḍuvē, it should be noted, was by no means an opponent of Kandy. On the contrary, it will be recalled that during the major conflict between the Kandyan and the low-country monks in the middle of the nineteenth century, he stood firmly behind Kandy against his own teacher, Valānē Siddhārttha, for whom he had the highest regard.[26] But it comes out clearly in his evidence that after a lapse of a few years even he found it difficult to derive much inspiration from Kandy. Asked for his 'opinion as to the state of learning among the priests of the Kandyan provinces', he commented: 'I think learning is on the decline in the Kandyan districts, but some priests come and study in the low-country. In former days, on the contrary, the priests from the low-country resorted to the Kandyan provinces for education'.[27]

Kandy, in other words, had been replaced by the low country as the effective 'centre' of Buddhism in Ceylon; and Hikkaḍuvē, however unwittingly, was himself a party to this process. In 1880, Olcott, having paid a visit to the Mahā Nāyakas in Kandy, wrote down in his diary: 'Under the Kandyan sovereigns, these officers were the royal functionaries, joint guardians of the Tooth Temple, and had precedence in all royal religious processions. [Hikkaḍuvē] Sumangala is their junior in rank, but immensely their superior in the public estimation, as in ability'.[28]

The political change of 1815 and all the other changes that followed in its wake were clearly detrimental to the interests of the religious establishment in Kandy. With the disestablishment of Buddhism, they lost a

[25] S.P. XVII: 1876, p. 11.

[26] See above, pp. 134–135.

[27] S.P. XVII: 1876, p. 11.

[28] *Old Diary Leaves*, vol. II, 1878–83 (Madras, 1928), p. 180.

good deal of their ecclesiastical *power*. Their *esteem* did not survive much longer. The privileged position that they traditionally enjoyed was closely dependent on the traditional social and political order. When that order faced its dissolution under the dominion of an alien and hostile power, their position suffered accordingly. What survived of the past—monastic lands, for example—only worsened their position, and made it all the more difficult for them to adapt to the changed circumstances.

What appeared, no doubt, as new and distressing conditions for the Kandyan monks were simply the normal state of affairs as far as the low-country monks were concerned. These monks lived within a territory which, for some three centuries, had been under the effective control of European Christian powers. Out of sheer necessity, therefore, they had had to learn to manage their affairs without the immediate and recurrent backing of a Buddhist political establishment. In no way can it be said that they relished the experience; yet, as it happened, it was evidently a very useful experience to have.

The low-country monks, of course, had their own problems. They had their controversies, and they had their schisms. Yet these controversies and schisms, rather than acting as impediments to their religiosity, contributed not a little to keeping it firmly alive. All the controversies, however motivated, were generally conducted on a highly scholastic plane. This was particularly so in the case of the two major religious controversies in the mid-nineteenth century—the 'Adhikamāsa Controversy' within the Siyam fraternity and the 'Sīmāsaṃkara Controversy' within the Amarapura fraternity. The letters and polemical pamphlets exchanged between the disputants in relation to these controversies reveal a high degree of familiarity with the scriptures as well as the vast corpus of exegetical literature. Indeed, the disputes and controversies led not merely to a closer study of the classical scriptures, but also to the production of *new* exegetical works dealing with the intricate problems of interpreting the scriptures.[29] The venue of all this was the low country, not the Kandyan provinces. It was no accident that all the individuals—seven monks and one former monk—referred to by Alwis (above) as the greatest Pali scholars of his time

[29] Some of these works have been cited earlier in the text. For others, see Polvattē Buddhadatta, *Pāli Sāhityaya*, 2 vols. (Ambalaṃgoḍa, 1962), *passim*.

were in the low country and were, furthermore, involved in one or the other of the controversies of the day.[30]

The controversies in the low country were not entirely confined to the religious sphere. In the early 1850s, for instance, there was a literary controversy, known as the Sav Sat Dam Controversy, which in fact attracted far more attention at the public level than any of the contemporary religious controversies. The Sav Sat Dam Controversy in the fifties was not so much a new controversy as a revival of an old one; the revival, however, witnessed greater public interest than the original.

The three words 'sav', 'sat' and 'dam' constituted the third prosodic foot (*gaṇa*) of the fourth stanza of a Sinhalese poem called *Gaṃgārōhaṇa Varṇanāva*, which was written by Tōmis Samarasēkara Disānāyaka in 1807 in praise of a grand religious festival that was celebrated in Mātara under the patronage of the leading headman of that town, David de Saram. 'Sav sat dam', together with the first and second feet of the stanza in question, read 'sasara saraṇa sav sat dam'; and the particular importance of these three feet was that, quite apart from constituting part of the stanza, they were also meant–according to clues given by the poet in the latter part of the stanza–to provide the name of the patron of the festival, Saram. The clues given by the poet were the initial *varṇa* (syllable) of the first foot; the middle *varṇa* of the second foot; and the last *varṇa* of the third foot. Evidently, what the poet had in mind, and what he expected the reader to take, were *sa* of the first foot (*sa*sara), *ra* of the second foot (sa*ra*ṇa), and *m* of the third foot (sav sat da*m*), which, when put together, formed the name Saram. But, in a critique of the poem, Mīripännē

[30] Alwis did not mean his list to be exhaustive. Among its noteworthy omissions were Yātrāmullē Dhammārāma (1828–72), a pupil of Bentara Atthadassī; and Vaskaḍuvē Subhūti (1835–1917), a pupil of Iňduruvē Sumaṃgala. Both Yātrāmullē and Vaskaḍuvē had considerable influence, not merely in Ceylon but also overseas. The founders of Pali studies in England, R. C. Childers and T. W. Rhys Davids, had their early training under Yātrāmullē, and they both held their teacher in very high esteem. See Yātrāmullē's obituary written by Childers in the *Trübner's Record*, 1872; and Rhys Davids, *The Origin and Growth of Religion as illustrated by some points in the history of Indian Buddhism* (The Hibbert Lectures, London, 1881), pp. 186–87. Vaskaḍuvē was frequently consulted on points of Pali scholarship by Childers and Rhys Davids and other Eruopean scholars as well as by H. C. Warren, the founder of systematic Pali studies in the United States. See C. R. Lanman, *Henry Clarke Warren (1854–1899): A Brief Memorial* (Cambridge, Mass., 1920), and Harischandra de Silva, 'Vaskaḍuvē Śrī Subhūti Himi', *Saṃskṛti*, XVI/4 (October–December 1969) 47–64.

Dhammaratana, who at this time had a great reputation as a Sinhalese poet,[31] contended that the last *varṇa* of the third foot was not *m* but *dam*, and that, therefore, the result of adding the three *varṇas* together would not be 'Saram' but 'saradam' (meaning 'jests')!

Mīripännē's interpretation was hardly complimentary either to the author of *Gaṃgārōhaṇa Varṇanāva* or to the distinguished headman who was eulogized in it. An exchange of letters soon followed between the author, Tōmis Samarasēkara Disānāyaka, and the critic, Mīripännē. The disagreement between them was not resolved by this exchange; but no large-scale controversy developed out of it, as Mīripännē, from the very beginning, was not in the least inclined to get involved in one. Indeed, he considered *Gaṃgārōhaṇa Varṇanāva* an 'excellent' poem; he came out with the above 'criticism' only when he was pressed hard by his patron, Abhayasiṃha Mudali of Galle, to show a blemish, however small, in it. (In pressing Mīripännē to show a blemish in the poem, Abhayasiṃha was merely accepting the friendly challenge of his relative, David de Saram, who had sent him a copy of it. Both de Saram and Abhayasiṃha, quite apart from being patrons of learning, were fairly accomplished scholars in their own right.)

The dispute was revived in the early 1850s because James Alwis, in the course of a classic survey of Sinhalese literature with which he introduced his translation of the thirteenth-century Sinhalese grammar, *Sidat Saňgarāva*, in 1852, referred to it at some length[32] and threw his own weight unequivocally behind Tōmis Samarasēkara Disānāyaka. Alwis called Mīripännē's critique 'no less unjust than wrong'; and 'with all the respect . . . for his eminent talents and truly poetic genius', he went on to cite some 'poetic blemishes' in the writings of Mīripännē himself.[33]

Mīripännē was not alive when Alwis's observations appeared in print; but his pupils, already saddened by their teacher's death in the previous year, and now provoked by the posthumous criticisms of him, took up his defence far more passionately than Mīripännē would ever have done himself.[34]

[31] See above, ch. IV, n. 20.

[32] 'Introduction' to *The Sidath Sangarawa* (Colombo, 1852), pp. ccxxxvii–cclv.

[33] *Ibid.*, pp. ccxl and ccxliii.

[34] Alwis consulted the opinions of Mīripännē's pupils before arriving at his conclusion regarding the 'sav sat dam' dispute. He was not convinced, however, by their arguments. *Ibid.*, p. ccxliii.

The details of the controversy as such has no relevance here;[35] the concern here is with some of its more significant results. Looking back at the controversy a decade later, Alwis wrote: 'That controversy awakened a spirit of inquiry previously unknown in Ceylon; and roused the dormant powers of a number of native scholars, who had been unknown to me, and had been content to remain buried in the obscurity and seclusion of their village *Pansalas* [monasteries]'.[36]

The 'native scholars' were, perhaps, not as 'obscure' as Alwis supposed; nor, considering the religious controversies that they were involved in, were their powers as 'dormant'. But, it must be noted, Alwis looked at them largely through the eyes of a sophisticated urbanite, and from that point of view it was only natural that he formed such an impression of them. The scholarly monks knew each other, and quite frequently disputed with each other. The laymen, in general, knew their monks well; but they knew very little of the disputes that the latter were involved in. Hence, even if the monks themselves were not exactly 'buried in the obscurity and seclusion of their village *pansalas*', a good many of their disputes certainly were.

The Sav Sat Dam Controversy, in contrast, was carried on almost entirely in the open. And what is particularly noteworthy, it provided the Buddhist monks with their very first opportunity to express themselves in print. All the printing establishments at this time (with the exception of the Government Press) were owned and managed by Christian organizations; and even though what they normally printed–Christian propaganda not infrequently coupled with attacks on Buddhism–was good material

[35] They have been dealt with by P. B. J. Hevawasam in 'The "Sav Sat Dam" Controversy', *UCR*, XVII (1959) 117–36.

[36] *Contributions to Oriental Literature*, Part I (Colombo, 1863), p. ix. Alwis entered into correspondence with many of these scholars, and he intended to publish parts of the correspondence as Part III of this work. This plan did not materialize, but a large portion of the correspondence has been preserved, of which a copy is available at the Ceylon National Archives: 5/63/94/(1). It was during the Sav Sat Dam Controversy that Alwis came into contact with Hikkaḍuvē Sumaṃgala, whom he described as 'a Priest of great intelligence and erudition'. 'I have profited much', he wrote, 'by cultivating an acquaintanceship with him, brought about by means of the controversy. . . . His letters to me in support of my views on the controversy are full of oriental learning. He not only quotes Sanskrit and Pali, but also Sinhalese writers; and he illustrates his position by arguments deduced from the art of Logic, and Rhetoric, not to mention writers on Prosody, on a matter directly bearing upon that branch of science'. *Contributions*, p. xiv.

for controversy, they resulted, in fact, in no real controversy, as Buddhists obviously had no access to the then existing printing establishments so long as their aim was to defend their religion. The Sav Sat Dam Controversy, however, had nothing whatsoever to do with religion; it was purely a literary controversy. The printing presses, therefore, were at the disposal of Buddhists, if they were so keen as to make use of them.

Mīripännē's pupil Koggala Dhammatilaka took the initiative in this regard. Not content merely with exchanging letters with Alwis, in February 1853 he published a defence of his teacher in the periodical *Śāstrālaṃkāraya* edited by John Pereira (Head Master of the 'Native Normal Institution') and published by the Wesleyan Mission Press. Soon many others joined in. But the editor of the journal being apparently somewhat partial to Mīripännē's point of view, no adequate representation was given to those who were in support of Alwis. Thus Alwis's teacher, Baṭuvantuḍāvē, started a rival periodical called the *Yatalaba Saňgarā* (printed at the Roman Catholic Press) in April 1854, and the controversy was continued in the columns of these two periodicals.[37]

The controversy itself came to no conclusive end.[38] But it created a wide interest among the Sinhalese literati, and to all those who participated in it, it provided a unique opportunity to develop their journalistic and polemical skills.[39] It was with these skills in hand, and in a background of widening interest in public controversies, that they began, in the next decade, their direct confrontation with Christian propagandists, a subject which we shall examine in some detail in the next chapter.

The effective, though not the formal, centre of Buddhism in Ceylon shifted, we noted earlier, from Kandy to the low country in the course of the nineteenth century. The question still remains: where exactly in the low country was this centre located?

The stronghold of Buddhism in the low country while Kandy was still

[37] Relevant extracts from the two periodicals were subsequently reprinted by Hendrick Perera Jayasuriya as a pamphlet called *Sav Sat Dam Vādaya* (Colombo, 1873).

[38] See Hevawasam, *op. cit.*

[39] Leading participants in the Sav Sat Dam Controversy, notably Koggala, Baṭuvantuḍāvē and Hikkaḍuvē, were among the pioneers of Sinhalese journalism. Koggala, in 1862, became the first editor of the first registered Sinhalese newspapers, *Lakmiṇipahana*. At this time, no longer a monk, he was known as Don Johannas Paṇḍitatilaka Koggala Gurutumā. See Kalukoňdayāvē Paññāsekhara, *Siṃhala Puvatpat Saňgarā Itihāsaya*, vol. I (Colombo, 1965), p. 80.

both the effective as well as formal centre of Buddhism was the area around the provincial town of Mātara in the Southern Province. This area did not really escape European intrusions after the sixteenth century; on the other hand, it was sufficiently removed from the citadels of European power, such as Colombo and Galle, to maintain its links with tradition reasonably unimpaired. The political influence of the kingdom of Kandy was high in this area, and it was also here that the impact of the mid-eighteenth century Buddhist revival in the Kandyan kingdom was most strongly felt (within the low country). Some of the leading monks in this area had their monastic training in Kandy; but once they had returned to the low country, they continued their religious and educational activities quite independently, under the patronage of their local headmen. In fact, with the literary contributions of these persons in mind, students of Sinhalese literature have come to speak of a specifically 'Mātara Period' of Sinhalese literature, a period extending roughly from about 1790 to 1830.[40]

Tennent, in 1850, described Mātara as a town 'which has always been pre-eminent as the stronghold of Buddhism and the residence of its most learned professors'.[41] But by 1850 the pre-eminence of Mātara as *the* stronghold was on the wane. As the movement which began there grew stronger, this provincial town became too small a place for its operations. It was replaced, about this time, by the much larger town of Galle which was also (still) the major port of the island.

The rise of Galle as a centre of Buddhist activity was closely related to the fact that it was in the immediate neighbourhood of Galle that all the major branches of the Amarapura fraternity (with the exception of its Kandyan branch) had their headquarters (at Välitara, Daḍalla, Doḍandūva and Mīripänna). All the monasteries of the Amarapura fraternity were new compared with those of the Siyam fraternity; but they were certainly very active. It is a clear indication of the enthusiasm of the Amarapura monks that they succeeded, within a short time, in equipping their monasteries with libraries which rivalled those in the older monasteries of the Siyam fraternity. Indeed, in 1875, the library at Daḍalla (founded at the beginning of the century by Kapugama Dhammakkhandha) was described in an official report on temple libraries as 'by far

[40] P. B. J. Hevawasam, *Mātara Yugayē Sāhityadharayan hā Sāhitya Nibandhana* (Colombo, 1966).

[41] Tennent, pp. 47–48.

the most extensive Buddhist library in the island'.[42] The libraries at Am̆bagahapiṭiya, Bōgahapiṭiya and Ganēgoḍälla—all Amarapura monasteries—also received special mention in the same report on account of the richness of their collections of manuscripts.[43]

The Amarapura monks were keen to maintain contacts with their co-religionists in Burma and Siam; and the proximity of their temples to Galle—for a long time, Ceylon's major gateway to the outer world—helped them to maintain these contacts. It was at Galle that Ceylonese delegations to southeast Asian countries were assembled prior to their departure; it was also there that Burmese and Siamese delegations were received and conducted with due ceremony to the monasteries in the vicinity of the port.[44]

The supremacy of Galle did not last very long; it was replaced by Colombo in the 1870s. Colombo, over the years, had been the administrative and political centre of the maritime provinces; and in the 1870s, it established its supremacy over Galle as the major port in the island as well. The city, at this time, was growing rapidly,[45] and the movement of Buddhists into this hub of events was a clear symptom of their growing strength.

Already, there were two large and ancient Buddhist temples in the neighbourhood of Colombo: one at Kälaṇiya, belonging to the Siyam fraternity, and the other at Kōṭṭe, belonging to the Kalyāṇi fraternity. Both these places had been active even in the early part of the nineteenth century when Buddhism, on the whole, was weak in the western part of the island. Tennent wrote of Kōṭṭe in 1850: 'Priests are still numerous, and Buddhism in that locality exhibits more activity and earnestness than is generally met with in the western section of the island'.[46] And in the course of the nineteenth century, Kōṭṭe and Kälaṇiya were supplemented

[42] Louis de Zoysa, *Reports on the inspection of Temple Libraries* (S.P. XI: 1875), pp. 11–12. For the impressions of a visitor to this library in 1816, see above, ch. II, n. 81.

[43] *Ibid.*

[44] For an account of the reception given by the Buddhists of Galle to the delegation sent by King Mongkut of Siam in 1852, see *The Dynastic Chronicles, Bangkok Era, the Fourth Reign (1850–1868)*, tr. Chadin Flood, vol. I (Tokyo, 1965), pp. 96 *et seq.*

[45] B. L. Panditharatna, 'The Harbour and Port of Colombo: a geographical appraisal of its historical and functional aspects', *CJHSS*, III (1960) 128–43, and 'Colombo City: its population growth and increase from 1824–1954', *The Ceylon Geographer*, XIV (1960) 1–10.

[46] Tennent, pp. 312–13. References to Buddhist activities at Kōṭṭe in the 1820s and 1830s can be found in James Selkirk, *Recollections of Ceylon* (London, 1844), pp. 378–79, 393–97, 412–13, 418–19, 442–50. Selkirk spent several years at Kōṭṭe as a missionary of the Church Missionary Society.

with newer Buddhist temples built much closer to the city of Colombo. The two most important of them belonged to the Saddhammavaṃsa (Amarapura) fraternity: the Jayasēkarārāmaya at Demaṭagoḍa, the residence, in his last years, of the founder of this fraternity, Laṃkāgoḍa Dhīrānanda, and the Dīpaduttārāmaya at Koṭahēna, the residence of Mohoṭṭivattē Guṇānanda, the leading anti-Christian polemicist of the 1860s and 1870s.

In the field of monastic educational institutions, the dominance of Colombo and its neighbourhood over other parts of Ceylon was firmly established with the founding of Parama Dhamma Cetiya Piriveṇa at Ratmalāna by Valānē Siddhārttha in 1845, followed by its two daughter-colleges: Vidyodaya Piriveṇa at Māligākanda, by Hikkaḍuvē Sumaṃgala in 1873, and Vidyālaṃkāra Piriveṇa at Pāliyagoḍa, by Ratmalānē Dhammāloka in 1875.

The rise of Colombo as the centre of Buddhism in Ceylon went further ahead as a result of the contest that the Buddhists, in and after the 1860s, were involved in with the Christian missionaries. For it was at Colombo that they established their main printing presses and publishing houses; new organizations like the Society for the Propagation of Buddhism, Buddhist Theosophical Society, Young Men's Buddhist Association; Buddhist schools; and so on. These will be discussed in detail in Part II.

The coincidence of the political and religious centres had been a common feature in the history of Sinhalese kingdoms, from Anurādhapura in the third century B.C. down to Kandy in the seventeenth and eighteenth centuries. The gradual shift of the religious centre to Colombo, after the political decline of Kandy, was therefore a continuation of the same process, though with an important difference. In Colombo, Buddhism was not favoured with the patronage of the political authority; hence its presence there was less conspicuous than in the earlier capitals.[47]

[47] Over the years, however, Buddhists seem to have gradually consolidated their position: fraternities which had no important monasteries there in the nineteenth century opened new ones in the early twentieth (the most important of which were Gōtamī Vihāre of the Kalyāṇivaṃsa fraternity and the Vajirārāma of the Dhammarakkhitavaṃsa fraternity); and at the symbolic level, although the traditional religio-political symbol par excellence, the Tooth Relic, continues to be at the old capital of Kandy, recent years have witnessed a proliferation of new Buddhist symbols all over the city of Colombo. See Gananath Obeyesekere, 'Religious Symbolism and Political Change in Ceylon', *Modern Ceylon Studies*, I (1970) 43–63.

Part Two

PROTESTANT BUDDHISM

Chapter VI

BUDDHISM VERSUS CHRISTIANITY: BEGINNINGS OF BUDDHIST PROTEST

i. THE CHALLENGE: CHRISTIAN MISSIONS IN CEYLON, 1800–1860

What was said in Part I of this study with regard to the activities of Christian missionaries in Ceylon in the nineteenth century related, in the main, to just one aspect of their activities, namely, to their involvement in the campaign to 'disestablish' Buddhism. This aspect was selected for special treatment because the disestablishment had important results for the traditional Buddhist organizations in Ceylon. In the 1840s and 1850s, the Christian missionaries were deeply involved in this issue; and in the decades that followed, they kept a watchful eye to ensure that the process that they had set in motion was not effectively reversed. Still, this involvement was just a part of their activities as missionaries, just one facet of their overall strategy to overthrow Buddhism and replace it with Christianity, into which, in fact, the attempt to deprive Buddhism of governmental support entered quite by accident owing to the special circumstances in which the Kandyan kingdom was ceded to the British in 1815. It is time now to focus attention on the more general and routine aspects of the missionary strategy, which began prior to and which were totally independent of the special issue of disestablishment.

Not long after the maritime provinces of Ceylon had fallen to the British (from the Dutch) in 1796,[1] attempts were made by the new rulers to reorganize the missionary efforts of their European predecessors. The first British governor in Ceylon, Frederick North (1798–1805), took the initiative in this regard, and his enthusiasm for the propagation of Christianity was shared by many of his successors. What the government

[1] For details, see Colvin R. de Silva, *Ceylon under the British Occupation, 1795–1833*, vol. I (3rd impression, Colombo, 1953), chs. II and III.

could directly do in this sphere remained somewhat limited, and the finances of the colony did not permit much governmental spending for religious and educational purposes. Yet, in Great Britain, the growth of the empire had witnessed the establishment of many missionary organizations, both Anglican and non-conformist, and these organizations received enough encouragement from the government to pursue their work in Ceylon. Thus, in 1805, there arrived in Ceylon four missionaries of the London Missionary Society; soon they were followed by others: Baptists in 1812; Wesleyans in 1814; and Church (of England) Missionaries in 1818. There was, in addition to these, a group of Congregationalist and Presbyterian missionaries sponsored by the American Board of Commissioners for Foreign Missions; they arrived in Ceylon in 1816.[2]

Of these five groups of missionaries, the first, the London Missionaries, did not expand beyond the original four who arrived in 1805 (one of the four was deported in 1807, and another left for South India in 1817); and the last group, the American Missionaries, though consistently active in the missionary field, was confined to the northernmost part of Ceylon where there were no Buddhists. The three groups of missionaries whose activities are relevant for the purposes of this study, therefore, are the Baptists, the Wesleyans and the Church Missionaries.

The Baptists, the smallest of the three groups, established their headquarters at Colombo (in 1812), and from there they gradually extended their activities eastward through Haṃvälla (1819) to Mātalē (1835) and then to Kandy (1841).[3] The Wesleyans, by far the most energetic of the three groups, had their mission stations along the populous southern and western coastline; beginning at the three key positions of Colombo, Galle and Mātara, they established, within two decades, new stations or substa-

[2] The earliest attempt to give a systematic account of the activities of all these missionary groups was Tennent's *Christianity in Ceylon* (London, 1850), a work which is useful, in addition to the historical data that it provides, as an exposition of the attitudes and aspirations of a prominent and influential administrator of the time. Of more recent studies, C. N. V. Fernando's 'A Study of the History of Christianity in Ceylon in the British Period from 1786–1903, with special reference to the Protestant Missions' (B.Litt. thesis, Oxford, 1942), gives a fairly useful general account. But its examination of the period 1868–1903 is rather superficial, and the study, as a whole, is lacking in a sufficiently critical approach to the subject.

[3] *A Historical Sketch of the Baptist Mission in Ceylon* (Kandy, 1850).

tions in thee intermediate towns and villages—Mīgamuva, Moraṭuva, Pānadurē, Kalutara, Ambalaṃgoḍa and Väligama.[4] The Church Missionaries, agents of the official Anglican Church, chose two places a little more inland: Baddegama (1819), twelve miles from Galle along the river Giṃ, and Kōṭṭe (1823), a one-time capital of Ceylon, five miles southeast of Colombo. They also had a third station at Kandy (1818), the last Sinhalese capital.[5]

In addition to the missionaries who were supported mainly by their own societies and by voluntary contributions, there was an official 'ecclesiastical establishment', which was maintained out of public funds. This establishment was placed under the jurisdiction of the Bishop of Calcutta in 1818, and an archdeacon was appointed in Ceylon for the administration of its local affairs. The ecclesiastical jurisdiction was transferred from Calcutta to Madras in 1837; in 1845 Ceylon was turned into a separate bishopric. Below the bishop and the archdeacon, there were within the ecclesiastical establishment several 'colonial chaplains', 'preachers' and 'catechists'; and there were also two much smaller non-episcopalian groups—the local branches of the Dutch Reformed Church and of the Church of Scotland. Members of the official establishment also took some part in the missionary enterprise; and a good many of the (non-official) missionaries received official grants, especially for their services in the field of education.

a. Education figured prominently as a means of diffusing Christianity, as it had done previously under the Portuguese and the Dutch. For primary instruction, there were schools of varying sizes attached to all mission stations; and for higher education there was a collegiate institution at Kōṭṭe, which, attached to the Church Mission, was founded in 1827 in order to train schoolteachers and candidates for the ministry. There were, in addition (a survival from the Dutch times), several 'parish schools' under the direction of the government, which had its

[4] W. M. Harvard, *A Narrative of the establishment and progress of the Mission to Ceylon and India* (London, 1823); and R. Spence Hardy, *Jubilee Memorials of the Wesleyan Mission, South Ceylon, 1814–1864* (Colombo, 1864).

[5] James Selkirk, *Recollections of Ceylon* (London, 1844); [anon.] *Jubilee Sketches: An Outline of the Work of the Church Missionary Society in Ceylon, 1818–1869* (Colombo, 1869).

own central collegiate institution at Colombo. These government schools came under the supervision of the Anglican clergy, and religious instruction constituted an essential part of their curriculum.[6]

The educational activities of the missionaries received high praise from the Colebrooke Commission in 1831. Dismissing the education provided by the Buddhist monks as scarcely meriting any notice, and reporting that government schools were 'extremely defective and inefficient', Colebrooke went on to remark: 'To the labours of these [missionary] societies . . . the natives are principally indebted for the opportunities of instruction afforded to them'.[7] He discouraged the retention of government schools in areas where the missionaries had already opened their own schools, and this advice was generally followed by the School Commission which was established in 1834 in implementation of Colebrooke's recommendations to 'facilitate the reform of government schools'.

The School Commission, with its subordinate committees at Kandy, Galle, Jaffna and Trincomalee, administered the funds allocated for educational purposes by the government; supervised the existing government schools, and made decisions on closing some of them and on opening new ones; appointed schoolmasters and fixed their salaries. They also made financial grants to non-government schools which were considered to be worthy of encouragement and assistance. The power and the patronage associated with these functions were enjoyed almost exclusively by the Anglican clergy who comprised an essential part of the commission, and whose head, the archdeacon, was also its president.[8]

[6] The following articles of L. J. Gratiaen deal with these government schools: 'The First English School in Ceylon', *CALR*, VII (1921–22) 141–47; 'The Parish Schools under Governor North', *ibid.*, VIII (1922–23) 35–44; and 'The Government Schools, 1804–1820', *ibid.*, IX (1923–24) 71–86.

[7] 'Report of Lieutenant-Colonel Colebrooke upon the Administration of the Government of Ceylon' (24 December 1831), in *The Colebrooke-Cameron Papers*, ed. G. C. Mendis, vol. I (Oxford, 1956), p. 73. In fact, the missionary schools, with very few exceptions, were confined to the northern and southwestern parts of Ceylon. In the Kandyan provinces, the decline of Buddhist monastic schools (see above, pp. 176–180) led to a steady decline in literacy during the early decades of the British administration. The neglect of the Kandyan provinces was suddenly realized by the administration after the disturbances of 1848 (see K. M. de Silva, *Social Policy and Missionary Organizations in Ceylon, 1840–1855*, London, 1965, pp. 176–79), but no effective steps were taken to remedy the situation.

[8] L. J. Gratiaen, *The First School Commission, 1832–1841*, Ceylon Historical Association, Pamphlet no. II (Colombo, 1927).

The Anglican monopoly was broken in 1841 when, under the new Central School Commission, membership was broadened to give representation to the Methodists, Presbyterians, and Catholics–the last being the largest Christian group in the island.[9] With regard to government schools, the Anglicans continued to hold their sway to a large extent; but over the control of the commission itself they no longer had the same monopoly. This led to much sectarian bickering within the Central School Commission, from its inception to its very end.[10]

Dissatisfaction with the Central School Commission resulted in 1865 in the appointment of a subcommittee of the Legislative Council 'to inquire into and report upon the state and prospects of Education in the Island'; and as a result of the recommendations of this subcommittee,[11] the School Commission was abolished and replaced with a (Government) Department of Public Instruction in 1869. As was made abundantly clear in the report of the subcommittee, the record of the School Commission was hardly a distinguished one. But the three and a half decades that it was in charge of education saw the firm entrenchment of Christian missionaries in the field. There were, to be sure, disagreements between the government and the missionaries; and there were also conflicts between the different missionary organizations. But from the point of view of the larger religious groups outside (Buddhists and Hindus), these conflicts amounted to scarcely more than family quarrels among the dominant minority of Christians.[12]

[9] The early decades of the nineteenth century saw a reorganization of the Catholic Church in Ceylon as a result of the re-establishment of contact with Europe. (After the expulsion of the Portuguese in the seventeenth century, there were no Catholic priests in Ceylon other than Indian priests of the Oratory of Goa.) Ceylon was made an Apostolic Vicariate by Rome in 1834, and soon afterwards European Catholic missionaries (Italian, French and Spanish) began arriving in the island. The first Catholic bishop was appointed in 1842. See 'The Letter of Father Francis Xavier to Governor Horton on the state of Catholicism in Ceylon, 1832', ed. R. Boudens, *CHJ*, III (1953) 86–92; and S. G. Perera, 'The First Catholic Bishop of Ceylon', *CALR*, VII (1921–22) 115–16.

[10] The following articles of L. J. Gratiaen deal with the history of the Central School Commission: 'The Central School Commission, 1841–1848', *JRAS(CB)*, XXXI (1928–30) 488–507; 'The School Commission, 1848–1859', *ibid.*, XXXII (1931–33) 37–54; and 'The Last Years of the Central School Commission, 1859–1869', *ibid.*, 328–46.

[11] For an examination of the recommendations and their impact, see L. A. Wickremeratne, '1865 and the changes in Education Policies', *Modern Ceylon Studies*, I (1970) 84–93.

[12] For a discussion of sectarian conflicts (especially between the Anglicans and the Methodists) within the School Commission during the years 1840–55, see K. M. de Silva, *Social Policy*, ch. IV.

It is worth noting that the lack of governmental assistance did not lead to the extinction of Buddhist monastic schools; in fact, the general decline which was manifest in the Kandyan provinces had no impact on the low country, where there was a steady strengthening of monastic education in the course of the nineteenth century. But, even at their best, Buddhist monastic schools were no match for Christian schools so far as the educational needs of laymen were concerned. Christian schools alone, with their more modern curricula, English education, and formal and informal contacts with the administration, had the capacity to provide laymen with secure avenues of secular advancement.

The missionaries were aware of this advantage and they were not slow to make capital out of it. But, though the largest portion of their time was probably spent on educational activities, the missionaries–particularly the more evangelically oriented ones like the Methodists and the Baptists–were not entirely satisfied with predominantly pedagogic roles. They, quite naturally, did not regard themselves as mere schoolteachers; nor did they cease to remind themselves, as well as others, that their aim was 'not making the natives learned men',[13] or helping them in their secular careers. If those things mattered, they mattered only as means to an end, in fact to *the* end–conversion to Christianity.

As far as the larger aim of conversion was concerned, education, despite its advantages, also had its obvious shortcomings. Even with government assistance, the number of schools that the missionaries could open, and effectively run, remained limited; and although by means of schools they came into contact with an important segment of the population, the number of 'heathens' outside the classroom always remained immeasurably larger than those inside.[14] Since those who were outside could not be made to come to the missionary, the missionary had to go to them; in other words, he had to tread the arduous path of the itinerant preacher.

[13] D. J. Gogerly, 'The Wesleyan Mission Free Schools', *Colombo Journal*, 16 February 1833.

[14] James Selkirk wrote to the Secretary of the Church Missionary Society at London in May 1833: 'The schools are at present badly attended. The Buddhist festivals occur about this season of the year, and many of the children are taken away by their parents and friends and relations to go with them to the temples. It is very discouraging, when we have been instructing our children all the year round in the truths of Christianity, to find their parents and relations step in between us and them, and say, "You must come with us to worship Buddha" '. Printed in Selkirk, *Recollections*, pp. 321–22.

b. Preaching, despite, or perhaps because of, the hardships and privations associated with it, had deep emotional significance for the evangelical missionary. He was highly conscious that this was the original and ordained means of spreading the gospel. Thus John Murdoch, who was about to embark on full-time missionary work, having, in October 1849, resigned his position as headmaster of the Government Central School at Kandy, wrote in his journal: 'I shall require to travel on foot, and shelter at night wherever I can, as I shall be unable to pay for lodgings; but even this has its associations which ought to render it pleasant. I shall be following the example of the Apostles, yea, of the Saviour Himself'.[15]

Buddhist villagers were not averse to listening to preachers, for preaching was as much an established Buddhist practice as it was a Christian one. Yet, for the same reason, the odds were heavily against the missionaries, for here they had to compete with Buddhist monks who were skilled preachers themselves, who greatly outnumbered the missionaries, and whose contacts with the villagers were of a far more enduring and recurrent nature.

Out in the villages scattered throughout the country, the missionary was very much on his own. Government support, if any, was of no great help to him; he had no secular incentives to offer his potential clientele—all he could offer was a new hope of salvation; his knowledge of English did not matter; what mattered rather was his knowledge of Sinhalese—and here he was greatly handicapped, and particularly so in comparison with the Buddhist monk who, as a speaker of Sinhalese, was clearly in a class of his own.

There were some, though not many, missionaries who gained considerable proficiency in Sinhalese. But their knowledge of the language was far from perfect; nor were their expressions in it always idiomatic or readily intelligible to their auditors, and this was made worse by the novelty of the content of the expressions.[16] With the highly complex system of Sinhalese

[15] Quoted in Henry Morris, *The Life of John Murdoch* (London, 1906), p. 56.

[16] Of the early missionaries who were able to speak and write Sinhalese, the most important were these: James Chater and Ebenezer Daniel of the Baptist Mission; John Callaway, Benjamin Clough, Robert Spence Hardy and Daniel J. Gogerly—all of the Wesleyan Mission; and Samuel Lambrick and James Selkirk of the Church Mission. They all wrote tracts and pamphlets; in addition, Chater wrote *A Grammar of the Cingalese Language* (Colombo, 1815); Callaway, *A Vocabulary in Cingalese and English* (Colombo, 1820) and *A School Dictionary* (Colombo, 1821); and Clough, *A Dictionary of the English and Singhalese Languages* (Colombo, 1821) and *A Dictionary of the Singhalese and*

honorifics, personal pronouns and their corresponding verbs and verbal-affixes,[17] the missionaries had virtually insurmountable difficulties. Clough wrote in the Preface to his English-Sinhalese Dictionary:

The Singhalese use an endless, and to Europeans a disgusting variety, in their modes of address, having about fourteen different terms to express the singular pronoun *you*, which must be varied, not only according to the rank of the person addressed . . . but likewise according to the character of the speaker. According to Singhalese etiquette a scrupulous adherence to the use of these terms is indispensable, as the least deviation is considered an insult.

'Nothing but an acquaintance with the language, and knowledge of the habits of the people can enable a foreigner to use them with propriety', he warned his readers;[18] but in practice this warning went unheeded. The missionaries tried, arbitrarily, to simplify the 'endless and disgusting variety', and in doing so, if they showed any method at all in their arbitrariness, it was only in preferring the less polite and the impolite forms to the more polite and the over-polite. Their standard Sinhalese equivalent for the English *you*, in addressing an audience, was *um̆balā*; and their vocabularies give, and their sermons and pamphlets use, for example, *varen* and *varellā*, *palayan* and *palayallā*, *karapan* and *karapallā* as the normal (singular and plural) equivalents of the imperatives *come*, *go*, *do*.[19]

These expressions were not necessarily offensive; it all depended on the relative statuses of the speaker and the person spoken to. In general, they were proper for use by two parties, mutually, in situations of social equality and familiarity, and by persons of high status to those of low (but not vice versa) in situations of marked inequality (e.g., parents and children, masters and servants). They were certainly inappropriate for general and promiscuous use in addressing persons of widely differing social status,

English Languages (Colombo, 1830); and Lambrick, *A Grammar of the Singhalese Language* (Cotta, 1834) and *A Vocabulary of the Singhalese Language* (Cotta, 1840). Even as pioneering efforts, the quality of these works was low, and compared very unfavourably with similar works produced in India. For a contemporary critique, see the comments of James Alwis in the 'Introduction' to *The Sidath Sangarawa* (Colombo, 1852), pp. ccliii–cclviii.

[17] On this subject, see James Alwis, 'Terms of Address and Modes of Salutation in use amongst the Singhalese', *JRAS(CB)*, III (1856–58) 219–76.

[18] *Op. cit.*, p. 627.

[19] See, for instance, Callaway, *A Vocabulary*; Lambrick, *A Vocabulary*, and *Sermons in Singhalese preached to Village Congregations* (Cotta, 1838).

either individually, or on occasions like preaching, collectively. Buddhist monks in their formal dealings with the laity successfully avoided the problem of (secular) status differences amongst the laity by resorting to terms like *pinvatni*–'(you) the meritorious'–which, while being flattering to all alike, had no relevance outside the religious context. Such terms, even if they were known, were not acceptable to the missionaries. Nor did they have the inclination to evolve a parallel terminology of their own. Their avowed aim was uprooting 'native prejudices', not coming to compromises with them. This attitude of mind strained their relationships not merely with those whom they looked upon as potential converts to Christianity, but also, as will be shown by the following example, with now a few of those who already professed Christianity.

The Church Missionaries at Kōṭṭe began, in the early 1820s, a new Sinhalese translation of the Bible. They did so because they were dissatisfied with the Sinhalese Bible, which had just been issued (1817–20) by the Colombo Auxiliary Bible Society, on the ground that it was written in 'high Sinhalese' and that it did not follow 'the beautiful simplicity of the original, which God himself had dictated'. Their projected 'simplifications' involved, among other things, the use of just one pronoun throughout for the second person singular–in strict conformity with the original, but in flat opposition to Sinhalese usage. The pronoun which they chose was *tō*: in sound close to the English 'thou', but in meaning far from it. Lambrick, the chief translator, evidently knew of the difficulties involved. 'To apply *tō* . . . to a man of respectable class', he admitted, 'is an actionable offence: and, I believe, damages have been actually awarded for it. . . . In the last complete version of the scripture into Singhalese, the Devil being represented as applying *tō* to our blessed Saviour, a Native professor of Christianity has declared, that he shudders whenever he reads that passage'.[20] Still, Lambrick was undaunted by these difficulties. For in his opinion, opposition to the use of *tō* was 'but a prejudice; and we have the surest grounds to conclude, that it will be constantly weakened, and diminished, when opposed by the mighty power of simplicity and truth'.[21]

The new translation of the whole of the Old and New Testaments,

[20] *An Essay to shew that every version of the Holy Scripture should conform to the Original in adopting one word throughout for each of the Personal Pronouns* (Cotta, 1826), pp. 8–9.

[21] *Ibid.*

known as the 'Cotta Version', appeared in 1834 (several individual books having been previously printed and used in Church Mission schools). Criticisms, not unexpected, followed from Sinhalese Christians;[22] but soon events took a somewhat less expected turn. When the new translation was introduced into Anglican churches in the 1840s (despite opposition from some congregations), the most prominent Sinhalese Christians in Colombo rose in a body and retired from the church on the ground that 'when language absolutely insulting, and in our opinion degrading, to our God and Saviour is used, we can only testify our abhorrence of it by withdrawing from the sound thereof'. In a petition to the Bishop of Colombo, they asked for a declaration that, until the Church had set forth an authorized version of the Bible, each congregation be free to choose a version that it preferred; and failure to make such a declaration, they insisted, would 'drive us to the necessity of seeking Christian privileges in some other branch of the Church Catholic, which will not impose on us, as terms of communion, a version of the Scriptures and of a Liturgy abounding . . . in blasphemous expressions towards our Creator, Redeemer, and Sanctifier'.[23]

Finally, but only after a prolonged controversy in which the Church Missionaries defended their translation with much tenacity,[24] causing not a little ill-feeling within the Christian community in Ceylon, the church authorities had to give way. Fresh translations of the Bible were undertaken in the 1850s with the active participation of prominent Sinhalese Christians like John Pereira and James Alwis.[25] These new and more acceptable translations did not appear in print until the early 1860s.

To return now to the subject of preaching—there is no evidence to indicate that the missionaries met with any active hostility in the villages either from the laymen or from the monks. Evidence is fairly clear, on the contrary, that they received a good deal of unexpected hospitality (as we shall see later in section ii of this chapter). Yet instances were not scarce,

[22] F. de Levera, *Remarks on the Cotta Version of the Scriptures into the Singhalese Language* (Colombo, 1835).

[23] The petition is given in Tennent, pp. 266–69.

[24] James Selkirk, *A Short Defence of the Cotta Version of the Scriptures into Singhalese* (Cotta, 1835).

[25] See James Alwis, *Contributions to Oriental Literature*, Part I (Colombo, 1863), pp. 27–48 and 89–95.

apparently, when the missionary, with his new doctrine of salvation and his limited knowledge of the language and customs of the people whom he visited, failed to attract the kind of serious attention that he expected from them. The Baptist missionary Ebenezer Daniel, who toured the area surrounding the mission station at Haṃvälla fairly extensively in the 1830s, dwelt at some length (in a letter, dated 8 July 1840, to the Committee of the Baptist Missionary Society in England) on the wide discrepancy between the ideal expectations of the missionary societies in England and the disappointing realities of the actual mission field in this regard. On the ideal expectations, he wrote:

People in England may think it an easy thing to go to a Singhalese village and preach to the people the good tidings of salvation through Jesus Christ. They may be ready to concede that . . . as soon as the missionary begins to open his commission crowds of willing hearers will flock around him, and receive his message with breathless attention and joy.

And, on the realities:

I enter a village, and, proceeding from house to house, I sit down on a seat, if I can procure one, or if not, I spread a mat upon the ground, and endeavour, in the plainest language, and with the most familiar illustrations, to explain the way of salvation. Sometimes, in answer to invitations to attend, the Singhalese ask, 'What will you pay us to do so? Will you give us arrack, if we listen to you?' If not thus coarsely insolent, they will invent some excuse to get away; and if sent to ask their friends to attend, they go, but do not return. We proceed to another house; and having thus spoken the word in one village, we pass on to the next. We often meet with little but contempt, opprobrium, and laughter.[26]

The refusal of Buddhist villagers to take missionary preachers seriously is hardly surprising, for, as heirs to a religious tradition in which preaching constituted an important element, they had rather fixed notions about the proper time, place and manner of preaching. The missionaries ignored those notions to their own cost.

Daniel's reference to demands for arrack is perhaps not without significance, for Europeans, particularly in the interior parts of Ceylon, had a well-established image as both consumers and distributors of liquor. 'The

[26] Quoted in Tennent, pp. 281–82.

Chingulays [Sinhalese] have a saying', wrote Knox in the seventeenth century, 'that Wine is as natural to white Men, as Milk to Children'.[27] This impression gained added confirmation during the early years of British rule in the Kandyan provinces, for one of the many ways in which the new regime differed from the old was on account of the facilities that it provided for the distribution of liquor. C. R. Buller, the government agent of the Central Province, pointed out in 1848 that the new government, which, during the first three decades of its existence, had established only four schools in his province, had granted licences for the erection of not less than 133 arrack taverns during the same period.[28] The association of Europeans with liquor was acutely embarrassing to the missionaries. Hardy, who in common with many of his contemporaries viewed the expansion of British power and influence as an act of God for the conversion of the heathen, found himself compelled to refer to the expansion in the liquor trade as 'the daemon that accompanies the spread of British influence'.[29] There were some missionaries who took some interest in temperance work, especially during or soon after the 1850s. But their opposition to the government's connection with the liquor trade never reached the same proportions as their earlier opposition to the government's connection with Buddhism.

Tennent, who quoted Daniel's letter in his *Christianity in Ceylon*, wrote on the *results* of preaching: 'It may safely be said, that of the whole number of real conversions in Ceylon, *five* at least have been made by means of preaching for one by the initiative of schools, or any other instrumentality'.[30] He provides no evidence to support this claim of 'safety'. The little he says on the subject, in fact, would warrant only a very different conclusion. His statement does reveal the high value placed on preaching as the ideal means of conversion, particularly because not all the missionaries were sufficiently qualified, or even inclined, to resort to it. Its validity as a statement of fact, however, remains doubtful in the extreme.

[27] *An Historical Relation of Ceylon* (1681), ed. James Ryan (Glasgow, 1911), p. 294. On the Sinhalese of that period Knox wrote: 'Drunkenness they do greatly abhor, neither are there many that do give themselves to it' (p. 159).

[28] 'Report on the Disturbances', enclosure to despatch no. 165 of 15 September 1848, Torrington to Grey, C.O. 54/251.

[29] *Eastern Monachism* (London, 1850), p. 319.

[30] P. 279.

c. Although the missionaries were handicapped as far as the *spoken* word was concerned, they nonetheless had, for what it was worth, a monopoly over the written, or more correctly, the *printed* word.

The printing press was first used for religious ends in Ceylon by the Dutch, who established a Sinhalese press in 1736 and used it extensively for printing religious works.[31] The need to revive this practice was felt in the early years of British rule, and as a first step a local branch of the British and Foreign Bible Society was formed at Colombo in August 1812 under the presidency of the governor (Brownrigg) and the active membership of the local clergy and the civil service.[32] While this society–the Colombo Auxiliary Bible Society–was busy arranging translations of the Bible and trying to get the old Dutch press repaired, the newly arrived Wesleyan missionaries established, on their own, a press at Colombo in 1815.[33] Since the Wesleyans already had a trained printer (Harvard) amongst them, the printing work of the Colombo Auxiliary Bible Society was soon entrusted to them. The Wesleyans did this work in addition to the work of their own mission, and also that of the Colombo Auxiliary Religious Tract Society, which was organized later in 1825. The Wesleyan lead was followed by the Church Missionaries and the Baptists, who, respectively, established presses of their own at Kōṭṭe in 1823 and at Kandy in 1841.

The task of co-ordinating the work of these different printing presses was done subsequently by the Sinhalese Tract Society, which was organized by John Murdoch in 1849.[34] Murdoch, who first arrived in Ceylon as headmaster of the Government Central School at Kandy and who resigned that post after four years of service, was a firm believer in the use of the press as a means of diffusing Christianity. His enthusiasm in this field gained due recognition when he was appointed 'Representative and Travelling Secretary in India' of the (interdenominational) Christian Vernacular Education Society, which was organized in England in 1858.[35] This new post kept Murdoch busy for the rest of his life; he travelled widely in Ceylon and India as well as in other parts of Asia; wrote many tracts and

[31] M. P. J. Ondaatje, 'A Tabular List of Oriental Works and Translations, published by the late Dutch Government of Ceylon at the Printing Press at Colombo', *JRAS*, n.s., I (1865) 141–44.

[32] *First Report of the Colombo Auxiliary Bible Society* (Colombo, 1813).

[33] Harvard, *A Narrative.*

[34] Morris, *Life of John Murdoch*, pp. 52 *et seq.*

[35] *Ibid.*, pp. 107–12.

pamphlets himself, and got others to do likewise; made arrangements for their publication and circulation; and periodically compiled catalogues of the publications already issued. The *Classified Catalogue of Printed Tracts and Books in Singhalese* which he published in 1868 with the collaboration of James Nicholson of the Wesleyan Mission, is a useful guide to the nature and contents of the works issued by missionary presses in Ceylon. It is particularly useful because not many of the works seem to have survived, some having disappeared even before the *Catalogue* was compiled.

In contrast to the Dutch missionaries, who used their printing press mainly to issue translations of the Bible, catechisms and prayer books for use in their schools and churches,[36] the British missionaries, from the outset, intended to use their presses for much wider ends. Their main aims were well expressed in the very first report of the Colombo Auxiliary Bible Society, which declared: 'To instruct the sincere Believer in the duties of his profession, to convert the nominal Christian into a faithful disciple of the Gospel, and to reclaim the deluded victim of Idolatrous superstition, are the great objects of this Society'.[37] In accordance with this policy, British missionary publications were, from the beginning, directed as much to the Buddhist as to the Christian. Tracts, pamphlets and (religious) periodicals figured as prominently amongst them as translations of the Bible, catechisms and prayer books. The launching of attacks on Buddhism received as high a priority as expositions of Christianity. Indeed, as the missionaries soon began to realize the extent to which 'the deluded victims of idolatrous superstition' and 'nominal Christians' outnumbered 'sincere believers', the expository publications gave way to the polemical in number as well as volume.

The traditional religion of the Sinhalese appeared to the missionary as a massive evil structure that had to be destroyed before conversion proper could begin. And the printed word provided the missionary with his most convenient outlet for his intense religiosity as well as the anger and frustrations that it necessarily engendered. Gogerly, the manager of the Wesleyan Press, was convinced in 1831 'that, at present, it is by means of

[36] Ondaatje, 'A Tabular List'.

[37] Pp. 20–21. This declaration was prompted by the more circumscribed policy adopted by the sister Society at Calcutta, which, because of fears of opposition from Hindus and Muslims, publicly disclaimed all intentions of making converts.

the Press our principal attacks must be made upon this wretched system. . . . We must direct our efforts to pull down this stronghold of Satan'.[38] Gogerly's imagery was not accidental. In missionary thinking and writing in the heyday of imperialism, attack and destruction, the metaphors of militarism, loomed larger than the milder imagery of spiritual husbandry–shepherds and lost sheep, seeds and harvests. They found their most violently eloquent expressions in the tracts and pamphlets written in English.[39] But the same spirit was unmistakably there, even in the Sinhalese writings.

Missionary tracts and pamphlets had a fairly extensive circulation in Ceylon, and for over four decades they had no competition from the Buddhists in this field. Figures of their total circulation are not available; but according to Murdoch and Nicholson, 1,500,000 had been circulated over the period 1849–61.[40] The significant result of this wide circulation was not that it helped the missionaries to achieve what they wanted to achieve–converts to Christianity–but rather that it provoked the Buddhists, though only after a time, to retaliate and meet the missionaries on their own ground.

ii. THE BUDDHIST RESPONSE, 1800–1860

British missionary efforts, in contrast to those of the Portuguese and the Dutch, were carried on during a period when Buddhism was fairly strong, and in fact (as we have seen in Part I of this study) was becoming stronger in the low country, where the missionary efforts were also most concerted. Even so, at first the British missionaries received no more resistance from the Buddhists than their Portuguese and Dutch predecessors. Buddhists, both laymen and monks, were more interested in fostering their religion in their own way than in competing with Christian missionaries. Tennent perceived the situation correctly when he wrote in 1850:

> Active hostility can scarcely be said to be manifested either by the Buddhists or their priesthood; and although more energetic exertions have been recently made by the latter, in the erection of banamaduas, the holding of pinkamas, and

[38] Quoted in M. Y. Gooneratne, *English Literature in Ceylon, 1815–1878* (Dehiwala, 1968), pp. 90–91.

[39] *Ibid.*, ch. VII.

[40] *Classified Catalogue of Printed Tracts and Books in Singhalese* (Madras, 1868), p. iv.

ceremonies, the efforts have been directed less to the discouragement of Christian religion than to the extension of their own.[41]

Christianity, of course, was nothing entirely new to many Buddhists; and they, in contrast to the missionaries, had no urge to regard the two religions as violently opposed to each other, to regard one as the 'Truth' and the other as 'Error'. Indeed, supporting both Christianity and Buddhism in different ways, and simultaneously, was an established practice in the maritime provinces, particularly among the more influential laymen who had connections with the government. These laymen had to cultivate the friendship of Buddhist monks in order to preserve their influence in the provinces; at the same time, in order to maintain their official positions, they had to gain the favour of Christian administrators and missionaries. It was not uncommon for them to be educated by Buddhist monks; but what helped them to achieve official positions was the education they received at government and missionary schools. Helping to build these schools and to maintain them, as well as looking after the comforts of the missionaries who ran and supervised them, constituted an important part of their official duties and obligations. Furthermore, whatever their personal religious convictions, in order simply to ensure the legal recognition of births, marriages and deaths in their families, they had to register them at Christian institutions, and therefore, according to Christian rites.

The situation was not new; it was already there when the British missionaries arrived in Ceylon. And it continued, after their arrival, with no noteworthy change except that the new Anglican form of Christianity now came to be regarded as the 'government religion'–in succession to Roman Catholicism under the Portuguese and 'reformed religion' under the Dutch.

With the right to register births, marriages and deaths taken over by the Anglican religious establishment, official membership of the Dutch Reformed Church declined rapidly. By 1850, its congregations were almost entirely limited to the few descendants of the old Dutch settlers in the major coastal towns.[42] The loss of the Dutch church was the gain of the Anglican. But the gain was mainly in terms of statistics of baptism, that is,

[41] *Christianity in Ceylon*, pp. 320–21.
[42] *Ibid.*, pp. 99–104.

in terms of a rite which for the Sinhalese had a legal rather than a religious significance. The ceremony of baptism, since the times of the Portuguese and the Dutch, was followed by the registration (in the *tombo*) of the name of the person baptized. This registration was of paramount importance in all civil and judicial matters relating to legitimacy and inheritance.[43]

Thus, the demand to be baptized, as the British missionaries discovered soon after their arrival in Ceylon, was never wanting among the (low-country) Sinhalese. But this was scarcely the sort of 'conversion' that the missionaries wanted. They discussed the subject of baptism at the highest levels;[44] at times, they reprimanded their Sinhalese assistants for the enthusiasm that they displayed in baptizing individuals with no regard to the 'worthiness' of the candidates themselves or of their sponsors;[45] and the (earlier) Dutch missionaries were freely criticized for having created 'nominal Christians' in Ceylon by means of indiscriminate baptisms.[46] Yet the British clergy were not in the least inclined to part with the same means as the Dutch clergy had used to bolster up their statistics. Indeed, over the question of exclusive rights to register births, marriages and deaths, there was a bitter struggle between the Anglicans and the non-conformists, just as there was one (as was mentioned earlier) over control of the School Commission. As in the field of education, so in the field of registration: the Anglican monopoly was broken in the 1840s, and the privileges were distributed on a formally equal footing among the different Christian groups.[47] But again the non-Christians were left out. And until the introduction of civil registration in 1868 they had no choice

[43] See the comments of James Alwis ('Terms of Address', pp. 241–43) in reply to Tennent's observations on baptism amongst the Sinhalese. Alwis concluded: 'The Singhalese resort to *baptism*, not as a religious duty, nor as a ceremony which conferred, as supposed by Sir Emerson Tennent, "*some civil distinction*"; but simply as an operation which alone secured the registration, which they prized so very high' (p. 242).

[44] Bishop Reginald Heber to the Church Missionaries of Kōṭṭe, 13 September 1825, in *Narrative of A Journey through the Upper Provinces of India*, vol. II (London, 1849), pp. 155–57.

[45] 'Extracts from Journal, 4 July 1838', in Selkirk, *Recollections*, pp. 515–16. Selkirk also wrote a small tract on the subject of baptism: *Bavtisma labā siṭina ayaval pradhāna koṭa siyaluma Siṃhala manuṣyayinṭa yakun ädahīmē ajñāṇakama saha pāpaya gäna danvana kāranā* (An Address to the Singhalese, particularly to such of them as have been baptized, on the Folly and Sin of Devil Worship) (Cotta, 1837).

[46] Selkirk, *Recollections*, pp. 244–45; Tennent, pp. 81–90.

[47] K. M. de Silva, *Social Policy*, pp. 51–58.

but to make a profession of Christianity, however nominal, in order simply to enjoy their essential civil rights.[48] Under these circumstances, it would appear hardly surprising that Buddhists continued to seek baptism, though not for the reasons that the missionaries preferred.[49]

The position of Buddhists in relation to education in Christian schools was not very different from their position in relation to baptism: they simply had *no alternative* to seeking instruction in Christian schools if they had any ambitions either to gain admission to new careers in the administrative service of the government or to keep within their reach such official careers as had previously been held by members of their families. An enthusiasm for education motivated by such ambitions was, again, not what the missionaries wanted; education, for the missionary, was essentially a means of conversion. They frequently noted with regret how the seminaries that they ran for the purpose of training young men for missionary work failed to realize their main objective. Of the Government Seminary at Colombo, it was said by a Colonial Chaplain in 1814: 'The Cingalese pupils consist chiefly of the sons and near relations of Modliars, Mohottiars and Mohandrams. They all know that the acquiring of the English language is the direct road to temporal honours and emolument'.[50] Similarly, the Church Missionaries at Kōṭṭe found out in the twentieth year of their 'Christian Institution' 'that the object for which it was established had not been fully effected; as many of the students after having completed their course, shrank from the trials and self-denial attendant on Mission work and made choice of the more lucrative and popular employment at the disposal of the Government'.[51]

So long as their children had an education that prepared them for respectable and lucrative secular careers, Buddhist parents had no seri-

[48] In the 1840s, there were demands from Buddhists for equal rights in the field of registration (e.g., C.N.A. 5/63/152/(7)), and the government was prepared to consider the immediate introduction of civil registration. The missionaries however managed to dissuade the government from taking this step. *Ibid.*, pp. 54–55.

[49] 'Indeed, almost all the Buddhist priests in the maritime provinces are persons who have been baptized in their infancy', wrote Selkirk, *Recollections*, p. 515. This was probably an exaggeration, though there were for certain Buddhist monks who had been baptized in their infancy. A noteworthy example was Hikkaḍuvē Sumaṃgala. See Yagirala Prajñānanda, *Śrī Sumaṃgala Caritaya*, vol. I (Colombo, 1947), pp. 17–18.

[50] Quoted in Gratiaen, 'The Government Schools', p. 83.

[51] *Jubilee Sketches*, p. 80.

ous objections to religious (i.e., Christian) instruction given in schools. Hence, although there was a 'conscience clause' adopted by the School Commission in 1841 (to the effect that religious instruction in government schools, as well as in those missionary schools which were supported by the government, be limited to the first hour of school, and that no child should be compelled to attend school during this hour if his parents objected to his doing so), this clause, in practice, was no real barrier to teaching Christianity to non-Christian children. Murdoch, the headmaster of the Government Central School at Kandy, reported in November 1844 that *all* children in his school read the Bible 'without offering any objections';[52] and Boake, the principal of the Colombo Academy, wrote that in his school, during a period of twelve years, 'not more than two instances occurred . . . in which any objection was expressed to the attendance of pupils, and, in each of these instances, the objection was abandoned when the matter was explained to the objector'.[53]

The manner in which the 'conscience clause' was formulated favoured the teacher rather than the parent; it was up to the parent to *object* to religious instruction (in person or in writing) rather than for the teacher to obtain the *consent* of the parent. Hence, indifference or reluctance on the part of parents to displease the teachers (who obviously had control over the children's future) may well have played some part in rendering the clause ineffective. But what was clearly of far greater importance was that Buddhists were not inclined to compare, and contrast, Buddhism and Christianity in the same way as the missionaries did; they were not given to considering respect or allegiance given to one as a root and branch rejection of the other. Theirs was a syncretistic religious tradition where 'pure Buddhism' mingled with 'non-Buddhist' beliefs and practices; and though they were not incapable of differentiating between these two aspects of their religious tradition, they were capable of seeing harmony between them. Likewise, though it gave no comfort to those who taught them Christianity, they were also capable, in their own way, of seeing similarities between Buddhism and Christianity. Gogerly, who, like all his colleagues in Ceylon, was puzzled and intrigued by this phenomenon, made an effort to understand the Buddhist point of view, and his obser-

[52] Morris, *Life of John Murdoch*, p. 27.

[53] *National Education in the East in general and in Ceylon in particular* (Colombo, 1855), pp. 6–7.

vations on the subject, which were supplied to Tennent, merit quotation at some length. Gogerly wrote:

In morals the Buddhists look on their own religion and that of the Christians as identical, so that without formal hypocrisy they fancy they can find themselves justified in making a profession of both. The doctrine of Christ shedding his blood for the redemption of men is not in opposition to their previous habits of thought; for they are taught by their own books that if all the blood lost by Buddhu himself in his different transmigrations for the benefit of sentient beings were collected, it would be more than the waters of the ocean.[54]

Nor were the attitudes of Buddhist monks, vis-à-vis Christianity, fundamentally different from those of laymen. As Gogerly continued:

Until Christianity assumed a decidedly opposing position, even the priests looked upon that religion with respect, and upon its founder with reverence. I have seen it stated in a controversial tract, written by a Buddhist priest of Matura not fifteen years since, that probably Christ in a former state of existence was a God residing in one of the six heavens (a position which they represented Gotama as having occupied immediately previous to his birth as Buddhu); that animated by benevolence he desired and obtained a birth as a man, and taught truth so far as he was acquainted with it. That his benevolence, his general virtue, and the purity of his doctrine rendered him worthy of reverence and honour. If, therefore, the supremacy of Buddhu and the absolute perfection of his system were conceded, they saw nothing inconsistent in respecting both systems–Buddhism as the perfection of wisdom and virtue; Christianity as an approximation to it, though mingled with errors.[55]

Buddhist monks, on the whole, looked upon Christian missionaries not so much as their adversaries as a group of religious virtuosi who preached to and instructed the laity, and therefore, as a group more or less akin to themselves. They did not shun the company of missionaries, or of Europeans in general–in contrast to many orthodox brahmins in India who shunned Europeans with the same sort of disgust as they shunned the low castes.[56] 'When not treated with disrespect, the priests of Ceylon rather court intercourse with Europeans than otherwise' wrote Hardy, who knew them as a missionary;[57] and Turnour, who came into repeated contact with

[54] Tennent, *Christianity in Ceylon*, p. 240.

[55] *Ibid.*

[56] See above, p. 44.

[57] Hardy, *Eastern Monachsim*, p. 312.

the monks of Malvatta ans Asgiriya both as Government Agent of the Central Province and as research worker in the libraries of these temples, wrote: 'Nothing can exceed the good taste, the unreserved communicativeness, and even the tact, evinced by the heads of the buddhistical church in Ceylon, in their intercourse with Europeans, as long as they are treated with the courtesy, that is due to them'.[58]

The monks did not regard their religious and literary knowledge as an exclusive possession. To those who sought it, they were ready to give instruction as well as access to their treasured collections of manuscripts. Furthermore, when translations of the Bible were undertaken by the Colombo Auxiliary Bible Society in 1812, two of the ablest and most scholarly monks in the low country, Karatoṭa Dhammārāma and Bōvala Dhammānanda, gave their assistance to the venture without the least reluctance.[59]

There are recorded instances of Buddhist monks assisting in the preparation of places of Christian worship in the immediate neighbourhood of their temples, and also of their placing the *baṇa maḍuvas* (preaching-halls) attached to Buddhist temples at the disposal of Christian missionaries.[60] They were genuinely puzzled when reciprocal requests on their part for the use of (missionary) schoolhouses for Buddhist preaching were indignantly turned down by the missionaries.[61]

The missionaries who took to itinerant preaching often spent the nights at Buddhist monasteries where they were received by the resident monks with the sort of hospitality with which they greeted their own brethren. As Hardy wrote:

In travelling through unfrequented parts of the interior, as was once my wont and my delight, I usually took up my abode at the pansal, and seldom was I refused a night's lodging or a temporary shelter during the heat of the day. The

[58] 'Introduction' to *The Mahāwanso in Roman Characters with the Translation subjoined* (Cotta, 1837), p. xliv.

[59] The translations were under the general supervision of William Tolfrey of the civil service. Tolfrey himself, with the assistance of Don Jacobus Dias Mudali and Paulus Perera Muhandiram, began translations from English into Sinhalese; and in order to obtain a final version, this direct translation was compared with an indirect one: from English into Pali by Don Abraham de Thomas (Älapāta) Muhandiram, and from Pali into Sinhalese by Karatoṭa Dhammārāma and Bōvala Dhammānanda. *The First Report of the Colombo Auxiliary Bible Society* (Colombo, 1813).

[60] Harvard, *A Narrative*, pp. 270, 272–73, 290.

[61] Hardy, *Eastern Monachism*, p. 313.

priests would bring out the alms-bowl, when they saw that I was hungry . . . ; or they would bring tobacco or some other luxury, to express their satisfaction at my visit.[62]

Hardy was perplexed by these kindnesses, and by the fact that the monks did not feel 'enmity to me as the teacher of another faith'–apparently assuming that to be the most natural feeling to have. He sought explanation in the stereotypical attitudes that were freely attributed to the Buddhists at the time: indolence, apathy and indifference in all matters concerning religion.[63] Interpreted thus, the tolerance and the lack of fanaticism and bigotry among the Buddhists appeared not so much as an uncommon virtue as a common vice, a vice all the more pernicious in its consequences as it stood in the way of conversion to Christianity. Tennent, writing his *Christianity in Ceylon* in the same year as Hardy wrote his *Eastern Monachism*, contrasted the problems (as they appeared to him) which beset the first apostles of Christianity with those which were currently being faced by the missionaries in Ceylon; and he concluded: 'Instead of the strife of theology, they have to overcome the apathy of indifference, and experience has proved that they encounter a more formidable opponent in the stupor of ignorance than in the dialectics of scepticism'.[64] Hardy, in the same vein, expounded the curious paradox: 'The carelessness and indifference of the people among whom the [Buddhist] system is professed are the most powerful means of its conservation'. And he concluded in a tone of some exasperation: 'It is almost impossible to move them, even to wrath'.[65]

Thus, it is not very surprising that when persistent attacks on Buddhism, in both the spoken and the written word, eventually provoked the Buddhists to withdraw their tolerance and to turn against Christianity, the missionaries–at the beginning, at any rate–instead of being disheartened by the reaction, welcomed it gladly as a great boon (even though they were a bit taken aback by the 'blasphemies' committed by the Buddhists). They were gratified to see that Christianity and Buddhism were at last in open combat, to find that all, in the end, would be compelled to make a definite

[62] *Ibid.*, 312–313.
[63] *Ibid.*
[64] P. 262. See also pp. 228–29.
[65] P. 430.

choice between the two opposing sides. As to which side would ultimately win, the missionaries, of course, entertained no doubts at all. Hardy himself, back in Ceylon (after an absence of fifteen years) just in time to witness the beginnings of the Buddhist reaction, wrote soon after his final return to England:

> A controversy, of great interest, has recently commenced in Ceylon, between the Christians and the Buddhists. The priests have purchased presses and type, and possess printing establishments of their own. They now refuse to render any assistance to the missionaries, as before, in explaining the native books, or lending those that are in their libraries for transcription. . . . Tracts, pamphlets, and serials issue in large number from the Buddhist presses. . . . I have formed bright anticipation as to the future. There can be no doubt as to the result of the contest now carried on; for although it may be prolonged and severe, it must end in the total discomfiture of those who have arisen against the Lord and his Christ, and in the renunciation of the atheist creed that now mars the happiness, and stays the enlightenment, of so many of the dwellers in Lankā.[66]

iii. THE BUDDHIST RESPONSE, 1860–1880

Although there were no organized and sustained expressions of anti-Christian feelings among Buddhists before the 1860s, signs of injury over attacks on their religion by the missionaries began to appear much earlier. To the Buddhists, these attacks appeared not merely distasteful and offensive, but also unjust, for they themselves made no similar attacks on Christianity. They could scarcely see that the missionaries needed no more provocation from them than their being Buddhists; that what was 'meritorious' to them was 'sinful' to the missionaries; that what they did as Buddhists—such as going to their own temples and worshipping at them, supporting Buddhist monks and listening to their sermons—were all utterly 'horrifying' and 'appalling', 'abominable' and 'wicked'[67] in the eyes of the missionaries.

The earliest Buddhist reaction to missionary attacks was to address petitions to the government. These petitions began to appear in the 1820s,

[66] *The Legends and Theories of the Buddhists, compared with History and Science* (London, 1866), pp. viii–ix.

[67] These were the common adjectives used to describe Buddhism and Buddhist practices at the time. See, for instance, Selkirk, *Recollections*, p. 378, and Hardy, *Eastern Monachism*, p. 321.

not long after the earliest missionary tracts and pamphlets had begun to appear in print. These petitions, in general, (1) affirmed the petitioners' deep concern for the welfare of Buddhism which had prevailed as their and their ancestors' religion for over two thousand years; (2) referred to the pain of mind caused to the Buddhists as a result of what was being written and preached against their religion by Christian missionaries; (3) pointed out that Buddhists themselves made no similar attacks on Christianity; and (4) urged the government to uphold religious toleration by (a) ordering the withdrawal of offensive publications which had been issued, and (b) making a general proclamation that no religious group should issue publications which are likely or calculated to offend and injure the feelings of other religious groups.[68]

These petitions failed to procure for the Buddhists the proclamation that they wanted, though there were isolated instances when the government did intervene to caution and restrain some of the overzealous missionaries. On 27 December 1833, Governor Horton wrote to Benjamin Clough of the Wesleyan Mission–almost certainly after protests by Buddhists–requesting the withdrawal of a tract which he felt to have 'the character of being prompted by hostile feelings', and expressing his wish that in future 'that mode of warfare should be avoided'. Writing to the Committee of the Wesleyan Missionary Society at London on the same issue, about a month later, the governor pointed out that 'true Religion' should be maintained against 'spurious religion' through 'a mild exposition of the truth of one and of the errors of the other, all personality should be excluded, and all imputations of bad intentions rather than of erroneous opinion'.[69]

Again, in 1852, when Benjamin Bailey, the archdeacon of Colombo, issued a pmaphlet called *Six Letters of Vetus . . . on the Re-connexion of the British Government with the Buddhist Idolatry of Ceylon*–in the words of the then governor, Anderson–'in language so violent and offensive as calculated to excite and exasperate the whole Buddhist population', the gov-

[68] Petitions of the following: 152 inhabitants of Pānadurē and the Rayigam, Salpaṭi and Hēvāgam Kōralēs to Governor Barnes, 15 September 1826, C.N.A. 5/63/152/(4); 96 monks of the Malvatu and Asgiri Chapters to the Commission of Enquiry, 13 September 1829, C.O. 416/31; (unspecified number of) monks and laymen of Daḍalla to Governor Barnes, n.d., C.N.A. 5/63/47/(3).

[69] Quoted in Gooneratne, *English Literature in Ceylon*, p. 91.

ernor protested to the Colonial Office (since its author refused to be cautioned either by the governor or by the Bishop of Colombo) and ensured that the archdeacon was compelled to resign his post.[70]

But such intervention on the part of the government was a very rare occurrence. The two (recorded) instances just referred to are noteworthy for the fact that they both took place on a background of noticeable nervousness on the part of the government created by its initial negligence, and then, under strong missionary pressure, by its subsequent refusal to honour the undertakings given to Buddhism in the Kandyan Convention of 1815.[71] The administrators, obviously, had to pay greater attention than the missionaries to the possible political consequences of causing discontent among the Buddhists. Hence they showed a general preference for a strategy of moderate rather than violent, and of indirect rather than direct, attack. Their basic attitudes towards Buddhism, however, did not differ significantly from those of the missionaries; all of them, to varying degrees, were supporters of the missionary enterprise; most of them had the same vision as the missionaries of a Buddhism that was doomed to decline and fall. It was not up to them to stand in the way of the inevitable; it was up to the Buddhists themselves to defend their ill-fated religion as best as they could.

As early as the 1830s, there were sporadic attempts on the part of individual Buddhists to reply to missionary tracts.[72] Yet these replies did not lead to an immediate and continuous debate between the two sides. For while the Buddhist defence was unorganized, the missionary attacks, on their own part, invited no serious rebuttals; they revealed all too plainly their unfamiliarity with what they held in contempt. The missionaries, at this stage, did not consider it worth their while to read Buddhist literature, to examine closely the religion they were trying to overthrow. Their general attitude to Buddhist literature was probably well summed up by

[70] K. M. de Silva, *Social Policy*, pp. 119–21.

[71] See above, pp. 115–127.

[72] The C.M.S. Tract no. 10—*Viruddhavādī Buddhagankārayāṭa Kristiyānikārayā visin dena Prativacanayi* (A Christian's Reply to a Buddhist Objector, Cotta, 1834)—is a rejoinder to a Buddhist reply, dated 18 October 1831, to an earlier tract. Gogerly, in a passage quoted earlier (p. 210), refers to a controversial tract written by a Buddhist monk of Mātara (*ca.* 1835). And B. M. Or. 2656 ff. 168–74 is an anti-Christian criticism of certain statements regarding Buddhism and the solar system which appeared in a calendar published by the missionaries in 1839.

George Conybeare Trimnell of the Church Mission, who, in 1833, recorded as one of the great achievements of his mission station at Baddegama that 'where there was nothing to be read but a few Buddhistical books, or foolish songs, written by hand on the leaf of a tree, there are now hundreds of printed copies of the Word of God'.[73] The situation changed mainly through the efforts (undertaken, incidentally, in the face of discouragement from headquarters) and the example of the two leading Wesleyan missionaries of the time, Hardy and, more particularly, Gogerly.

Hardy, who first arrived in Ceylon in 1825, soon applied himself to the task of learning Sinhalese; and, in 1835, returning to the mission field after a furlough of two years in England, he began reading Sinhalese religious works systematically so 'that I might ascertain, from authentic sources, the character of the religion I was attempting to displace'.[74] Hardy's reading was limited, however, to Sinhalese, and therefore secondary, sources; and the more important results of his studies were published only after his return to England in 1847. His *Eastern Monachism* (1850) and *Manual of Buddhism* (1853) were widely read in Ceylon by the missionaries as well as by the English-educated Ceylonese, by whom they were acclaimed as 'authoritative' works on Buddhism.[75] They failed, however, mainly because of the language barrier, to reach the Buddhist monks, who might, had they been able to read the works, have pronounced opinions rather less complimentary.

In contrast to the studies of Hardy, Gogerly's were based on the Pali sources. Gogerly, who arrived in Ceylon in 1818, began the systematic study of Pali in 1833 at Mātara, where, while in charge of the Wesleyan mission station, he came into contact with some of the leading Buddhist monks of that town and gained the benefit of their knowledge and access to their libraries. Gogerly's writings, again, were largely in English.[76] But

[73] Quoted in Selkirk, *Recollections*, p. 248.

[74] Hardy, *Eastern Monachism*, 'Preface'.

[75] James Alwis reflected this opinion when he referred to Hardy as 'an undoubted authority on matters connected with Buddhism'. 'Preface' to *The Attanagalu-Vansa*, translated from Pali (Colombo, 1866), p. cliii. In appreciation of his works on Buddhism, Hardy was elected to an honorary membership of the Royal Asiatic Society in 1856. See his obituary in *JRAS*, n.s., III (1868) v–viii.

[76] *Ceylon Buddhism: The Collected Writings of Daniel John Gogerly*, ed. A. S. Bishop, 2 vols. (Colombo, 1908).

in 1849, putting his knowledge of Pali to its immediate practical use, he published in Sinhalese a treatise of 144 pages called *Kristiyāni Prajñapti* (The Evidences and Doctrines of the Christian Religion), which immediately superseded all the previous polemical writings issued by the missionary presses and sounded the effective beginnings of the Christian-Buddhist controversy.

Kristiyāni Prajñapti was inspired partly by William Paley's *Evidences of Christianity* (1794), which, in its popularity at the time as a text for religious instruction, ranked second only to the Bible itself. Gogerly followed Paley–and his anti-Deist precursors like Charles Leslie and Joseph Butler–in Part II of his treatise. Following their arguments, he put forward prophecy and miracles as 'evidences' of Christianity.

Kristiyāni Prajñapti was not merely about the *evidences* of Christianity; it was also about its *doctrines*. Hence, in addition to the 'facts' of divine revelation, it also had to show the 'necessity' of divine revelation. Part I of the treatise was devoted to this purpose; and since it was intended mainly for a Buddhist audience, Gogerly made a comparison of Buddhist and Christian doctrines in relation to key theological issues such as causality, the uniqueness of man, sin and the problem of evil, sources of morality and religion, and salvation. The aim of this comparison (which was the more original contribution of Gogerly) was to 'refute' the Buddhist doctrines and to establish the 'truth' of the Christian.

After its first publication in 1849, *Kristiyāni Prajñapti* was reissued in 1853, and again in 1857 (at the rate of 2,000 copies in each edition).[77] And then in 1861 Gogerly added to it a long introduction of 78 pages: an elaboration of some of the ideas already expressed in Part I of the original work, it was called 'Proofs that Buddhism is Not a True Religion'. This was, on the whole, a new approach to Buddhism: an approach characterized by appeals to 'evidences' and 'proofs', to reason rather than to emotion. The underlying assumption of this new approach (already discernible in works like that of Paley) was the superiority of Christianity over other religions on the intellectual plane, on account of the soundness of its own principles and the unsoundness of the principles of other religions.

[77] Murdoch and Nicholson, *Classified Catalogue*.

The new approach was reflected in the style and tenor of *Kristiyāni Prajñapti*; in it there were no violent outbursts on the 'sin and folly of idolatry and devil worship'. In this respect it differed noticeably from the bulk of the earlier publications as well as from the current English publications (intended mainly for Christian readers) by missionaries like Bailey and Boake. Indeed, with its relatively restrained style and numerous quotations from the Pali scriptures (which far exceeded those from the Bible), *Kristiyāni Prajñapti* approximated, at least in its outward appearance, to the polemical works written about this time by Buddhist monks in relation to disputes within the Buddhist order.

Kristiyāni Prajñapti repeatedly challenged Buddhists to disprove, if they could, its main theses.[78] This challenge was repeated again and again soon after its publication. In addition to the work itself, several small tracts, based on it and written in a still more controversial style by Gogerly's Sinhalese protégé, David de Silva, were circulated widely.[79] And the Wesleyans as well as other missionaries quoted the work frequently in their sermons throughout the country.

Buddhist monks, with their polemical skills sharpened as a result of their participation in the earlier internal religious and literary controversies, accepted the challenge. They realized, at the outset, that the new controversy needed an effort rather different and more organized than the earlier ones; for even though the basic issues of the new controversy—the evidences and the doctrines of the Christian and Buddhist religions—were perhaps as esoteric as those which were involved in the earlier—'Adhikamāsa', 'Sīmāsaṃkara' and 'Sav Sat Dam'—controversies,[80] a contest between Christianity and Buddhism was bound to have much wider popular interest. The tracts and pamphlets written in relation to the Adhikamāsa and the Sīmāsaṃkara controversies were addressed almost exclusively to the monks themselves; and those in relation to the Sav Sat Dam Controversy were written mainly with the Sinhalese literati in mind. Polemical exchanges with the missionaries, in contrast, had to be addressed to the largest possible audience; and for this reason the monks had to have

[78] Pp. 43, 78 (Colombo, 1849); p. 76 (Colombo, 1861).

[79] Murdoch and Nicholson, *Classified Catalogue*.

[80] Regarding these controversies, see above, pp. 129–136, 153–160, 182–185.

the same means that the missionaries, all this time, had been using against them: printing presses.[81]

Ironically enough, the first Buddhist press (at Colombo) was the selfsame press which for over three decades had belonged to the Church Missionaries at Kōṭṭe, and which during that period had been used extensively to issue pro-Christian and anti-Buddhist publications. It was sold by the missionaries in 1855 (to a person who had been employed for some time in the printing office) because they found it difficult to spare sufficient time for its management, and also because, by that time, several other printing presses had been established in Colombo or elsewhere, by other missionary organizations. The decision to part with the press, however, caused them no little regret in retrospect. 'It is a sad fact', they wrote in their *Jubilee Sketches*, 'that this press, which had been so long instrumental in diffusing truth and knowledge, was, soon after its transference to other hands, used in opposition to Christianity, and that from it came forth the first of the Buddhist tracts, naturally filled with blasphemy'.[82]

Immediately afterwards, a second Buddhist press, called Laṃkopakāra Press, was established independently at Galle on the initiative of Bulatgama Sumana of Paramānanda Vihāre. It began in July 1862 with the help of small local contributions; and once it had begun to operate, Bulatgama managed to obtain more substantial grants for its maintenance, notably from his friend, King Mongkut of Siam,[83] and also from a wealthy Kandyan chief, Rahupola Abhayakōn Jayasundara Hērat Baṇḍāra of Ūva.[84]

[81] As far as the more 'serious' Buddhist works were concerned, it appears that, initially, not all the monks were enthusiastic over the advantages of printing. Rhys Davids, the founder of the Pali Text Society, wrote: 'I once tried in vain to persuade my friend and tutor, the learned and high-minded monk Yātrāmullē Unnānse, that it would be a good thing to print the Pitakas. He said they would be no longer copied; and he would not be convinced that books printed on our flimsy paper were safer than those written on substantial palm leaves'. *Buddhism* (London, 1877), pp. 235–36 (footnote).

[82] Pp. 66–67.

[83] Mongkut himself, during his monkhood, was the first Siamese to establish a printing press (which was housed in his own monastery). R. Lingat, 'History of Wat Pavaraniveça', *Journal of the Siam Society*, XXVI (1933) 80–81.

[84] Bulatgama to Rahupola (a message of thanks), 23 February 1863. C.N.A. 5/63/150/(17).

The Galle publications were largely the work of Hikkaḍuvē Sumaṃgala, still in his thirties, and already a respected scholar who had displayed his abilities in the Adhikamāsa and the Sav Sat Dam controversies. The leading Buddhist figure at Colombo, Mohoṭṭivattē Guṇānanda (1823–90), was by five years Hikkaḍuve's senior, but until now a relatively unknown monk of the Amarapura (Saddhammavaṃsa) fraternity. In outlook and temperament very different from Hikkaḍuvē as well as from the majority of his other contemporaries, Mohoṭṭivattē, popularly known as Migeṭṭuvattē Hāmuduruvō, soon became the leading champion and popular hero of the Buddhists in the Christian-Buddhist confrontation. Though born in the Southern Province, Mohoṭṭivattē lived at Koṭahēna (a suburb of Colombo) at Dīpaduttārāmaya, a temple founded in 1832 by his uncle and teacher, Sīnigama Dhīrakkhandha. On the founder's death in 1843,[85] Mohoṭṭivattē succeeded to the incumbency jointly with two of his fellow-pupils; and then in 1858 the full incumbency devolved on him. The experience of living in Colombo at a time when–compared with the more rural areas in his native province–Christianity was dominant and Buddhism was at a low ebb, made a deep impression on Mohoṭṭivattē in his young days. In the main, this experience had the result of hardening his attitudes toward Christian missionaries, whom, on account of their preachings and writings against Buddhism, he identified as his and his religion's major adversaries. And once he had set his mind on the task, he combatted them with a zeal that equalled, if not exceeded, that of his opponents, coupled with verbal skills far superior to theirs.

Mohoṭṭivattē's first major step in mobilizing resistance to the missionaries was the organization, in 1862, of a 'society' which was called Sarvajña Śāsanābhivṛddhidāyaka Dharma Samāgama. The name of the society was translated into English as 'Society for the Propagation of Buddhism', in evident imitation of 'Society for the Propagation of the Gospel', which had been active in Ceylon since 1840. This was the first clear sign of the shape of things to come: the attempt on the part of the Buddhists to meet the missionaries on their own ground, with weapons deliberately modelled on those of their opponents. It was this society–the Society for the Propagation of Buddhism–that acquired (after a change of hands) the printing press which in 1855 had been sold by the Church Missionaries. And the

[85] C.N.A. 5/63/47/(134) is a copy of his will dated 3 July 1843.

funds of the society were devoted mainly to the publication and distribution of polemical tracts, pamphlets and periodicals.

The first publication of the Society for the Propagation of Buddhism was *Durlabdhi Vinodaniya*, a reply written by Mohoṭṭivattē to Gogerly's *Kristiyāni Prajñapti*. It began as a monthly periodical in June 1862; and soon after the appearance of its first number, the Wesleyans–in fact Gogerly himself–started a rival periodical in July called *Sudharma Prakaraṇaya*. While the exchanges between these two periodicals were going on, Hikkaḍuvē Sumaṃgala, from Galle, joined in, in October of the same year, with the first issue of *Sudarśanaya*. For the next three years or so, the claims and counter-claims of Christianity and Buddhism were argued out mainly through periodical publications of this sort, each generally lasting about a year, sometimes less, to be followed immediately afterwards by another under a different name but containing the same sort of material. Thus: from the Society for the Propagation of Buddhism came forth *Kristiyāni Vāda Mardanaya* (1862–63) and *Samyak Darśanaya* (1863–64), both by Mohoṭṭivattē; written by Hikkaḍuvē and printed at the Laṃkopakāra Press at Galle, there appeared *Bauddha Vāksāraya* (1863), *Sumati Saṃgrahaya* (1864) and *Labdhi Tulāva* (1864–65); and the Wesleyans, who were leading the Christian front, wrote and published *Bauddha Vākya Khaṇḍanaya* (1863) and *Satya Dvajaya* (1863–64).

The subjects discussed in the columns of these periodicals were broadly akin to those raised by Gogerly in *Kristiyāni Prajñapti*–the evidences and the doctrines of the Christian and Buddhist religions. But as the controversy progressed, the actual range of topics widened, and the number of arguments and counter-arguments multiplied. The Buddhists, taking their cue from the Christians, devoted as much of their effort to attacking the religion of their opponents as to defending their own.

Gogerly himself did not live long enough to see the progress of the controversy that he, more than anybody else, had helped to originate. Ending a forty-four-year stay in Ceylon, he died on 6 September 1862 when the controversy was just beginning. To succeed Gogerly as General Superintendent of the South Ceylon Mission, Hardy, who had been away in England since 1847, returned to Ceylon in 1863. Hardy at once began to evince a great interest in the controversy; and in the hope of making his own contribution to it, he began the study of the Pali Scriptures with the help of oral translations given by Don Johannas Paṇḍitatilaka of Koggala (former monk and leading participant in the Sav Sat Dam Controversy). But after a time, Koggala 'was unwilling to proceed further . . . , probably deterred by the supporters of Buddhism; and . . . no one of competent information could be induced to continue the task, even for high reward'.[86] Undeterred by such difficulties, which he did not have to encounter during his previous stay in Ceylon, Hardy managed to write a polemical treatise called *The Sacred Books of the Buddhists compared with History and Modern Science* (Colombo, 1863), which was also issued in Sinhalese under the title *Sudharma Nikaśaya* (Colombo, 1865). But Hardy's sojurn in Ceylon did not last very long. He returned to England soon, in 1865, leaving the superintendence of the South Ceylon Mission to his son-in-law, John Scott. With the death of Gogerly and the subsequent departure of Hardy, the task of leading the Christians in the Christian-Buddhist confrontation devolved on the Sinhalese Wesleyan minister, David de Silva. He, among the Christians, came to occupy a position that perhaps came closest to that which was occupied by Mohoṭṭivattē among the Buddhists.

The encounter between de Silva and Mohoṭṭivattē, which had been going on for several years through rival publications, took a dramatic turn in August 1873 when the two faced each other in a two-day public debate at Pānadurē (a coastal village a few miles south of Colombo) on the relative merits of Christianity and Buddhism. This debate, though far-reaching in its consequences, was not unique in the mode of its occurrence, it was simply the culmination of a series of debates which began almost a decade earlier.[87]

British missionaries, from the very beginning of their stay in Ceylon, showed a keenness to have public discussions on religious subjects with Buddhist monks. Thus:

Influenced by a desire to become intimately acquainted with the superstitions of the natives, that he might be the better prepared to expose their absurdity and sinfulness, Mr. Clough [one of the original Wesleyan missionaries who, subsequently from 1826–38, was General Superintendent of the South Ceylon

[86] Hardy, *Legends and Theories*.

[87] Regarding interreligious debates in the eighteenth century, see above, ch. I, n. 60 and n. 145.

Mission] took every opportunity of being present at their religious services, and endeavoured on such occasions to engage the priests in conversations on religious topics, in the hearing of their followers.[88]

At first, the Buddhist monks, though not uncommunicative, showed no eagerness to be drawn into argument. Their general attitude was probably well summed up by an unnamed monk of the Kōṭṭe temple who, when visited for the first time by Selkirk (who was then in charge of the Church Mission station in the neighbourhood of the temple) on 17 June 1827 told the latter 'that the English people worshipped Jesus Christ, and that the Singhalese people worshipped Buddha, that they were both good religions'.[89]

Such expressions, of course, gave no satisfaction to the missionaries, and they took every opportunity to display their disagreement. Particularly at temples situated close to mission stations, the missionaries were seen frequently on occasions of important Buddhist festivals and ceremonies; and on those occasions they made efforts to distribute tracts and make speeches denouncing Buddhism and Buddhist practices. When in July 1835 a grand religious festival, attracting thousands of devotees, was held at the Kōṭṭe temple (on account of the consecration of twenty-four Buddha images in the new verandah that had been built around the main shrine-room), the Church missionary in the village (Selkirk) and his catechist were there on every evening during the entire festival-week with copies of a special tract–on the common theme of the 'sin and folly of image worship' with particular reference to the consecration ceremony that was then being held–which they had ready, written and printed, a month in advance of the ceremony. Their provocative conduct during the festival brought to an end the–outwardly, at least–friendly relations that they, until then, had managed to maintain with the monks of the temple.[90] Still the intrusions, at Kōṭṭe as well as elsewhere, continued over the years, indeed with increasing vigour, until they reached a peak soon after the publication of *Kristiyāni Prajñapti* (which gave the missionaries the confidence that Buddhism had been conclusively 'refuted' after an

[88] Harvard, *A Narrative*, p. 234.

[89] 'Extracts from Journal' in Selkirk, *Recollections*, p. 379.

[90] *Ibid.*, pp. 441–50.

examination based on its 'most authentic sources') which the monks found quite unbearable.

In the mid 1860s, with their campaign against Christianity through the printing press already well organized, the monks decided to come out into the open. Their first major opportunity arose at Baddegama–a Church Mission station since 1819, to which the first Anglican church built in Ceylon was also attached–when members of the local Anglican seminary (which had been transferred to Baddegama from Kōṭṭe in 1863), having previously had several discussions with the monks of the Buddhist temple in the village, challenged them, in the presence of several Buddhist laymen who had gathered at the temple on 21 November 1864, to a public debate. The monks accepted the challenge, and after an exchange of letters the meeting was fixed for 8 February 1865.

On the appointed date, the missionaries were in for some surprise. Shattering their theories of a Buddhism that was losing its hold over its adherents, the defenders and supporters of Buddhism appeared at the meeting in formidable force. Under Bulatgama Sumana's leadership, nearly fifty monks–from different temples scattered right along the coastal belt from Colombo to Galle–were there at the meeting. Amongst them were Hikkaḍuvē Sumaṃgala of the Siyam fraternity, Potuvila Indajoti of the Kalyāṇi fraternity, Kahavē Ñāṇānanda of the Amarapura Mūlavaṃsa fraternity, Mohoṭṭivattē Guṇānanda of the Amarapura Saddhammavaṃsa fraternity, and Väligama Sumaṃgala of the Amarapura Kalyāṇivaṃsa fraternity–five of the ablest representatives of their respective fraternities assembled for the first time, in all probability, on a common platform. Along with the monks, there were also about two thousand Buddhist laymen. The leaders and supporters of Christianity–ministers, catechists and laymen–apparently numbered about sixty or seventy.

The impact of the show of strength was immediate. George Parsons, who was in charge of the mission station, wrote to his headquarters soon afterwards:

> The spirit of controversy broke out in November last, and though I was partly prepared for it, I was slow to believe it would become such a serious matter until urged by our people to prepare for a fierce contest. The result fully justified their anxieties, for never before in Ceylon was there such a marshalling of the enemy

against Christianity. The one aim of the fifty priests and their two thousand followers who assembled here on February 8, was not to defend Buddhism but to overthrow Christianity. . . . Knowing the people we had to encounter, we felt that our victory would be more triumphant and complete, by attacking Buddhism, while we defended Christianity. It was not, however, till we were somewhat advanced in the controversy, that we could fairly estimate the difficulties of our position, and day by day, we had to commend ourselves in prayer to God and confide in Him for wisdom and direction at every step.[91]

The 'Baddegama Controversy' was in fact held not in the form of a public debate—because of disagreements between the two sides on the exact mode of holding one—but in the form of questions and answers exchanged in writing. The letters thus exchanged, signed by Bulatgama Sumana on behalf of the Buddhists and by George Parsons on behalf of the Christians, were printed for general circulation in May 1865.[92]

In August of the same year, a similar exchange of letters took place at Varāgoḍa (a village close to Kälaṇiya in the Western Province).[93] And this was followed by the first public debate proper at Udanviṭa (in the Four Kōralēs) on 1 February 1866.[94] A second debate occurred at Gampola (in the Central Province) on 9 and 10 January 1871;[95] and the more famous debate at Pānadurē on 26 and 28 August 1873 was the third of the series.[96]

The spokesmen for Christianity varied somewhat from debate to debate. At Udanviṭa, the spokesman was John Edward Hunupola, a former Buddhist monk and convert to Christianity employed by the Anglican missionaries as one of their preachers. At Gampola, Hunupola was joined

[91] Quoted in J. W. Balding, *The Centenary Volume of the Church Missionary Society in Ceylon, 1818–1918* (Madras, 1922), pp. 119–20.

[92] *Baddēgama Vādaya*, ed. Bulatgama Sumana (Galle, 1865). Bulatgama, in his introduction, gives a brief account of the meeting on 8 February 1865 and the series of events that led to it.

[93] Summaries of questions and answers were published under the title *Varāgoḍa Vādaya* (Colombo, 1865) by the Society for the Propagation of Buddhism.

[94] *Udanviṭa Vādaya* (Colombo, 1866) is a summary of the proceedings published by the Society for the Propagation of Buddhism.

[95] A summary of the proceedings was published by the Society for the Propagation of Buddhism under the title *Gampola Vādaya* (Colombo, 1873).

[96] *Pānadurē Vādaya* (Colombo, 1873) gives a summary of the proceedings in Sinhalese. An English translation of the proceedings, together with brief observations on the debate by the *Ceylon Times* special correspondent (John Perera, a Sinhalese Christian), was published by the editor of the *Ceylon Times*, John Capper, as *A Full Account of the Buddhist Controversy held at Pantura* (Colombo, 1873).

by two others: F. S. Sirimanne, a catechist of the Church Missionary Society, and Samuel Perera, a Sinhalese non-conformist minister. The main Christian speaker at Pānadurē, as was mentioned earlier, was David de Silva of the Wesleyan Mission; but of the four (one-hour) speeches delivered there on the Christian side, one was by Sirimanne. The change of speakers was, partly at least, due to the difficulty of finding a proper match for Mohoṭṭivattē, the Buddhist spokesman at all the debates, 'a consummate master of public haranguing'.[97]

Mohoṭṭivattē's style of oratory differed noticeably from that of the traditional Buddhist preacher. In contrast to his seated and motionless traditional counterpart, he stood up when he spoke, and he also made free and skilful use of gestures.[98] His style was perhaps influenced by that of Christian evangelical preachers. But if this was so, he, by all accounts, outdid the more legitimate heirs of that tradition in Ceylon in arresting the attention of audiences. Mohoṭṭivattē's hold over the massive and unprecedented gathering at Pānadurē (about five thousand on the first day, and over ten thousand on the second) was seen perhaps even more vividly at the close of the debate than during it.

> Scarcely had the last words of the above lecture [Mohoṭṭivattē's concluding address] been uttered when cries of 'Sadu' ascended from the thousands who were present. Endeavours were made by the handful of Police to keep order, but nothing induced them to cease their vociferous cries until at the request of the learned High Priest of Adam's Peak [Hikkaḍuvē Sumaṃgala], the Priest Migettuwatte again rose, and with a wave of hand, beckoned to men to be quiet, when all was still.[99]

Of their victory at Pānadurē, as well as elsewhere, the Buddhists themselves had no doubts whatsoever. But this was not a victory that the Christians were willing to concede. The issues of the controversy were such that no agreement between the two sides on its final outcome was indeed conceivable. What the general trend of the Christian-Buddhist confrontation did show clearly, however, was the degree to which the Christian

[97] *Ibid.*, p. 4. David de Silva, though learned, was a poor orator; Sirimanne, though not learned, was more fluent. It was for this reason that Sirimanne was asked by the Christian clergy who were at Pānadurē to open the proceedings of the second day of the debate. *Ibid.*, p. 35.

[98] *Ibid.*, p. 3.

[99] *Ibid.*, p. 73.

missionaries had misjudged the religious situation in Ceylon, in particular the degree to which they had overestimated their own abilities and underestimated the abilities of their opponents.

'The countenances of the priests in Ceylon', wrote Hardy in a work that was held to be highly authoritative, 'are frequently less intelligent than those of the common people; indeed there is often an appearance about them of great vacancy, amounting almost to imbecility. . . . The same appearance of mental inertness has been noticed by nearly all those who have travelled in countries where Buddhism is professed'.[100] Of their general standing amongst the laity, he wrote: 'In no part of the island that I have visited do the priests as a body, appear to be respected by the people'.[101] Even the monks' competence in the field of Buddhist literature was put in doubt—'the priests exhibit no enthusiasm of study, and many of them are unable to read at all'[102]—and the handful of Europeans who had managed to acquire some knowledge of the subject (indirectly, if not directly, from the monks themselves) were considered distinctly more competent. As early as 1850, Gogerly was hailed as 'the best Pali scholar in existence'.[103] And though he never put forward the claim in so many words, Hardy, in his own writings, assumed for himself a position not very dissimilar in relation to Sinhalese literature.[104]

Hardy himself took some precautions not to press his generalizations (about monks) too far; he did refer to 'individual exceptions'. But what really defined the situation for the missionaries was not the exceptions but the generalities, or rather, what appeared to them as such. Hence, instead of concentrating all their efforts on indirect attacks on Buddhism, they dared the monks to come out into the open on the assumption that they would thereby be able to humiliate the monks in public and thus

[100] Hardy, *Eastern Monachism*, pp. 311–12.

[101] *Ibid.*, p. 319.

[102] *Ibid.*, p. 366.

[103] *Ibid.*, p. vii. Six years after Gogerly's death, William Skeen, the government printer, recalled the years

> When Gogerly's great powers were felt,
> Before whom the ablest pundits knelt;
> Who first of Pali scholars known,
> Resplendent as a preacher shone.

The Knuckles, and Other Poems (Colombo, 1868), p. 89.

[104] See above, ch. V, n. 7.

speed up the downfall of Buddhism. In the end, the monks turned the tables on their challengers, and rendered the missionaries victims of their own miscalculations.

The greatest miscalculation of the missionaries was perhaps with regard to the religious attitudes of Buddhist laymen. The laymen were taken to be 'indifferent' to Buddhism and lacking in respect for the monks. In fact, however, the attacks on Buddhism drove the laymen to depend more and more on the monks, and to look to them for leadership. Thus no sooner than the monks had risen to the occasion, the Christian-Buddhist controversy, at the public level, turned out to be pretty much a one-sided affair. The audience to which the missionaries addressed themselves, in the spoken as well as the written word, was not an impartial audience, but one which was already heavily biased against them. The monks, on the other hand, had an audience that was overwhelmingly convinced of the 'truth' of Buddhism; what it needed in addition was simply reassurance.

Many of the dilemmas and paradoxes raised by the Christian missionaries in relation to fundamental Buddhist doctrines like karma and rebirth, nirvana and Buddhahood were not new in the basic structure of their logic. Such problems had been raised, discussed and resolved (as far as the Buddhists were concerned) in their exegetical works, as well as, in more succinct form, in non-exegetical works like the *Milindapañha*. (The Questions of King Milinda). It is significant that Mohoṭṭivattē himself took the initiative in bringing out an edition of the eighteenth-century Sinhalese translation of the *Milindapañha*. Published in 1878, it was a volume of nearly 650 pages, the largest single work to be issued from the Buddhist press. The 'Preface' to this edition introduced the work as 'a priceless book, unsurpassable as a means for learning the Buddhist doctrine, or for growth in the knowledge of it, or [no doubt with Christian objectors to Buddhism in mind] for the suppression of erroneous opinions'.[105]

There was one noteworthy sphere where the missionaries did strike a new note, and that was with regard to criticisms of (Hindu-) Buddhist cosmology. This subject received rather disproportionate importance during the controversy because Christian writers–Gogerly and others–had

[105] *Milinda Praśnaya*, tr. Hīnaṭikum̆burē Sumaṃgala, ed. Mohoṭṭivattē Guṇānanda et al. (Koṭahēna, 1878).

chosen it deliberately for attack, as the traditional theories were 'in antagonism to the most obvious teachings of science'.[106] Still, even here, the Christians were scarcely able to realize their desired end. For one thing, the public at large, along with the monks, were believers in the traditional cosmology. And in addition, the Buddhists soon began to throw the questions back at the Christians. When asked to locate Buddhist heavens and hells, they in turn asked the Christians to locate their own heaven and hell; when David de Silva, at one point during the Pānadurē debate, pointed out that European explorers who had ventured into all corners of the globe had not come across the Mahā Mēru (the cosmic mountain at the centre of the world), Mohoṭṭivattē, in his reply, raised the question whether they had come across the Garden of Eden.

The same tactics were adopted by the Buddhists on many other counts as well. Problems regarding the omniscience of the Buddha were matched with counter-problems regarding the omniscience (and omnipotence) of Jehovah. Questions on the historicity of events recorded in Buddhist works were matched with counter-questions of the historicity of events recorded in the Bible.

In raising objections to Christianity, the monks, at first, were left entirely to their own resources and to their own readings of the Bible. But as the controversy progressed, they began, with the help of English-educated laymen, to search more widely for additional weapons. Thus in the early 1860s, Bishop Colenso's writings (on the Pentateuch) caused 'much excitement in Ceylon'.[107] And so did, soon afterwards, the writings of free thinkers, Charles Bradlaugh and others.[108] European criticisms of Christianity were used by the Buddhists to taunt their opponents with the claim that Christianity was losing ground even in its traditional homeland. And to drive the point further, they combined these claims with expressions of sympathy for Buddhism which, about this time, began to emerge gradually from Western sources. Reginald Copleston, the Bishop of Colom-

[106] John Scott's 'Introduction' to Gogerly's lecture on 'Buddhism', *JRAS(CB)*, IV (1867–70) 88.

[107] R. Spence Hardy, *The Sacred Books of the Buddhists compared with History and Modern Science* (Colombo, 1863), p. 1. Hardy described his own work thus: 'The method that Bishop Colenso employs, unsuccessfully, in his attack upon the Pentateuch of Moses; we may employ, successfully, in exposing the "unhistorical" character of the Pitaka of Buddha'. *Ibid.*, p. 3.

[108] Translations of their writings were published in the Sinhalese periodical *Vibhajjavādaya* (1872), edited by D. P. Vijayasiṃha and published by the Society for the Propagation of Buddhism.

bo, who was clearly irritated by the phenomenon, commented upon it thus in 1879 in a letter to the Society for the Propagation of the Gospel:

At the present day it [i.e., Buddhism] is receiving an *impetus* . . . from the prestige given to it by the interest taken in Pali scholarship and Buddhist literature in Europe. The Secretary of an obscure Society–which, however, for all the Sinhalese know, may be a distinguished one–has been writing, it appears, to several Buddhist priests here, hailing them as brothers in the march of intellect, and congratulating one or two of them on the part they took so nobly against Christianity in a certain ill-judged but insignificant 'public controversy', which took place years ago in a village called Panadure. These letters the priests have printed in a little pamphlet, along with some selections from an English book, which describe some spiritualistic performances of Buddhist priests in Thibet. . . . This nonsense has a good deal of effect, I think, on the common people, while the more educated, having really become free thinkers, welcome the extravagant encomiums passed on the true original Buddhism by European writers, and thereby justify their own adherence to the national religion. . . . It is, I fancy, considered a mark of culture in England to say that Buddhism is very like Christianity, if not almost as good; and no doubt many think there can be no harm in praising Buddhism in England, because no one there is in danger of adopting it. Now both these are errors. Buddhism is not like Christianity. . . . And it is also an error to suppose that Buddhism can be safely praised in England. All that comes out here and is made the most of.[109]

'The Secretary of an obscure Society' that Copleston referred to was Olcott, President-Founder of the Theosophical Society, who, some time before the transfer of the Society headquarters to India (in 1879), opened a correspondence with Mohoṭṭivattē (and other Buddhists of Ceylon), having come to know of him through *A Full Account of the Buddhist Controversy held at Pantura*. The 'English book, which describe[s] some spiritualistic performances . . .' was Madame Blavatsky's *Isis Unveiled* (1877), a copy of which had been presented by the author to Mohoṭṭivattē at about the same time.[110] The contacts thus established paved the way for the arrival of Olcott and Blavatsky in Ceylon in May 1880. Their arrival marked the beginning of a new era in the Buddhist reaction to Christian

[109] *Classified Digest of the Records of the Society for the Propagation of the Gospel in Foreign Parts, 1701–1892* (London, 1894), pp. 664–65.

[110] H. S. Olcott, *Old Diary Leaves*, II (1878–83), 1910 (Madras, 1928), p. 157.

missionary activities. But even before this event, the Buddhists, by their own efforts, had shown the missionaries a good deal of their real and potential strength.

Hardy, in 1863, had prophesied in his usual eloquence:

> The cross must triumph, wherever it is upheld in its simplicity, by men who are willing to be nothing in its presence, that the name of the Redeemer may be high over all. Where are the old idols of Europe, Jupiter and Mars, Woden and Thor, and all the other lords many, and gods many, whom my own forefathers worshipped? Not one of them has now a single votary in the whole world. And thus it shall be with Buddha, and the myriads of deities in the east. The time will come when the wihāra will be deserted, the dāgoba unhonoured, and the bana unread.[111]

This millennialist optimism was not dampened for a long time to come, and even as late as 1874 Bishop Jermyn of Colombo was inclined to report that 'by the testimony of all Buddhism is effete; its hold on the people is as slight as it is possible to be'.[112] But only five years later, Jermyn's successor, Copleston, having taken the trouble to examine his surroundings a little more closely, conceded: 'Buddhism as a whole is not conquered, or near it. It remains in the fullest sense the religion of the mass of the Sinhalese. . . . There is little doubt that Buddhism is far more vigorous in Ceylon than it was a hundred and fifty years ago'.[113]

[111] Hardy, *Sacred Books*, pp. 162–63. See also pp. 173–174, above.

[112] *Classified Digest of the Records of the S.P.G.*, p. 664.

[113] *Ibid.*

Chapter VII

PROTEST CONSOLIDATED

i. CRISIS IN THE BUDDHIST RESPONSE TO CHRISTIAN MISSIONARY ACTIVITY

Education, preaching and the press were the three major expedients resorted to by the missionaries in their efforts to diffuse Christianity in Ceylon. Two of these, preaching and the press, were used, in turn, against Christianity by the Buddhists after the early 1860s.[1] On both these fronts the Buddhists were able, within two decades, to thrust themselves forward decisively in opposition to the missionaries. But on the third front, education, the missionaries held their ground with no difficulty whatsoever, during the same period. Why?

For one thing, the attacks made on Buddhism in the classrooms were less direct and less visible than those made in public through the spoken and the written word. The monks, who were exposed in particular to missionary tracts and pamphlets, and who, consequently, were driven to the necessity of starting rival publications, were not to the same degree exposed to missionary education. Opposing the missionaries in the field of education may have appeared less urgent, therefore, than opposing them on the other two fronts.

This is only part of the explanation, however, and possibly a rather unimportant part at that. What is clearly more to the point is that the monks were not sufficiently equipped to oppose the missionaries in the fields of education, even if they wanted to. To meet–and 'beat'–the

[1] In ch. VI, sec. iii (above), where this subject was discussed, emphasis was laid on the use of the press, and as far as the spoken word was concerned, on public debates rather than preaching. It is worth noting here that preaching too constituted an important part of the Buddhist campaign. Mohoṭṭivattē Guṇānanda, the leading Buddhist polemicist, claimed in 1887 that, during the preceding twenty-five years, he had given over 4,000 public lectures in different parts of the country. 'Preface' to *Bauddha Praśnaya* (Colombo, 1887). The claim seems quite plausible.

missionaries in the fields of preaching and writing, the traditional skills of the monks needed only minor modifications. The situation was not quite the same with regard to education.

The monks, to be sure, did have their traditional role as teachers, and they continued to play this role in a large area of the country. Especially in many interior parts of Ceylon, which were not adequately cared for by either the government or the missionaries, the monks were almost solely responsible for whatever instruction afforded to the inhabitants. Their services in this sphere received little or no official recognition; the *pansala* (monastic) schools were frequently dismissed as worthless, and sometimes, because of their connections with Buddhism, condemned as worse than useless.[2] Yet pleas for their recognition were not altogether scarce even in official circles. A provincial administrator in one of the Kandyan districts argued in 1869:

> The question how to educate the Kandyan people is a puzzling one. I do not see that there is any better course left than to encourage the Buddhist priesthood. I doubt not that an objection may be found to this course by those whose charity begins and ends at home; but I contend that the question of religion is one entirely foreign to the subject. That the Buddhist priesthood will take the opportunity of inculcating Buddhism I have no doubt; and the books read must be Buddhistical, for the simple reason that there are no others. Wherever there is a pansala, there are always to be found a few village boys learning to read and write. They pay nothing, and instruction is imparted to them in a very desultory and unsystematic manner, but be it remembered that this is the only school where they learn their own language.[3]

Quite apart from the *pansala* schools, which were scattered in the villages throughout the country, there were also larger and more advanced *piriveṇas* (monastic colleges) in the same areas where the missionaries also

[2] See above, pp. 176–177.

[3] 'Annual Report on the Kegalla District', *Administration Reports: 1869*, p. 32. The Report of the Legislative Council subcommittee on education, which was published in 1867, while objecting to *pansala* schools as a medium of primary education on religious grounds (see above, ch. V, n. 14), also asserted that they were 'not as numerous as they once were'. Though there is little doubt that their number in the Kandyan provinces had declined since 1815 (see above, pp. 177–180), the number which remained was quite substantial. It was much later that an attempt was made to enumerate them, and in 1885 the figure was given as 'no less than 1,769' (see below, n. 10 of this chapter).

had their educational establishments. But monastic schools and colleges, even at their highest levels, were not, either in their intent or in their effect, a real challenge to the educational establishments of the missionaries. The *piriveṇas* did attract a fair proportion of laymen (in addition to monks); but the traditional curricula which were followed in them were geared unmistakably to the requirements of monks rather than of laymen.

For the laymen, education was basically a training for a secular career, a means for secular advancement. It was by providing an education that satisfied this need that the missionaries were able to attract children of all religions to their schools. Hence Buddhist children could be distracted from missionary schools only by providing them with genuine alternatives: non-missionary schools with general (secular) instruction comparable to that of the missionary schools. In other words–as in using the spoken and the printed word for religious propaganda, so in education–the Buddhists, in order to compete with the missionaries, had to emulate them. They were slow to accomplish this; still, the basic strategy was evidently not unknown to them.

In 1868, Doḍandūvē Piyaratana (1826–1907) of the Amarapura Kalyāṇivaṃsa fraternity organized a society called Lokārtthasādhaka Samāgama, and on the initiative of this society and with the help of funds collected by it, the first non-monastic Buddhist school was opened at Doḍandūva in 1869.[4] The person employed by the society as headmaster of the school was a Sinhalese convert from Christianity who had had his education in a missionary school.[5]

The policies of the government with regard to education at this time were not unfavourable to the opening of Buddhist schools. The Department of Public Instruction, which was established in 1869 (as successor to the earlier Central School Commission), adopted an attitude of formal neutrality in relation to various religious bodies. All schools which had been, or were being, opened privately or by different religious organizations qualified for government grants-in-aid on the basis of the quality of secular instruction (i.e., instruction in non-religious subjects) offered in them.

The Buddhist school at Doḍandūva, which was registered as a private

[4] Doḍandūvē's obituary in *The Buddhist* (June 1907). C.N.A. 5/63/150/(7) is a text book written by Doḍandūvē to be used in this school. See also P. B. J. Hevawasam, 'Where are the Buddhist Pioneers?' *Ceylon Daily News*, 3 September 1969.

[5] *Ibid.*

Anglo-vernacular school under the management of J. Peiris Mudali of the Vällabaḍa Pattuva of the Galle district, qualified for a government grant in 1872.[6] By 1880 there were more private schools under the management of Buddhists; and there were also four schools which were specifically registered as Buddhist and which received government grants-in-aid.[7] Of these four schools, three were in the Western Province (at Koratoṭa, Hōmāgama and Hañdapāngoḍa), and the manager of all three was Koratoṭa Sobhita (1829–1903), a monk regarding whom little is known save that he was well known among his contemporaries as a militant and colourful personality.[8]

Between 1869 and 1880 there was thus an increase in the number of Buddhist schools; but progress was very slow indeed. Buddhists were lacking in men, resources and overall organization to compete with the Protestant missionaries who were already well established in the field. Hence the bulk of public funds for education still went in fact to the Protestant missionaries. Only the Catholics, under the leadership of their own European missionaries, had the capacity to compete with them.

The inability of the Buddhists to compete with the missionaries in the field of English education was hardly surprising. But in the field of Sinhalese education, the already existing *pansala* schools, with only minor modifications, had the capacity to qualify for government grants. Indeed in the 1880s, the government itself, indicating a belated but unmistakable change in its attitude towards *pansala* schools, made an effort to help them and to incorporate them into the general scheme of education. H. W. Green, the Director of Public Instruction (1883–89), argued in 1887: 'In my opinion, with a very little money, and with supervision and conditions exacted before this money were paid over (as in ordinary grant schools), the existing Pansala schools might be made very good "village schools in connection with the vihāras" '.[9]

The government, at this time, was more prepared than it was before to demonstrate in action the principle of religious neutrality that it professed; the Anglican church was disestablished in 1880, and in 1884 the Vesak full-moon day was declared a public holiday. In the field of education, the

[6] 'Report of the Director of Public Instruction', *A.R.: 1872*, p. 375.

[7] 'Report of the Director of Public Instruction', *A.R.: 1880*, Part IV, pp. 59, 60, 62, 79. All these were 'vernacular' schools.

[8] V. D. de Lanerolle, *Atītaya*, 2nd ed. (Colombo, 1944), pp. 42–48.

[9] 'Report of the Director of Public Instruction', *A.R.: 1887*, Part IV, p. 31.

government recognized the necessity of gaining the cooperation of Buddhist monks in addition to that of Christian missionaries. In fact, as far as the interior parts of the country were concerned, the government had little choice but to seek the cooperation of Buddhist monks; the financial difficulties of the time (mainly because of the decline in the revenue from coffee) necessitated economies in the field of education, and the system of grants-in-aid showed no signs of having attracted the missionaries to the interior parts of the country. The missionaries, on the whole, preferred to compete with each other in the more urban and populous parts of the country.

Buddhist monks were not quite ready, however, to make use of the new sympathetic attitude of the government. They showed no eagerness to formalize the organization of their schools: to keep regular school-hours and insist on the regular attendance of their pupils (a difficult task, in any case, in a rural agricultural society where children took some part in domestic and economic activity);[10] to maintain registers and annual returns, and so forth, which were necessary to meet the formal requirements of the Department of Public Instruction. Disappointed in his effort to incorporate the *pansala* schools into the national scheme of education, Green reported two years later:

> In the *pansala* schools, which are schools attached to Buddhist monasteries, . . . the priests will not take a money grant from the Department, and prefer to follow their old-fashioned methods of instruction in learning by heart passages out of the sacred Buddhist books, and in acquiring a small amount of astrology and medicinal knowledge; all of which means something better than nothing, but it is a great pity that every effort to turn them on to more modern lines has failed, through no fault of mine, but through inveterate conservatism of the most obsolete type.[11]

The only monastic educational institution which by this time had qualified for a regular government grant (since 1877) was Vidyodaya

[10] 'There are no less than 1,769 pansala schools, and yet they have only an attendance of 9,701 scholars, about five to a school. Now, this is partly due to the floating nature of the attendance, that is to say, the priest does not usually want more than four or five boys at once; . . . Then these boys go away, and others take their place, so that there is little instruction of a regular set of boys, only *some boys* are always there, and those who are there are taught'. 'Report of the Director of Public Instruction', *A.R.: 1885*, Part IV, p. 74.

[11] *Ibid., A.R.: 1889*, Part IV, p. 1.

Piriveṇa at Māligākanda. This Piriveṇa was efficiently organized as a result of the enthusiasm of its principal, Hikkaḍuvē Sumaṃgala, and of its Committee of (Lay) Managers (Vidyādhāra Sabhā).[12] But despite the efficiency of its organization, the curriculum that was adopted and followed was ill-balanced from the point of view of the newly accepted standards of the day. While the students were given fairly advanced instruction in subjects such as oriental languages and literature, not even elementary instruction was imparted to them in the 'new' subjects which were being taught in the missionary schools. The official 'examiners' of the Piriveṇa in 1878, at the end of a favourable report, noted 'that no attention is paid to arithmetic or geography, which might, they think, be introduced with advantage, into the lay classes at least, if not throughout all the classes of the institution'.[13] Subjects such as arithmetic and geography (and English) were clearly outside the competence of Buddhist monks; they had little opportunity to acquire a knowledge of them, and they evinced little or no enthusiasm to go out of their way to study them. The result was a devaluation of their position (in comparison with that of the missionaries) as teachers of the laity.

Since the monks were lacking in competence as well as organizational skills to compete with the missionaries in the field of (lay) education, the leadership of the campaign against the missionaries, if it were to have any further success, had to be taken over by the laity. Once they had taken over this leadership, Buddhist laymen joined hands with administrators like Green in expressing disillusionment over the 'conservatism' of the monks. Their paper, *The Buddhist*, minced no words about the matter: 'The Sangha of Ceylon is a very conservative body, and is only slowly induced to give up their own methods'.[14]

It was not without considerable difficulty, however, that the laymen were induced to give up *their* own methods.

ii. LAY PARTICIPATION BEFORE 1880

The voluntary participation of Buddhist laymen in religious activity and organization was customarily in the capacity of *dāyakas* (literally 'donors').

[12] For an account of the early days of the Piriveṇa, see Yagirala Prajñānanda, *Śrī Sumaṃgala Caritaya*, vol. I (Colombo, 1947), pp. 185–242.

[13] 'Report of the Director of Public Instruction', *A.R.: 1878*, Part IV, p. 16.

[14] 7 October 1892.

The *dāyakas* supplied the material requisites of the monks at their local temple and made contributions, as and when the need arose, for the building and maintenance of shrines, dwelling-houses, libraries and so forth, attached to the temple.[15]

The *dāyakas* worked essentially on a local basis. The organization of religious activity at the national level was traditionally the function of the central political authority, the king. The king, while working at the national level, also made arrangements for supplying the obligatory services (*rājakāriya*) of certain groups of laymen to religious institutions (over and above the voluntary services of the *dāyakas*) through the system of temple lands.[16]

Historically, the *dāyakas* played a crucial role in the development of Buddhist monastic institutions in the low country, as the system of *rājakāriya* had no significance there (temple lands having been abolished by the Europeans). Monasteries of the Amarapura and Rāmañña fraternities, as well as of the Siyam fraternity in the low country, were maintained essentially through the help of their local *dāyakas*.

Attempts to widen the scope of the *dāyaka* role in order to meet the new problems facing Buddhism at the time first became visible in the early 1860s. Not surprisingly, there were difficulties at first. When the idea of establishing a Buddhist press at Galle for the purpose of issuing replies to missionary tracts was first mooted, the organizers found it difficult to collect contributions for the project. As their report for 1865 explained, not many Buddhists were convinced of the 'merits' (*ānisaṃsa*) of helping to establish a Buddhist press.[17] The idea of a Buddhist press was new; it did not fall within the sphere of activity for which laymen customarily made contributions. Still, the difficulties were soon overcome and the press was eventually established. Indeed, at about this time, Buddhist leaders became increasingly aware that they themselves had to work in a voluntary but well-organized manner for the welfare of their religion, as that function was no longer being performed by the central political authority. This

[15] The term *dāyaka*, which is still in use, occurs in the same sense in the tenth century 'Tablets of Mahinda IV'. See *EZ*, I (1904–12), p. 100, n. 5.

[16] See above, pp. 17–18, 89–90.

[17] The Report is reproduced in full in Kalukoňdayāvē Paññāsekhara, *Siṃhala Puvatpat Sañgarā Itihāsaya*, vol. I (Colombo, 1965), pp. 97–104.

realization comes out clearly in a letter written by two prominent Buddhist laymen in Colombo, Don Philip de Silva Āpā Appuhāmi and Don Velon Vikramatilaka Appuhāmi, to the editor of *Lakmiṇipahana* (published in the issue of 14 December 1864) suggesting the establishment of a college of Buddhist studies. The letter read:

Buddhism was introduced to Ceylon 2,200 years ago. From that time until the end of the Sinhalese kingdom fifty years hence, the kings of Ceylon took the initiative in maintaining Buddhism. The citizens of the country followed the leadership of their kings; it was not their practice to have organizations of their own for the maintenance of Buddhism. For this reason, it is difficult nowadays to organize Buddhists for the purpose of maintaining their religion.

In the days when Buddhism was receiving the patronage of kings, there were ample opportunities for the pursuit of Buddhistic studies. The kings appointed learned *bhikkhus* to the incumbencies of important temples, and made generous endowments for the benefit of both teachers and pupils alike.

But now, because of the absence of a Buddhist king and the lack of experience among the Buddhists in organizing their religious affairs, there is a decline in all branches of Buddhistic studies. Results of this process would be harmful not merely to the Buddhists, but also to the population of Ceylon as a whole. Learning in Ceylon has always been closely associated with Buddhism; a decline in Buddhist education, therefore, would soon reduce the masses to a condition of ignorance. It is the duty of all Sinhalese—not merely Buddhists—to take measures to avert this prospect.

A few of us who have reasoned on these lines have decided to put forward the following plan for the consideration of all Ceylonese. If our plan meets with a favourable response, we shall take steps to implement it; if it does not, we shall abandon it.

Our aim is to establish a Buddhist College—for the benefit of all Ceylonese—for the purpose of teaching subjects such as Pali, Sinhalese and Sanskrit, Buddhist texts, history, logic, medicine and astrology. The following are the major features of our plan:

1. A capital fund of not less than £10,000 must be raised.
2. The Society or the Committee of Trustees which raises this fund must deposit it in a bank and administer the interest.
3. A sum of not more than £200 should be spent on building the College (a hall and residential quarters consisting of about twenty rooms) in a place not far removed from any part of the country.
4. About three or four teachers must be appointed to the College. Lay teachers

must be paid with moderate salaries. In the case of clerical teachers, maintenance allowances must be handed over to their *käpakaruvō*.

5. Students aged between fifteen and thirty years, who have already had some previous education, will be admitted to the college.
6. The number of students to be given admission at any time will depend on the interest due on the capital fund.
7. In the case of clerical students, an allowance for the supply of their meals (only) will be handed over to a *käpakaruvā*. Lay students will be expected to provide for themselves; they shall not be required to make tutorial-gifts (*gurupaňḍuru*) to their teachers at the conclusion of their courses of study.
8. A special official should be appointed by the Society (which will manage the institution) to be in charge of monthly payments to teachers and (clerical) students.
9. The teachers appointed should prepare courses of instruction; remove from the institution students whose general performance does not reach the required standards; and make arrangements to award small prizes to the students who perform well at the annual examinations.
10. The prior consent of the Governor should be obtained to the effect that the government would take charge of the fund and use it to promote the teaching of Sinhalese–in the event of the failure of the College to continue its teaching functions.[18]

This letter clearly reflects not only the growing realization on the part of a few articulate Buddhist lay leaders of the need for new voluntary organizations, but also the nature of their anxieties over the feasibility of such measures. The anxieties were not altogether unfounded, for it took almost a decade to put into effect the plan proposed by Ǟpā Appuhāmi and Vikramatilaka Appuhāmi. Contributions were slow to come, and when the proposed college was finally established in 1873 (under the name of Vidyodaya Oriental College), a good measure of the financial burden had to be borne by its Committee of Managers (Vidyādhāra Sabhā) until the government was successfully persuaded to make an annual grant from 1877 onwards.[19]

Of the new voluntary organizations of the time, the Vidyādhāra Sabhā of Vidyodaya College was by far the most viable as well as that which was destined to last with no break in its continuity. Of the others, the

[18] The above is a somewhat abbreviated translation of the original.

[19] Yagirala Prajñānanda, *op. cit.*

Laṃkopakāra Press at Galle, after a four-year period of highly enthusiastic activity, became almost totally defunct in the early 1870s;[20] the Society for the Propagation of Buddhism in Colombo continued longer, but the intensity of its activities fluctuated considerably, mainly because of financial difficulties.[21] In the field of printing and publishing, it was not impossible for an organization to continue despite fluctuations in its finances and efficiency. But the situation was different in the field of education. All schools which qualified for government grants were subject to periodic inspection by government officials. In order to receive the grants continuously, therefore, schools had to be managed with consistent efficiency. It is an indication of the inability of the Lokārtthasādhaka Samāgama at Doḍandūva to maintain such efficiency that their school, which qualified for a grant in 1872, ceased to receive it just two years afterwards.[22] Similarly, of Koratoṭa Sobhita's three schools which received grants, two–those at Haňdapāngoḍa and Hōmāgama, which had been receiving grants since 1878 and 1880 respectively–were removed from the register of aided schools in 1882.[23]

What the Buddhists lacked at the time was not concern for their religion; nor was it realization of what they really wanted. What was clearly wanting was organizational capacity and experience. It is not without significance that by far the most successful new organization of the time, the Vidyādhāra Sabhā of Vidyodaya College, counted among its members some of the leading Sinhalese entrepreneurs in Colombo. The best known of them were Hewavitharanage Don Carolis, a furniture dealer, and his father-in-law, Lansage Don Andris Perera, who was a timber merchant. Of the others, Āpā Appuhāmi and Wettasinghage Don Cornelis de Silva were joint owners of Laṃkābhinava Viśṛta Press (1864); Gurunnānselāgē Don Pālis was editor and publisher of a successful satirical newspaper, *Kavaṭa Katikayā* (1872–1910).

In addition to deficiencies in organizational capacity and experience, there were also differences amongst Buddhists–based on such factors as

[20] *Samaya Saṃgrahava*, 15 June 1873.

[21] It was with great difficulty that its publications were maintained. There were repeated appeals in them for more subscribers, and for current subscribers to pay their fees in time.

[22] The school at Doḍandūva does not appear in the grant-in-aid lists of the Department of Public Instruction after 1874.

[23] 'Report of the Director of Public Instruction', *A.R.: 1882*, Part IV, p. 83.

caste and locality–which stood as real or potential barriers to unified efforts at the national level. It was the good fortune of the Buddhists that they were able, at this critical juncture, to enlist the cooperation of a group of experienced propagandists, the Theosophists, to do a good part of this organizational work much better than they could have done it themselves.

The arrival of the Theosophists brought to a high pitch the religious enthusiasm of the Buddhists, which had already been awakened as a result of the controversies in the preceding years between Christian missionaries and Buddhist monks. This heightened enthusiasm was of immense help in collecting funds at the national level for organized religious activity. Furthermore, the Theosophists, simply by virtue of being outsiders, had the capacity to bring together different groups and factions of Buddhists who, on their own, might not have been inclined perhaps to work closely with each other.

iii. LAY PARTICIPATION AFTER 1880: THE BUDDHIST THEOSOPHICAL SOCIETY

The founders of the Theosophical Society, Colonel Henry Steel Olcott and Madame Helena Petrovna Blavatsky, arrived in Ceylon on 17 May 1880 accompanied by an English Theosophist (Edward Wimbridge) and five Indian delegates (three Hindus and two Parsees) from the Bombay branch of the Theosophical Society.[24] Olcott, who led the Theosophist party, had little or no idea, at the time of his arrival, of the role that Buddhists in Ceylon had already assigned him–of the role that he himself was to play later on.

Olcott had established contact with Mohoṭṭivattē and Hikkaḍuvē even before the headquarters of the Society were transferred to India (in May 1879); and one of Mohoṭṭivattē's lay supporters, John Robert de Silva, became a 'Fellow' of the Theosophical Society while the headquarters were still in New York.[25] When the Society's journal, the *Theosophist*, was started in July 1879, Olcott invited Hikkaḍuvē and Mohoṭṭivattē, among many others, to contribute articles to it;[26] and de Silva was later appointed its agent in Ceylon. Olcott was keen to consolidate these contacts and

[24] H. S. Olcott, *Old Diary Leaves*, II (1878–83), 1910 (Madras, 1928), pp. 151 *et seq.*

[25] *Ibid.*, pp. 156–57.

[26] *Ibid.*, p. 93.

organize a branch of the Theosophical Society in Ceylon. It was primarily to achieve this end that he led the Theosophical delegation in 1880. As he explained in the lecture on Theosophy and Buddhism which he delivered at Vidyodaya College about two weeks after his arrival in Ceylon:

> . . . So much for the history of our Society and its principles. Let me now tell you why this delegation has come to Ceylon.
>
> While investigations of other religions had been afoot, and learned Hindus and Parsees had begun to assist us, we had made no proper alliance with Buddhists. We felt how great an anomaly this was, for to conduct a Theosophical Society without counting in the Buddhists would be the height of absurdity. . . .[27] Our Society had long been in correspondence with the High Priest Sumangala and others, but nothing could be done without organization and system. We felt that. . . a Branch Society must be formed in Ceylon, which should embrace all the scholarship and practical ability among the priests and the laity. . . . And so, after taking everything into account and leaving our business in India, we sailed for Ceylon, and here we are.[28]

A role as narrow as forming a branch of the Theosophical Society in Ceylon for a purpose as esoteric as aspiring towards 'wisdom and universal brotherhood' was not what the Buddhists wanted of Olcott. Their primary concern at the time was the contest that they were involved in with the Christian missionaries; and what they wanted most of all was sympathy, support and guidance in this contest. As far as this local contest was concerned, Olcott had already made his position clear in the letters which he had written to Mohoṭṭivattē and others—letters which were given much publicity well before his arrival in Ceylon.[29] It was thus as a Western champion of Buddhism that Olcott was welcomed into Ceylon; and his behaviour, since his arrival, sufficiently confirmed the eager expectations of the Buddhists. Though he never ceased to remind his audiences that Theosophy, as a movement, had no connection with any particular religion, a week after their arrival, both Olcott and Blavatsky (as well as

[27] At the end of his presidential address to the fourth anniversary meeting of the Theosophical Society (the first to be held in India) on 17 November 1879, Olcott observed: 'There is one regret that comes to mar the pleasure of this evening, and somewhat dim the lustre of all these lamps—our Buddhist brothers of Ceylon are absent'. *A Collection of Lectures . . . delivered in India and Ceylon* (Madras, 1883), p. 25.

[28] *Ibid.*, p. 34.

[29] See above, p. 230.

one Hindu delegate, Damodar K. Mavalankar), acting in their personal capacity, embraced Buddhism through the customary means of reciting the Three Refuges and the Five Precepts.[30]

Olcott realized, before long, that the motives which brought him and his associates to Ceylon did not quite tally with those of their hosts who, throughout their tour of the island, greeted them with almost embarrassingly flattering ceremony. A week before the close of the triumphant two-month tour, Olcott told a convention of Buddhist monks:

> You all know the circumstances under which our party of Theosophists visited Ceylon, how we came as private persons, expecting to travel as such, and quietly organize the Buddhist Branch of our Society; and how the people prevented this by catching us up, as it were, in their arms, and, with one glad shout of welcome that ran from end to end of the island, hailing us as champions of their faith.[31]

This was scarcely intended as a protest; indeed, once the role that the Buddhists wanted him to play—that of a champion of their faith—had become clear, Olcott not merely accepted it gladly, he almost considered himself obliged to do so. As he explained, a year and a half later, in his Presidential Address to the Sixth Anniversary of the Theosophical Society:

> During our visit of 1880, the Sinhalese people *en masse* gave us a princely reception. . . . Triumphal arches; flags flying in every town, village and hamlet; roads lined with *olla* fringes for miles together; monster audiences gathered together to hear and see us—these evidences of exuberant joy and warm affection astounded us. In India we had been so reviled by Christians, so frowned upon by the authorities . . . , and so given the cold shoulder by the Natives, to stay with whom and work for whose welfare we had come so far, that this greeting of the Sinhalese profoundly moved us to gratitude. We felt a sincere desire to do something, even if only a little, to show them that we were not insensible to such kindness.[32]

Intending 'to do something, even if only a little' for the Buddhists, Olcott was soon drawn into the Buddhist movement in a big way. From his first visit in 1880 until his death in 1907, he visited the island practically every year. He took the leadership in organizing the Buddhists himself with the vast resources at his command as lawyer (which he was by

[30] *Old Diary Leaves*, II, pp. 167–68 and 371.

[31] The address (dated 4 July 1880) was printed in *The Buddhist* of 6 June 1890.

[32] Olcott, *A Collection of Lectures*, p. 121.

training), as colonel (which he was during the American Civil War), and as anti-missionary missionary (which he was by force of circumstance). And in doing this he articulated and expounded as a general policy what the Buddhists themselves had until then realized and practised more implicitly:

> If you ask how we should organise our forces, I point you to our great enemy, Christianity, and bid you look at their large and wealthy Bible, Tract, Sunday-school, and Missionary Societies—the tremendous agencies they support to keep alive and spread their religion. We must form similar Societies, and make our most practical and honest men of business their managers. Nothing can be done without money. The Christians spend millions to destroy Buddhism; we must spend to defend and propagate it. We must not wait for some few rich men to give the capital: we must call upon the whole nation.[33]

The confidence of the Buddhists in Olcott, in the early years at any rate, was universal; in 1884, he was sent as their representative to the Colonial Office with full powers 'to ask for such redress and enter into such engagements as may appear to him judicious'. And before his departure from Ceylon, he was also given the following commission:

On the 12th day of the waxing moon of January-February in the year A.B. 2427 (1883), this letter is written

KNOW ALL GOOD MEN THIS

That the great minded man who is called Colonel Henry Steel Olcott who is a scrupulously faithful follower of Lord Buddha who observes the precepts of Buddha is empowered by the undersigned to accept and register as Buddhists persons of any nation who may make to him application to administer to them the Three Refuges and Five Precepts and to organize societies for the promotion of Buddhism.

In proof whereof the present commission is issued to him by the undersigned Senior Priests (Thero) of the Siam and Amarapura Sects in the Island of Ceylon.

1. Sumangala Nayaka Thero
2. Sri Sumangala Thero
3. Dhammalankara Nayaka Thero
4. Subhuti Thero
5. Amaramoli Thero
6. Gunaratana Thero
7. Dewamitta Thero[34]

[33] *Old Diary Leaves*, IV (1887–1892), 1910 (Madras, 1931), p. 120.

[34] Yagirala Prajñānanda, *op. cit.*, pp. 151–52. See also *Old Diary Leaves*, III, p. 118.

The result of all this was that, in Ceylon, Theosophy began and developed not so much as a new exogenous movement as a further stage of an older indigenous movement. 'Buddhist Theosophy' had very little Theosophy in it; what it did have was a good deal of Buddhism. Its Buddhism, however, was not of the traditional type; it was rather of the type which has recently been called Protestant Buddhism.

'The term "Protestant Buddhism" in my usage has two meanings', writes Obeyesekere, who has introduced this term: '(a) . . . many of its norms and organizational forms are historical derivatives from Christianity (b) . . . it is a protest *against* Christianity . . . '.[35] Both these features were discernible in Ceylon even before 1880. But it was only after 1880 that a third feature (which, in fact, would be part of (a) above, but which is worth being considered separately) became clearly noticeable–the increasing involvement of laymen in roles of religious leadership, and its concomitant, the displacement of monks from some of their traditional positions of leadership.[36] A brief examination of the history of the different branches of the Theosophical Society founded by Olcott in Ceylon in 1880 will make this development quite clear.

Olcott, during his first visit in 1880, founded two main branches of the Theosophical Society, a Buddhist branch and a non-Buddhist branch. The non-Buddhist (or 'scientific') branch, which was called the Lanka Theosophical Society, was described at its inception as 'composed of Freethinkers and amateurs of occult research'.[37] This Lanka Theosophical Society was scarcely heard of again, and the reasons for its still-birth are not difficult to imagine. Buddhists had no interest in 'occult research', and non-Buddhists had little or no interest in Theosophy.

The Buddhist branch of the Theosophical Society, which came to be called the Buddhist Theosophical Society (B.T.S. for short), had two divisions within it: a lay division (with local subdivisions) and a clerical one (not itself subdivided).[38]

The clerical division, under Hikkaḍuvē Sumaṃgala's chairmanship, counted among its members all the leading monks of all the different

[35] 'Religious Symbolism and Political Change in Ceylon', *Modern Ceylon Studies*, I (1970) 46–47.

[36] Regarding the process of laicization in the (Christian) Protestant tradition, see J. F. MacLear, 'The Making of the Lay Tradition', *Journal of Religion*, XXXIII (1953) 113–36, and Bryan R. Wilson, *Religion in Secular Society: A Sociological Comment* (London, 1966), pp. 38–39, 132–33.

[37] *Old Diary Leaves*, II p. 189.

[38] *Ibid.*, p. 179.

fraternities. Olcott, at the time, considered this a great achievement—bringing together into one organization monks of different fraternities.[39] In fact the achievement was not as significant as it appeared to him at first. The monks, even before the formation of the clerical division of the B.T.S., had worked in close cooperation with each other on certain important occasions. In, and after, the 1860s, they had worked in unison with each other in the controversies with Christian missionaries.[40] Even before these controversies, however, enduring personal ties existed between monks of different fraternities, especially in the field of monastic education. Generally, monks who were well known for their learning gathered around them several junior monks, not merely from their own fraternities but also from others. The willingness of the monks to work jointly in the field of religious studies was well demonstrated at the revision of the Buddhist canon at Pälmaḍulla during the years 1865–74. Leading Pali scholars of all the fraternities participated in the project under the patronage of Iddamalgoḍa Basnāyaka Nilamē and several other laymen of Sabaragamuva.[41] Such cooperation among the monks as previously existed continued over the years. On the other hand, the formation of the clerical division of the B.T.S. in no way helped to infuse a new unity into the order, or a new enthusiasm. 'I have not been able, during an intimate intercourse of twenty-two years, to arouse their zeal', Olcott himself wrote of the monks in 1903.[42]

In contrast to the clerical division of the B.T.S., the lay division, from its very beginning, was a significant organizational success. With its branches in several provincial towns and headquarters in Colombo, the lay division of the B.T.S. came to provide Buddhist laymen with what in the preceding decades they had been wanting to create, a strong and unified organization.[43] Its original membership was drawn mainly from Sinhalese Buddhist laymen who had already been active in religious work in some

[39] *Ibid.*, pp. 202–3.

[40] See above, ch. VI, sec. iii.

[41] References to this 'revision' (*Tripiṭaka Śuddhiya*) may be found in *Satya Mārgaya*, 13 March 1868; 'Revision of the Sinhalese Buddhist Scriptures', *Indian Antiquary*, I (1872) 31; W. A. de Silva, *Catalogue of Palm Leaf Manuscripts in the Colombo Museum*, I (Colombo, 1938), 'Introduction'; Yagirala Prajñānanda, *op. cit.*, pp. 172–82; and Kalukoňdayāvē Paññāsekhara, *op. cit.*, pp. 239–54.

[42] 'Preface' to the thirty-sixth edition of *The Buddhist Catechism* (Madras, 1947), p. xii.

[43] On the history of the B.T.S., see G. P. Malalasekara (ed.), *Diamond Jubilee Souvenir of the Buddhist Theosophical Society, 1880–1940* (Colombo, 1940).

capacity or other. Don Andris Perera; his son, Don Simon Perera; and son-in-law, H. Don Carolis–all of whom were members of the Vidyādhāra Sabhā of Vidyodaya College–became prominent members of the Colombo branch of the B.T.S. (Don Andris was also its president from 1883-90.) Don Carolis's son, H. Don David (later Anagarika Dharmapala), worked in several capacities–travelling companion and interpreter to Olcott and other Theosophists in their tours of the country, general manager of the B.T.S. press, and so forth–during the years 1886-90.[44] The assimilation of prominent Buddhist laymen into the B.T.S. occurred in the provinces as well–for example, Iddamalgoḍa at Ratnapura, T. B. Panabokke at Kandy and E. R. Gooneratne at Mātara and Galle.[45]

Under the auspices of the B.T.S., these laymen found an opportunity not merely to collaborate more closely with each other but also to work shoulder to shoulder with foreign Theosophists and new local recruits to the movement. Among the Theosophists who worked in Ceylon in the late nineteenth century were (in addition to Olcott) C. W. Leadbeater (1886-89), C. F. Powell (1889-90), and B. J. Daly (1890-93). Their activities helped to bring into one organization not only Buddhists of different castes and localities who had already been active in religious work, but also English-educated Ceylonese who, before the 1880s, had evinced little or no interest in Buddhist propagandist work. Nearly all the new recruits were Sinhalese; a notable exception was A. E. Buultjens (a Burgher). He played a leading role within the B.T.S. during the last decade of the nineteenth century as principal of the Buddhist English School (later Ananda College) at Colombo (1889-98), editor of *The Buddhist* (1890 and 1892), and as general manager of Buddhist schools (1892-1900).[46]

The propagandist and polemical work begun in the earlier decades by organizations such as the Society for the Propagation of Buddhism were continued by the B.T.S. through the columns of its two (Sinhalese and English) newspapers, the *Sarasavi San̆darӓsa* (1880) and *The Buddhist*

[44] See his 'Reminiscences of my early life', *The Maha Bodhi*, XLI (1933).

[45] These last three were members of the local aristocracy. Most of the other Buddhist leaders were from the new entrepreneurial class. For a discussion of 'the prominence of the trader elements' in the Buddhist movement, see L. A. Wickremeratne, 'Religion, Nationalism and Social Change in Ceylon, 1865-1885', *JRAS*, 1969, especially pp. 135-39.

[46] See his obituary in *Ananda College Journal*, III (1916); and Visakha Kumari Jayawardena, *The Rise of the Labour Movement in Ceylon* (Durham, North Carolina, 1972), pp. 80-84 *et passim*.

(1888). But the most concerted effort of the new organization was directed to that sphere where the Buddhists, all this time, had been noticeably lagging behind–education.

Olcott himself, during his very first visit, came to be convinced, as he put it, of 'the risk they [i.e., the Buddhists] ran in leaving their children to be prejudiced against their ancestral religion by its professional enemies, who were in the country for no other object than this'.[47] The subject of education was discussed at the convention of the lay branches of the B.T.S. which was held at the conclusion of the visit;[48] and on the appeal of the Buddhists, Olcott returned to Ceylon in the following year (1881) for the purpose of 'raising an Education Fund and the rousing of popular interest in the subject of education generally'.[49]

To achieve this object, Olcott, with the assistance of several monks and laymen, began touring the country from village to village. These fund-raising tours were continued over the years by Olcott himself, by other Theosophists such as Leadbeater and Daly, and by Sinhalese Buddhists like Dharmapala. Work in connection with the Education Fund did not proceed altogether smoothly; the sums of money collected were frequently less than what was needed and expected, and there were squabbles over the control of the Fund.[50] Even so, compared with the earlier years, the progress made in the field of Buddhist education since the formation of the B.T.S. was phenomenal. The position at the end of the nineteenth century was summarized as follows in a government report on education:

> Though the portals of religious neutrality in education were since that year [1869, the year in which the Department of Public Instruction was established] thrown open to all engaged in this enterprise without distinction, native Buddhists were still slow to avail themselves of the opening for educational activity in the interests of their co-religionists that thus presented itself. For fifteen years or more after that . . . Christian societies continued to be in almost undisputed possession of the field. With the Buddhist Theosophical movement in 1886 [*sic*] the Buddhist community awakened to the responsibility to their

[47] *Old Diary Leaves*, II, p. 179.

[48] *Ibid.*, p. 204.

[49] *Ibid.*, p. 296.

[50] *Ibid.*, pp. 307–8; 369–71.

co-religionists. . . . A society was formed to resist the inroads of the foreign faith and, by the establishment of Buddhist schools for Buddhist children, to narrow the scope and the opportunities of the opponents of their religion. . . . In ten years' time 63 Buddhist schools have been registered under the management of the Buddhist Theosophical Society.

A few Buddhist priests, too, have in the meanwhile interested themselves in education, and three of their number share the management of 13 schools. A few wealthy lay Buddhists are the managers of 27 schools well attended and in many instances admirably housed. The total number of what may be termed avowedly Buddhist schools . . . now stands at 103, and there is every indication that this number will be increased year by year. For the present no less than 20 applications for Buddhist schools are under consideration.[51]

The schools opened and managed by the B.T.S. were modelled on missionary schools (with Buddhism taking over the position occupied by Christianity). The problem of providing education in English was soon solved by the steady inflow of British and American Theosophists, and by the increasing involvement of English-educated Ceylonese in the activities of the B.T.S. In relation to these schools, the monks had no significant role, either as teachers or as managers. In fact, the success of the (lay division of the) B.T.S. clearly witnessed the relegation of monks into the background of the Buddhist movement.

This was a reversal of the pre-1880 situation. For, although laymen did indeed take part in the pre-1880 organizations, the activities of those organizations were closely identified with, and to a good measure dependent on, the vision and energy of some outstanding monks: Mohoṭṭivattē Guṇānanda (Society for the Propagation of Buddhism), Bulatgama Sumana (Laṃkopakāra Press), Doḍandūvē Piyaratana (Lokārtthasādhaka Samāgama) and Hikkaḍuvē Sumaṃgala (Vidyodaya Piriveṇa). The lay division of the B.T.S., in contrast, was—naturally—a lay organization; monks had no place in it except, at most, in a purely advisory capacity in the background.

The transition from one stage to the other was not devoid of its element of drama. In the mid-1880s, there occurred a direct confrontation between the old hero, Mohoṭṭivattē, and the new, Olcott, a confrontation which

[51] *An Account of the System of Education in Ceylon* (S.P. XXXIII: 1898), p. 12.

reached its climax in February 1887. Olcott's own account of it was as follows.

At the time in question I had every reason to be dissatisfied with the behaviour of Megittuwatte, the orator, the champion of Buddhism at the famous intellectual tournament at Panadure which proved a terrific blow to Missionary work. . . . From having been my enthusiastic panegyrist, he had now turned to the other side, and, always a specious and silvery-tongued man, had begun to drag the amiable High Priest Hikkaduvē Sumangala into his way of thinking, and to make inevitable a breach between us. . . . He had asked me to lecture at his temple at Kotahena on the 18th February 1887 which I did to a great crowd; but one may guess my feeling of anger and disgust when I learnt that the fiery discourse in Sinhalese, with which he followed my lecture, was a venomous attack on the Colombo B.T.S. and myself. Sumangala was present and seemed shaken in his friendship for me, but joined Megittuwatte in asking me to lecture on the following evening at the same place. The next morning, while thinking how I could escape the trap that was being fixed for me to walk into, I learnt that a steamer . . . would sail that afternoon for Bombay, so I got my things quickly packed, called a carriage, bought my ticket, and by 11.30 a.m. was on the wide ocean, sailing away from the wily fowler who had spread his net for a bird too old to be caught so very easily.[52]

Despite his sudden exit, Olcott, backed by his admirers and followers in the lay division of the B.T.S., won the duel in the end. Reflecting on the episode later on, he recorded with a sense of triumph:

Megittuwatte did his best to crush our brave little group of hard workers in the Colombo Branch. He even started a small paper [*Riviräsa*, begun in January 1888], in which, for months, he exhausted his armory of invectives, but all to no purpose. The only result was to weaken his influence, lessen his popularity, and expose himself as a selfish, uncharitable, and pugnacious man, while actually strengthening our hold on public sympathy.[53]

No doubt with some justification, Olcott considered Mohoṭṭivattē's opposition to be motivated by the desire to maintain his old supremacy in the Buddhist movement. Tracing the conflict back to 1881, he noted:

[52] *Old Diary Leaves*, III (1883–87), pp. 406–7.
[53] *Ibid.*, pp. 407–8.

He was a man of mixed characteristics and motives. He had helped me to raise the Sinhalese National Buddhistic Fund in the Western Province, and when the Trust Deed was being drafted had given us no end of bother. His aim seemed to have been to get the absolute control of the money, regardless of the rights of all who had helped in the raising of the funds.[54]

Quite apart from this struggle for power, it also seems very likely that by 1887 Mohoṭṭivattē had become suspicious of the attitudes of the Theosophists towards Buddhism. In fact, in the same year he had his final breach with Olcott, Mohoṭṭivattē wrote the first part of his *Bauddha Praśnaya*, a Buddhist catechism of his own, as a rival, in all probability, to Olcott's more famous one of 1881. In the preface to this work, Mohoṭṭivattē emphasized the need to re-assert the 'true' doctrines of Buddhism, as many Western sympathizers of Buddhism–he claimed–had begun to incorporate into Buddhism many doctrines which were 'false' (*mithyā*) and alien to it. The same thesis was elaborated in *Rivirāsa*, the weekly which he began in January 1888, which proved to be a short-lived and unsuccessful rival to *Sarasavi Sañdaräsa* of the B.T.S.

Scepticism regarding many Theosophical ideas–or, at any rate, ideas which were held dear by many leading Theosophists–was not limited to Mohoṭṭivattē, but was common among many other monks as well as among many laymen. By Olcott's own admission, only one monk in the whole of Ceylon believed in the existence of the 'Mahatmas';[55] and Väligama Sumaṃgala, a close associate of Olcott, categorically denied their existence in the course of an interview with Edwin Arnold in 1886.[56]

Room for disagreements over issues of this sort, and for disappointments over the intellectual trends of the Theosophical movement in general, widened over the years. This became particularly so at the turn of the century with the growing identification of the Theosophical Society with Hinduism, mainly as a result of Annie Besant's rise in the Society's hierarchy. Anagarika Dharmapala, who knew the Indian scene well, began to part company with Olcott, Besant and other Theosophists as well as the B.T.S. in the mid-1890s, and not long afterwards he turned out to be one

[54] *Ibid.*, p. 406.

[55] *Ibid.*, p. 388. The monk in question was Ilukvattē Medhaṃkara of the Rāmañña fraternity, regarding whom see above, p. 168.

[56] *India Revisited* (London, 1886), p. 273.

of their most outspoken critics in Ceylon. His relations with them reached the breaking point between November 1897 and July 1898 when he made an attempt to eliminate the word 'Theosophical' from the name of the Colombo branch, an attempt which was prompted by his dissatisfaction with the intellectual trends of Theosophy in general. He wrote in his diary on 12 April 1898: 'Theosophists rose into prominence by borrowing Buddhist expressions. Their early literature is full of Buddhist terminology. Now they are kicking the ladder'.[57] Dharmapala's move was personally, and successfully, resisted by Olcott[58] but the latter's problems did not end there. Hikkaḍuvē Sumaṃgala, after a twenty-five-year association with Olcott, decided to resign his membership of the Theosophical Society in 1905 on the grounds that 'the platform of the Society had been changed and that it was no longer an eclectic body'. It was only after a moving personal appeal and assurance by Olcott that Hikkaḍuvē was led to withdraw his letter of resignation.[59] In his *Old Diary Leaves*, Olcott wrote of Sumaṃgala:

> He is a good man and very learned but, at the same time, so susceptible to the criticisms of his people, that I am never sure of not finding him temporarily upset by some doubt created in his mind as to my orthodoxy in Buddhism; it is never anything very serious, and I can always dispel it by getting him to compare the state of Sinhalese Buddhism to-day with what it was when he and I first met in 1880.[60]

Though a little beside the point, Olcott's self-defence was rarely lacking in its desired effect. Not even his sternest critic could deny him credit for what he did for Sinhalese Buddhists.

Paradoxically Olcott's popularity in Ceylon was closely related to a basic failure—his failure to attract Buddhists to Theosophy. The vast majority of the members of the B.T.S. remained uninterested in the Theosophical

[57] 'Diary Leaves of the Late Ven. Anagarika Dharmapala', ed. Devapriya Valisinha, *The Maha Bodhi*, LIX/3–4 (March-April, 1961). Also relevant are entries of 9 November 1897, 2 and 26 March 1898, 13 May 1898, and 4–8 July 1898.

[58] *Old Diary Leaves*, VI (April 1896–September 1898) (Madras, 1935), pp. 349–50.

[59] Olcott's letter (dated 18 November 1905) and a draft of Hikkaḍuvē's reply are reproduced in Yagirala Prajñānanda, *op. cit.*, pp. 778–79.

[60] *Old Diary Leaves*, VI, pp. 5–6. This sixth series of the diary leaves was first published in *The Theosophist* between January 1905 and December 1906, at the time that relations between Olcott and Hikkaḍuvē were somewhat strained.

movement outside Ceylon, and the essentially local character of their interests continued over the years, helped in some measure by the behaviour of visiting Theosophists themselves.[61] Thus, despite its repeated contacts with several leading Theosophists, and despite its physical proximity to the headquarters of the Theosophical Soceity, the B.T.S., on the whole, remained outside the mainstream of Theosophy.[62] Olcott himself tried to account for this in the following words:

The Sinhalese are not much given to study, being rather practical than ideal, more workers than dreamers, besides which they have no class like that of the Brahmins, who have a hereditary proclivity for philosophical and metaphysical speculation. Although Branches which we organised in 1880 are still active. . . , it is altogether within the lines of Buddhism. They neither understand nor wish to understand the contents of other religious systems; and when they speak of themselves as Branches of our Society, it is always with this reservation, that they do their best for Buddhism and acknowledge the President-Founder as their principal adviser and leader.[63]

As it happened, this very parochialism was not without its blessings. The B.T.S. remained unmoved by the jealousies, scandals and upheavals in the branches of the Theosophical Society in India, Europe and America,[64] and it was able to devote its undivided attention to the immediate organizational tasks–especially in the field of education–that the Buddhists of Ceylon were interested in, rather than to those metaphysical speculations to which many Theosophists outside Ceylon were attracted. 'Our Society Branches [in Ceylon] have, with a few exceptions, been inert and useless as centres of Theosophy, but all have the right to take credit for

[61] The precedent set by Olcott and Blavatsky of formally embracing Buddhism was followed by several others who came to Ceylon subsequently: for instance, Leadbeater in 1884 (*Old Diary Leaves*, III, p. 196); E. F. Fawcett (*The Buddhist*, 7 February 1890); B. J. Daly (*ibid.*, 25 July 1890).

[62] The only Ceylonese to be drawn into and remain in the mainstream of Theosophy was C. Jinarajadasa, but he spent nearly all his adult life outside Ceylon. A pupil of Leadbeater at the Buddhist English School at Colombo, Jinarajadasa accompanied the master to England in 1888, and later entered St. John's College, Cambridge. References to his career in the Theosophical Society–in which he became vice-president (under Annie Besant) in 1921, and president in 1945–can be found in Arthur H. Nethercot, *The Last Four Lives of Annie Besant* (London, 1963), *passim*.

[63] *Old Diary Leaves*, IV, pp. 216–17.

[64] See Nethercot, *Last Four Lives*.

a great total of work done along philanthropical [i.e., educational] lines', was Olcott's own verdict.[65]

It is also indicative of the limited interests of the Buddhists of Ceylon that the Hindu 'revival' in neighbouring India had no noticeable impact on them. India as a matter of fact had no importance for the most of them except as 'Buddhist Jerusalem', an idea which inspired Dharmapala to form the Maha Bodhi Society in 1891 with the avowed aim of regaining control over Buddhist holy places and taking Buddhism back to India. Dharmapala spent a good part of his adult life in India and came into contact with Hindus, but these contacts, rather than bringing him closer to them, made him react against them. And, as was noted earlier, he reacted against Theosophists, too, precisely because of their close associations with Hinduism in India. Jinarajadasa, who, in contrast to Dharmapala, had been completely absorbed in the Theosophical movement, complained many years later:

> Speaking frankly to the young generation, who are doing much work today, I would like to mention one profound cause for my dissatisfaction when I tried to do something for Buddhism and for Ceylon. It is the complete mental separation which exists between Ceylon and the great tradition of India. Anyone who has had even a glimpse into Hindu traditions knows at once that all that is of real significance in Sinhalese civilization is closely linked to Hindu civilization, if not fully derived from it. . . . All those who considered themselves intelligent Buddhists—particularly the leading priests—never seemed to realize that it was scarcely possible to understand any Buddhist philosophical term without a thorough knowledge of the Hindu philosophies of the time of the Lord Buddha.[66]

Somewhat similar ideas had been expressed previously by yet another well-known Ceylonese in exile, Ananda Coomaraswamy.[67] But to the vast majority of Sinhalese Buddhists these ideas had no appeal. They remained indifferent to the 'great tradition' of India; and so far as they had any interest in it at all, it was mainly in relation to defining their own separate identity in opposition to that of the Hindus.

[65] *Old Diary Leaves*, II pp. 325–26.

[66] 'The Y.M.B.A. in 1901', *The Buddhist*, n.s., IV (1933–34) 13.

[67] *Mediaeval Sinhalese Art*, 1908, 2nd ed. (New York, 1956), p. 18.

CONCLUSION

The expression 'Buddhist revival' was used widely by contemporary observers to characterize the state of Buddhism in Ceylon at the end of the nineteenth century. These observers, with only a few exceptions, traced the beginnings of the revival to the arrival of the Theosophists in Ceylon in 1880. 'Thanks to Colonel Olcott and Madame Blavatsky . . . truer ideas of Buddha's teaching have been spread, and a remarkable revival has occurred under leaders of high character', wrote Arunachalam in 1901.[1] The common assumption behind such statements was that Buddhists were relatively inactive until they were stirred into activity by their new friends from overseas. Bishop Copleston, a much less sympathetic observer than Arunachalam, went on to dub the revival 'external and artificial'.[2]

This was hardly an accurate description of events. Buddhists were by no means dormant before the arrival of the Theosophists; in fact the Theosophists were enthusiastically welcomed and absorbed into the Buddhist movement precisely because the Buddhists were already active at the time of their arrival. It is not surprising, all the same, that many contemporary observers assigned the origins of the revival to the Theosophists. For it was only after 1880 that the activities of the Buddhists began to attract the serious attention of official circles, of Westerners and of the westernized Ceylonese.[3] Olcott himself had no reticence about claiming his due share in the revival; but describing his visit in 1880 as 'the

[1] *The Review of the Census Operations and Results*, Census of Ceylon, vol. I (Colombo, 1902), p. 89. Arunachalam was Police Magistrate at Kalutara in 1880, and he entertained the Theosophists at his home there on 28 May. Olcott was very impressed with his young host and described him as 'one of the most intellectual and polished men we have met in Asia'. *Old Diary Leaves*, II (Madras, 1928), p. 172.

[2] *Buddhism: Primitive and Present in Magadha and in Ceylon* (London, 1892), p. 467.

[3] For other contemporary accounts of the 'revival', see G. B. Ekanayake, 'The Revival of Buddhism in Ceylon', *The East and the West*, XII (1915) 447–59; and James B. Pratt, *India and its Faiths: A Traveller's Record* (New York, 1915), chs. XVI–IX.

beginning of the second and permanent stage of the Buddhist revival', he attributed the first and original stage to Mohoṭṭivattē.[4]

Mohoṭṭivattē, of course, though certainly the most colourful figure of the 1860s and 1870s, was not an isolated one; quite apart from the backing of several Buddhist laymen, he also had a substantial number of his brethren to work alongside him in roles less conspicuous than his, though equally important. The strength, energy and enthusiasm which these monks possessed at the time, and which alone enabled them to start their campaign against well-established missionary organizations, had their roots, historically, in the internal changes within the Buddhist order which occurred in the first half of the nineteenth century. But, though there were more than a few, even as early as the 1860s, who saw signs of revival in Buddhism in the campaign against the Christian missionaries,[5] very few indeed saw signs of revival in the internal changes. These changes, which generally manifested in the form of controversies and schisms, were viewed as signs of decline and fall. A Sinhalese Christian, in an essay on the Amarapura fraternity written in 1847, did discern signs of 'reformism' and 'revivalism' in the new fraternity. But even he, with characteristic (Christian) optimism of the time, wrote: 'It is to be hoped that if Buddhism can be brought back to its early principles and doctrines, it will be simply a kind of abstruse and metaphysical philosophy much above the comprehension of the ignorant and unlearned Singhalese, who will thus be more open to instruction of a simpler nature from the Christian Missionaries who are settled amongst us'.[6]

Revival in such a literal sense as an attempt to take Buddhism 'back to its early principles and doctrines' does not provide an entirely satisfactory description of the rise and development of the Amarapura fraternity, nor of the other new fraternities of the time, and still less of the Buddhist reaction to Christian missionary activity. Even when such ideals were present, the actual processes of revival were always intertwined with processes of change. Hence the focus of the present study on revival and change.

What were the major changes? First and foremost, there was the

[4] *Old Diary Leaves*, II, pp. 156 and 166.

[5] E.g., John Murdoch and James Nicholson, *Classified Catalogue of Printed Tracts and Books in Singhalese* (Madras, 1868).

[6] A. de Silva, 'On the Corruptions of Buddhism and the Different Tenets, Opinions and Principles of the Amarapoora and Siamese Sects', Appendix XII to Ribeyro's *History of Ceylon*, tr. G. Lee (Colombo, 1847), p. 78.

breakdown of the traditional interdependence between Buddhism and political authority. The connection between these two, as was noted in the Introduction (following Weber), was a crucial feature of the 'transformation' of Buddhism from a virtuoso religion to a mass (or world) religion, and in the first chapter we dealt with the nature and vicissitudes of this connection in the course of the history of Ceylon from the time of the introduction and establishment of Buddhism until the time of Kīrti Śrī Rājasiṃha in the eighteenth century, when it was revived and re-established in its classical form, as it happened, for the last time in the history of Ceylon. The breakdown of the connection between Buddhism and political authority was a direct result of the ascendancy of European colonial powers in Ceylon, and along with this political change, it occurred in stages and over a long period of time. It began in the sixteenth century with Dharmapāla's conversion to Roman Catholicism and his transfer of Buddhist temple villages to the Franciscans and his subsequent bequest of his whole kingdom to the King of Portugal. In the low country, the old politico-religious order was never restored again–in fact under the Portuguese as well as their colonial successors governmental machinery was used against Buddhism–though there were towards the end of the eighteenth century some monks and monasteries in the low country who received some amount of support from the kings of Kandy. In Kandy itself, as was shown at length in chapter III (section i), there was no immediate withdrawal of state patronage to Buddhism after the cession of the kingdom to the British in 1815; but in stages the withdrawal was made all the same.

The withdrawal of state support accelerated a process which had already begun–the segmentation of the order of monks. The process had begun initially as a result of the political division of the country into coastal and interior regions (chapter II). Because of this division, the authority of the ecclesiastical hierarchy in Kandy over monks in the coastal regions was generally weak, and over the new low-caste fraternities, non-existent. European colonial rule had directly and indirectly facilitated the emergence of these fraternities in two main ways: one, by the upward mobility of certain low castes under colonial rule which led them to challenge high-caste monopolies in many fields including that of religion; and two, by the lack of (Buddhist) political and religious establishments working in close cooperation with each other in the low country, which, had they existed, could have prevented the emergence of autonomous fraternities. The liberalized religious attitudes of the colonial government at the time also helped; for even though it was committed to promoting the spread of Christianity in the colony, there was no concerted effort on the part of the colonial government (in contrast to Portuguese and early Dutch times) to directly interfere with the attempts of the Buddhists to promote their own religion.

Once begun, and with no political backing to a central ecclesiastical hierarchy to hold the order together, there was no effective check to the process of segmentation (chapters III and IV). It could proceed almost endlessly on the basis of caste, subcaste or regional differences, or clashes of personalities or doctrinal disputes. Thus in place of the unified and centralized order which had been established in Kīrti Śrī's time, there were, a hundred years later, several autonomous fraternities with their own *sīmās* for granting higher ordination and their own chief monks for the internal administration of the fraternities.

Results of the disestablishment of Buddhism and the wide prevalence of controversies and schisms within the order were viewed by contemporary observers as signs of a general decline (chapter V, section i). What in fact happened, however, was a shift of the religious centre from Kandy, where there was a decline after the disestablishment, to the low country, where there was a revival inspired to a large extent by the controversies and schisms themselves (chapter V, section ii). In the low country the collapse of the high-caste monopoly of the religious life facilitated more intimate incorporation of non-Goyigama castes into religious activity; the multiplication of fraternities led to an increase in the number of monks and monasteries; and competition and rivalry between different fraternities made the monks more watchful of the behaviour and religious knowledge of one another. Furthermore, since there were no royal endowments in the low country, the monks had to depend on the support of their local patrons. This, on the one hand, compelled the monks to try to make themselves worthy of the patronage of their supporters; on the other hand, it enabled laymen to take an active part in religious affairs on a voluntary basis. The economic and social changes initiated under colonial rule in the meantime had expanded the number of strata who could afford and who wished to perform this role of local benefactors.

The nineteenth century, in this manner, witnessed the passing away of the classical era of Sinhalese Buddhism, when the maintenance of religion depended on the support of political authority, and the beginning of a new era with a decentralized monastic structure which directly and constantly depended on the laity for its support. The new situation had a curious resemblance to the pre-'transformation' period of Buddhism, and Tambiah has thus observed that 'modern Buddhism appears as a reincarnation of Weber's ancient Buddhism'.[7]

Perceptive and interesting though Tambiah's observation is, it is necessary to add that there are other aspects of modern Buddhism which cannot be adequately grasped by viewing them in this light; for ancient Buddhism was (and is) only one of the models which were (and are) available to Buddhists. There were (and are), in addition, two other models–diametrically opposed to each other, but equally important in their direct and indirect influence on shaping the attitudes, organizations and aspirations of the Buddhists–namely, the models of Protestant Christianity and traditional Buddhism.

The emulation of the model of Protestant Christianity was the outcome of the confrontation between Buddhism and missionary Christianity, and the resultant changes in Buddhism were discussed in Part II of this book under the general title 'Protestant Buddhism'. Noteworthy among those changes were the imitation by the Buddhists of the organizational forms, tactics and expedients of Christian missionary bodies, and also the acquisition by them of a new militancy, which had more in common with the spirit of the Christian missionaries of the time than with their own more traditional attitudes towards other religions. In keeping with the same developments were also the process of laicization, or the increasing involvement of laymen in roles of religious leadership, and its concomitant, the displacement of monks from some of their traditional positions of leadership. In this book attention has been concentrated only on some of the activities of the new lay leadership–in particular their contribution (mainly through education) to the continuation and consolidation of the Buddhist campaign against Christian missionary organizations; other activities–such as their attempts to reinterpret Buddhism to bring it into harmony with modern concepts and ideals like science, democracy and

[7] S. J. Tambiah, 'Buddhism and This-worldly Activity', *Modern Asian Studies*, VII (1973) 8.

socialism—which had their clearer manifestations in the twentieth century were left out altogether or were only touched upon incidentally.

Protestant Buddhism, which was a direct result of the colonial experience, indicated a curious adaptation consisting of an acceptance of that experience as well as a reaction against it. Variations between these two extremes of acceptance and reaction were also discernible in what we might call 'traditionalist Buddhism', that is, in ideals and activities inspired by the model of traditional Buddhism. At one extreme, there were the millennial episodes, briefly referred to in the Introduction, which visualized the overthrow of colonial rule and restoration of Sinhalese-Buddhist monarchy. At the other extreme, however, there was willingness to come to terms with the de facto political power and place it in a position comparable to that of Sinhalese-Buddhist kings, and if possible, to get it to perform some of the latter's functions in relation to Buddhism. Thus the fifth clause of the Kandyan Convention, in contrast to its other clauses, became a matter of concern and debate for a very long time; and even in the low country, the different branches of the Amarapura Nikāya, which had originally rejected the right of secular authorities to regulate the affairs of the order of monks, eagerly sought formal recognition by the colonial government, just as institutions like Vidyodaya Piriveṇa solicited the friendship and patronage of colonial governors. It was not uncommon among scholarly monks of the time to eulogize colonial governors or British royalty with epithets which had traditionally been used to refer to Sinhalese-Buddhist heroes, and this practice was continued by Yagirala Prajñānanda (subsequently, the biographer of Hikkaḍuvē Sumaṃgala) in his continuation of the *Mahāvaṃsa* published in 1935. This deep-rooted desire to be on good terms with the established political authority was probably one of the reasons why the Buddhist 'revival' of the nineteenth century did not develop into an organized political movement for national independence.

All the same, Buddhism, in both its Protestant and traditionalist forms, did indeed have a good deal of nationalist potential, and in making this potential politically manifest in post-colonial times the organizational changes which had begun in the nineteenth century played an important part. The new lay organizations functioned as powerful pressure groups; and members of the *saṃgha*, with no effective body to control their activities either internally (by a centralized hierarchy) or externally (by the government), displayed their independent power and influence. At the level of ideology the old problem of the relationship between Buddhism and political authority reappeared in the limelight in the form of the cry to restore Buddhism to its 'rightful place' (i.e., the position that it had occupied in pre-colonial times). Behind this cry was the assumption, and quite often the explicit argument, that the colonial period was a time of decline of Buddhism; but on balance this hardly appears accurate, for what had really happened was the passing away of the classical era of Sinhalese Buddhism and the emergence of a new era in which it had made adaptations in accord with changes in other spheres–political, economic and social. The changes which had occurred in these other spheres during the colonial period were profound, and the way that Buddhism not merely survived these changes but also, in the end, came out even stronger than before in many respects is a clear indication of its strength and resilience. For a religion which emphasizes the impermanence of all worldly things, it was certainly an impressive achievement.

Developments similar or comparable to those we have examined in this study occurred in other Buddhist countries, notably Burma, and in other Asian religions, especially Hinduism and Islam, during the nineteenth and early twentieth centuries. In all these instances, (a) changes in the traditional social and political order, and (b) the challenge of Christian missions, provided a common background for changes and revivals in religion. A comparative survey of these different religions in their different societal contexts, however, is beyond the scope of the present study. The primary aim of this study has simply been to provide a fairly detailed case study of a single religion within the confines of a single society.

APPENDIX I

Chronological Table, 1750–1900

1753 Arrival in Ceylon of the Siamese mission under Upāli; reintroduction of *upasampadā* ordination

1756 Arrival of the second Siamese mission

1760 Abortive conspiracy against Kīrti Śrī Rājasiṃha

1765 (*ca.*) *Upasampadā* ceremonies confined to Kandy

1766 Treaty between the King of Kandy and the Dutch

1778 Death of Välivița Saraṇaṃkara Saṃgharāja

1782 Death of Kīrti Śrī Rājasiṃha and the accession of Rājādhi Rājasiṃha

1785 Karatoṭa Dhammārāma's return to the Southern Province

1796 Transfer of power in the maritime provinces of Ceylon from the Dutch to the British

1798 Death of Rājādhi Rājasiṃha and the accession of Śrī Vikrama Rāmasiṃha

1803 Return of Aṁbagahapiṭiyē Ñāṇavimala from Burma and the beginning of the Amarapura fraternity

1805 Arrival of London Missionary Society missionaries in Ceylon

1809 Return of Kapugama Dhammakkhandha from Burma

1810 Return of Kataluvē Guṇaratana from Burma

1811 Return of Bōgahapiṭiyē Dhammajoti from Burma

1812 Arrival of Baptist missionaries in Ceylon
Formation of the Ceylon Branch of the British and Foreign Bible Society

1813 Return of Attuḍāvē Dhammarakkhita from Burma

1814 Arrival of Wesleyan missionaries in Ceylon

1815 Deposition of Śrī Vikrama Rājasiṃha and the cession of the Kandyan kingdom to the British Crown under the Kandyan Convention

1817–18 Great Rebellion

1818 Arrival of Church Missionary Society missionaries in Ceylon

1825 Aṁbagahapiṭiyē Ñāṇavimala appointed 'High Priest in and over the

Buddhist Priests belonging to the Mahabadda of the Maritime districts of Ceylon'

1826 Gāllē Medhaṃkara appointed chief monk of Śrīpāda

1827 Death of Karatoṭa Dhammārāma

1829–31 Commission of Eastern Enquiry

1831 Beginning of the Adhikamāsa Vādaya

1833 Administrative amalgamation of the Kandyan and maritime provinces

1835 Death of Aṁbagahapiṭiyē Ñāṇavimala and the appointment of Bōpāgoḍa Sumana as chief monk of the Amarapura fraternity

1837 Beginning of the missionary campaign to dissociate the government from Buddhism

1842 Appointment of the first Roman Catholic Bishop of Ceylon

1845 Appointment of the first Anglican Bishop of Ceylon
Founding of the Parama Dhamma Cetiya Piriveṇa at Ratmalāna by Valānē Siddhārttha

1848 Disturbances in Mātalē and Kuruṇāgala

1849 Appearance of Gogerly's *Kristiyāni Prajñapti*

1851 Beginning of the Sīmāsaṃkara Vādaya

1852 Beginning of the Sav Sat Dam Vādaya

1855 Establishment of the Śri Kalyāṇi Sāmagarīdharma Saṃgha Sabhā
Establishment of the Amarapura Saddhammavaṃsa fraternity

1856 Temple Lands Ordinance

1862 Death of Bentara Atthadassī
Death of Daniel J. Gogerly
Return of Aṁbagahavattē Indāsabhavara Ñāṇasāmi from Burma
Establishment of the Laṃkopakāra Press at Galle
Organization of Sarvajña Śāsanābhivṛddhidāyaka Dharma Samāgama (Society for the Propagation of Buddhism) by Mohoṭṭivattē Guṇānanda in Colombo

1863 Return of Puvakdanḍāvē Paññānanda from Burma

1864 Death of Bōpāgoḍa Sumana
Beginning of the Rāmañña fraternity

1865 Buddhist-Christian debate at Baddegama
Buddhist-Christian debate at Varāgoḍa
Beginning of the revision of the Buddhist Canon at Pälmaḍulla

1866 Buddhist-Christian debate at Udanviṭa

1868 Lokārtthasādhaka Samāgama organized by Doḍandūvē Piyaratana

1869 Establishment of the Department of Public Instruction

1870 Service Tenures Ordinance

1871 Buddhist-Christian debate at Gampola
Beginning of the Dēvapūjā Vādaya

1873 Buddhist-Christian debate at Pānadurē
Founding of Vidyodaya Piriveṇa at Māligākanda by Hikkaḍuvē Sumaṃgala

1875 Founding of Vidyalaṃkāra Piriveṇa at Pāliyagoḍa by Ratmalānē Dhammāloka

1880 Arrival of Theosophists in Ceylon
Beginning of the publication of *Sarasavi Sañdaräsa*
Disestablishment of the Anglican Church in Ceylon

1882 Founding of the Pali Text Society

1883 Catholic-Buddhist clash at Koṭahēna

1886 Death of Am̆bagahavattē Indāsabhavara Ñāṇasāmi

1887 Clash between Olcott and Mohoṭṭivattē

1888 Beginning of the publication of *The Buddhist*

1889 Buddhist Temporalities Ordinance

1890 Death of Mohoṭṭivattē Guṇānanda

1891 Establishment of the Maha Bodhi Society

1893 Dharmapala represents Buddhism at the World Parliament of Religions in Chicago

1898 Clash between Olcott and Dharmapala
Formation of the Colombo Young Men's Buddhist Association

APPENDIX II

Pupillary Succession of Välivița Saraṇaṃkara in the Low Country

NOTE ON THE DIAGRAM

Buddhist monks trace their spiritual genealogies (*sāsana paramparā*) through their teachers. But the terms teacher (*guru*) and pupil (*gōla* or *śiṣya*), as commonly used, lack precision with regard to the nature and scope of the relationship. A teacher may mean:

1. a monk who has initiated a layman into the order by robiņg him, and thus acts as preceptor (*upajjhāya*) to the novice (*sāmaṇera saddhivihārika*), whom he trains and eventually presents to his fraternity for ordination (*upasampadā*); or
2. a tutor (*ācariya*) who instructs his student (*antevāsika*) in the doctrine and other branches of traditional knowledge such as languages, literature, astrology and medicine; or
3. both (1) and (2) above combined in one person.

As is evident from this classification, it is possible for one pupil to have two (or more) teachers, and therefore two (or more) genealogies as well: one relating to his admission to the order (*pävidi paramparā*) and another (or more) relating to his education (*śāstra paramparā*).

Of these two types of genealogies, the first (*pävidi paramparā*) is more exclusive than the other because recruits to the order are usually selected from localities and families well known to the teachers. Not infrequently, the recruits are younger kinsmen, especially nephews. Such selection is fundamental to the establishment and continuity of individual (caste-, subcaste- or locality-based) fraternities. Genealogical relationships of this first type are indicated in the diagram by thick lines.

Thin lines, in contrast, indicate relationships of the second type (*śāṣtra paramparā*), which are more 'open' than the first type in that they often exist irrespective of *nikāya* (and caste) boundaries, the lay-cleric distinction, and occasionally even differences in terms of nationality and religion.

It will be observed in the diagram that with regard to some monks both the *pävidi* and the *śāstra paramparā* have been indicated separately, while for others only one of them has been shown. Where only the *pävidi paramparā* is shown (by a thick line), it may or may not have coincided with the *śāstra paramparā*. In a few instances where only the latter is shown (by a thin line), genealogical relationships of the other (*pävidi paramparā*) type also may have existed; but evidence has been insufficient to establish them conclusively.

The diagram has been drawn on the basis of information gathered from a variety of sources, such as biographies of monks, and histories of individual monasteries or fraternities, nearly all of them written in Sinhalese. Most of them are listed in the bibliography, but are too numerous to be mentioned here separately. A few wills written by monks transferring their property to their pupils have also proved very useful. Though easily the best source for this purpose, they are unfortunately not easily available.

It is hardly necessary to add that the diagram is a very selective one indicating only some of the more important lines of pupillary succession. Where information is available, the years of birth or death or both of individual monks have been mentioned.

BIBLIOGRAPHY

Several items which are cited in full in footnotes, but which are marginal or incidental to the main theme of this book, have been excluded from the following list. On the basis of the same criterion of relevance, a few items which have appeared after the text of this book had been substantially or fully completed have been included.

I. REFERENCE WORKS

Alwis, James. *A Descriptive Catalogue of the Sanskrit, Pali and Sinhalese Literary Works of Ceylon*. Vol. I (Colombo, 1870).

Anthonisz, R. G. *Report on the Dutch Records in the Government Archives at Colombo* (Colombo, 1907).

Codrington, H. W. *Glossary of Native, Foreign and Anglicised Words, commonly used in Ceylon in official correspondence and other documents* (Colombo, 1924).

De Silva, W. A. *Catalogue of Palm Leaf Manuscripts in the Library of the Colombo Museum*. Vol. I (Colombo, 1938).

De Zoysa, Louis. *A Catalogue of Pali, Sinhalese and Sanskrit Manuscripts in the Temple Libraries of Ceylon* (Colombo, 1885).

Encyclopaedia of Buddhism (Colombo, 1961–). In progress; two volumes completed by 1968.

Encyclopaedia of Religion and Ethics. 13 vols. (Edinburgh, 1908–1926).

Gard, Richard A. *A Bibliography for the Study of Buddhism in Ceylon in Western Languages*. 2nd ed. Mimeographed (Berkeley, 1957).

Goonetileke, H. A. I. *A Bibliography of Ceylon*. 2 vols. (Inter Documentation Company, Zug, Switzerland, 1970).

Hanayama, Shinsho. *Bibliography on Buddhism* (Tokyo, 1961).

Historical Manuscripts Commission (Ceylon). *First Report* (S.P. IX: 1933).

________. *Second Report* (S.P. XXI: 1935).

________. *Third Report* (S.P. XIX: 1951).

Juriaanse, M. W. *Catalogue of the Archives of the Dutch Central Government of Coastal Ceylon, 1640–1796* (Colombo, 1943).

Lawrie, A. C. *A Gazetteer of the Central Province of Ceylon*. 2 vols. (Colombo, 1896–1898).

Murdoch, J., and Nicholson, J. *Classified Catalogue of Printed Tracts and Books in Singhalese* (Madras, 1868).

Ondaatje, M. P. J. 'A Tabular List of Oriental Works and Translations, published by the late Dutch Government of Ceylon, at the Printing Press at Colombo'. *JRAS*, n.s., I (1865) 141–44.

Paññāsekhara, Kalukoňdayāvē. *Siṃhala Puvatpat Sañgarā Itihāsaya*. Vol. I, 1832–1887 (Colombo, 1965); vol. II, 1888–1900 (Colombo, 1966).

Wainwright, M. D., and Mathews, Noel. *A Guide to Western Manuscripts and Documents in the British Isles Relating to South and South-East Asia* (London, 1965).

Wickremasinghe, D. M. de Z. *Catalogue of the Sinhalese Manuscripts in the British Museum* (London, 1900).

———. *Catalogue of the Sinhalese Printed Books in the Library of the British Museum* (London, 1901).

II. MANUSCRIPT MATERIAL

i. Ceylon National Archives

Photostat copies of documents collected by the Ceylon Historical Manuscript Commission; series 5/63.

ii. Colombo Museum Library

Johnston Papers.
Palm Leaf Manuscripts.

iii. British Museum Library (Oriental Section)

Hugh Nevill Collection.
Sinhalese Manuscripts.

iv. Public Record Office

Colonial Office papers relating to Ceylon: Despatches from Ceylon with enclosures, etc., C.O. 54/; and Evidence collected by the Commissioners of Eastern Enquiry (1829–31), C.O. 416/.

III. PERIODICALS AND NEWSPAPERS
(in chronological order with dates of first publication)

i. English

The Ceylon Government Gazette (1802).
The Colombo Journal (1832).
The Friend (1837).
Journal of the Ceylon Branch of the Royal Asiatic Society (1845).
The Friend (1870). Second Series.
The Theosophist (1879).
The Buddhist (1888).

ii. Sinhalese

Durlabdhi Vinodaniya (1862).
Sudharma Prakaraṇaya (1862).
Sudarśanaya (1862).
Kristiyāni Vāda Mardanaya (1862).
Bauddha Vākśāraya (1863).
Bauddha Vākya Khaṇḍanaya (1863).
Satya Dvajaya (1863).
Samyak Darśanaya (1863).
Sumati Samgrahaya (1864).
Labdhi Tulāva (1864).
Satya Mārgaya (1867).
Vibhajjavādaya (1872).
Samaya Saṃgrahava (1873).
Sarasavi Sañdaräsa (1880).

IV. BOOKS, ARTICLES, PAMPHLETS, COLLECTIONS OF DOCUMENTS AND UNPUBLISHED DISSERTATIONS

i. English (originals and translations)

Alwis, C. 'On the Principles of Singhalese Chronology'. *JRAS(CB)*, III (1856–58) 181–94.

Alwis, James. 'On the Elu Language, its Poetry and its Poets'. *JRAS(CB)*, II (1850).

———. 'Introduction' to the *Sidath Sangarawa* (Colombo, 1852).

———. 'Terms of Address and Modes of Salutation in use amongst the Singhalese'. *JRAS(CB)*, III (1856–58) 219–76.

———. *Contributions to Oriental Literature*. 2 parts (Colombo, 1863).

———. 'Buddhism: Its Origin, History and Doctrines' (1865). Reprinted in *JPTS* (1883).

———. 'The Buddhist Scriptures and their Language, the Pali' (1865). Reprinted in *JPTS* (1883).

Ames, Michael M. 'Ideological and Social Change in Ceylon'. *Human Organization*, XXII (1963) 45–53.

———. 'Magical-animism and Buddhism: A Structural Analysis of the Sinhalese Religious System'. *Journal of Asian Studies*, XXIII (1964) 21–52.

———. 'The Impact of Western Education on Religion and Society in Ceylon'. *Pacific Affairs*, XL (1967) 19–42.

Arasaratnam, S. *Dutch Power in Ceylon, 1658–1687* (Amsterdam, 1958).

———. 'Oratorians and Predikants: The Catholic Church in Ceylon under Dutch Rule' (Review Article). *CJHSS*, I (1958) 216–22.

———. 'Vimala Dharma Surya II (1687–1707) and his relations with the Dutch'. *CJHSS*, VI (1963) 59–70.

Ariyapala, M. B. *Society in Mediaeval Ceylon* (Colombo, 1956).

Arnold, Edwin. *India Revisited* (London, 1886).

[Bailey, Benjamin]. *Six Letters of Vetus . . . on the re-connexion of the British Government with the Buddhist Idolatry of Ceylon* (Colombo, 1852).

Bailey, J. *Statement of the Ceylon Mission of the Church Missionary Society for the year 1832* (Cotta, 1833).

Balding, J. W. *The Centenary Volume of the Church Missionary Society in Ceylon, 1818–1918* (Madras, 1922).

Baptist Mission. *A Historical Sketch of the Baptist Mission in Ceylon* (Kandy, 1850).

Bechert, Heinz. 'Theravāda Buddhist Sangha: Some General Observations on Historical and Political Factors in its Development'. *Journal of Asian Studies*, XXIX/4 (August, 1970) 761–78.

Bell, H. C. P. *Report on the Kegalla District* (Colombo, 1892).

———. *Report on the Kuṭṭāpiṭiya Sannasa* (Kandy, 1925).

Bell, H. C. P., and Gunasekera, A. M. 'Kelani Vihāra and its Inscriptions'. *CALR*, I (1916) 145–61.

Boake, B. *A Brief Account of the origin and nature of the connection between the British Government and the idolatrous systems of religion prevalent in the island of Ceylon* (Colombo, 1855).

———. *National Education in the East in general and in Ceylon in particular* (Colombo, 1855).

Boudens, R. *The Catholic Church in Ceylon under Dutch Rule* (Rome, 1957).

Boudens, R. (ed.). 'The Letter of Father Francis Xavier to Governor Horton on the state of Catholicism in Ceylon, 1832'. *CHJ*, III (1953) 86–92.

Bouglé, C. 'The Essence and Reality of the Caste System' (1900). *Contributions to Indian Sociology*, II (1958).

Boxer, C. R. 'Christians and Spices: Portuguese Missionary Methods in Ceylon, 1518–1658'. *History Today*, VIII (1958) 346–54.

———. 'A Note on Portuguese Missionary Methods in the East: 16th–18th centuries'. *CHJ*, X (1960–61) 77–90.

———. *The Dutch Seaborne Empire, 1600–1800* (London, 1965).

Buddhist Temporalities. *Report of the Commissioners appointed to inquire into the administration of the . . .* (S.P. XVII: 1876).
Capper, John. *A Full Account of the Buddhist Controversy held at Pantura* (Colombo, 1873).
Chapman, James. *Memorials of . . . , first Bishop of Colombo* (London, 1892).
Childers, R. C. Obituary of Yātrāmullē Dhammārāma in *Trübner's Record* (1872).
Church Missionary Society. *Jubilee Sketches: An Outline of the . . . in Ceylon, 1818–1869* (Colombo, 1869).
Clough, M. M. *Extracts from the Journal and Correspondence of the late Mrs. . . .* (London, 1829).
Codrington, H. W. 'The Date of Kirttisri's Accession'. *CALR*, II (1917) 156–57.
______. *Ancient Land Tenure and Revenue in Ceylon* (Colombo, 1938).
______. *A Short History of Ceylon*. Rev. ed. (London, 1939).
______ (tr. and ed.). 'A Letter from the Court of Siam, 1756'. *JRAS(CB)*, XXXVI (1945) 97–99.
Colombo Auxiliary Bible Society. *The First Report of the . . .* (Colombo, 1813).
______. *Correspondence between the Rev. J. Bailey, Church Missionary, and the Rev. B. Clough, Wesleyan Missionary, on the affairs of the . . .* (London, 1835).
Coomaraswamy, Ananda K. *Mediaeval Sinhalese Art*. 2nd ed. (New York, 1956).
Copleston, R. S. *Buddhism: Primitive and Present in Magadha and in Ceylon* (London, 1892).
Cordiner, James. *Description of Ceylon*. 2 vols. (London, 1807).
Coser, Lewis A. *The Functions of Social Conflict* (London, 1956).
Cronin, Vincent. *A Pearl to India: The Life of Roberto de Nobili* (London, 1959).
Cūlavaṃsa, being the more recent part of the Mahāvaṃsa. Tr. by Wilhelm Geiger, and from the German into English by C. M. Rickmers. 2 vols. (Colombo, 1953).
Daly, J. B. *Report on the Galle Convention* [of the Buddhist Theosophical Society] (Galle, 1891).
Daniel, Ebenezer. *Reminiscences of Two Years Missionary Labours in the Jungles of Ceylon* (Kandy, 1843).
[Davids, T. W. Rhys]. 'Revision of the Sinhalese Buddhist Scriptures'. *Indian Antiquary*, I (1871) 31.
Davy, John. *An Account of the Interior of Ceylon and of its Inhabitants* (London, 1821).
De Levera, F. *Remarks on the Cotta Version of the Scriptures into the Singhalese Language* (Colombo, 1835).
De Melo, Carlos Merces. *The Recruitment and Formation of Native Clergy in India*

(16th–19th Centuries): An Historico-Canonical Study (Lisbon, 1955).

De Queyroz, Fernão. *The Temporal and Spiritual Conquest of Ceylon* (1687). Tr. S. G. Perera. 3 vols (Colombo, 1930).

De Silva, A. 'On the Corruptions of Buddhism and the Different Tenets, Opinions and Principles of the Amarapoora and Siamese Sects'. Appendix XII to Ribeyro's *History of Ceylon* (1685), retranslated from the French edition (with an appendix) by George Lee (Colombo, 1847).

De Silva, Carolis. *The Life of Dhammaratana of Miripenna* (Galle, 1868).

De Silva, Colvin R. *Ceylon under the British Occupation, 1795–1833*. 2 vols. 3rd impression (Colombo, 1953).

De Silva, K. M. 'The Development of British Policy on Temple Lands in Ceylon, 1840–55'. *JRAS(CB)*, n.s., VIII (1963) 312–29.

———. *Social Policy and Missionary Organizations in Ceylon, 1840–1855* (London, 1965).

De Silva, K. M. (ed.). *Letters on Ceylon 1848–50: The Administration of Viscount Torrington and the 'Rebellion' of 1848* (Colombo, 1965).

Dewaraja, L. S. 'History of Buddhism in Ceylon during the Nayakkar Period (1739–1815)'. M.A. thesis, University of Ceylon, 1965.

———. *A Study of the Political, Administrative and Social Structure of the Kandyan Kingdom of Ceylon, 1707–1760* (Colombo, 1972).

De Young, John E. *Village Life in Thailand* (Los Angeles, 1955).

De Zoysa, Louis. *Reports on the inspection of Temple Libraries* (S.P. XI: 1875).

———. *Report on the inspection of Temple Libraries* (S.P. XXV: 1879).

Dharmapala, Anagarika. 'Reminiscences of My Early Life'. *The Maha Bodhi*, XLI (1933) 151–62.

———. 'Diary Leaves of the Late Ven. . . .'. Ed. Devapriya Valisinha. *The Maha Bodhi*, LI (1943)–LXXII (1964).

Dhani Nivat. 'Religious Intercourse between Ceylon and Siam in the Bangkok Period of Siamese History'. In N. A. Jayawickrama (ed.), *Paranavitana Felicitation Volume* (Colombo, 1965), pp. 135–41.

Dickson, J. F. 'The *Upasampadā-Kammāvācā*, being the Buddhist Manual of the Form and Manner of Ordering of Priests and Deacons: The Pali Text, with a Translation and Notes'. *JRAS*, n.s., VII (1875) 1–16.

———. 'The *Pātimokkha*, being the Buddhist Office of the Confession of Priests: The Pali Text, with a Translation and Notes'. *JRAS*, n.s., VIII (1876) 62–130.

———. 'Notes illustrative of Buddhism as the daily religion of the Buddhists of

Ceylon'. *JRAS(CB)*, VIII (1884) 207–31.

D'Oyly, John. *The Diary of . . . 1810–1815*. Ed. H. W. Codrington (Colombo, 1917).

———. *A Sketch of the Constitution of the Kandyan Kingdom*. Ed. L. J. B. Turner (Colombo, 1929).

Dubois, J. A. *Letters on the state of Christianity in India* (London, 1823).

Dumont, L. 'World Renunciation in Indian Religions'. *Contributions to Indian Sociology*, IV (1960) 33–62.

Durkheim, Emile. *The Elementary Forms of the Religious Life*. Tr. J. W. Swain (London, 1915).

Dynastic Chronicles, Bangkok Era, The Fourth Reign (1850–1868). Tr. Chadin Flood. vol. I (Tokyo, 1965).

Ekanayake, G. B. 'The Revival of Buddhism in Ceylon'. *The East and the West*, XII (1915) 447–59.

———. 'The Story of the Anglican Communion in Ceylon, 1796–1845' (n.d., *ca.* 1930s). In Percy Wickremesinghe, *Canon Ekanayake of Colombo: Priest, Missionary and Theologian* (Colombo, 1949), pp. 211–28.

Evers, Hans-Dieter. *Monks, Priests and Peasants: A Study of Buddhism and Social Structure in Central Ceylon* (Leiden, 1972).

Ferguson, Donald. 'Mulgirigala'. *JRAS(CB)*, XXII (1911) 197–235.

Fernando, C. N. V. 'A Study of the History of Christianity in Ceylon in the British Period from 1796–1903, with special reference to the Protestant Missions'. B.Litt. thesis, Oxford, 1942.

Fernando, P. E. E. 'The Authorship of Sangharājasādhucariyāva'. *UCR*, XVI (1958) 53–55.

Fernando, P. E. E. (ed. and tr.). 'An Account of the Kandyan Mission to Siam in 1750 A.D.'. *CJHSS*, II (1959) 37–83.

——— (ed. and tr.). 'India Office Land Grant of King Kīrti Śrī Rājasiṃha'. *CJHSS*, III (1960) 72–81.

Forbes, J. *Eleven Years in Ceylon*. 2 vols. (London, 1840).

Galpin, C. A. 'The Johnston Manuscripts: Relation of a Conspiracy against the King of Candy in the year 1760, given by Appoohamy de Lanerolles'. *CALR*, II/4 (April 1917) 272–74.

Geertz, Clifford (ed.). *Old Societies and New States: The Quest for Modernity in Asia and Africa* (Glencoe, Ill., 1963).

Geiger, W. *Culture of Ceylon in Mediaeval Times*. Ed. Heinz Bechert (Wiesbaden, 1960).

Gluckman, Max. *Order and Rebellion in Tribal Africa* (London, 1963).

Godakumbura, C. E. (ed. and tr.). 'Kaḍadora Grant'. *JRAS(CB)*, n.s. II (1952) 141–58.

———. 'Postscript to the Kaḍadora Grant'. *JRAS(CB)*, n.s. III (1953) 72–79.

——— (ed. and tr.). 'Medawala Copper-plate'. *EZ*, V (1965) 466–90.

Gogerly, D. J. 'The Wesleyan Mission Free Schools'. *Colombo Journal*, 16 February 1833.

———. *Ceylon Buddhism: The Collected Writings of. . . .* Ed. A. S. Bishop. 2 vols. (Colombo, 1908).

Gombrich, Richard F. *Precept and Practice: Traditional Buddhism in the Rural Highlands of Ceylon* (Oxford, 1971).

Gooneratne, E. R. *Mid XIX Century: From the Diaries of. . . .* Ed. P. E. Pieris (Colombo, n.d.).

Gooneratne, M. Y. *English Literature in Ceylon, 1815–1878* (Dehiwala, 1968).

Goonetileke, W. A. (tr.). *Syāmūpasampadā: The adoption of the Siamese order of priesthood in Ceylon* (Bangkok, 1914).

Gratiaen, L. J. 'The First English School in Ceylon'. *CALR*, VII (1921–22) 141–47.

———. 'The Parish Schools under Governor North'. *CALR*, VIII (1922–23) 35–44.

———. 'The Government Schools, 1804–1820'. *CALR*, IX (1923–24) 71–86.

———. *The First School Commission, 1832–1841* (Colombo, 1927).

———. 'The Central School Commission, 1841–1848'. *JRAS(CB)*, XXXI (1928–30) 488–507.

———. 'The School Commission, 1848–1859'. *JRAS(CB)*, XXXII (1931–33) 37–54.

———. 'The Last Years of the Central School Commission, 1859–1869'. *JRAS(CB)*, XXXII (1931–33) 328–46.

Griswold, Alexander B. 'King Mongkut in Perspective'. *Journal of the Siam Society*, XLV (1957) 1–14.

Hardy, Robert Spence, *The British Government and the Idolatry of Ceylon* (Colombo, 1839).

———. *Eastern Monachism* (London, 1850).

———. *The Sacred Books of the Buddhists compared with History and Modern Science* (Colombo, 1863).

———. *Jubilee Memorials of the Wesleyan Mission, South Ceylon, 1814–1864* (Colombo, 1864).

———. *The Legends and Theories of the Buddhists, compared with History and Science* (London, 1866).

———. Obituary in *JRAS*, n.s., III (1868) v–viii.

Harvard, W. M. *A Narrative of the establishment and progress of the Mission to Ceylon and India* (London, 1823).

Harvard, W. M. (ed.). *Memoirs of Mrs. Elizabeth Harvard*. 3rd ed. (London, 1833).

Heber, Reginald. *Narrative of a Journey through the Upper Provinces of India*. 2 vols. (London, 1849).

Hevawasam, P. B. J. 'The "Sav Sat Dam" Controversy'. *UCR*, XVII (1959) 117–36.

———. 'Where are the Buddhist Pioneers?' *Ceylon Daily News*, 3 September 1969.

Hocart, A. M. *Caste: A Comparative Study* (London, 1950).

Horner, I. B. 'The Monk: Buddhist and Christian'. *Hibbert Journal*, XXXIX (1940–41) 168–78.

Hutton, J. H. *Caste in India*. 3rd ed. (Bombay, 1961).

Jayatilaka, D. B. *Saranankara: The Last Sangha-rāja of Ceylon* (Colombo, 1934).

Jayawardena, V. K. *The Rise of the Labour Movement in Ceylon* (Durham, North Carolina, 1972).

Jinarajadasa, C. *The Golden Book of the Theosophical Society* (Madras, 1925).

Johnston, Alexander. *Important Public Documents, to and from . . .* (n.d.).

———. 'Account of a Flag representing the introduction of the caste of Chalias or Cinnamon-peelers to Ceylon'. *Transactions of the R.A.S.*, III (1835) 332–34.

Kaufman, Howard K. *Bangkhuad: A Community Study in Thailand* (New York, 1960).

Kotelawele, D. A. 'New Light on the Life of Sangharaja Welivita Saranankara'. *Journal of the Vidyalankara University of Ceylon*, I/1 (January 1972) 119–24.

Knox, Robert. *An Historical Relation of Ceylon* (1681). Ed. James Ryan (Glasgow, 1911).

Lambrick, Samuel. *An Essay to shew that every version of the Holy Scripture should conform to the Original in adopting one word throughout for each of the Personal Pronouns* (Cotta, 1826).

Leach, E. R. (ed.). *Aspects of Caste in South India, Ceylon and North-West Pakistan* (Cambridge, 1960).

——— (ed.). *Dialectic in Practical Religion* (Cambridge, 1968).

Legislative Council (Ceylon). *Papers on the Subject of Vernacular Education* (S.P. XXVII: 1866–67).

———. *Report of a Sub-Committee of the Legislative Council appointed 'to inquire into and report upon the state and prospects of Education in the Island . . .'* (S.P. VIII: 1867).

———. *Papers on Service Tenures* (S.P. XVIII: 1869).

———. *Papers on the Subject of Literary and Scientific Work carried out by the Government of Ceylon* (S.P. I: 1878).

———. *Report of a Commission appointed by the Governor to inquire into the causes which led to the recent riots at Kotahena* (S.P. IV: 1883).

———. *An Account of the System of Education existing in Ceylon* (S.P. XXXIII: 1898).

Lingat, R. 'History of Wat Mahādhātu'. *Journal of the Siam Society*, XXIV (1930).

———. 'History of Wat Pavaraniveça'. *Journal of the Siam Society*, XXVI (1933).

Loten, Joan Gideon. *Memoir*, 1757. Ed. and tr. E. Reimers (Colombo, 1935).

MacLear, J. F. 'The Making of the Lay Tradition'. *Journal of Religion*, XXXIII (1953) 113–36.

The Mahāvaṃsa, or the Great Chronicle of Ceylon. Tr. Wilhelm Geiger, with an Addendum by G. C. Mendis (Colombo, 1950).

Malalasekara, G. P. *The Pali Literature of Ceylon* (London, 1928).

Malalasekara, G. P. (ed.). *Diamond Jubilee Souvenir of the Buddhist Theosophical Society, 1880–1940* (Colombo, 1940).

Malalasekara, G. P., and De Silva, D. N. W. (eds.). *The Colombo YMBA: Golden Jubilee Souvenir* (Colombo, 1948).

Malalgoda, Kitsiri. 'Millennialism in Relation to Buddhism'. *CSSH*, XII/4 (October 1970) 424–41.

———. 'Sinhalese Buddhism: Orthodox and Syncretistic, Traditional and Modern' (Review Article). *CJHSS*, n.s., II/2 (July–December 1972) 156–69.

———. 'The Buddhist-Christian Confrontation in Ceylon, 1800–1880'. *Social Compass*, XX/2 (1973) 171–200.

Marriott, McKim. 'Cultural Policy in the New States'. In Geertz (ed.), *Old Societies and New States.*

Martin, David A. *Pacifism: An Historical and Sociological Study* (London, 1965).

Mendis, G. C. (ed.). *The Colebrooke-Cameron Papers.* 2 vols. (Oxford, 1956).

Mills, Lennox A. *Ceylon under British Rule, 1795–1932.* New Impression (London, 1964).

Modder, F. H. 'Ridi Vihara'. *JRAS(CB)*, XIV (1896) 118–24.

———. *The Principles of Kandyan Laws* (London, 1914).

Moffat, Abbot L. *Mongkut, the King of Siam* (New York, 1961).

Morris, Henry. *The Life of John Murdoch* (London, 1906).

Nash, Manning. *The Golden Road to Modernity: Village Life in Contemporary Burma* (New York, 1965).

Nash, Manning, et al. *Anthropological Studies in Theravada Buddhism* (New Haven, 1966).

Nethercot, Arthur H. *The First Five Lives of Annie Besant* (London, 1959).

_______. *The Last Four Lives of Annie Besant* (London, 1963).

Obeyesekere, Gananath. 'The Great Tradition and the Little in the Perspective of Sinhalese Buddhism'. *Journal of Asian Studies*, XXII (1963) 139–53.

_______. 'The Buddhist Pantheon in Ceylon and its extensions'. In Nash et al., *Anthropological Studies*.

_______. 'Theodicy, Sin and Salvation in a Sociology of Buddhism'. In Leach (ed.), *Dialectic in Practical Religion*.

_______. 'Religious Symbolism and Political Change in Ceylon'. *Modern Ceylon Studies*, I (1970) 43–63.

Olcott, Henry Steel. *The Buddhist Catechism*, 1881. 44th ed. (Madras, 1947).

_______. *A Collection of Lectures on Theosophy and Archaic Religions, delivered in India and Ceylon* (Madras, 1883).

_______. *Old Diary Leaves*. 6 vols. 2nd ed. (Madras, 1928–35).

Palm, J. D. 'The Educational Establishment of the Dutch in Ceylon'. *JRAS(CB)*, II (1846–47) 105–33.

_______. 'An Account of the Dutch Church in Ceylon, collected from the local records deposited in the Wolfendahl Church, Colombo'. *JRAS(CB)*, III (1847–48) 5–68.

Paññāsāmi. *Sāsanavaṃsa* (1861). Tr. B. C. Law (London, 1952).

Paulusz, J. H. O. 'Prince Crumpty-Pippit and Governor van Eck'. *Journal of the Dutch Burgher Union of Ceylon*, XXI/2 (October 1931) 92–95.

Peggs, J. *The Present State of the British Connection with Idolatry in Ceylon* (London, 1853).

Peiris, Edmund. 'Sinhalese Christian Literature of the XVIIth and XVIIIth Centuries'. *JRAS(CB)*, XXXV (1943) 163–81.

Perera, S. G. 'The First Catholic Bishop of Ceylon'. *CALR*, VII (1921–22) 115–16.

_______. *Historical Sketches* (Jaffna, 1938).

_______. *Jesuits in Ceylon* (Madura, 1941).

_______. *The Life of Father Jacome Gonçalvez* (Madura, 1942).

Pieris, P. E. 'Papers of Sir Alexander Johnston'. *Buddhist*, n.s. III/3 (20 January 1917) 1.

_______. *Ceylon and the Hollanders, 1656–1796* (Tellippalai, 1918).

_______. *Tri Sinhala: The Last Phase, 1795–1815*. 2nd ed. (Colombo, 1939).

_______. 'Appointments within the Kandyan Provinces'. *JRAS(CB)*, XXXVI (1945) 112–16.

_______. *Sinhalē and the Patriots, 1815–1818* (Colombo, 1950).

Pieris, Ralph. *Sinhalese Social Organization: The Kandyan Period* (Colombo, 1956).

Pocock, D. F. 'The Movement of Castes'. *Man* (1955) 71–72.

Pratt, James B., *India and its Faiths: A Traveller's Record* (New York, 1915).

Rahula, Walpola. *History of Buddhism in Ceylon: The Anuradhapura Period* (Colombo, 1956).

[Rājapakṣa] 'Abridgement of the history of the CHALIAS by Adrian Ragia Pakse, a Chief of that Caste'. Appended to J. Joinville, 'On the Religion and Manners of the People of Ceylon'. *Asiatick Researches*, VII (1801) 444–45.

Rajapakse, Sampson. *A Memoir, with a sketch of the Salagama Sinhalese* (Colombo, 1912).

The Rājāvaliya, or A Historical Narrative of Sinhalese Kings from Vijaya to Vimala Dharma Surya II. Ed. and tr. B. Gunasekara (Colombo, 1900).

Redfield, Robert. *Peasant Society and Culture* (Chicago, 1956).

Ryan, Bryce. *Caste in Modern Ceylon* (New Brunswick, New Jersey, 1953).

Sarathchandra, E. R. *The Sinhalese Novel*. Rev. ed. (Colombo, 1950).

Schreuder, Jan. *Memoir*, 1762. Ed. and tr. E. Reimers (Colombo, 1946).

Selkirk, James. *A Short Defence of the Cotta Version of the Scriptures into Singhalese* (Cotta, 1835).

———. *Recollections of Ceylon* (London, 1844).

Seneviratne, H. L. 'The Äsaḷa Perahära in Kandy'. *CJHSS*, VI (1963) 169–80.

Service Tenures Commission. *Reports* (A.R. 1870, 1871 and 1872).

Sharma, J. P. *Republics in Ancient India, c. 1500 B.C.–500 B.C.* (Leiden, 1968).

Shils, Edward. 'The Intellectuals and the Powers: Some Perspectives for Comparative Analysis'. *CSSH*, I (1958) 5–22.

———. 'Centre and Periphery'. In *The Logic of Personal Knowledge: Essays Presented to Michael Polanyi* (London, 1961).

———. 'On the Comparative Study of the New States'. In Geertz (ed.), *Old Societies and New States*.

Skeen, W. *Adam's Peak* (Colombo, 1870).

Smith, Donald E. (ed.). *South Asian Politics and Religion* (Princeton, New Jersey, 1966).

Society for the Propagation of the Gospel in Foreign Parts. *Classified Digest of the Record of the . . . , 1701–1892* (London, 1894).

Spiro, Melford E. *Burmese Supernaturalism: A Study in the Explanation and Reduction of Suffering* (Englewood Cliffs, New Jersey, 1967).

———. *Buddhism and Society: A Great Tradition and its Burmese Vicissitudes* (New York, 1970).

Srinivas, M. N. 'The Social System of a Mysore Village'. In McKim Marriott (ed.), *Village India: Studies in the Little Community* (Chicago, 1955).

———. *Social Change in Modern India* (Berkeley and Los Angeles, 1966).

Stevenson, H. N. C. 'Status Evaluation in the Hindu Caste System'. *JRAI*, LXXXIV (1954) 45–65.

Suraweera, A. V. 'The Imprisonment of Sangharāja Saraṇaṃkara'. *Vidyodaya Journal of Arts, Science and Letters*, I/1 (January 1968) 53–57.

Tambiah, S. J. 'The Ideology of Merit and the Social Correlates of Buddhism in a Thai Village'. In Leach (ed.), *Dialectic in Practical Religion*.

———. *Buddhism and the Spirit Cults in North-East Thailand* (Cambridge, 1970).

———. 'Buddhism and This-worldly Activity'. *Modern Asian Studies*, VII (1973) 1–20.

Temple Lands Commission. *Reports*, 1857–58 (Colombo, 1859); 1859 (S.P. II: 1861); 1860 (S.P. I: 1862); 1861 (S.P. X: 1862); 1862 (S.P. XI: 1863); 1863 (S.P. IX: 1864); 1864 (S.P. X: 1865); 1865 (S.P. XIX: 1866).

Tennent, J. Emerson. *Christianity in Ceylon* (London, 1850).

Theosophical Society, *A Full Report of the Proceedings of the Seventh Anniversary Meeting of the . . .* (Calcutta, 1883).

Tillekeratne, John F. 'The Life of Karatota Kīrti Srī Dhammārāma, High Priest of Matara in the Southern Province of the Island of Ceylon'. *The Orientalist*, III (1889) 204–7.

Troeltsch, E. *The Social Teachings of the Christian Churches*. Tr. O. Wyon. 2 vols. (London, 1931).

Turnour, George. 'Introduction' to *The Mahāwanso in Roman Characters with the Translation subjoined* (Cotta, 1837).

University of Ceylon. *History of Ceylon*. Vol. I, part I (Colombo, 1959); vol. I, part II (Colombo, 1960); vol. III (Colombo, 1973).

Vella, Walter F. *Siam under Rama II, 1824–1851* (New York, 1957).

Warnasuriya, W. M. A. 'Inscriptional Evidence bearing on the nature of Religious Endowment in Ancient Ceylon'. *UCR*, I (1943) 69–82; II (1944) 92–96.

Weerasinghe, S. J. de S. 'The Sinhalese Bible from early beginnings to our times'. *New Lanka*, III/3 (April 1952) 69–75.

Weber, Max. *Essays in Sociology*. Tr. and ed. H. H. Gerth and C. W. Mills, 1946 (New York, 1958).

———. *The Theory of Social and Economic Organization*. Tr. A. M. Henderson and Talcott Parsons (New York, 1947).

———. *The Religion of India*. Tr. H. H. Gerth and Don Martindale (Glencoe, Ill., 1958).

———. *The Sociology of Religion*. Tr. E. Fischoff, 1963 (London, 1965).

Wickremeratne, L. A. '1865 and the changes in Education Policies'. *Modern Ceylon Studies*, I (1970) 84–93.

———. 'Religion, Nationalism and Social Change in Ceylon, 1865–1885'. *JRAS* (1959) 123–50.

Wickremasekera, S. B. W. 'The Social and Political Organization of the Kandyan Kingdom'. M. A. thesis, London, 1961.

Wilson, Bryan R. 'An Analysis of Sect Development'. *American Sociological Review*, XXIV (1959) 3–15.

———. *Religion in Secular Society: A Sociological Comment* (London, 1966).

Woodhouse, G. W. 'Sissiyānu Sissiya Paramparāwa, and other Laws relating to Buddhist Priests in Ceylon'. *CALR*, III (1918) 174–86; 281–90.

Wriggins, Howard. *Ceylon: Dilemmas of a New Nation* (Princeton, New Jersey, 1960).

Yalman, Nur. 'The Ascetic Buddhist Monks of Ceylon'. *Ethnology*, I (1962) 305–28.

———. 'The Structure of Sinhalese Healing Rituals'. *Journal of Asian Studies*, XXIII (1964) 115–50.

ii. German

Bechert, Heinz. *Buddhismus, Staat und Gesellschaft in den Ländern des Theravāda-Buddhismus*. 3 vols. (Frankfurt am Main and Berlin, 1966–73).

iii. Sinhalese (originals and translations)

Ariyasēna, Kam̆burupiṭiyē, 'Sīmāva hā ehi aitihāsika saṃvardhanaya piḷiban̆da tulanātmaka vimarśanayak'. Ph.D. thesis, University of Ceylon, 1967.

Adrian Appuhāmi, H. L. *Dussīla Mardanaya* (Colombo, 1895).

Buddhadatta, Polvattē. *Kalyāṇi Sāsanavaṃsaya* (Colombo, 1935).

———. *Samīpātītayehi Bauddhācāryayō* (Ambalaṃgoḍa, 1950).

———. *Pāli Sāhityaya*. 2 vols. (Ambalaṃgoḍa, 1962).

———. 'Lakdiva Buruma Nikāyē Itihāsaya'. In N. A. Jayawickrama (ed.), *Paranavitana Felicitation Volume* (Colombo, 1965).

Buddharakkhita, Dikvällē. *Kāvya Dīpanī* (1778). Ed. Māpalānē Paññālaṃkāra (Colombo, 1913).

Buddharakkhita, Tibboṭuvāvē Siddhārttha. *Siyāmopasampadāvata*. Ed. Giridara Ratanajoti (Colombo, 1892).

Buddha Sāsana Commission. *Report* (S.P. XVIII: 1959).

Church Missionary Society. *Viruddhavādī Buddhāgankārayāṭa Kristiyānikārayā visin dena Prativacanayi* (Cotta, 1834).

De Lanerolle, V. D. *Atītaya*. 2nd ed. (Colombo, 1944).

De Silva, Lionel W. *Baṭuvantuḍāvē Caritaya* (Colombo, 1913).

De Silva, Harischandra. 'Vaskaḍuvē Śrī Subhūti Himi'. *Saṃskṛti*, XVI/4 (October–December, 1969) 47–64.

Dhīralaṃkāra, Välitara. 'Mahā Vihāra Vaṃśaya hā Amarapura Nikāya'. *Itihāsa Kathā*, II (1926) 146–225.

Dussīla Dāna Viniścaya (Colombo, 1897).

Dussīla Katura (Colombo, 1897).

Godakumbura, C. E. (ed.). *Sāsanāvatīrna Varṇanāva* (Colombo, 1956).

Gogerly, D. J. *Kristiyāni Prajñapti* (Colombo, 1849 and 1861).

Guṇānanda, Mohoṭṭivattē. *Dussīla Dāna Vibhāga* (Colombo, 1887).

_______. *Bauddha Praśnaya* (Colombo, 1887).

Hardy, R. Spence. *Sudharma Nikaśaya* (Colombo, 1865).

Hevawasam, P. B. J. *Mātara Yugayē Sāhityadharayan hā Sāhitya Nibandhana* (Colombo, 1966).

Jayasūriya, Hendrick Perera (ed.). *Sav Sat Dam Vādaya* (Colombo, 1873).

Jayatilaka, D. B. (ed.). *Katikāvat Saṅgarā* (Colombo, 1922).

Jñāṇavimala, Kiriällē. *Saparagamuvē Päraṇi Liyavili* (Colombo 1942).

Lambrick, Samuel. *Sermons in Singhalese preached to village congregations* (Cotta, 1838).

Lamkananda, Labugama. *Jayavardhanapura Kōṭṭē Śrī Kalyāṇi Sāmagrīdharma Mahā Saṃgha Sabhāva* (Colombo, 1964).

Laṃkānanda, Labugama (ed.). *Mandāram Pura Puvata* (Colombo, 1958).

Muṃkoṭuvē Rāḷa. *Saṅgarajavata*, 1780. Ed. Śrī Charles de Silva (Colombo, 1955).

Nandārāma, Veheragampiṭa. *Karatoṭa Vata* (Mātara, 1940).

Ñāṇissara, Nitalava. *Śrī Saraṇaṃkara Mahā Sthavira Caritaya* (Mīrigama, 1928).

Pānadurē Vādaya (Colombo, 1873).

Paññāmoli, Toṭagamuvē. *Sadācāra Vibhāvaniya* (Colombo, 1904).

Paññāsena, Nāhällē, and Sannasgala, P. B. (eds.). *Saṃgharāja Sādhucariyāva* (Colombo, 1947).

Peiris, P. A. *Śramaṇa Dussīla Saraṇāgamana Vibhāgaya* (Colombo, 1893).

Perera, S. L. *Rāmañña Vāda Bhaṃgaya* (Colombo, 1893).

Prajñānanda, Yagirala. *Śrī Sumaṃgala Caritaya*. 2 vols. (Colombo, 1947).

Rāhula, Panamvela. *Bädigama Nāhimiyō* (Mātara, 1967).

Rāmacandra, Piyadāsa. *Śrī Dharmārāma Mahā Svāmi Caritaya* (Colombo, 1913).

Rāmañña Nikāya. *Katikāvata* (Colombo, 1925).

Ratanapāla, Gammullē. *Siṃhala Vimānavastu Prakaraṇaya*, 1770. Ed. Telvattē Mahānāga Sīlānanda (Colombo, 1901).

Saddhammavaṃsa, Kotmalē. *Aṁbagahavattē Indāsabhavara Ñāṇasāmi Mahā*

Nāyaka Svāmīndrayan Vahansēgē Jīvana Caritaya (Kalutara, 1950).
Sannasgala, P. B. *Siṃhala Sāhitya Vaṃśaya* (Colombo, 1961).
Sāsanatilaka, Mātalē. *Rāmañña Vaṃśaya* (Colombo, 1964).
Selkirk, James. *Bavtisma labā siṭina ayaval pradhāna koṭa siyaluma Siṃhala manuṣyayanta . . . , danvana kāranāvalya* (Cotta, 1837).
Sēnānāyaka, H. J. M. Vikramaratna. *Amarapura Śrī Saddhammavaṃsa Nikāya piḷibaňda ati saṃkṣipta Itihāsa Katāva* (Ambalaṃgoḍa, 1928).
Siri Sumana, Ratgama. *Abhayatissa Nāyaka Sthavira Caritaya* (Balapiṭiya, 1909).
Sumana, Bulatgama (ed.). *Baddēgama Vādaya* (Galle, 1865).
Suvaṇṇajoti, Uḍugampola. *Dussīla Saṃgraha Bhedaya* (Colombo, 1888).
———. *Ilukvattē Medhaṃkarasabha Svāmīn Vahansēgē Jīvita Katāva* (Colombo, 1889).
———. *Bhikṣu Śīlaya* (Colombo, 1893).
———. *Bauddha Labdhi Viśodhaniya* (Colombo, 1898).
Udanviṭa Vādaya (Colombo, 1866).
Vācissara, Koṭagama. *Saraṇaṃkara Saṃghrāja Samaya* (Colombo, 1960).
Varāgoḍa Vādaya (Colombo, 1865).
Vīraratna, D. P. *Upavihāravaṃsaya hevat Lakdiva Paurāṇika Siddhasthāna* (Colombo, 1930).

iv. Pali

Bode, Mabel (ed.). *Sāsanavaṃsa* (London, 1897).
Buddhadatta, Polvattē (ed.). *Pāli Sandesāvalī* (Ambalaṃgoḍa, 1962).
Dhammālaṃkāra, Randoṁbē. *Sīma Naya Dappana* (Colombo, 1885).
Minayeff, I. P. (ed.). 'Sandesa-Kathā'. *JPTS*, (1885) 17–28.
——— (ed.). 'Sīma Vivāda Vinicchaya Kathā'. *JPTS*, (1887) 17–34.
Paññāsena, Keselvattē. *Siri Sumaṃgalatthera Caritaṃ* (Colombo, 1906).
Ratanajoti, Mātalē. *Siri Sumaṃgala Caritaṃ* (Colombo, 1901).
Vimalasāra, Aṁbagahapiṭiyē. *Sīmālakkhana Dīpanī* (Colombo, 1881).

INDEX

This index is also intended to serve as a glossary. In defining non-English words the main aim has been to indicate the senses in which they occur in the text of this book rather than to explain all their possible variations. The following abbreviations are used: nl., name of a layman; nm., name of a monk; pl., name of a place in Ceylon.

Abhayagiri, ancient monastery in Anurādhapura, 14

Abhidhamma, special or higher doctrine, classical Buddhist philosophy, 20–21

Abhidhamma piṭaka, division of the *tipiṭaka* containing the *abhidhamma*

Abhiṣeka, royal consecration ceremony, 12

Adam's Peak. *See* Śrīpadā

Adhikamāsa, intercalary month or leap-month added to the lunar year at thirty-month intervals to bring the lunar year into harmony with the solar year, 131

Adhikamāsa Vādaya, Controversy on the Intercalary month, 131ff, 158, 162, 163, 181, 218, 220

Adigar = Adikāram. *See* Maha Adikāram

Aḍu jāti = *aḍu kula*, low castes, 87. *See also* Caste

Aḍukku, cooked provisions supplied to officer or chief monk on tour, 82

Ähälēpola Adikāram (1), Kandyan chief, 63

Ähälēpola Adikāram (2), Kandyan chief, 79, 80–81, 113n, 140

Akmīmana, pl., village close to Galle, 162

Akmīmana Sobhita, nm., 162, 163

Alagalla, pl., 58, 59

Alms. See *Piṇḍapāta*; *Sāṃghika dāna*

Aluvihāre, Buddhist temple in Mātalē, 18, 53, 108

Alwis, James, 174–175, 181, 183–184, 185, 200, 207n, 216n

Amarapura, a former capital of Burma, 98, 144, 150

Amarapura Dhammarakkhitavaṃsa Nikāya, 147ff, 188n; derivation of name, 149–150

Amarapura Kalyāṇivaṃsa Nikāya, 147ff, 188n; derivation of name, 151

Amarapura Mūlavaṃsa Nikāya, 151ff; derivation of name, 161

Amarapura Nikāya, Amarapura fraternity, so named because its founder received ordination from Burmese monks in Amarapura, 87, 92, 98ff, 126, 131, 161–169 *passim*, 186–187, 238, 257, 261; in the Kandyan provinces, 139–143, 162; contrasted with the Siyam Nikāya, 144–146; segmentation of, 146ff, 258–259

Amarapura Saddhammavaṃsa Nikāya, 151ff, 188; derivation of name, 161

Am̆bagahapiṭiyē Ñāṇavimala, nm., 97–100 *passim*, 145n, 149, 150, 151, 152, 156, 161

Am̆bagahapiṭiyē Vimalasāra, nm., 145n, 156, 160n

Am̆bagahavattē Saraṇaṃkara (later Indāsabhavara Ñāṇasāmi), nm., 135n, 162ff, 170n

Ambalaṃgoḍa, pl., 139, 193

Ambarukkhārāmaya, Buddhist temple at Välitara, headquarters of Amarapura Mūlavaṃsa fraternity, 97, 187

Ames, Michael M., 1, 2, 3, 15n

Ananda College, 248, 254n

Anderson, George William, British Governor of Ceylon (1850–55), 214–215
Anglican Church and clergy in Ceylon, 193, 194, 195, 200, 206–207, 224, 235. *See also* Bishops of Colombo, Anglican
Animism. *See* Magic; Supernatural beings
Anu Nāyaka, Deputy Supreme Chief Monk, deputy head of a fraternity, 68
Äpā Appuhāmi, Don Philip de Silva, nl., 239, 240, 241
Appuhāmi, a term of respect added to a man's name
Anurādhapura, pl., capital of ancient Ceylon, 67, 68n
Arakan, a district in Lower Burma; missions from, 56–57
Ārāmaya, ārāme, in its general sense a synonym of *vihāraya*
Ārāmikas, attendants and servants of a monastery, 51
Araññа, forest hermitage, 168
Araññavāsī, forest dwelling (monks), 19, 67n, 168
Aristocracy: Kandyan, 53, 65–66, 75ff, 79n, 80–81, 90, 93, 94, 107, 112–113, 140–141; low-country, 29–30, 45–46, 47–48, 75–76, 92, 93, 96, 206, 208
Arnold, Edwin, 252
Arunachalam, Ponnambalam, nl., 256
Äsaḷa (Sinhalese), Āsāḷha (Pali), lunar month, June–July, 130
Äsaḷa Perahära, a series of religious processions held in the month of Äsaḷa, 64, 69n
Asceticism, 104–105, 172
Ascetic monks. See *Araññavāsī*, *Paṃsukūlikas*
Asgiri Alut Vihāre, also known as Vijayasundarārāmaya, more recent part of Asgiri Vihāre, 122n
Asgiriya, Asgiri Vihāre, Buddhist temple in Kandy, headquarters of the Asgiri chapter of the Siyam fraternity, 54, 63, 67–69, 86, 110, 116, 124, 125–128 *passim*, 134, 139, 140, 141, 142, 162, 179, 180, 211
Asoka, Emperor of India, 12
Astrology, 23–24, 25, 26, 31, 58, 236, 239. *See also* Calendar, Buddhist
Attaragama Rājaguru Baṇḍāra, nl., 171
Attuḍāvē Dhammarakkhita, nm., 100, 147n, 149
Augustinian missionaries, 40
Ava, Burmese city, also known as Ratanapura, 99, 144n
Avalokiteśvara, Mahāyānist Bodhisattva, in Sinhalese Buddhism identified with Nātha, 24

Baḍahäla, Sinhalese caste, 'potters', 89–90
Badda, rent or tax, a caste organized as a department for paying tax and performing service to the Crown, 93. *See also* Koṭṭalbadda; Kuruvēbadda; Maḍigēbadda; Mahabadda
Baddegama, pl., 193, 216, 224
Baddegama Saraṇaṃkara, nm., 137
Baddegama Vādaya, Christian-Buddhist controversy at Baddegama in 1865, 224–225
Bailey, Benjamin, 214–215, 218
Balapiṭiya, pl., *sīmā* at, 98, 139, 151, 153, 154ff
Balapiṭiyē Dhīrānanda, nm., 156
Baldaeus, Philippus, 42n
Bana, Buddhist sermon, 231. *See also* Preaching
Bana maḍuva, preaching hall (usually in a *vihāraya*), 205, 211
Baṇḍāra, lord, prince, nobleman
Baptism, 32, 206–208
Baptist missionaries, 192, 196, 210, 203
Barnes, Edward, British Governor of Ceylon (1824–31), 116n, 118–119
Basnāyaka Nilame, title and office of principal lay officer of a *dēvāle*
Batgama. *See* Padu
Bathurst, Earl of, 109
Baṭuvantuḍāvē Devarakṣita, nl., 134, 135, 175, 185
Batvaḍana Nilame, officer in charge of purveying food to the king, 66
Bechert, Heinz, 3
Begging by monks. See *Piṇḍapāta*
Bentara, also known as Bentoṭa, pl., 128
Bentara Atthadassī, nm., 128–138 *passim*, 158, 163, 175, 182n
Bēratuḍuvē Dhammādhāra, nm., 145n, 153, 155, 156
Berava, Sinhalese caste, 'drummer', 48, 90
Besant, Annie, 252, 254n
Bhikkhu, Buddhist monk, 25–26, 54–55, 57. *See also* Monks, Buddhist
Bhuvanekabāhu VII, King of Kōṭṭe (1521–51), 28–29
Bible, translations into Sinhalese, 199–200,

203, 204, 211
Bishops of Colombo, Anglican, 193, 200, 215, 230, 231. *See also* Copleston, Reginald Stephen
Bisset, George, 100n
Blavatsky, Helena Petrovna, 230, 242, 243–244, 254n, 256
Boake, Barcroft, 209, 218
Board of Commissioners for Kandyan Affairs, administrative authority established in the Kandyan provinces after their cession to the British government, 86, 122n, 123, 125
Bodawpaya, King of Burma (1782–1819), 98, 99, 161
Bodhi, enlightenment
Bodhi tree, tree of wisdom, type of tree (*ficus religiosa*) under which the Buddha attained enlightenment, and hence held sacred by Buddhists, 13, 107
Bodhisattva, a being who is determined to become a Buddha, 23
Bōgahapiṭiyē Dhammajoti, nm., 143, 151n, 153 n
Bōpāgoḍa Sumana, nm., 99n, 132n, 149, 152, 153, 155–161 *passim*
Bouglé, Celestin, 44
Bōvala Dhammānanda, nm., 97n, 211
Boxer, C. R., 39
Bradlaugh, Charles, 229
Brahmins, 42, 44–45, 46, 64, 254
British: relations with the Kandyan kingdom, 76ff; attitudes and policies towards Buddhism, 83–84, 108ff, 120ff, 133, 173, 174, 176, 177, 178, 215, 259, 261, 262, *see also* Disestablishment of Buddhism; colonial government and Christianity, 191–192, 193–195, 203, 215, 259; reactions against colonial government, 7–8, 112, 261
British and Foreign Bible Society, 203
Brownrigg, Robert, British Governor of Ceylon (1812–20), 94, 100n, 103n, 108, 109, 110, 111n, 112n, 113, 114, 118, 203
Buddha, 22–26, *passim*, 73n, 210, 228, 229, 255; doctrine of, see *Dhamma* (1)
Buddhadāsa, King of Ceylon (337–365), 21
Buddhaghosa, Buddhist commentator, 171, 175
Buddhism: recent sociological studies of, 1, 2, 3; ancient, 1, 11–12, 24–25, 230, 260; transformation into a world religion, 1, 11–12, 25, 258; Theravāda, *see* Theravāda; Mahāyāna, 22, 23, 51n; reforms and revivals of, 27, 37, 56, 58ff, 101ff, 172, 256–262 *passim*; traditional, 260, 261; traditionalist, 261; Protestant, 246, 260–261; modern, 260; and secular authorities, 1, 2, 12–14, 26–27, 101, 172, 188, 238, 239, 257–262 *passim*. *See also* Kingship; Religious establishment; and caste, *see* Caste and Buddhism; and Colonial government, *see* British attitudes and policies towards Buddhism, Disestablishment of Buddhism
Buddhist, The, English newspaper begun by the Buddhist Theosophical Society, 237, 248
Buddhist canon. See *Tipiṭaka*
Buddhist Congress, All Ceylon, 9
Buddhist holy days. See *Upsoatha* (1)
Buddhist laymen. *See* Laymen, Buddhist
Buddhist monastic discipline. See *Vinaya*
Buddhist monks. *See* Monks, Buddhist
Buddhist philosophy. See *Abhidhamma*
Buddhist temporalities. *See* Religious endowments
Buddhist Temporalities Commission (1876), 52–53, 127, 170, 179
Buddhist Theosophical Society, 9, 188; clerical division of, 246–247; lay division of, 246, 247ff
Bulatgama Sumana, nm., 160, 163, 164, 165, 219, 224, 225, 250
Buller, C. R., 119, 202
Burghers, descendants of Portugese and Dutch settlers in Ceylon, 43, 248
Burma: anthropological studies of Buddhism in, 1; relations with Ceylon, 37, 56–57, 97–100 *passim*, 143, 144–147 *passim*, 159–160, 163–165, 187; revival of Buddhism in, 262
Būssē Paññāmoli, nm., 156, 159
Buultjens, A. E., 248

Calendar, Buddhist, 129ff. *See also* Astrology; Adhikamāsa Vādaya
Callaway, James, Wesleyan missionary, 197n
Campbell, Colin, British Governor of Ceylon (1841–47), 117, 119, 120
Caste: Sinhalese system contrasted with the Hindu, 46–47; mobility, 48–49, 88, 93ff, 258; and Christianity, 43–49; and Buddhism,

Caste, *continued*
59, 87ff, 145ff, 167, 242, 258–259. See also *Nikaya* (2); statistics, 150n
Catholic Church and clergy in Ceylon, 28–49 *passim*, 61n, 195n, 235, 258
Celibacy, 26, 58
Central School Commission, 195, 234
Cetiya = *dāgäba*, dome-shaped monument containing relics of the Buddha or other great persons, 13, 231
Ceylon: sociological studies of Buddhism in, 1–3; introduction of Buddhism and its establishment in, 12–14; continuity of Buddhism in, 2; guardian deities of, 7, 24–25; contacts with other countries, 20. *See also* India; Burma, relations with Ceylon; Siam, relations with Ceylon; Portuguese power and activity in Ceylon; Dutch power and activity in Ceylon; British
Chakri dynasty of Siam, 132
Chalia. *See* Salāgama
Chater, James, Baptist missionary, 197n
Chief monks. *See* Nāyaka; Anu Nāyaka; Mahā Nāyaka; Saṃgharāja
Chiefs. *See* Aristocracy
Chilaw = Halāvata, pl., 49
Childers, Robert Ceasar, 182n
Christian missionaries: Dutch Calvinist, 28–49, 203, 204, 206–207; American, 192; British, 9, 114, 115, 117, 119, 124, 173, 191ff, 242, 243, 249, 257, 260; Roman Catholic. *See* Catholic Church and clergy in Ceylon. *See also* Anglican Church and clergy in Ceylon; Wesleyan missionaries
Christian sectarian movements, 102–103
Chronicles, 13, 16, 18, 46. See also *Mahāvaṃsa*
Church Missionary Society missionaries, 192–193, 199–200, 203
Cinnamon department. *See* Mahabadda
Clough, Benjamin, Wesleyan missionary, 197n, 198, 214, 222–223
Colebrooke, W. M. G., 114–115, 117, 118n, 121, 176, 177; Colebrooke Commission, British Royal Commission (officially known as the Commission Eastern Enquiry) which investigated into and reported on Ceylon (1829–31), 86, 123, 126, 147–148, 194
Colenso, Bishop John William, 229
Colombo, 38, 43, 186, 187, 194; as a centre of Buddhist activity, 187–188; Christian mission stations in, 192
Colombo Auxiliary Bible Society, 199, 203, 204, 211
Colombo Auxiliary Religious Tract Society, 115n, 203
Colonial Office, British, 9, 113, 114, 115, 117, 119, 173, 215, 245; documents, 4–5
Commentaries, on the *tipiṭaka*, 16, 18, 20, 155
Congregation of the Oratory, Goa, 42. *See also* Oratorian missionaries
Conversion, 30–32, 196, 202. *See also* Christian missionaries
Coomaraswamy, Ananda K., 64, 65, 255
Copleston, Reginald Stephen, Bishop of Colombo, 105, 172, 230, 231, 256
Cosmology, Buddhist, 228–229
Cūlavaṃsa, continuation of *Mahāvaṃsa*, 107

Daḍalla, pl., one of the two main centres of Salāgama monks, 98, 126, 151, 152, 153, 155, 157, 161, 186
Dāgäba, relic-container. See *Cetiya*
Dakkhiṇā Vibhaṃga Sutta, Discourse on the Analysis of Offerings, part of the Majjhima Nikāya of the Sutta Piṭaka, 16, 128, 170, 171
Däkuma, literally seeing, customary gift from tenant to landlord, 90
Daḷadā, Tooth Relic (of the Buddha): brought to Ceylon and festivals held in its honour, 13–14; palladium of Sinhalese kings, 14, 118; after the cession of the Kandyan kingdom to the British, 110, 117 ff; other references, 135, 188n
Daḷadā Māligāva, Temple of the Tooth Relic, 64, 118, 120
Daḷadā perahära, Tooth Relic procession, 14, 64, 118
Daly, B. J., 248, 249, 254n
Daṁbadeṇi Katikāvata, an edict to regulate the affairs of the Buddhist order in Ceylon promulgated on the initiative of King Parākramabāhu II (1236–70) whose capital was at Daṁbadeṇiya, 90
Daṁbulu Vihāra Tuḍapata, an early eighteenth-century document relating to Daṁbulu Vihāre, 54n
Daṁbulu Vihāre, Buddhist temple at Daṁbulla, 127, 128
Dāna, offering, giving. See *Sāṃghika dāna*
Daniel, Ebenezer, Baptist missionary, 197n, 201–202
Davids, T. W. Rhys, 182n, 219n

Davy, John, 73, 88n, 93n, 121, 176n
Dāyaka, literally donor; lay supporter or patron of a Buddhist monastery, its activities and its monks, 141, 237–238. *See also* Laymen, Buddhist
Debates and controversies: inter-religious, 34, 35, 60n, 105, 215ff, 242, 247, *see also* Baddegama Vādaya, Gampola Vādaya, Pānadurē Vādaya, Udanviṭa Vādaya; within Buddhism, 105, 181–182, 184, 218, 257, 259. *See also* Adhikamāsa Vādaya, Dēvapūjā Vādaya, Dussīla Vādaya, Sīmāsaṃkara Vādaya. Literary, *see* Sav Sat Dam Vādaya
De La Nerolle, Nanclars, 34
De Melo, Carlos Merces, 41
Demons. *See* Supernatural beings
De Nobili, Roberto, 30, 44–45
Department of National Archives (Ceylon), 5, 6
Department of Public Instruction, 195, 234, 236, 249
De Queyroz, Fernão, 57n, 90
De Saram, David, 182, 183; de Saram family, 96
De Silva, A., 103, 139–141 *passim*, 257
De Silva, David, Sinhalese Wesleyan Minister, 218, 222, 226, 229
De Silva, George Nadoris, 100n, 103n. *See also* Kapugama Dhammakkhandha
De Silva, John Robert, 242
De Silva, Wettasinghage Don Carolis, 241
Deva, deity, god. *See* Supernatural beings; Ceylon, guardian deities of
Dēvālagam, villages granted by the king to *dēvālayas*. *See* Religious endowments
Dēvālaya, dēvāle, abode of god(s), shrine dedicated to a god or gods of the Sinhalese Buddhist pantheon, 108, 109, 110, 118, 169, 170
Devānampiya, beloved of the gods, a Mauryan royal title, adopted also by some kings of Ceylon, 12
Devānaṃpiya Tissa, King of Ceylon (250–210 B.C.), 12
Dēvapūja Vādaya, Controversy on the propitiation of deities, 169–170
Devātideva, god above gods, epithet of the Buddha, 24, 25, 171
Devundara, pl., 100, 149, 150
De Young, John E., 1
Dhamma (1), doctrine or teaching of the Buddha, one of the *tiratana*, 17, 18, 26, 56
Dhamma (2) = *Sutta piṭaka*
Dhammadīpa, island of *dhamma* (1), Ceylon viewed as a country having a special connection with Buddhism, 22
Dhamma kamma, regulative act performed by the *saṃgha* in accordance with the *vinaya* and on the orders of a king in order to 'purify' the *sāsana*, 27
Dhammakathikas, preachers of the doctrine, monks specializing in the learning and teaching of the *dhamma*, 19
Dhammarakkhitavaṃsa fraternity. *See* Amarapura Dhammarakkhitavaṃsa Nikāya
Dhammayuttika Nikāya, monastic fraternity in Siam, 133, 165
Dharmapāla, Don Juan, King of Kōṭṭe (1551–97), 29, 38, 258
Dharmapala, Anagarika, 9–10, 248, 249, 252–253, 255
Dikvällē Buddharakkhita, nm., 97, 156
Dīpaduttārāmaya, Buddhist temple at Koṭahēna, Colombo, 188, 220, 251
Dīpēgoḍa Sīlakkhandha, nm., 163, 164
Disānāyaka, Tōmis Samarasēkara, nl., 182, 183
Disāva (1), province, 79n
Disāva (2), officer in charge of a province, 39–40, 107
Discipline, monastic. See *Vinaya*
Disestablishment of Buddhism, 8, 27, 28–29, 115ff, 173, 174, 177, 191, 258–259
Diyavaḍana Nilame, principal lay officer of the Daḷadā Maligāva, 120
Doḍandūva, pl., centre of Karāve monks, 150, 151, 155, 186; Buddhist school at, 234–235, 241
Doḍandūvē Piyaratana, nm., 158, 164, 165, 234, 250
Dominican missionaries, 40
Don Carolis, Hewavitharanage, 241, 248
Don David, Hewavitharanage. *See* Dharmapala, Anagarika
Doranāgama Muhandiram, Sinhalese envoy to Siam in 1741 and 1745, 61
Downing, John, 123
D'Oyly, John, 77n, 81, 84n, 94, 110, 111, 115, 116, 118, 119
Dubois, Abbé J. A., 33–34, 45
Dūllāve, Kandyan chief, 113n, 179
Dūllāve Loku Baṇḍā, nl., 127, 179
Dunuwille, C. B., 179
Durāve, Sinhalese caste, 'toddy-tappers', 92ff, 148, 150, 161, 167; Durāve monks, 91n, 100, 145, 146, 147ff, 161, 166. *See also*

Durāve, *continued*
Amarapura Dhammarakkhitavaṃsa Nikāya
Durayā, headman of low caste, 93
Durkheim, Emile, 14, 172
Dussīla Vādaya, Controversy on impious monks, 170–172
Dutch power and activity in Ceylon, 28–29 *passim*, 57n, 61, 62, 66n, 75–77 *passim*, 82–83, 94–95, 108, 152n, 203, 204, 206–207
Duṭṭhagāmaṇī, King of Ceylon (161–137 B.C.), 16–17

Ecclesiastical establishment, Christian, 117n, 193, 235. *See also* Anglican Church and clergy in Ceylon
Education, Buddhist monastic, 20, 60, 176–180 *passim*, 188, 194n, 196, 232–234, 235–237, 247; Buddhist non-monastic, 234–235, 249f, 260; Christian missionary, 30, 32, 176–177, 193–196, 208–209, 232, 234, 235, 236, 249, 250
English education, 176, 208, 250

Fa-Hsien, 14
Falck, Iman Willem, Dutch Governor in Ceylon (1765–85), 83, 91
Five Precepts (*pansil*), the five precepts for Buddhist laymen, 129, 244, 245
Forbes, J., 174
Forest-dwelling monks. See *Araññavāsī*
Franciscan missionaries, 28–29, 32n, 38, 40, 41, 258

Gabaḍāgam, villages set apart for the maintenance of the king's establishment, 65, 74, 116
Gajanāyaka, chief officer of the Kuruvēbadda, 93n
Galle, pl., 31, 32, 104, 194; as a centre of Buddhist activity, 186–187, 219; Christian missions in, 192, 193
Gāllē Medhaṃkara, nm., 86, 128, 135, 140
Gāmavāsī, village-dwelling (monks), 19, 20, 26, 67n, 101
Gaṃgārōhaṇa Varṇanāva, a Sinhalese poem written in 1807, 182, 183
Gammullē Ratanapāla, nm., 56
Gampola Vādaya, Christian-Buddhist debate at Gampola in 1871, 225, 226
Gaṇēbaṇḍāra, chief *gaṇinnānse*, title in early Kandyan times, 50
Ganēgoḍälla Vihāre, Buddhist temple at Kosgoḍa, 158, 187
Gaṇinnānse, quasi-monk of early Kandyan times who was resident in a monastery but who had not been formally admitted to the order as a *sāmaṇera* and who was not necessarily celibate, 54, 57–58, 59, 65
Gantha-dhura, vocation of books (learning and teaching) among monks, 19, 20, 21
Garhita vidyā, despised sciences, sciences prohibited for monks, 26
Giffard, Hardinge, 112n, 116, 119n
Gluckman, Max, 106
Goa, 30; Provincial Councils of, 43–44
Goḍamunnē Ratanajoti, nm., 127
Gods. See *Dēvālaya*; Supernatural beings
Gogerly, Daniel John, Wesleyan missionary, 196, 197n, 204–205, 209–210, 216–218, 221, 222, 227, 229
Gombrich, Richard F., 1
Gonçalvez, Jacome, Oratorian missionary, 34, 35n
Gooneratne, Edmund Rowland, 175n, 248
Goonetileke, H. A. I., 4
Gordon, Arthur Charles Hamilton, British Governor of Ceylon (1883–90), 122n
Goyigama, Sinhalese caste, 'farmers', 6, 47, 48, 87, 89, 90, 92, 94, 95, 104, 148, 167; Goyigama monks, 90, 91, 92, 139, 145, 146, 148, 149, 161–162, 166. *See also* Siyam Nikāya; Kalyāṇi fraternity; Uḍaraṭa Amarapura Nikāya; Rāmañña Nikāya
Green, H. W., Director of Public Instruction (1883–89), 235, 236, 237
Gurunnānselāgē Don Pālis, nl., 241

Hakuru. *See* Vahumpura
Haṃsāvatī. *See* Pegu
Haṃvälla, pl., 192, 201
Hardy, Robert Spence, Wesleyan missionary, 115n, 122n, 123, 173, 174, 175, 197n, 202, 210, 211–213, 216, 221–222, 227, 229n, 231
Harvard, W. M., Wesleyan missionary, 99n, 100n, 203
Hat Kōralē, seven *kōralēs*, a Kandyan province, 67, 79, 168
Hatara Kōralē, four *kōralēs*, a Kandyan province, 50n, 81
Hikkaḍuvē Sumaṃgala, nm., 134–138 *passim*, 169n, 170n, 175, 179–180, 184n, 185n, 188, 208n, 220, 221, 224, 226, 237, 242, 243, 245,

246, 250, 251, 253, 261
Hīnaṭikum̆burē Sumaṃgala, nm., 171
Hindus and Hinduism, 29, 31, 33–34
44–46, 252–255 *passim*, 262
Hinnāvō, Sinhalese caste, 'washermen for Salāgamas', 93n
Historical Manuscripts Commission (Ceylon), 5, 6
Horton, Robert Wilmot, British Governor of Ceylon (1831–37), 117, 121, 123, 214
Huduhumpola Vihāre, Buddhist temple at Huduhumpola near Kandy, 126, 127, 128, 139, 141–142
Hunu, Sinhalese caste, makers of *hunu* (lime), 90
Hunupola, John Edward, 225

Iddamalgoḍa, nl., 170n, 247, 248
Ilipängamuvē, nm., 59
Ilangakkōn, Don Joan Abhayasirivardhana, nl., 96n, 103n
Ilukvattē Medhaṃkara, nm., 168, 252n
India, relations with Ceylon, 12, 27, 255
Indra = Śakra, king of gods, 24
In̆duruvē Sumaṃgala, nm., 182n
Islam, 29, 44, 262

Jaffna, pl., 32, 39, 194
Jāgara, nm., 160n
Jātaka, story of a former life of the Buddha, whilst still a Bodhisattva, 16
Jayasēkarārāmaya, Buddhist temple at Demaṭagoḍa, Colombo, 152n, 188
Jermyn, Bishop of Colombo (1871–74), 231
Jesuit missionaries, 30, 41, 49
Jinarajadasa, C., 254n, 255
Johnston, Alexander, 84n, 122

Kaḍadora Grant, an early eighteenth-century document relating to Kaḍadora Vihāre, 53–54
Kaḍadora Vihāre, Buddhist temple at Kaḍadora, 53–54
Kadirāgoḍa, nm., 59
Kahavē Ñāṇānanda, nm., 155, 156, 157, 175, 224
Kälaṇi river, 137
Kälaṇi Vihāraya, Buddhist temple at Kälaṇiya, 38–39, 67, 68n, 136, 137, 187
Kälaṇiya (Sinhalese), Kalyāṇi (Sanskrit), pl., 38, 136, 137, 151n
Kalutara, pl., 134, 151, 157, 193, 256n
Kalyāṇi. *See* Kälaṇiya
Kalyāṇi fraternity, 136–138, 151n, 163
Kalyāṇi Sāmagrīdharma Saṃgha Sabhā. *See* Kalyāṇi fraternity
Kalyāṇivaṃsa fraternity. *See* Amarapura Kalyāṇivaṃsa Nikāya
Kam̆burupiṭiyē Guṇaratana, nm., 85
Kam̆burupiṭiyē Guṇaratana, Kuḍā (i.e. Junior), nm., 86n
Kammācariya (Pali), *karmācārya* (Sanskrit), senior monk to whom a newly-ordained *bhikkhu* is assigned for further training, 55, 137
Kanda uḍa raṭa, country above the mountain (Kandyan kingdom), 49. *See also* Kandyan kingdom
Kandy, pl., derivation of name, 49n; as a centre of Buddhism, 29, 36–38, 49ff, 73, 86–87, 180, 185, 188, 259; Buddhist temples in, *see* Daḷadā Māligāva, Malvatta, Asgiriya; four *dēvāles* (Nātha, Viṣṇu, Kataragama, Pattini) in, 110, 118; Christian missions in, 192, 193, 203
Kandyan chiefs. *See* Aristocracy
Kandyan Convention, the treaty by which the Kandyan kingdom was ceded to the British in 1815, 81, 106–107, 109, 110, 111n, 112, 114, 138, 141–142, 174, 215, 261
Kandyan kingdom, Sinhalese kingdom of which Kandy was the capital, 7, 29, 35, 36–37, 49ff, 73ff; political and administrative divisions, 79n; and European colonial powers, 29, 35, 36–37, 62, 66n, 75ff; structure and process of politics, 65–66, 73ff, 106, 111ff. *See also* Nāyakkar dynasty
Kandyan religious establishment. *See* Religious establishment, Kandyan
Käpakaruvā, a lay assistant to a monk, 240
Käppiṭipola, Kandyan chief, 112n
Kapugama Dhammakkhandha, nm., 98–100, 144n, 147, 151, 152, 156, 161, 186. *See also* De Silva, George Nadoris
Kapurāla, kapuvā, priest of a *dēvāle*, 109n, 110, 111
Kapuvatte, Kandyan chief, 112n
Karapuṭugala Dhammadinna, nm., 156, 158
Karatoṭa Dhammārāma, nm., 83, 84–86, 112, 128, 211
Karāve, Sinhalese caste, 'fishers', 48–49, 92ff, 103n, 148, 150, 167; Karāve monks, 100,

Karāve, *continued*
145, 146, 147ff, 155, 158, 160, 161, 164, 165, 166. *See also* Amarapura Kalyāṇivaṃsa Nikāya

Karma (Sanskrit), *kamma* (Pali), action, deed, ethical law of cause and effect, 22, 23, 25, 228

Kataluvē Atthadassī, nm., 137

Kataluvē Guṇaratana, nm., 100, 144n, 147n, 150, 164

Kataragama, pl.

Kataragama = Skanda, a guardian deity of Ceylon, 24, 118

Kataragama Dēvālaya, shrine dedicated to god Kararagama (at Badulla), 109

Katikāvata, an edict to regulate the affairs of the order of monks or of a fraternity within it. See *Dam̆badeṇi Katikāvata*

Kaufman, Howard, K., 1

Kingship, 12–13, 14, 22, 27, 46, 51. *See also* Buddhism and secular authorities

Kiralagama Devamitta, nm., 122n

Kīrti Śrī Rājasiṃha, king of Kandy (1747–82), 35n, 39n, 50n, 62–69 *passim*, 73, 84, 88, 90, 125, 132, 258, 259

Knox, Robert, 57n, 90, 105n, 202

Kobbǟkaḍuve family, 52–53

Kobbǟkaḍuvē Gaṇēbaṇḍāra, nm., 50

Kobbǟkaḍuvē Sirinivāsa, nm., 116

Kobbǟkaḍuve Vihāre, Buddhist temple at Kobbǟkaḍuva, 52–53

Kōdāgoḍa Sumaṃgala, nm., 163, 164

Koggala Dhammasāra, nm., 155

Koggala Dhammatilaka, nm., later Don Johannas Paṇḍitatilaka Koggala Gurutumā, nl., 185, 185n, 222

Kōrāla, officer in charge of a *kōralē*, 107

Kōralē, district within a *disāva* (1)

Koratoṭa Sobhita, nm., 235, 241

Koṭagama Guṇaratana, nm., 116, 123

Koṭahēna, a suburb of Colombo, 220

Koṭikāpola Ratanajoti, Mahā Nāyaka of Malvatta (1825–26), 116, 125

Koṭṭalbadda, artificer's department; a group of people who, in return for enjoying service land, provided services to the Crown as artificers, 93n. *See also* Navandanna

Kōṭṭe, pl., 187, 193, 203; kings of, *see* Bhuvanekabāhu VII; Dharmapāla, Don Juan

Kōṭṭe Vihāre, Buddhist temple at Kōṭṭe, 134, 136, 187, 223

Kristiyāni Prajñapti, 'The Evidences and Doctrines of the Christian Religion', a polemical pamphlet written by D. J. Gogerly, 217–218, 221, 223

Kurun̆dukāra, cinnamon-peeler, subcaste of Salāgama, 95, 152n

Kuruvēbadda, elephant department; people who, in return for enjoying service land, provided services to the Crown in capturing and taming of, and caring for, elephants, 93n

Lambrick, Samuel, C. M. S. missionary, 197n, 199

Laṃkāgoḍa Dhīrānanda, nm., 146, 152, 153, 154ff, 175, 188

Laṃkopakāra Press, 219, 221, 238, 241, 250

Land: royal, see *Gabaḍāgam*; chiefly, see *Nindagam*; religious, see *Vihāragam, Dēvālagam*, Religious endowments; registers, see *Lēkam miṭi, Tombos*

Lanka Theosophical Society, 246

Laymen, Buddhist: religious needs and interests of, 1, 2, 11–12, 15, 22–25, 169, 228, 260–261; involvement in religious activities, 9, 64, 129, 130, 170, 237ff, 246, 247ff, 259, 260, 261; laymen and monks, 16–17, 20, 21, 26, 96–97, 103–105, 121–122, 129, 141, 145, 170–172, 178, 199, 228, 237–238, 246, 259

Leadbeater, C. W., 248, 249, 254n

Legislative Council of Ceylon, 117, 177n, 195

Lēkam miṭi, Sinhalese records of property, land holdings and services, 120

Levkē Rāḷahāmi (1), Kandyan chief, 59, 61n

Levkē Rāḷahāmi (2), Kandyan chief, 79

Liquor, 201–202

Lokārtthasādhaka Samāgama, Society for the Welfare of the World, a Buddhist educational society, 234, 241, 250

London Missionary Society, 192

Loten, Joan Gideon, Dutch Governor in Ceylon (1752–57), 62

Low country (*pāta raṭa*), as contrasted with the central hill country (*uḍa raṭa*); the term refers to the southern and western lowlands rather than to the whole of the maritime provinces of Ceylon; 7, 9, 37, 75, 76, 82, 87, 94; emergence as a centre of Buddhist

activity, 73, 180–182, 185ff, 259
Low-country aristocracy. *See* Aristocracy, low-country
Low-country monks, contrasted with Kandyan monks, 92, 104, 178, 181, 259

MacKenzie, Alexander Stewart, British Governor of Ceylon (1837–41), 123–124
Maḍigēbadda, transport department; people who, in return for enjoying service land, provided transport services to the Crown, 93n
Maetsuyker, Joan, Dutch Governor in Ceylon (1646–50), 94
Magic, 23–26, 31, 58
Maha Adikāram, title and office of Chief Minister of King of Kandy, 67n, 78n, 107, 122
Mahabadda (low country), Cinnamon Department, the term was also used as a name for the Salāgama caste, 94f, 99n, 103n, 148
Maha Bodhi Society, 255
Maha Gabaḍāva, royal storehouse, 116
Maha Mudali, title and office of highest-ranking Sinhalese official in the colonial administration in the low country, 77n
Mahā Nāyka, Supreme Chief Monk, head of a fraternity, 68; of the Siyam fraternity, 8, 120, 126–128, 133, 140, 153, 180
Mahāsammata, mythical first king, so named because he was elected or agreed upon (*sammata*) by the people, 46n
Mahā Tammarāja (Boromkot) II, King of Siam (1733–58), 61, 62, 63
Mahatmas, in Theosophy, a brotherhood of adepts from whom the leaders of the movement claimed to receive knowledge and guidance, 252
Mahāvaṃsa, Great Chronicle, 16, 18n, 22, 27, 50n, 132, 261. *See also* Chronicles; *Cūlavaṃsa*
Mahāyāna. *See* Buddhism, Mahāyāna
Mahiyaṃgana Vihāre, Buddhist temple at Mahiyaṃgana, 67, 68n
Maitland, Thomas, British Governor in Ceylon (1805–12), 77n, 83–84
Maligaspē Dhammapāla, nm., 163
Maligaspē Maṃgala, nm., 134–138 *passim*
Mālimbaḍa Dhammadhara, nm., 85
Malvatta, Malvatu Vihāre, Buddhist temple in Kandy, headquarters of the Malvatu chapter of the Siyam fraternity, 63, 66, 67–69, 85, 86–87, 108, 110, 116, 125–127 *passim*, 134ff, 140, 141, 162, 165, 179, 180, 211
Mandalay, Burmese city, also called Ratanapuṇṇa, 164
Mandāram Pura Puvata, Story of the City of Mandāram, a versified Sinhalese historical work, 60, 88–89n
Mannar, pl., 32
Māpiṭigama Saṃgharakkhita, nm., 136–138 *passim*
Mārga, path (to salvation), 45
Mass religiosity. *See* Laymen
Mātalē, pl., 18, 165, 168, 192
Mātara, pl., 32, 83–84, 96n, 182; as a centre of Buddhism, 185–186; Christian missions in, 192, 216
Mavalankar, Damodar K., Indian Theosophist, 244
Mayilavävē Guṇaratana, nm., 126, 139, 143
Meditation, 19. See also *Araññavāsī*
Medicancy. See *Piṇḍapāta*
Merit-making. See *Puñña kamma*
Methodists. *See* Wesleyan missionaries
Mīgamuva, pl., 37n, 193
Milindapañha, Questions of Milinda, noncanonical Buddhist text, 170–171, 228
Millǟve, Kandyan chief, 113n, 118n
Millennial movements, 7–8, 112, 261
Mindon, King of Burma (1853–78), 160
Mīripänna, pl., 150, 186
Mīripännē Dhammaratana, nm., 150, 182–183, 185
Missionaries. *See* Christian missionaries
Mleccha, non-Indian, barbarian, 44
Mohoṭṭāla (alternatively, Mohoṭṭi, Mohoṭṭiyar), scribe, secretary, an officer in charge of keeping records, 94, 107
Mohoṭṭivattē (or Migeṭṭuvattē) Guṇānanda, nm., 188, 220–221, 222, 224, 226, 228, 229, 230, 242, 243, 250–252, 257
Moladaṇḍē Batvaḍana Nilamē, Kandyan chief, 66
Molligoḍa (the elder), Kandyan chief, 79, 80–81, 112n
Molligoḍa (the younger), Kandyan chief, 81, 113n
Monastery, Buddhist. See *Vihāraya*

Monastic discipline. See *Vinaya*
Monastic fraternity. See *Nikāya* (2)
Monastic landlordism. *See* Religious endowments
Monastic libraries, 5, 186–187
Monastic ritual. See *Pabbajja*; *Upasampadā*; *Uposatha* (2); *Vassa*
Monastic schools and colleges. *See* Education, Buddhist monastic
Mongkut, Siamese prince, monk and later king, known as Vajirañāṇa during his monkhood, 133, 133n, 134, 155, 165, 187n, 219
Monks, Buddhist: order of, see *Saṃgha*; admission, see *Pabbajja*; ordination, see *Upasampadā*; other rites and practices, see *Uposatha* (2), *Vassa*; different grades of, see *Sāmaṇera*, *Bhikkhu*, *Thera*; disciplinary regulations of, see *Vinaya*; chief monks, *see* Nāyaka, Anu Nāyaka, Mahā Nāyaka, Saṃgharāja; vocational differentiation, see *Paṃsukūlikas, Dhammakathikas, Vipassanā-dhura, Gantha-dura*; residential differentiation, see *Araññavāsī*, *Gāmavāsī*; regional differentiation, *see* Low-country monks, contrasted with Kandyan monks; caste differentiation, *see* Goyigama monks, Salāgama monks, Karāve monks, Durāve monks; organizational differentiation, see *Nikāya* (2); medicant monks, see *Piṇḍapāta*; monks and laymen, *see* Laymen, Buddhist, and monks
Moratoṭa Dhammakkhandha, nm., 85–86, 97n, 148
Moraṭuva, pl., 193
Mudali (alternatively, Mudaliyar, Modeliar), high-ranking title or administrative office or both, 93n, 94, 208
Mudali-pēruva = Mudiyanselā, aristocratic segment of the Goyigama caste. *See* Aristocracy, Kandyan
Muhandiram, high or middle rank in the official administration, 208
Mūlavaṃsa fraternity. *See* Amarapura Mūlavaṃsa Nikāya
Mulgirigala Vihāre, Buddhist temple at Mulgirigala, 67, 83–84
Mulhiriyāvē Lēkam, nl., 137
Murdoch, John, 197, 203–204, 205, 209
Muslims. *See* Islam
Mutteṭṭu, landlords' fields as distinguished from the fields of tenants in *gabaḍa-, ninda-, vihāra-,* and *dēvāla-gam*, 89

Näkäti, astrologer, polite term for Berava caste, 91n
Nallur, pl., 43
Narendrasiṃha, Śrī Vīra Parākrama, King of Kandy (1707–39), 34, 58, 60, 61
Nash, Manning, 1
Nātha, a guardian deity of Ceylon, 118
Navandanna, Sinhalese caste, artificers, 48, 89, 93n. *See also* Koṭṭalbadda
Nāyaka, Chief Monk of a monastery or a region, 68; rights and privileges, 82; manner of appointment in the Kandyan kingdom, 122; granting of Acts and Certificates of Appointment by the British colonial administration, 99–100, 122ff
Nāyakkar dynasty, princes of South Indian descent (from the Nāyaks of Madhura) who ascended the throne of Kandy (1739–1815), 35, 60, 61, 65–66, 110
Nayide, title of a headman of the
Navandanna caste, 61
Negombo = Mīgamuva
New nations, 3, 4, 262
Nicholson, James, Wesleyan missionary, 204, 205
Nikāya (1) (textual), one of the five subdivisions of the *sutta piṭaka*
Nikāya (2) (organizational), monastic fraternity, 87n, 98n, 141. *See also* Siyam Nikāya; Amarapura Nikāya; Rāmañña Nikāya
Nindagam, villages granted by the king to noblemen, 65, 74
Nirvana (Sanskrit), *nibbāna* (Pali), Buddhist salvation, 15, 228
Niyamakanda, pl., 60
Nock, A. D., 31
North, Frederick, British Governor in Ceylon (1798–1805), 77n, 80, 191
Novices, Buddhist. See *Sāmaṇera*
Nugavela Baṇḍāra, nl., 140
Nuvara Kalāviya, a Kandyan province, 168

Obeyesekere, Gananath, 1, 3, 104, 246
Olcott, Henry Steel, 166–167, 168, 180, 230, 242ff, 256–257

Oratorian missionaries, 34–35, 48, 61n, 195n
Ordination. See *Pabbajja; Upasamapadā*

Pabbajja, formal admission of a layman to the order as a *sāmaṇera*, 54
Padu = Batgama, Sinhalese caste, 'palanquin bearers', 90
Pali language and its study, 20, 59, 60, 175–176, 179, 182n
Palkuṁburē Atthadassī, nm., 59n
Pälmaḍulla, pl., a *vihāragama* attached to Śrīpāda, 84n, 247
Paṃsukūlikas, monks who wore robes made out of rags, 19
Pānadurē, pl., 151, 193
Pānadurē Sumaṃgala, nm., 136, 137
Pānadurē Vādaya, debate at Pānadurē in August 1873 between Christians and Buddhists, 222, 225, 226, 229, 230, 251
Panditaratna, Henricus Philipsz, Sinhalese predikant, 43n
Panividakāra, messenger, subcaste of Salāgama, 95, 152n
Pansala, building in which monks reside, in general sense a synonym of *vihāraya*, 184, 211, 233; *pansala* schools, *see* Education, Buddhist monastic
Pantheon, Sinhalese Buddhist. *See* Supernatural beings
Päpiliyānē Sīlavaṃsa, nm., 136, 137
Parākramabāhu I, King of Ceylon (1153–83), 14, 66n
Parakuṁburē Vipassī, Mahā Nāyaka of Malvatta (1850–62), 135–138 *passim*
Parama Dhamma Cetiya, *vihāre* and *piriveṇa* at Ratmalāna, Colombo, 134, 188
Paramānanda Vihāre, Buddhist temple in Galle, 219
Paramparāva, genealogy; *sāsana paramparāva*, spiritual or religious genealogy, 52; *ācāri paramparāva*, genealogy of teachers, 165; *śiṣyānuśiṣya paramparāva*, teacher-pupil genealogy, pupillary succession, 51, 52, 67, 145; *sivuru* or *jñātiśiṣya paramparāva*, genealogy of teachers and pupils who are also kin of one another, 52–54, 145n
Paritta (Pali), *pirit* (Sinhalese), protection, ceremony at which certain *suttas* are chanted to avert misfortune and bring fortune, 26
Pariyatti, learning the *dhamma* (as distinguished from practising it), 17, 18, 19, 21n
Parsons, George, C.M.S. missionary, 224–225
Pātimokkha, *vinaya* text containing two hundred and twenty-seven rules for *bhikkhus* recited at *uposatha* (2), 64n, 129–130
Paṭipatti, practising the *dhamma* (as distinguished from the mere learning of it), 17, 18, 19, 21n
Paṭṭapola Mohoṭṭāla, Sinalese envoy to Siam in 1750, 62
Pattini, a goddess of the Sinhalese pantheon, 118
Pegu, Burmese city, also known as Haṃsāvatī, 61, 144n, 150, 151, 164
Peiris, J., 235
Pērādeṇiyē Indajoti, nm., 127
Pereira, Affonso, 37n
Pereira, John, 185, 200
Perera, Lansage Don Andris, 241, 248
Perera, Lansage Don Simon, 248
Perera, Samuel, 226
Piḷimatalavvē Jr., Kandyan chief, 79n, 112n
Piḷimatalavvē Sr., Kandyan chief, 78–80
Piṇḍapāta, begging for alms by monks, mendicancy, 17, 60, 104
Piṇḍapātika Samāgama, mendicant fraternity. *See* Silvat Samāgama
Pinkama. See *Puñña kamma*
Piriveṇa (Sinhalese), *pariveṇa* (Pali), in ancient Ceylon the living quarters of monks in a *vihāre*, in more recent times monastic school or college, 188, 233–234. *See also* Education, Buddhist monastic
Plakaats, proclamations of the Dutch colonial government, 38
Planetary influences, 23, 24, 25. *See also* Astrology
Pōhaddaramullē Vanaratana, nm., 156, 159, 163
Polonnaruva, pl., 14, 67, 68n
Portuguese power and activity in Ceylon, 28–49 *passim*, 75–77 *passim*, 94–95, 107–108, 109
Potuvila Indajoti, nm., 135n, 224
Poverty, 59–60. See also *Piṇḍapāta*
Pōya (Sinhalese) = *uposatha* (Pali)
Pōyagē (Sinhalese) = *uposathāgāra* (Pali)
Pōyamalu Vihāre, older part of Malavatu Vihāre, 50, 59n

Preaching: Buddhist, 9, 16, 21, 105, 197, 199, 201, 211, 226, 232n; Christian missionary, 197–202 *passim*, 211, 226, 232
Priests. See *Kapurāla*
Printing presses, 6, 9, 184–185; Dutch, 203, 204; Wesleyan Mission Press, 185, 203, 204–205; C.M.S., 203, 219; Roman Catholic Press, 185; Baptist, 203; Buddhist, 188, 213, 219, 220–221, 228, 238, 241, 248
Proponent, clerical officer of the Dutch Reformed Church below the rank of a predikant, 43
Pudgalika, private, personal or individual (as against *sāṃghika*, communal or collective), 51–52, 129
Puñña kamma (Pali), *pinkam* (Sinhalese), meritorious deeds, religious ceremonies and festivals, 14–17, 22, 23, 90, 205
Puññakkhetta, merit-field (in which one could sow seeds of merit and reap good harvests), an epithet of the *saṃgha*, 17
Puñña potthaka, merit-books, kept by important laymen in which their meritorious deeds were recorded, 16–17
Pupillary succession. See *Paramparāva*
Puvakdanḍāvē Paññānanda, nm., 162, 164–165, 166, 168

Radā, Sinhalese caste, 'washermen', 48, 90
Rahula, Walpola, 16
Rājādhi Rājasiṃha, King of Kandy (1782–98), 65, 66, 84–85
Rājakāriya, primarily and literally service to the king; extended to cover services to a nobleman, a *vihāre* or a *dēvāle* by tenants of *nindagam*, *vihāragam* and *dēvālagam* respectively, 74, 114, 115, 121, 238
Rājapakṣa, Adrian de Abrew Vijaygunaratna, 98, 102
Rajaraṭa, the northern of the three ancient divisions of Ceylon, 67
Rājasiṃha II, King of Kandy (1635–87), 50, 81n, 108, 109
Rājāvaliya, Sinhalese historical work, 48
Rakkhaṃga Dēśa = Arakan
Rama III, King of Siam (1824–51), 132, 133, 134n
Rāmañña, Lower Burma, 144n, 150, 164,
Rāmañña Nikāya, 6, 104, 146, 150–151, 161ff, 238; contrasted with the Siyam and Amarapura Nikāyas, 166–169
Ram̆bukkana Sobhita, nm., 108
Ram̆bukvällē Sobhita, nm., 126, 139, 141–142
Ram̆bukvällē Sonuttara, nm., 179
Random̆bē Dhammālaṃkāra, nm., 156, 160n, 245
Raṭa, in general sense country or region (e.g. *pāta raṭa*, low country), more specifically an administrative division within the Kandyan kingdom, 79n
Ratanapuṇṇa. *See* Mandalay
Ratmalānē Dhammāloka, nm., 188
Ratvatte, Kandyan chief, 112n
Reischauer, A. K., 105
Relics. See *Cetiya; Daḷada*
Religious endowments, 8–9, 17, 18, 26–27, 29 38, 40, 50–54, 58, 65, 66, 68, 74, 89–90, 114, 115, 120–121, 124, 126–127, 142, 177–178, 179, 238, 239, 258, 259
Religious establishment, Kandyan, 53, 67–69, 73–74, 86–87, 90–91, 97, 98, 124–125, 126–127, 139–142 *passim*, 180–181, 258–259
Religious festivals and ceremonies, 13–15, 16. See also *Daḷadā perahära; Puñña kamma*
Religious organizations. See *Nikāya* (2); Religious establishment, Kandyan; Voluntary associations
Ricci, Matteo, 30, 45n
Ridī Vihāre, Buddhist temple in Kuruṇāgala District, 67, 68n
Rohṇa, the southern of the three ancient divisions of Ceylon, 14
Ruel, Johannes, Dutch predikant, 42n

Sabaragamuva, a Kandyan province, 66, 67, 79, 80, 81, 84, 85, 86, 139–141, 143, 247
Saddhammavaṃsa fraternity. *See* Amarapura Saddhammavaṃsa Nikāya
Saddhivihārika, novice under the guidance of an *upajjhāya* (preceptor), 52
Sādhu, religious exclamation used to express approval and joy, 226
Salāgama (alternatively Halāgama, Chalia), Sinhalese caste, 'cinnamon-workers', 48, 92ff, 102–103, 148, 161, 167; subcastes, 152n; Salāgama monks, 97ff, 145, 146, 147, 148, 150, 151ff, 161, 166. *See also* Amarapura Nikāya; Amarapura Mūlavaṃsa Nikāya; Amarapura Saddhammavaṃsa Nikȳa
Salvation, primary and secondary, 15, 17, 24–25
Samāgama (1), fraternity of monks, synonym

of *nikāya* (2), 98n
Samāgama (2), voluntary association or society of both monks and laymen or entirely of laymen. *See* Voluntary associations
Saman, a guardian deity of Ceylon
Samaṇa, monk, 170, 171
Saman Dēvālaya, shrine dedicated to god Saman (at Ratnapura), 108, 109, 170n
Samanakkoḍi Adikāram, Kandyan chief, 66
Sāmaṇera, Buddhist novice, 54, 55, 57, 59, 63
Samanola Kanda, Abode of Saman. *See* Śrīpāda
Saṃgha, order of Buddhist monks, 16, 22, 26–27, 67n, 73n, 88, 89; changes in, 17ff. *See also* Monks, Buddhist
Saṃgharāja, literally king or ruler of the *saṃgha*, highest ecclesiastical office in a Buddhist country; of Ceylon, 66, 67n; of Burma, (1) 98, 99, 100, (2) 146, 158n, 159, 160, 163, 164n
Sāṃghika dāna, offerings made to the order of monks, 16, 17, 116, 128–129, 131, 170, 171
Sannasa, a royal grant
Sannyāsi, world-renouncer in the Indian religious tradition, 89
Sarasavi Sañdaräsa, Sinhalese newspaper published by the Buddhist Theosophical Society, 248, 252
Sarvajña Śāsanābhivṛddhidāyaka Dharma Samāgama. *See* Society for the Propagation of Buddhism
Sāsana, Buddhist teachings, institutions and practices, 19, 22, 26–27, 51, 55, 56, 58, 69
Sav Sat Dam Vādaya, a literary controversy on the three Sinhalese words, *sav, sat* and *dam*, 182–185, 218, 220, 222
Śayilabimbārāmaya, Buddhist temple at Doḍandūva, headquarters of Kalyāṇivaṃsa fraternity, 155
School Commission, 194, 209
Schools. *See* Education
Scott, John, Wesleyan missionary, 222
Selkirk, James, C. M. S. missionary, 187n, 196n, 197n, 207n, 208n, 223
Seminaries, Roman Catholic, 41, 45; Calvinist, 43; Anglican, 208, 224. *See also* Education, Christian missionary
Senkaḍagala Sirivardhana Pura, Sinhalese name of Kandy, also called Maha Nuvara (Great City), 49n
Service Tenures Commissioner, 127
Shils, Edward, 4
Siam: anthropological studies of Buddhism in, 1; relations with Ceylon, 37, 61–64, 66, 67, 132–134, 165, 187
Silvat Samāgama, fraternity of the pious, 59–60, 91, 101
Silvat täna, pious one, member of the Silvat Samāgama, 59–60
Sīmā, consecrated boundary within which *upasampadā* and other *saṃgha kamma* (ecclesiastical acts) are performed: term and significance explained, 153–154; in the Siyam Nikāya, 63, 68–69, 125–126, 139, 153; in the Amarapura Nikāya, 98, 145, 151ff; Kalyāṇi, 151, 164
Sīmāsaṃkara Vādaya, Controversy on the Confused Boundary, 155ff, 162, 163, 181, 218
Siṃhalē = Siṃhala Raṭa, Sinhalese name of the Kandyan kingdom, 49n, 91
Sinhalese language, 21, 34, 42n, 60, 176–177
Sinhalese Tract Society, 203
Sīnigama Dhīrakkhandha, nm., 220
Sirimanne, F. S., 226
Siri-Meghavaṇṇa, King of Ceylon (301–28), 14
Siṭināmaluvē Dhammajoti, nm., 59, 91, 92, 97n
Siyam Nikāya, Siamese fraternity, so named because its founders received ordination from Siamese monks, 6, 98, 104, 131, 138, 139–142 *passim*, 144, 145, 146, 161–169 *passim*, 186, 238. *See also* Religious establishment, Kandyan
Skanda, in Sinhalese Buddhism a guardian deity of Ceylon. *See* Kataragama
Social stratification, 2, 241, 248n, 259. *See also* Aristocracy; Caste
Society for the Propagation of Buddhism, 188, 220–221, 241, 248, 250
Society for the Propagation of the Gospel in Foreign Parts, 220, 230
Spiro, Melford E., 1
Śrīpāda, Sacred Foot Print, also called Samanola Kanda and Adam's Peak, 67, 68n, 84–86, 140
Śrī Vijaya Rājasiṃha, King of Kandy (1739–47), 35, 60, 61
Śrī Vikrama Rājasiṃha, King of Kandy (1798–1815), 50, 78ff, 85, 107, 109, 110, 112, 140
Stephen, James, 119

Supernatural beings, beliefs and practices relating to, 23–26, 64, 74n, 169–170
Sūriyagoḍa Rājasundara, nm., 57n, 58, 61n
Sutta, discourse, sermon
Sutta piṭaka, division of *tipiṭaka* containing the *suttas*, also referred to as *dhamma* (2), 21, 56, 57, 63

Talpiṭiya Vihāre, Buddhist temple in Kalutara, 157
Tambiah, S. J., 1, 260
Tamil language, 34, 42n, 45
Tangalla, pl., 97
Temperance, 9, 202
Temple of the Tooth. *See* Daḷadā Māligāva
Temple libraries. *See* Monastic libraries
Temple property. *See* Religious endowments
Temples. See *Dēvālaya; Vihāraya*
Tennent, James Emerson, 33, 46, 173, 176, 186, 187, 192n, 202, 205, 207n, 210, 212
Terunnānse (Sinhalese), derived from *thera* (Pali), senior monk, 57n, 90
Thailand. *See* Siam
Theosophical Society and Theosophists, 105, 168n, 230, 242ff, 248, 249, 250, 252–255, 256. *See also* Buddhist Theosophical Society
Theosophist, The, journal of the Theosophical Society, 242, 253n
Thera, a *bhikkhu* with more than ten years' standing from his *upasampadā,* 55n, 57n
Theravāda, School of the Elders, the kind of Buddhism accepted and followed mainly in Ceylon, Burma and Thailand, 20, 25
Three Refuges (*tisaraṇa*, same as *tiratana*), 244, 245
Tibboṭuvāvē Siddhārttha Buddharakkhita, Mahā Nāyaka of Malvatta (1753–73), 62n, 66
Tibboṭuvāvē Siddhārttha Buddharakkhita, Kuḍā (i.e. Junior), nm., 116
Tipiṭaka (Pali), *tripiṭaka* (Sanskrit), literally 'three baskets', collective name for the Buddhist canon which falls into three divisions: *vinaya piṭaka, sutta piṭaka* and *abhidhamma piṭaka*; committed to writing, 18; study by monks, 20; suggestion to print, 219n; revision at Pälmaḍulla, 247
Tiraścīna vidyā, beastly sciences, sciences prohibited for monks, 58
Tiratana, three 'gems' of Buddhism: Buddha, *dhamma, saṃgha*, 26
Tōlaṃgamuvē Siddhārttha, nm., 65n, 139–140, 143, 163
Tolfrey, William, 211n
Tombos, registers of land compiled under the Portuguese and Dutch administrations, 30, 207
Tooth Relic. See *Daḷadā*
Torrington, Viscount, Governor of Ceylon (1847–50), 120, 124, 141
Toṭagamu Vihāre, Buddhist temple at Toṭagamuva, 97, 148
Trimnell, George Conybeare, C. M. S. missionary, 216
Trincomalee, pl., 194
Troeltsch, Ernst, 87n, 103
Tun Kōralē, three *kōralēs*, a Kandyan province, 80, 81
Turnour, George, 86, 118, 175–176, 179, 210–211
Tuvakkugala Vihāre, Buddhist temple in Galle, 162

Udanviṭa Vādaya, Buddhist-Christian debate at Udanviṭa in 1866, 225
Uḍaraṭa Amarapura Nikāya, Kandyan branch of the Amarapura fraternity. *See* Amarapura Nikāya, in the Kandyan provinces
Uḍugampiṭiyē Sumana, nm., 158, 164, 165
Ulaṃkulamē Saraṇaṃkara, nm., 168
Unnānse, 'his reverence', a respectful term used to refer to a monk
Upajjhāya (Pali), *upādhyāya* (Sanskrit), senior monk who acts as preceptor to a *saddhivihārika* (novice), 52, 137
Upāli, nm., leader of the Siamese mission to Ceylon in 1753, 62, 63, 144
Upāsaka, Buddhist lay devotee, 65. *See also* Laymen, Buddhist
Upasampadā, higher ordination by which a *sāmaṇera* (novice) is admitted to the order as a *bhikkhu* (monk): term defined and explained, 54–55; re-establishment in Ceylon by Arakanese monks, 37, 56–57; re-establishment in Ceylon by Siamese monks, 37, 63, 73; in the Siyam fraternity, 6, 68–69, 88, 90, 91; outside Kandy, 97, 148; brought back to Ceylon from Burma, 97–100 *passim*, 164–165; in the Kalyāṇi fraternity, 136–138; in the Uḍaraṭa Amarapura fraternity, 143; in the Rāmañña fraternity, 165–166
Uposatha (1), Buddhist holy day occurring four times in each lunar month at new

moon, full moon and the two intermediate days, 129, 130
Uposatha (2), confessional meeting of *bhikkhus* held on two of the *uposatha* (1) days at new moon and full moon, 60, 129–130
Uposathāgāra, building in a monastery in which monks assemble to perform *uposatha* (2) and other *vinayakamma*, 129

Vādaya, debate, controversy. *See* Debates and controversies
Vādduvē Dhammānanda, nm., 138
Vagēgoḍa Dhammakusala, nm., 97n
Vahumpura = Hakuru, Sinhalese caste, makers of *hakuru* (jaggery), 104, 161n
Vajirañāṇa. *See* Mongkut
Valagedara Dhammadassī, nm., 131
Valānē Siddharttha, nm., 134–135, 136, 137, 175, 180, 188
Väligama, pl., 193
Väligama Dhammapāla, nm., 163, 164
Väligama Sumaṃgala, nm., 175, 224, 245, 252
Välitara, pl., one of the two main centres of Salāgama monks, 96, 97, 98, 151, 152, 153, 155, 157, 186
Välivita Samāgama, fraternity of Välivita (Saraṇaṃkara). *See* Silvat Samāgama
Välivita Saraṇaṃkara, nm., 58–61, 66, 67n, 84, 85, 91, 92n, 97n, 171
Välivita Saraṇaṃkara, Kuḍā (i.e. Junior), nm., 86n, 116, 123n
Vālukārāmaya, Buddhist temple at Daḍalla, 98, 99n, 157
Vanavāsa Vihāre, Buddhist temple at Bentara, 128, 162–163
Vanavāsī = *araññavāsī*
Van de Graff, Willem Jacob, Dutch Governor in Ceylon (1785–93), 83
Van Eck, Lubbert Jan, Dutch Governor in Ceylon (1761–65), 66n
Varāgoḍa Vādaya, Buddhist-Christian controversy at Varāgoḍa in 1865, 225
Varañāṇamuni, nm., leader of Siamese mission to Ceylon in 1756, 63
Varāpitiyē Sumitta, nm., 162, 165–166
Vāriyapola, nm., 126
Vaskaḍuvē Subhūti, nm., 156, 159n, 182n, 245 163
Vaskaḍuvē Saraṇapāla Sīlakkhandha, nm., 156, 159
Vaskaḍuvē Subhūti, nm., 156, 159n, 182n, 245
Vassa, a three-month stay in one place observed by Buddhist monks during the rainy season, 130, 131, 135
Vassāna, rainy season lasting for four months from the day after the full moon of Āsāḷha (June–July) until the full moon of Kattikā (October–November), 69n, 130
Vaṭabuluvē Unnānse, nm., 59n
Vaṭṭagāmaṇī, King of Ceylon (89–77 B.C.), 18n
Vattegama Sumaṃgala, nm., Mahā Nāyaka of Asgiriya (1869–85), 127
Vaz, Joseph, Oratorian missionary, 42
Vēhällē Dhammadinna, nm., 85, 91
Vellāla, Tamil caste, 'farmers', the term was also used to refer to the comparable Sinhalese caste, Goyigama, 103n, 148, 149
Victoria, Queen, petitions to, 120, 138
Vidānē, headman of a caste group organized into a *badda*, 93, 107
Vidyādhāra Sabbhā, Society for aiding knowledge, Committee of Managers of Vidyodaya Piriveṇa, 237, 240, 241, 248
Vidyālaṃkāra Piriveṇa, monastic college at Pāliyagoḍa, Kälaṇiya, 188
Vidyodaya Piriveṇa, monastic college at Māligākanda, Colombo, 180, 188, 236–237, 239–241, 243, 248, 250, 261
Vihāragam, villages granted by the king to Buddhist monasteries. *See* Religious endowments
Vihāragē = *piḷimagē*, image house, containing image(s) of the Buddha and other objects of religious art, part of the complex of buildings in a *vihāraya*
Vihāraya, vihāre, dwelling of monks, also referred to as *ārāme* or *pansala*, translated as monastery or temple; in addition to living quarters of monks, a *vihāre* also has other important features such as a *cetīya*, a *bodhi* tree, a *vihāragē*, a *pōyagē* and a *bana maḍuva,* 21, 64–65, 169, 231
Vikramabāhu, King of Kandy (*ca.* 1475–1510), 52, 53
Vikramatilaka Appuhāmi, Don Velon, nl., 239, 240
Vilbāgedara, Sinhalese envoy to Siam in 1745 and 1750, 61, 62
Vilēgoḍa Puññasāra, nm., 147–148, 149
Vimaladharmasūrya I, King of Kandy (1591–1604), 50n, 56
Vimaladharmasūrya II, King of Kandy (1687–1707), 38, 50, 56, 57

Vinaya, monastic discipline, disciplinary regulations, 26–27, 51, 54–58 *passim*, 59, 63, 73n, 88, 91, 136, 154, 155, 158, 170
Vinayakamma, acts of *vinaya* like *uposatha* (2) and *upasampadā*
Vinaya piṭaka, division of the *tipiṭaka* concerned with monastic discipline
Vipassanā-dhura, vocation of meditation among monks, 19
Viṣṇu, in Sinhalese Buddhism a guardian deity of Ceylon, 24, 118
Visuddhācariya, nm., leader of Siamese mission to Ceylon in 1756, 63
Vitārandeṇiyē Indasāra, nm., 164
Voluntary associations, 9, 188, 238ff

Warren, H. C., 182n
Weber, Max, 1, 2, 11n, 23, 87n, 106, 258, 260
Wesleyan missionaries, 176–177, 192–193, 195, 196, 203, 214, 216, 221–222. *See also* Gogerly, Daniel John; Hardy, Robert Spence
Wijesinha, Louis Corneille, 170, 175n
Wilberforce, William, 114
Wilson, Bryan R., 7, 102
Wriggins, Howard, 3

Yagirala Prajñānanda, nm., 261
Yakkha, demon. *See* Supernatural beings
Yalman, Nur, 1
Yaṭanvala Sunanda, nm., Mahā Nāyaka of Asgiriya (1824–35), 125, 126, 139
Yaṭavattē Suvaṇṇajoti, nm., Mahā Nāyaka of Asgiriya (1853–69), 138
Yātrāmullē Dhammārāma, nm., 135n, 182n, 219n
Young Men's Buddhist Association, 188

[redacted]